# The Cup of The Harlot

The End Times
We Were
Never Taught

**Bob Morley**

The Cup of The Harlot
© 2013 Bob Morley
All rights reserved
Printed in the United States of America

Unless otherwise noted Scriptures are from the
HOLY BIBLE: NEW INTERNATIONAL VERSION. 1973,
1978, 1984 by International Bible Society.
Used by permission of Zondervan Publishing House.
All rights reserved.

Scriptures marked kjv are from the Holy Bible,
King James Version

Footnoting information included in text.

Copyright: May, 2013
U.S. Library of Congress
TXu

# Dedication

This book is dedicated to
my daughters who I love dearly,
Tondra, Beth, Heather, and Michelle,
who awaits me in heaven.

# Table of Contents

| Title | Page |
|---|---|
| The End Times We Were Never Taught | 6 |
| Days of Noah | 11 |
| Nephilim After The Flood | 21 |
| The Start of the End Times | 38 |
| End Time Prophecies | 47 |
| Opening Revelation | 52 |
| What John Witnessed | 57 |
| The Scroll | 59 |
| A Prophecy from God? | 67 |
| Fathers Know Best | 70 |
| Have Trumpets Been Blowing? | 81 |
| Trumpet Six Is Deafening | 91 |
| The Timing of the Tribulation | 101 |
| The Source of Teaching | 109 |
| Timing of the Rapture | 115 |
| Antichrist | 128 |
| The Little Scroll | 150 |
| The Two Witnesses | 152 |
| The Woman and the Dragon | 153 |

# Table of Contents Continued

| **Title** | **Page** |
|---|---|
| Parables, Allegory, and Swine | 159 |
| There are Two Sides to Everything | 175 |
| John's Teaching | 191 |
| The Heavens | 212 |
| Seals, Trumpets, and Bowls | 241 |
| The Harlot and Babylon | 244 |
| The Cup of the Harlot | 261 |
| The Great Tribulation | 272 |
| Orchestrated Shadows | 275 |
| Hard Times | 284 |
| The Just Ending | 295 |
| Off We Go | 301 |
| Non Stop Action | 304 |
| The Jews | 312 |
| It Ends At Jerusalem | 324 |
| King of Kings | 338 |
| Into Heaven | 362 |
| Final Thoughts from Me and God | 372 |

# The "End Times" We Were Never Taught

You may find this book to be startling. Had I read it a few years ago, it certainly would have been to me. Quite frankly, much of what we will cover in this book is nothing like you or I have been taught about the end times. But now, after extensive research, I find that traditional teaching on the end times is exactly that, teaching based more on tradition than on actual information given us by God.

One of my favorite stories is about the girl who watched her mother cut the end off the roast before she put it in the oven and asked her mother "why." The mother said it was the way her mother cooked a roast, but the curious little girl wasn't satisfied with the answer and pressed her mother with another "why." Not being able to come up with a justifiable reason for the lopping off of the end of the roast, the mother said, "Let's call Grandma and find out." When reached by phone, Grandma explained that she did it because her mother prepared a roast that way. Naturally, the mother's curiosity was now peaked to match her daughter's, so the two decided to drive to the nursing home and talk to Great Grandma in person to find the obviously important underlying cause for shortening the hunk of beef to make a perfect roast. Great Grandma was found rocking in her chair and fortunately was still extremely alert for a woman of her advanced age of 102. After the important question was posed, and mother and daughter sat poised for the true revelation that resulted in gourmet roast preparation. Great Grandma announced the underlying recipe secret, "My baking pan was a very small one and I always had to chop off the end of the meat in order to get it to fit." And such was born a tradition that as time went on became part of the never to be ignored cooking instructions for a perfect roast.

Unfortunately the more I really dig into why we Christians believe as we do about many of the "sacred" doctrines and teachings of our religion, the more I find that the origins of them more often than I might hope are almost as baseless as lopping off the end of the roast was for the descendants of Great Grandma in the above story. We believe things, and do things, because they have been taught to us, or repeated so many times, that we almost think they were instructions from Jesus Himself. But contrary to coming from the mouth of our Lord, traditions came from men. And unlike we normally are instructed, my experience is that traditions should be questioned.

In so doing, however, we may find that the traditions are good things, such as rituals that have been kept in tack since the very beginning of Christianity. One example was what I found when trying to trace back as far as I could the way we handle communion in church. My journey took me all the way back to Justin Martyr, who in the first half of the second century explained communion to the Romans by writing:

"On finishing the prayers we greet each other with a kiss. Then Bread and a cup of water mixed with wine are brought to the leader and he, taking them, sends up praise and glory to the Father of the Universe through the name of the Son and of the Holy Spirit, and offers thanksgiving at some length that we have been deemed worthy to receive these things. When the leader has finished the prayers and thanksgivings, the whole congregation assents, saying, "Amen." ("Amen" is Hebrew for "So be it.") Then those whom we call deacons give to each of those present a portion of the consecrated bread and wine and water, and they take it to the absent."

From <u>The First Apology</u> by Justin Martyr.

In such a case as that, it is very gratifying for me to find that we are still following a tradition the same way as those who were taught by the original apostles.

On a different level, in researching our traditions or traditional teaching I sometimes find things that may help in our understanding of God's working throughout history, and that also is a good thing. For instance, we have a traditional teaching in our churches that talks about how God used Alexander the Great's "Common Greek" language to facilitate the spread of the Gospel. Although the Bible prophesies much about Alexander the Great in the book of Daniel, it does not mention anything about the Common Greek language. History, however, written by man, does explain why Alexander formulated the Common Greek language and made it mandatory that all the people groups he conquered from Greece to Egypt learn to speak it. Later on, this was extremely helpful for the spread of Christianity by the apostles and their followers. Therefore, in this instance, historical fact shows us one traditional teaching that is not based on the information in the Bible, but still is helpful for us in seeing God's hand in the building of His early church.

Of course, my favorite tradition as a boy growing up in the mountains of North Carolina was the "covered dish suppers," when each of the church ladies brought their very best dishes. Wow! Some of the best fried chicken you have ever tasted. And baked beans, potato salad, biscuits that would melt in your mouth with honey, and every possible desert you could imagine. And all of it you wanted. I can attest that I was really big on traditions back then. In fact, I would love to relive that tradition again, weekly. Anyone for "dinner on the grounds?"

But sometimes traditions and traditional teaching can actually lead us away from what the Word of God teaches, and if so, they can be destructive. The end result is that our relying on traditional teaching without ever questioning it can be a big part of the reason why Jesus wrote to our modern church in Revelation 3:16 with the frightening words, *"I am going to spit you out of my mouth."*

This book is not a book that will attempt to cover all of the traditions that we hold dear. It will, however, challenge some of the traditional thinking that we have about the end times. The search may result in some positions that at first might appear to be extremely radical. But please know that these positions were not arrived at nonchalantly. I mentioned in the first paragraph that extensive research went into what you are about to read. And quite naturally, much prayer time, too.

What I have come to realize is that the end times will probably be a lot different from what you might have been taught if you ever were involved in a Bible study on Revelation and the end times. This book, therefore, will challenge what you have come to believe about the period known as the tribulation. Your view of the future of the world you live in is about to be changed forever. I think you will be amazed.

Some of the things we will be discussing may sound far fetched and unbelievable. Remember, however, that what will be presented comes from God's Word, the Bible, which we proved in earlier books is completely true and one hundred per cent reliable. That proof stemmed from the fact that of the more than six thousand prophetic verses that should have come to pass by now, every single one has indeed been fulfilled exactly as the Bible said they would. Such an astounding number of fulfilled prophecies, with never a mistake, could only have been made by someone outside of our time limitations. Someone who could actually see the future; something that no mortal human being could ever do. And that someone is God, the Author.

There are more than two thousand remaining prophetic verses in the Bible that have not been fulfilled. They all deal with the end times, and we can be fully confident that they, too, will be fulfilled as accurately as the first six thousand were. We need to be aware, though, that exactly how those prophecies will be fulfilled is not always as plain as we might think. In retrospect, fulfilled prophecies can elicit an "aha, now I see how He did it." Fulfilled prophecies are normally easy to see.

Unfulfilled prophecies, however, are always a matter of speculation. So, when a "Bible prophecy expert" says that such and such will definitely happen in a specific way, he may in fact turn out to be way off base. By the same token, some parts of this book that propose future events may also turn out to be off the mark.

I will say, though, that there is one ingredient that I endeavored to utilize that I feel will make those interpretations based on a much more solid footing than most of what is taught today. That ingredient is the fact that as much as possible I used the teaching that came directly from the Apostle John, after he had written Revelation, rather than from some idea that sprang to someone's mind as being plausible hundreds of years later, and was then repeated so often that everyone came to believe it was gospel. In other words, I have attempted to question very hard "traditions" created by man when they disagreed with what John taught to his students like Polycarp.

The oral teaching about the end times that John passed on to his students was strictly adhered to by Polycarp as he in turn taught his student, Irenaeus, and so it was by Irenaeus when he in turn instructed students such as Hippolytus. Unfortunately it seems that following that third generation, people felt the need to add their own ideas to the prescribed oral teaching of John. And so, as time went on, every succeeding generation of "prophecy scholars" felt that they could increase their standing by adding something to the mix. The end result is a teaching today that is so far removed from what the Apostle John told his students that it is almost unrecognizable in many ways.

So, yes, as with any discussion of future events, part of what you will read in this book will be speculative. However, after doing the research necessary, I feel that sticking closely to John's interpretation reduces greatly the speculative nature. Who better to teach us than someone who was taught directly by Jesus as John was?

To start with, though, we will go back in the Bible to things that include no speculation at all. Although not normally discussed, we will be examining things that God's Word tells us actually happened. And even though we can be sure that they are true, we will find things that will be utterly mind boggling.

All footnoting information is included in body of the text.

# Days of Noah

There is an intriguing and often misunderstood teaching from our Master, Jesus. The disciples once questioned Christ about his second coming by asking,

*"When will this happen, and what will be the sign of your coming and of the end of the age."* Matthew 24:3.

The answer Jesus gave was,

*"As it was in the days of Noah, so it will be at the coming of the Son of Man."* Matthew 24:37.

Most of Christianity teaches that the reference by Jesus was based on the rampant sin that was in the world at the time of Noah. But let's think about it, sin has always been here, and every age seems to have had evil periods that were way too horrible for God to have put up with. If sin had been the reason for the flood, God would have been wiping out mankind every few years. There had to be more to it than that. But what else was happening that could have made God do something as drastic as to cause the flood?

Immediately before the introduction of Noah in Genesis 6 there are four verses that may be one of the most important parts in the Bible; however, after listening to thousands of sermons I have found that these verses are seldom studied. Those rarely mentioned verses say:

*"When man began to increase in number on the earth and daughters were born to them, the **sons of God** saw that the daughters of men were beautiful, and they married any of them that they chose. ... Then the Lord said, 'My Spirit will not contend with man forever'... The **Nephilim** were on the earth in those days - and **also afterward** - when the **sons of God** went to the daughters of men and had children by them."* Genesis 6:1-4.

The Hebrew term translated here as *sons of God* was B'Nai HaElohim, which is consistently used throughout the Old Testament to mean angels. In fact, the 270 B.C. Septuagint simply used the word *angels* in these verses.

Wow! Now there's a thought that is kind of hard to swallow. Angels had sex with regular women and had children. We can understand why most ministers don't particularly want to open that can of worms. But even Josephus Flavius, the noted first century Jewish historian, wrote in <u>Antiquities</u>:

"They made God their enemy, for many angels of God accompanied with women, and begat sons that proved unjust, and despisers of all that was good."

Obviously these angels were rebellious and had to be punished. And punished they were, for we read in the New Testament,

*"For if God did not spare angels when they sinned, but sent them to hell, putting them into gloomy dungeons to be held for judgment; if He did not spare the ancient world when he brought the flood on its ungodly people, but protected Noah..."*  2 Peter 2:4-5.

God did punish them severely by putting these rebellious angels in hell, and as an aside, *hell* in this verse is the Hebrew word Tatarus, which means "dark abode of woe." Even Jude, the half-brother of Jesus, told us,

*"And the angels who did not keep their positions of authority but abandoned their home - these He has kept in darkness, bound with everlasting chains for judgment on the great Day."*  Jude 6.

When Jude says that the angels he is talking about *"abandoned their home,"* he is referring to the fact that they left their home in heaven and visited earth to take for themselves human women. It was only these angels that are currently bound over in chains awaiting their judgment. This action has not been taken against Satan and the other angels that rebelled with him. We must remember that a third of the angels had earlier joined Lucifer, Satan, in his rebellion against God, for we read in the scriptures,

"His (Lucifer's) tail swept a third of the stars (angels) out of the sky and flung them to the earth."     Revelation 12:4.

OK, so some really bad angels left their spiritual dimension, materialized as we know they can from numerous scriptures, and had sex with women, fathering children. But why?

Satan knew, from the time he was caught seducing mankind in the Garden of Eden, that God would send a Messiah to destroy him. God had told him of his future punishment, something Satan has never forgotten:

*"I will put enmity between you and the woman, and between your offspring* (seed) *and hers; he will crush your head, and you will strike His heel."*     Genesis 3:15.

Satan's plan, therefore, was to get some of his angel cronies to have sex with Eve's line and pollute the gene pool. By doing this, that cunning old devil figured he could outsmart God. Of course, God foiled the plan by sending a flood to wipe out Satan's bad seed. That's where Noah comes in.

*"Noah was a righteous man, blameless among the people of his time, and he walked with God."*     Genesis 6:9.

The King James Version says, *"perfect in his generation."* In reality, the word interpreted in these two versions as "blameless" or "perfect" was the Hebrew word tamiym, which actually means "without blemish, without spot, or unimpaired." It is the same word used when the Bible later instructs the children of God to bring animals that are "without spot or blemish" to sacrifice to God. This physical perfection is the real key for God selecting Noah. Yes, he was righteous, and he walked with God, but much more than that, his genes had not been polluted by Satan's seed. This is gigantic. This is the real reason for the flood.

And as confirmation that this was the reason for the flood we can look to the oral teaching of the Apostle John as recorded by Irenaeus who was mentored by John's student Polycarp. We will be discussing Polycarp and Irenaeus and this oral teaching in detail later, but the important point now is for us to understand that Irenaeus, in chapter twenty nine, section two of his book, Against Heresies, stated of the flood that it was "due to the apostasy of the angels."

End of story. Right? The flood occurred, and all the Nephilim, the seed of Satan, were destroyed. But there's a hitch. If this corruption of the gene pool was the big thing that had happened, and God took care of the problem with the flood, why did Jesus make the following extremely important statement?

*"As it was in the days of Noah, so it will be at the coming of the Son of Man."*

Could it be that there will be Nephilim on the earth at the time of Christ's second coming? And if so, are there Nephilim on the earth today? How well do you know your next door neighbor?

The plot thickens.

## Nephilim

*"The **Nephilim** were on the earth in those days - and **also afterward** - when the **sons of God** went to the daughters of men and had children by them."* Genesis 6:4.

Obviously the disconcerting phrase is "also afterward." This states plainly that the Nephilim were going to continue to be a problem even after the flood. And, boy oh boy, have they ever been a problem.

There are two books that were around in the time of Jesus that He very conceivably studied. The first one, The Book of Enoch, was written in four sections from 200 BC to 100 BC, and personally I am totally convinced that it was inspired by God, very much as our normal sixty six Bible books were. In fact, St. Origin was quite upset when the Catholic Church did not include The Book of Enoch in our Bible at the Nicene Council. He said it was a conspiracy to keep the people from knowing that there were still Nephilim in the world, and that they would play a part in the end times. He may have been right, although I think that if God had wanted it in our Bible He certainly could have made it happen. My personal view is that although I do believe it was inspired by God, the sixty six books we have in our Bible also comprise the "Book of Life," with all our names, etc., written in code underneath the surface text, whereas The Book of Enoch is not a part of that. That being said, I will mention that The Book of Enoch is included to this day in the Coptic Christian Bible.

My reason for believing it was inspired by God is that it was quoted several times in our Bible, most notably in the letter by Jude, the half brother of Jesus, which says,

*"Enoch, the seventh from Adam, prophesied about these men: 'See, the Lord is coming with thousands upon thousands of his holy ones."* Jude 1:14.

Jude got that quote directly from the ancient text which says:

"And behold! He cometh with ten thousands of His holy ones to execute judgment upon all, and to destroy all the ungodly: and to convict all flesh of all the works of their ungodliness which they have ungodly committed, and of all the hard things which ungodly sinners have spoken against Him." Book One, verse 9, The Book of Enoch.

Since we know that God wrote every word in the Bible, I can not imagine God quoting from The Book of Enoch unless He was quoting from a source He Himself had already written (inspired).

The book is ostensibly written by one of Enoch's descendants, who believed the "oral tradition" that had been passed down through the centuries were words from Enoch himself. As you know, oral tradition back then was quite reliable, since each person made sure they memorized each word to pass on to the next generation. So, the book was written as if Enoch himself is doing the talking. And in the above quote from the Biblical book of Jude, the writer, God Himself, when quoting from The Book of Enoch, states that in fact Enoch himself was being quoted when He says *"Enoch, the seventh from Adam, prophesied about these men."*

The Book of Enoch is interesting because it talks quite a lot about the Nephilim, giving much more detail than Genesis does, even listing the names of the angels who were involved in this horrendous act. For instance, we read in it:

"And it came to pass when the children of men had multiplied that in those days were born unto them beautiful and comely daughters. And the angels, the children of the heaven, saw and lusted after them, and said to one another: 'Come, let us choose us wives from among the children of men and beget us children.' And Semjaza, who was their leader, said unto them: 'I fear ye will not indeed agree to do this deed, and I alone shall have to pay the penalty of a great sin.' And they all answered him and said: 'Let us all swear an oath, and all bind ourselves by mutual imprecations not to abandon this plan but to do this thing.' Then sware they all together and bound themselves by mutual imprecations upon it. And they were in all two hundred; who descended in the days of Jared on the summit of Mount Hermon, and they called it Mount Hermon, because they had sworn and bound themselves by mutual imprecations upon it. And these are the names of their leaders: Samlazaz, their leader, Araklba, Rameel, Kokablel, Tamlel, Ramlel, Danel, Ezeqeel, Baraqijal, Asael, Armaros, Batarel, Ananel, Zaq1el, Samsapeel, Satarel, Turel, Jomjael, Sariel. These are their chiefs of tens.
And all the others together with them took unto themselves wives, and each chose for himself one, and they began to go in unto them and to defile themselves with them, and they taught them charms and enchantments, and the cutting of roots, and made them acquainted with plants. And they became pregnant, and they bare great giants, whose height was three thousand ells."

Chapters 6 and 7, The Book of Enoch.

Did you notice, by the way that the angels "descended in the days of Jared?" Jared was the fifth in line from Adam, the father of Enoch, and the great, great grandfather of Noah. This information on the timing of this angelic disobedience and the birth of the original Nephilim is not given to us in Genesis, but if every detail about those early years that we might be interested in knowing had been put in Genesis, it might have ended up being a million pages long.

To me, however, the real eye opener of the sections of The Book of Enoch that deal with the Nephilim is a paragraph that tells us:

"Now the Nephilim, who have been born of spirit and of flesh, shall be called upon the earth evil spirits, and on earth shall be their habitation. Evil spirits shall proceed from their flesh. ... Evil spirits shall they be upon the earth, and the spirits of the wicked shall they be called. The habitation of the spirits of heaven shall be in heaven, but upon earth shall be the habitation of terrestrial spirits, who are born on earth. The spirits of the Nephilim shall be like clouds, which shall oppress, corrupt, fall, contend, and bruise those upon the earth." Chapter 15, The Book of Enoch.

People think of demons as being the fallen angels, but that is not so. The fallen angels are kept in Tatarus, a place of hell. They are no longer on the earth. As for the Nephilim, however, that is not the case. When they died, their spirits were not kept in Tatarus. Those spirits were obviously not allowed to go to heaven, and they were not even sent to what we might think of as hell. Therefore, the spirits of the Nephilim had no place to go. They remained on earth, and **they became what we now refer to as demons**.

You read that right. **Demons are the spirits of the Nephilim**. What we just read from The Book of Enoch described them by saying "The spirits of the Nephilim shall be like clouds, which shall oppress, corrupt, fall, contend, and bruise those upon the earth." The demons that Jesus cast out of people and **the demons on the earth today are in fact the spirits of the Nephilim** who died, the offspring of fallen angels and human women.

Interestingly, the word, demon, is not found in the Old Testament until after the flood, after the death of Nephilim had occurred. And we can see that these spirits of the Nephilim started their evil work immediately, on the very next generation of humans. One source that refers to that is the second book we mentioned above, Book of Jubilees, which was written about 150 BC. Although I am not as firmly convinced that it was inspired by God, like I am The Book of Enoch, the Book of Jubilees (or just Jubilees) was a very highly regarded book by early church leaders and is included in the Ethiopian Bible today. The Book of Jubilees does give us good insight at how quickly the demons went to work on mankind:

"And in the third week of this jubilee the evil demons began to lead astray the sons of Noah and deceive them. And the sons came to Noah their father and told him concerning the demons which were leading astray, darkening, and slaying the sons of their sons. And he prayed before the Lord his God and said; 'Lord of the spirits of all flesh, thou hast shown mercy to me and hast delivered me and my children from the waters of the deluge, and hast not suffered me to be destroyed as thou didst the children of destruction (the Nephilim), for thy grace was great over men, and great was thy mercy over my soul; may thy grace be exalted over the sons of thy sons, and may **the evil spirits (spirits of Nephilim)** not rule over them to destroy the earth. And thou hast verily blessed me and my sons that we increase and multiply and fill the earth. And thou knowest how the Watchmen (angels), the fathers of these spirits, acted in my day; and these spirits also which are alive, cast them into prison and hold them in the places of judgment." Jubilees 10:1-4.

We all know that God answers our prayers with "yes, no, or wait until I am ready to do it." In this case Noah asked that the demons, the spirits of the Nephilim, be taken from the earth and thrown in prison, but God gave him the "wait" answer we all hate to get. God needed the demons to remain on earth to fulfill His plan.

There was another part of the "also afterward" in the Genesis 6:4, *"The **Nephilim** were on the earth in those days - and **also afterward.**"* First, as we have learned, the spirits of the Nephilim who died in the flood remained on the earth and became the demons who are still here today. But secondly, more Nephilim appeared in the flesh in Biblical history after the flood. But how could that have been possible if God had sent the flood in order to do away with them? Weren't they all destroyed? Had the bad seed not been eradicated? Evidently not. So, how did the Nephilim seed continue to comingle with normal human seed after the flood? These are questions we need to answer, and we will.

The Nephilim were always giants. And, of course, when Moses sent the twelve spies out hundreds of years after the flood to look over the Promised Land, they encountered giants. In fact, the ten frightened spies lamented,

*"We saw the Nephilim there. We seemed like grasshoppers in our own eyes, and we look the same to them."*                      Numbers 13:13.

That, of course, was a bit of an exaggeration by intimidated men, but they were gigantic compared to normal humans. As an aside, although the Hebrew word Nephilim normally means "fallen ones," it is sometimes translated "giant" because the Greek word for nephilim is "gigantes." At any rate, Satan was up to his old tricks, trying to stop the birth of Jesus who he knew would be born in the promise land. So Satan had established more Nephilim as a front guard to try to keep the Israelites out of the promise land and thwart God's plan of the first coming of His Messiah.

With this information we can better understand why Joshua, when he led the Jews into that land of promise forty years later, was instructed by God to kill every one of those tribes, including the women and children. God wanted all the living Nephilim destroyed. Reading those passages without understanding the story of the Nephilim makes God look ruthless. When we understand that He only wanted demonic beings destroyed, we get a different picture of God's character. Unfortunately, Joshua did not fully obey God, and later David had to deal with Goliath and his brothers.

For us to understand demons we need to know that demons understand the Bible, probably better than most of us do. They know that they will not be resurrected, for the demons themselves read in places like Isaiah 26:14, which talks about them by saying,

*"They are now dead, they live no more; those departed spirits do not rise,"*

That is why they seek embodiment. They want to be in human bodies. Jesus, of course, cast many demons out of people. They know they are completely doomed if they remain only spirits. The "wait" part of God's answer to Noah's prayer will end. The demons, the spirits of the Nephilim, can see that their time is limited. Is it any wonder that they hate you and me so much? They can see that our future is eternity in heaven, while theirs is complete destruction.

But God's plan is to use them for a while longer. In fact, they will even be present on the last day of the tribulation, for we read about John's vision,

*"Then I saw the evil spirits that looked like frogs; they came out of the mouth of the dragon, out of the mouth of the beast and out of the mouth of the false prophet. They are spirits of demons performing miraculous signs, and they go out to the kings of the whole world, to gather them for the battle on the great day of God Almighty."* Revelation 16:13-14.

I must tell you that in the early years of my Christian walk I had a hard time wrapping my mind around the existence of demons. It was easy to learn about and grasp the notions of God's love, grace, and forgiveness, as well as thoughts of heaven, peace, and eternal bliss. But Satan and demons were not pleasant subjects for me, and my mind wanted to either not believe in them or at least relegate them to obscurity. That may be true of you as well. One of the things that changed that type of thinking for me was a period of musing and honesty with myself about a statement made by Saint Augustine. He profoundly said, "If you believe some of the Bible, but not all of it, it is yourself you believe and not the Bible." When we let that truly sink in and take hold of us, unbelief in demons or Satan is done away with.

# Nephilim After The Flood

The reason for this book is to delve into the future, and since I began this book with an introduction to the Nephilim, I am sure it is obvious to you that I believe Nephilim are going to play a part in the end times. With that in mind it is important to see how the Nephilim survived the flood and whether or not they are in the world today in bodily form and not solely surviving among us as demons. Even more important may be a discussion of why God allowed all of this to happen. Although we obviously do not know the mind of God, let's first consider what reason He may have had to allow Nephilim to be born in the first place. We can be sure that if the Nephilim were not going to play a part in His overall plan, He would have put a stop to them at the very outset. We need to realize that everything that happens is ultimately in God's control. In <u>Unlocking God's Secrets</u> I wrote:

God created mankind because "God is love," and a love that indescribable must be manifested in a love relationship with an "other." That love should not, dare we say "could not," exist for all of eternity with no "other" to love and be loved in return. Mankind is the necessary "other." God made man as His "other."

In order to have an "other" to love, and to be loved by, any being would want the other to be of like nature. A robin seeks a robin, a dolphin seeks a dolphin, and a giraffe seeks a giraffe.

In the very same manner, we read,

*"Then God said, 'Let us make man in our own image, in our likeness. ... So God created man in His own image, in the image of God He created him; male and female He created them."*   Genesis 3:26-27.

The problem is that love that is manipulated or coerced in any way is not true love. God obviously knew that. In the sixty six books of the Bible we find the word love used 808 separate times. God is the expert on love. He knew that He could not create an "other" that expressed only a robotic kind of love, and be satisfied with that kind of love. You and I are made "in His image" and we can fully understand that fact.

In order for love to be real and meaningful, it must be returned to us by choice. Anything else is not truly love. Therefore, God had to create us with free will. We had to have the ability to return His love or reject it. In the end, it had to be our choice to love Him or not. The idea of predestination dies with that one simple fact. Mankind was not created as robots. You and I have free will, just like God does. That is the only way God would have it. It is the only way to have honest love.

The necessity of free will, of choice, brings with it the necessity of two things to choose from. Mankind could have been given free will, but it would have been completely meaningless without something other than God to choose. We could tell a child that he could have any puppy in the pet store to bring home and love, but if there is only one puppy in the store, the child's free will in the matter is actually non existent.

With that as a fundamental fact, God had to also create an alternative for His longed for love recipient. He was forced to give mankind someone else to choose to love. The created angel, Lucifer, was the needed possible "other suitor" for you and me; a being so opposite from God that a real choice could be made.

Everything about God is crystal clear. There are no gray areas. Let's examine just a few of God's attributes:

> *"The Lord is righteous in all His ways."* Psalm 145:17
> *"God is light; in Him there is no darkness."* 1 John 1:5
> *"There is no one holy like the Lord."* 1 Samuel 2:2
> *"All His ways are just. Upright and just is He."* Deut. 32:4
> *"All Your words are true."* Psalm 119:160

We could go on and on for page after page, but the bottom line is that everything about God is good, pure, holy, righteous, honest, faithful, etc., etc., etc. It is easier to just say that God is perfect, and He can not be in the presence of darkness (sin).

Satan, on the other hand is the total opposite. In John 10:10 Jesus said that he *"comes only to steal and kill and destroy."*

He went on to tell us, *"He was a murderer from the beginning, not holding to the truth."* John 8:44

Everything that God is, Satan is not, and vice versa.

The other problem lies in the fact that if mankind had been created perfect like God, not being able to even be in the presence of sin, we would have been forced to choose Him. We would once again be devoid of free will. If you and I had been created exactly like God, our choice between returning God's love or choosing Satan and sin would have been moot. Once again, we would have had no true free will, and our love would have been robotic in nature. Remember, God wants us to be able to choose to love Him. He wants honest love.

The truth is obvious, though. Mankind was not made perfect. And it was by God's choice that we weren't. Psalm 51:5 states clearly, *"Surely I was sinful at birth, sinful from the time my mother conceived me."*

We were not just born with a sin nature, but we were also conceived that way. Ponder that. It had to be so. This is the only way that you and I and the rest of mankind could have a choice. It was a risk on God's part to design His plan that way, but it had to be. Every single person could reject him, but He had to give mankind an honest to goodness choice in the matter. Eternity would be a long time to spend with a love that He knew was not truly and freely given. Remaining alone would actually be preferable. And lest we forget, the end result of this entire creation was to determine how God would spend eternity. It is His Story.

He also knows that in order to make that choice a real choice, He must also create that other possible suitor that His beloved could choose, one totally opposite from Himself, such as Satan, who incidentally also was the most beautiful angel God ever created. Creating Satan so beautiful was done so as not to stack the deck in His own favor. God did not want the choice to be an obvious one. He made Satan and sin desirable. God also knew that He must instill in His beloved the ability to actually choose Satan. To choose Satan took the ability to be able to tolerate sin, the very thing that Satan would use to court her with."     <u>Unlocking God's Secrets</u>, by Bob Morley.

God's desire for us to love him solely from a position of free will is in my opinion the reason why he allowed the Nephilim in the world in the first place. In order for you and I to truly make an honest choice, there needed to be a way for us to be tempted. That is the main job of the demons, to push us in the direction of Satan. And only the spirits of the Nephilim could become demons. This obviously is speculation on my part, but it is the one thing that truly makes sense of what otherwise would seem to be a senseless part of Biblical history.

Now, if we assume that to be correct, why the flood? Nephilim, not being eternal creatures, would eventually die without the flood anyway, so God would still have had the needed demons to tempt us. Obviously the flood was not to altogether eliminate the Nephilim. The reason for the flood was to preserve a bloodline from Eve that did not have the corrupted seed so that Jesus could be born. By the time of the flood, Noah and his family were the only pure humans left. And maintaining a pure bloodline for His Son to be born into was of utmost importance for all of God's plan. Jesus could not be born with Nephilim genes. That was the reason for the flood.

As an aside, seldom do Biblical "scholars" who write commentaries on the Nephilim ever get into the question of why they existed in the first place. But if they do, their answer revolves around how Satan orchestrated their arrival in his battle against God. Well, let's clear something up. There is no battle between Satan and God. There may be one in Satan's mind, but that is the extent of it. Satan is not omnipresent. He is not omniscient. And he is not omnipotent. Satan is nothing more than a created being. An angel to be sure. And possibly one on the order of Michael. But that is it. Thinking that there is a battle going on between God and Satan is as ludicrous as saying that there is a battle between a one hour old baby bunny and a full grown elephant. The instant Satan ever became the slightest thorn in God's side would be the instant he would cease to exist. He was created for the purpose of being a part of God's plan, and he is fulfilling his role. As far as God is concerned, Satan is a tool He is using to achieve His goal, and when that goal is achieved, Satan will be done away with.

But now let's get to the question of how the Nephilim surfaced again after the flood. We know that the spirits of those Nephilim who perished in the flood became demons, but how did any Nephilim surface again after the flood if Noah and his family were the last of the humans whose blood line was not corrupted by the Nephilim seed?

# The "N" Gene Thrives

In Genesis 6:4 God tells us about the situation on the earth at the time of the flood,

*"The Nephilim were on the earth in those days, **and also afterward…**"*

The verse above makes it clear that Nephilim giants returned after the flood. Nowhere in scripture is it again written that angels ever cohabited and/or had relations with human women after the flood. Genesis 6 was the only instance of this. So how did the Nephilim return? How could this have happened? The Bible, of course, holds the answer:

*"Noah was six hundred years old when the floodwaters came on the earth. And Noah and his sons and his wife and his sons' wives entered the ark to escape the waters of the flood."* Genesis 7:6-7.

While Noah and his sons were one hundred per cent human, we are not told the same about the wives of his three sons, Shem, Ham and Japheth. What is clear is that one or more of these women must have been carrying the Nephilim gene. This had to be the source of the post-flood Nephilim. As we said, nowhere in the Bible is it ever stated that angels once again cohabited with human women, so the gene was planted prior to the flood.

The first time Nephilim giants are mentioned by name after the flood is in Numbers 13, after the Exodus, in which Moses led the Israelites out of Egypt to go to God's designated Promised Land. Moses sent twelve spies to scout out the land in advance. Two of the spies, Caleb and Joshua, spoke of the land in glowing terms and urged the Israelites to enter and rightfully claim the land God had promised them. But the other ten spies had a different opinion for we read in Numbers 13:31-33,

*"Then Caleb silenced the people before Moses and said, 'We should go up and take possession of the land, for we can certainly do it.' But the men who had gone up with him said, 'We can't attack those people; they are stronger than we are.' And they spread among the Israelites a bad report about the land they had explored. They said, 'The land we explored devours those living in it. All the people we saw there are of great size. We saw the*

*Nephilim there (the descendants of Anak come from the Nephilim). We seemed like grasshoppers in our own eyes, and we looked the same to them."*

A few things should be noted in the above verses. First, the giants living in the Promised Land at that time were descendants of a specific person named Anak. This description, where a Nephilim is referred to as "[so and so] who was born of the giant" shows that the Nephilim hybrids after the flood were the offspring of other giants and not angels. And in Numbers 13, the giants the spies saw were the sons of the Nephilim giant Anak.

Second, they were so large that the Israelites spies were like insects to them. And third, these giants had special agricultural knowledge because they knew how to grow grapes so large that it took two Israelite men using poles to carry a cluster. This is one thing that most people forget when thinking about the Nephilim, they had knowledge that normal people did not have.

So, how did the giants return after the flood and how did they know to be in the exact place that God was going to send His chosen people, namely the land of Canaan? The answer starts with the lineage after the flood.

The Bible provides a specific genealogy of the Nephilim giants after the flood that can be traced back to Noah's own sons. What seems to be consistent with the presence of the Nephilim gene was an affinity for evil, due to their fallen angelic parentage. And among Noah's sons, Ham was by far the most wicked.

*"The sons of Noah who came out of the ark were Shem, Ham and Japheth. (Ham was the father of Canaan.)"* Genesis 9:18.

From the first time Ham is introduced, he is described as "the father of Canaan." Notice that none of his brothers get any similar distinction. Whenever special descriptions are included in a genealogy in God's Word it is the Bible's way of saying something significant happened with that particular event. In this case, it is clear that Canaan carried the Nephilim gene. This could only happen through his mother, Ham's wife, having the Nephilim gene herself, since we know that Noah "in all his generations" was one hundred per cent human. If Ham was wicked and not a follower of God, the chances of him taking a wife who was a part of the Nephilim hybrid pagan culture was much greater than that of his two brothers. We can say that because throughout Scripture men who fell into sin often ended up marrying wives who worshiped false gods. And from what the Bible tells us, Ham was certainly not a follower of God. In fact, he was involved in an inappropriate incident with Noah that led to a curse:

*"Noah, a man of the soil, proceeded to plant a vineyard. When he drank some of its wine, he became drunk and lay uncovered inside his tent. Ham, the father of Canaan, saw his father's nakedness and told his two brothers outside. But Shem and Japheth took a garment and laid it across their shoulders; then they walked in backward and covered their father's nakedness. Their faces were turned the other way so that they would not see their father's nakedness.*
*When Noah awoke from his wine and found out what his youngest son had done to him, he said, 'Cursed be Canaan! The lowest of slaves will he be to his brothers.' He also said, 'Blessed be the Lord, the God of Shem! May Canaan be the slave of Shem."*          Genesis 9:20-26.

The details of this incident are strange to say the least, but it can be concluded that Ham, out of evil intent, looked at his father's nakedness and then made it public. The Hebrew term for *"outside"* in that verse is "chwuts," which means "outside, in the street," so obviously Ham made the incident of his father getting drunk public knowledge. And there is proof of how God looks at what Ham did as an evil thing or an immoral act in Habakkuk when God says:

*"Woe to him who gives drink to his neighbors, pouring it from the wineskin till they are drunk, so that he can gaze on their naked bodies. You will be filled with shame instead of glory. Now it is your turn! Drink and be exposed! The cup from the Lord's right hand is coming around to you, and disgrace will cover your glory."*          Habakkuk 2:15-16.

Shem and Japheth, the righteous children of Noah, were much different than Ham because they tried to respect their father's dignity by not looking at him, and instead carefully covered him. Ham's sin was so severe that it resulted in his youngest son, Canaan, becoming the second person in the

Bible to be cursed by God. The first to be cursed was Cain, the wicked son of Adam and Eve who was the world's first murderer.

What is interesting for us in this study is that Canaan, of Ham's three sons, was the one cursed. Why? And why is Ham distinguished as *the father of Canaan*? Is it possible that Canaan was already showing the appearance of being a Nephilim? This is not stated in scripture, but we will see a similar distinction made for another infamous hybrid being below. What we can know with certainty is that from the line of Ham we find the resurgence of the Nephilim giants.

The lineage of the post-flood giants can be traced specifically to three of Ham's sons, Cush, Mizraim and Canaan. The first grandson of Ham who receives special designation is King Nimrod who led the Tower of Babel rebellion. Was he a Nephilim?

*"The sons of Ham: Cush, Mizraim, Put and Canaan. The sons of Cush: Seba, Havilah, Sabtah, Raamah and Sabteca. The sons of Raamah: Sheba and Dedan. Cush was the father of Nimrod, who grew to be a mighty warrior on the earth. He was a mighty hunter before the Lord; that is why it is said, 'Like Nimrod, a mighty hunter before the Lord.' The first centers of his kingdom were Babylon, Erech, Akkad and Calneh, in Shinar. From that land he went to Assyria, where he built Nineveh, Rehoboth Ir, Calah and Resen, which is between Nineveh and Calah; that is the great city."* Genesis 10:6-12.

Just as Canaan received a special distinction in his genealogy, Nimrod gets several extra verses, too. Clearly this is someone of special significance. Nimrod was the first murderer and conqueror in the post flood world. He was the founder of the city of Babylon, which became a center of pagan, satanic idolatry, much of it with various versions of Nimrod himself being worshiped as a god. His name, which means "to rebel" or "let us rebel" indicates his disposition. He was an enemy of God and at the time was Satan's main servant on Earth. He is credited for leading the effort to build the Tower of Babel, a religious temple used to access the angelic realm through pagan ritual. The Tower of Babel was also the first attempt at a global government, led by Nimrod, and an attempt for man to reach the spiritual realm and "godhood" without the Lord, to which God swiftly responded by destroying the tower, confusing the languages of all the people of the world and scattering them all over the Earth. Was this grandson of Ham possibly a Nephilim?

It is interesting to note that the above verse states that Nimrod *"began to be a mighty one in the earth."* The term for "mighty one," gibborim, is the same Hebrew phrase used to describe the Nephilim giants in Chapter 6 of Genesis who were *"mighty men."* It is also the same term used to describe the giant Goliath in 1 Samuel 17:51.

In mythology, Nimrod is known by many names, among them Gilgamesh and Osiris, who were worshiped as gods. In Sumerian texts he is described as "2/3 god, 1/3 man." The Hebrew word for "began" in the verse *"began to be a mighty one in the earth"* is chalal, which means, "to profane, desecrate or pollute oneself, ritually or sexually."

Matthew Henry's Bible commentary, which was written in 1706 and is still relied on heavily by Christian scholars, talks about that verse. It states: "That which is observable and improvable in these verses is the account here given of Nimrod, v. 8-10. He is here represented as a great man in his day: He began to be a mighty one in the earth, that is, whereas those that went before him were content to stand upon the same level with their neighbors, and though every man bore rule in his own house yet no man pretended any further, Nimrod's aspiring mind could not rest here; he was resolved to tower above his neighbors, not only to be eminent among them, but to lord it over them. The same spirit that actuated the giants before the flood, who became mighty men, and men of renown, now revived in him, so soon was that tremendous judgment which the pride and tyranny of those mighty men brought upon the world forgotten."

The final piece of evidence we can look at is the Septuagint, the oldest version of the Old Testament. The same verse from Genesis in the Septuagint reads:

*"And [Cush] begot [Nimrod]: he began to be a giant upon the earth. He was a giant hunter before the Lord God; therefore they say, As [Nimrod] the giant hunter before the Lord."*         Genesis 10:8-9 Septuagint (LXX).

So it appears that Nimrod, the grandson of Ham, was very likely a giant containing the Nephilim gene.

Looking further in Genesis we find,

> *"Mizraim was the father of the Ludites, Anamites, Lehabites, Naphtuhites, Pathrusites, Casluhites (from whom the Philistines came) and Caphtorites."*                Genesis 10:13-14.

We can see that Ham's son, Mizaraim, also contributed to the Nephilim lineage. In the above verse we have the first mention of the Philistines in *"(from whom the Philistines came)."* This is the nation of the giant Goliath. Calshuhim was the father of Phillistim and his family later resided in Capthor in the Promised Land. So we see the direct origins of the Philistines, one of the most hated enemies of the Israelites, who also obviously carried the Nephilim gene.

In fact, the Philistine nation was a big "hideout" for the remnant of the Nephilim giants. And they can be traced back to Casluhim, the son of Mizraim and grandson of the evil Ham.

Then, too, we have the important name, Canaan, which should be very familiar as it was the land that bore his name that was the Promised Land that The Lord reserved for the Israelites after they escaped from Egypt. The fact that Nephilim were in the Promised Land the Israelites were supposed to inhabit was no coincidence. The Philistines were worshipers of demons, fallen angels, and Satan. And the Nephilim giants among the Philistines were placed there by Satan to try to keep God's chosen people from getting in. Canaan's line also contains many other enemies of the Israelites for continuing on in Genesis God tells us,

> *"Canaan was the father of Sidon his firstborn, and of the Hittites, Jebusites, Amorites, Girgashites,"*                Genesis 10:15-16.

The Jebusites, the Amorites and Gegusites, all cousins of Nimrod, are mentioned time and time again with reference to the Israelites capturing the Promised Land. These families were usurpers in the Promised Land and carried lots of the Nephilim gene. This is once again why God had to deal mercilessly with these nations. It cannot be stressed enough that the Nephilim threatened not only the existence of the human race itself, but the ability of an all-human Messiah to eventually be born as well. Look at God's instructions to Moses on how to battle against these children of the cursed Canaan:

*"When the Lord your God brings you into the land you are entering to possess and drives out before you many nations—the Hittites, Girgashites, Amorites, Canaanites, Perizzites, Hivites and Jebusites, seven nations larger and stronger than you— and when the Lord your God has delivered them over to you and you have defeated them, then you must destroy them totally. Make no treaty with them, and show them no mercy. Do not intermarry with them. Do not give your daughters to their sons or take their daughters for your sons,"* Deuteronomy 7:1-3.

Notice that God describes these peoples as *"larger and stronger than you"* to the Israelites. The physical and military advantage was clearly on the side of the enemies of God's people, the nations that were home to the Nephilim giants. But what gave the Israelites the ultimate edge was that the Lord Himself was going to supernaturally intervene in the conflict to deliver the enemies of Israel so they could be defeated. This point is clear: God fought against and defeated the early post-flood Nephilim. This shows the severity of the matter to Him. The Lord was not allowing these superhuman, powerful hybrids to keep His people out of the land He had set aside for them. Plus, He not only tells the Israelites to wipe out these nations totally, but makes a specific point of prohibiting any marriage between them.

## Israelites and Nephilim

We all know that Moses was not allowed to take God's children into the Promised Land. That job fell to his predecessor, Joshua, the man we all look at as a phenomenal warrior and general. What most Biblical teaching seldom mentions is that Joshua did not follow God's instructions to the letter. As we saw, the plan from God was to completely annihilate the nations that contained the Nephilim seed. In that regard, Joshua failed. For instance,

*"Now the five kings had fled and hidden in the cave at Makkedah. When Joshua was told that the five kings had been found hiding in the cave at Makkedah, he said, "Roll large rocks up to the mouth of the cave, and post some men there to guard it. But don't stop! Pursue your enemies, attack*

*them from the rear and don't let them reach their cities, for the Lord your God has given them into your hand."*

*So Joshua and the Israelites destroyed them completely—almost to a man—but the few who were left reached their fortified cities."*
Joshua 10:16-20.

The last sentence tells the tale. *"Almost to a man"* is not complete annihilation. *"Almost to a man"* means that some survived. But that was not the only place where Joshua was not perfect in carrying out orders.

*"At that time Joshua went and destroyed the Anakites from the hill country: from Hebron, Debir and Anab, from all the hill country of Judah, and from all the hill country of Israel. Joshua totally destroyed them and their towns. No Anakites were left in Israelite territory; only in Gaza, Gath and Ashdod did any survive."* Joshua 11:21-22.

Again the last sentence tells the tale. *"Only in Gaza, Gath and Ashdod did any survive."* I find it extremely interesting that Gaza was one of those areas, since it is the home of trouble for Israel to this day. Additionally, Gath is now referred to as "Gath of the Philistines" and is the city where Goliath later came from. That area is what is currently known as the West Bank, once again a thorn in Israel's side. So even though God had been quite specific in his instructions, Joshua did not completely obey, allowing the Nephilim gene to continue, and possibly even being felt by Israel today. In fact, the Bible says the same,

*"But the Israelites did not drive out the people of Geshur and Maacah, so they continue to live among the Israelites to this day."* Joshua 13:13.

We must not be too hard on Joshua for his disobedience in this matter, however, because God obviously knew that His instructions would not be completely followed, and He allowed it anyway. We can only surmise that God actually wanted some of Satan's seed to survive. We must surmise that having Nephilim on earth in the future is a part of His master plan.

# Nephilim Evolve

In doing the research on the Nephilim it seemed that God was showing us that as time went on at least one of the traits that we might have thought to be dominant traits, were actually not. Whereas brown eyes is a more dominant trait when determining a baby's eye color than blue eyes, the same evidently is not the case with one thing we think of as being a distinctively Nephilim trait, gigantic size. And as Nephilim blended with normal society we can see subtle changes in that trait evolve.

One thing that did seem to remain constant was that women, although obviously carriers of the Nephilim gene, such as in the case of Ham's wife, never exhibited the giant quality. At least there is no instance in the Biblical scriptures of a giant Nephilim female.

So, let's examine Nephilim size and see what we find.

As we recall when God was talking to Moses about the Promised Land He said,

*"When the Lord your God brings you into the land you are entering to possess and drives out before you many nations—the Hittites, Girgashites, Amorites, Canaanites, Perizzites, Hivites and Jebusites, seven nations larger and stronger than you, and when the Lord your God has delivered them over to you and you have defeated them, then you must destroy them totally. Make no treaty with them, and show them no mercy."* Deuteronomy 7:1-2.

Later, in Amos, we hear the Lord talking about that earlier time and he says,

*"I destroyed the Amorite before them, though he was tall as the cedars and strong as the oaks."* Amos 2:9.

The Amorites obviously were listed in the Deuteronomy verses as one of the groups that were standing in the way of the Israelites first incursion into the Promised Land. What may be of importance in the Amos verse is God's reference to them being as *"tall as the cedars."*

The cedar is described in many places in the Bible and is normally described like it is in Ezekiel 31:3-5,

*"A cedar in Lebanon, ... it towered on high, its top above the thick foliage. ... So it towered higher than all the trees of the field."*

God obviously was telling us in Amos that the Amorites were by far much taller than normal men. Most Nephilim scholars put the height of the original Nephilim the Israelites encountered between 24 and 35 feet. We can consider that range to be speculative but they may well be fairly accurate. However, as we move along in Biblical history we find that God's Word is much more precise in giving us the heights of later Nephilim. For instance, in Deuteronomy we encounter Og, the king of Bashan,

*"Only Og king of Bashan was left of the remnant of the Rephaites. His bed was made of iron and was more than thirteen feet long and six feet wide. It is still in Rabbah of the Ammonites."* Deuteronomy 3:11.

There are some things about that verse we need to explore more closely. First, it is plausible that by *"bed"* Moses in fact meant his final bed, or his sarcophagus (coffin). This would make sense from the fact that there is no unique word for sarcophagus in Hebrew other than bed and this *"bed"* was apparently on display. It would seem strange to just have the bed of their former king lying around apparently on display. However, being able to visit the sarcophagus of their fallen king is very plausible. If that is the case, then it would suggest that the *"bed"* was not for nightly sleeping but was made just big enough for his body to be placed in. Thus, those dimensions more aptly describe the true size of this Rephaim king.

Second, the true dimensions were probably bigger than the above New International Version (NIV) quote. The New King James Version says of the dimensions, *"Nine cubits is its length and four cubits its width."* Cubits varied, and it is more probable that the cubit Moses used was the Egyptian Royal Cubit which was 20.63 inches. This would make the coffin almost fifteen feet six inches long and its width six feet ten inches. Thus we can assume that Og must have been slightly shorter than the coffin, therefore making him roughly fifteen feet tall. Either way, thirteen or fifteen feet is a big man.

Of course, the most famous of all the giant Nephilim was David's foe, Goliath.

*"A champion named Goliath, who was from Gath, came out of the Philistine camp. He was over nine feet tall. He had a bronze helmet on his head and wore a coat of scale armor of bronze weighing five thousand shekels (about 125 pounds); on his legs he wore bronze greaves, and a bronze javelin was slung on his back. His spear shaft was like a weaver's rod, and its iron point weighed six hundred shekels (about 15 pounds)."*
1 Samuel 17:4-7.

As an aside, Goliath came from an entire family of Nephilim for we are told,

*"Again there was war at Gob with the Philistines, where Elhanan the son of Jaare-Oregim the Bethlehemite killed the brother of Goliath the Gittite, the shaft of whose spear was like a weaver's beam."*
2 Samuel 21:19 NKJV.

In the famous 1952 novel, East of Eden, John Steinbeck wrote, "I believe there are monsters born in the world to human parents." In Goliath's case, it seems he was a monster born in this world of a total family of monsters of the Nephilim variety.

Actually, about this same time, roughly fifteen hundred years after the flood, the Bible relates quite a few specific incidents with giant Nephilim. For instance,

*"Then Ishbi-Benob, who was one of the sons of the giant, the weight of whose bronze spear was three hundred shekels, who was bearing a new sword, thought he could kill David. But Abishai the son of Zeruiah came to his aid, and struck the Philistine and killed him. Then the men of David swore to him, saying, "You shall go out no more with us to battle, lest you quench the lamp of Israel."*

*Now it happened afterward that there was again a battle with the Philistines at Gob. Then Sibbechai the Hushathite killed Saph, who was one of the sons of the giant."*                           2 Samuel 16-18 NKJV.

What we are seeing is that as the Nephilim gene was passed down through the generations, their size seemed to more closely replicate the normal population. The sizes we have been discussing are more dramatically noted in the following depiction:

Like me, you probably have seen pictures on the internet or passed around in e-mail of bones that were supposedly dug up recently that were the bones of Nephilim when they were still giants. Unfortunately, some of these have proven to be hoaxes. Although it may be unfair of me, this has reduced the credibility I give to any of these purported finds. However, in addition to the word of God in his Bible, which we can be certain is true, I do find intriguing the reports from others who lived two thousand years ago and were obviously much closer in time than we are to the days when the giant trait of Nephilim was still in evidence.

Tertullian, for example, who lived from 160 AD to 225 AD, and was a prolific early Christian author from Carthage, wrote that the giants' bodies were still around in his day.

And then we can read from the famous and extremely reliable Jewish historian, Josephus, who wrote of the Jews about a hundred years earlier than Tertullian,

"For which reason they removed their camp to Hebron; and when they had taken it, they slew all the inhabitants. There were till then left the race of giants, who had bodies so large, and countenances so entirely different from other men, that they were surprising to the sight, and terrible to the hearing. The bones of these men are still shown to this very day, unlike to any credible relations of other men." (xiii) Josephus.

So, in summery, we know that Nephilim, the seed of Satan, flourished prior to the flood, as well as after. We know that the souls of the Nephilim who died in the flood became the demons that were cast out of people by Jesus and are still on the earth today doing Satan's bidding. We also know that after the flood the seed of the Nephilim came about through Ham's wife, they multiplied and existed as giants, causing problems for God's chosen people all the way from the time of Noah to the time of David, about 1,000 BC. We also have seen that during that time the Nephilim seemed to reduce in size, blending in more naturally with their neighbors. Yes, truth is stranger than fiction. But unlike fiction, truth can not be dismissed.

With that as a starting point, let us leave the discussion of Nephilim for the time being and see where we stand on God's prophetic timetable and what we have to look forward to. Much of what we will learn will be far different from what you have probably learned through traditional, "man invented" teaching of the end times, the Tribulation, the Millennial Kingdom of Jesus, and beyond that into heaven. We will find that this initial discussion of the Nephilim will be useful because we will discover how they will play a part in God's plan right up until the second coming of Jesus.

Your current conception of the things that are going to happen on this planet in the future is about to be blown away, but the peace it will bring to your mind will be solid and durable. So put aside what you think you know, open your minds, and go with me on a mental adventure that will be as exciting for you as it has been for me these past several years that I have been searching and researching for the truth. You may find that predicted events of the future actually make a lot more sense after we take this mental excursion.

# The Start of the End Times

The belief in modern Christianity concerning where we are on God's timeline today is that we have not begun to see the unfolding of the Revelation scriptures because the seven year peace treaty that the antichrist will sign with Israel has not yet happened.

It makes sense that we would all believe that because that is what we have always heard, read, and been taught. Could it be, however, that we are "lopping off the end of the roast" for no good reason? It is a fact that if we hear something enough times we begin to think it is truth, but could it be that we are falling for a myth?

Popular prophecy teachers are all well intentioned, and they believe very strongly in what they have been teaching us, but they are just human like we are. They, too, have been taught the idea of the seven year peace treaty with Israel. And they read each others' books, which only serves to reinforce the concept for them. So quite naturally, they never even think to challenge what they believe to be proven interpretation.

What caused me to initially question the validity of the peace treaty interpretation was the seven year part. Think back, have you ever heard of a peace treaty that was scheduled to end at a particular time?

I can't. A peace treaty basically says that two nations are going to quit fighting and are going to try to be friends. You don't put an end date on something like that. It just makes no sense at all.

Granted, peace treaties are broken all the time, but they don't start out with the premise that they will end at a particular time. The idea of a peace treaty set up to end after seven years does not pass the "common sense" rule, yet none of our "prophecy scholars" seem to have ever even considered that.

So, let's be totally radical for a change. Let's do the unthinkable and look directly at the Word of God, with the crazy notion that if we don't find proof to back up what we have been taught, it might be time to reconsider our belief. I fully understand that what I am proposing may sound like heresy, but let's live on the wild side for a moment.

The first thing we need to understand is that all of the detailed writings about this foretold peace treaty stem from mainly one line in the Bible, and that line is not all that clear. That verse reads,

*"He will confirm a covenant with many for one 'seven.' In the middle of the 'seven' he will put an end to sacrifice and offering. And at the temple he will set up an abomination that causes desolation, until the end that is decreed is poured out on him."*                                        Daniel 9:27.

The single line in the Bible that has caused almost every Christian to think the antichrist must make a peace treaty with Israel is the very first line:

*"He will confirm a covenant with many for one 'seven.'"*

That is it. That is the sole "proof" we modern Christians have that the events foretold in Revelation can not start until the antichrist signs a peace treaty with Israel. And by the way, we are told that the signing of that peace treaty will allow the world to know for the first time who the long awaited antichrist really is. Do you think it might be wise to look a little more closely at those apparently extremely important few words? I do.

I dare say that millions of words are currently in print that paint elaborate pictures of the events surrounding the day this historic event will take place. It also seems that each expert adds a little bit more to the tale of this forthcoming monumental event. But being a tad bit skeptical, let's forget we ever read all those hallowed and enshrined words and see if we can take a stab at what God might have actually been saying in Daniel 9:27.

One thing we probably should confirm is that Israel is actually involved at all. We might expect to see the word "Israel," or maybe "Jew," or possibly "Judah" or some other word the Bible uses to allude to the nation of Israel. However, the only word we can see in the sentence, *"He will confirm a covenant with many for one 'seven.'"* is the word, *"many."* Now, here is a bold and somewhat telling statement: In not one single place in the entire Bible is Israel ever referred to as the *"many."* Not one time. But that word *"many"* is what the entire notion of a peace treaty with Israel is based on.

A very few scholars evidently have actually seen that truth so they instead insist the *"many"* refers to the nations surrounding Israel. Their contention is that the antichrist will be in Jerusalem and will make a peace treaty with the *"many"* nations in the region. But again, they don't seem to have paid attention to the fact that peace treaties are not made for a specific period of years.

Allow me to submit that if we had never heard the theory of the peace treaty before, we might actually be more inclined to picture the *"many"* as being those described in Revelation which says,

*"The ten horns you saw are ten kings who have not yet received a kingdom, but who for one hour will receive authority as kings along with the beast. They have one purpose and will give their power and authority to the beast. The beast and the ten horns you saw will hate the prostitute. They will bring her to ruin and leave her naked; they will eat her flesh and burn her with fire. For God has put it into their hearts to accomplish his purpose by agreeing to hand over to the beast their royal authority, until God's words are fulfilled."* Revelation 17:12-13,16-17.

It seems to make more sense to me that the antichrist will strike a deal with ten power brokers who are not kings themselves but are more like behind the scenes, powerful people. These would be people, or the "many," *"who have not yet received a kingdom, but who for one hour will receive authority as kings along with the beast. They have one purpose and will give their power and authority to the beast."*

One thought that comes to my mind concerns the Illuminati and the Bilderberg Group, among others, which have for years been seeking to run a one world government through the use of what has been referred to as a "shadow government." Once they felt they had the one world government in place, they would need a person to be the figurehead. Could it be that they might give the antichrist that top position in exchange for being made "kings" over their own nations or regions? Could this be the covenant mentioned in Daniel?

We are told *"He will confirm a covenant with many,"* and nowhere in the Bible does it say that the antichrist previously made a covenant with Israel prior to this that he could confirm. Had he, that would probably be included in the Biblical text. However, since there is nothing in the scripture that says whether this initial covenant making, or the mentioned confirming of it, ever occurs, it may make more sense that what we are looking at could be a secretive deal by folks who have been planning a "one world" takeover.

The fact is that this verse from Revelation is the only verse in the Bible, other than the one in Daniel 9, in which the antichrist makes a deal with anyone.

From my vantage point, a peace treaty with Israel is a theory fraught with problems. But it is a theory, like the lopping off of the end of the roast, that virtually no one has ever questioned. Someone came up with the notion some years back, and almost everyone has taken it as undeniable truth. In reality, the only covenant the antichrist will make that is mentioned anywhere in the Bible will be with the "ten" described in Revelation, and the chances are that no one other than those ten people who are involved would ever have any knowledge of it. So, this is one possibility.

Another possibility could be that the covenant that we are looking at is one of the Biblical covenants, and the idea that the antichrist confirms it only means that he asserts that he will stand by it. Let's look at the possibility that the antichrist might be elected to an office that has a term of seven years. The Secretary Generals of the United Nations currently serve five year terms. That length, of course, could be extended in the future. Or another organization may be in place at that time that has seven year terms for its top position. In the verse, *"He will confirm a covenant with many for one 'seven"* might possibly mean that he will confirm a Biblical covenant by stating that he will follow it for his term.

There are numerous covenants in the Bible that God made, and interestingly they all involve cutting and the shedding of blood. Consider the second covenant God made in the Bible in which by killing an animal, shedding its blood, and covering Adam and Eve's nakedness with the animal's skin, God was making a covenant that He personally would cover the sins of mankind; which He did by coming in the form of Jesus and dying on the cross for those of us who accept His sacrifice and make Him the Lord of our lives.

One of the most detailed covenants is referred to as the Abrahamic Covenant or Covenant of Circumcision. We read:

*"When Abram was ninety-nine years old, the Lord appeared to him and said, 'I am God Almighty; walk before me and be blameless. I will confirm my covenant between me and you and will greatly increase your numbers.'*

*Abram fell facedown, and God said to him, 'As for me, this is my covenant with you: You will be the father of many nations. No longer will you be called Abram; your name will be Abraham, for I have made you a father of many nations. I will make you very fruitful; I will make nations of you, and kings will come from you. I will establish my covenant as an everlasting covenant between me and you and your descendants after you for the generations to come, to be your God and the God of your descendants after you. The whole land of Canaan, where you are now an alien, I will give as an everlasting possession to you and your descendants after you; and I will be their God.'*

*Then God said to Abraham, 'As for you, you must keep my covenant, you and your descendants after you for the generations to come. This is my covenant with you and your descendants after you, the covenant you are to keep: Every male among you shall be circumcised. You are to undergo circumcision, and it will be the sign of the covenant between me and you. For the generations to come every male among you who is eight days old must be circumcised, including those born in your household or bought with money from a foreigner—those who are not your offspring. Whether born in your household or bought with your money, they must be circumcised. My covenant in your flesh is to be an everlasting covenant. Any uncircumcised male, who has not been circumcised in the flesh, will be cut off from his people; he has broken my covenant."*            Genesis 17:1-14.

Notice that in the above scripture God promises to give Abraham's descendants the whole land of Canaan, and Abraham and his descendants must be circumcised, once again involving cutting and the shedding of blood. As an aside, I find it interesting that every single Hebrew seed that passes to the woman must pass through that everlasting symbol of the covenant.

We could be looking in the Daniel verse at an antichrist who takes away the "whole land of Canaan" from Abraham's descendants half way through his seven year term, after originally having promised to abide by the Abrahamic Covenant. Confirming a Biblical covenant and then breaking it is not unheard of by world leaders. To investigate a recent case in which that actually happened, we can look at the very first covenant God made:

*"So the Lord God caused the man to fall into a deep sleep; and while he was sleeping, he took one of the man's ribs and closed up the place with flesh. Then the Lord God made a woman from the rib he had taken out of the man, and he brought her to the man.*

*The man said, 'This is now bone of my bones and flesh of my flesh;*

*she shall be called woman, for she was taken out of man.'*
    *For this reason a man will leave his father and mother and be united to his wife, and they will become one flesh."*           Genesis 2:21-24.

    The cutting and bloodshed part obviously occurred when God took Adam's rib to create Eve. And the promise part came with the part that a man will *"be united to his wife, and they will become one flesh."* With this statement God established the Covenant of Marriage as being a union between a man and a woman. This brings up the perfect example of a world leader confirming a covenant and then breaking it.

    As you know, Barack Obama initially "confirmed" God's covenant by stating that he was for marriage only being between a man and a woman. It was news worldwide. Then, three and a half years later, Obama held a press conference stating that his thinking had "evolved" to the point where he was now for "same sex" marriage, thus publicly breaking the very first covenant God had made.

    We should truly take note that the Covenant of Marriage was the very first covenant God made. That being the case, we can assume that He looks at that covenant very solemnly, and protectively. For that reason I predict that the rush to enact same sex marriage laws worldwide, which was hastened by Obama's public and much ballyhooed endorsement, will not be taken lightly by the Creator of everything. Obama was speaking not only as the president of the United States, but also as the leader of the free world. He truly was speaking to the *"many."* And his endorsement of this sacrilege was not only heard world wide, but also acted upon. In fact, as I am typing this, I am looking at my local newspaper that came today which had an article stating that "yesterday the British House of Commons voted 400 to 175 in favor of legislation permitting same sex couples to get married in both civil and religious ceremonies," including supposed Christian ceremonies. Do we think God is happy about these snowballing events worldwide that were ushered in with fanfare by Barack Obama? God's wrath falls on the breaking of His solemn covenants, and I repeat, the Covenant of Marriage being solely between a man and a woman was the very first covenant God entered into.

    A day of reckoning is coming. We have not heard God's response yet, but we will.

    Am I saying that I think Obama is the antichrist? Not at all. We won't be able to know who that person is unless we happen to be alive when he declares himself to be the true Christ. However, in later chapters we will find out a lot about that person in the teaching of the Apostle John to Polycarp that was passed on to those he mentored. Most of that information has been lost to our modern church and I'm confident you will find it stunning. But even with that information, we will not be able to pinpoint exactly who the antichrist is, if indeed he happens to be alive today. So, no, I am not stating that Obama is the antichrist. There are several men worldwide who could be possibilities. But the highly publicized breaking of God's very first covenant with mankind can not be ignored. It was a bold and totally astonishing slap in the face of the one true Sovereign God of the universe. Obama may well not turn out to be the antichrist, but with that unbelievable act by the leader of the free world he could be seen as auditioning for the role.

    However, the reason I even chronicled that event was to further show that there are several other possible ways to interpret the Daniel 9:27 verse other than it being a seven year peace treaty with Israel. We have looked at just a few, including the possibility that the verse may be looking at a covenant between the antichrist and his ten kings, or even more probable in my estimation, the confirming of one of the Biblical covenants. And quite naturally, there are even other possibilities that could play out. What does seem evident is that there never will be a seven year peace treaty between the antichrist and Israel, one that defies common sense by being set up at the beginning to end seven years later That means that there is no single event mentioned in the Bible that will alert us as to when the events described in Revelation will begin.
    Of course, you might be thinking that the starting point for any end time prophecies will be the rapture. That is what most, including myself, have been taught. I even have written and taught that exact thing myself. We will, in fact, cover that subject in detail later in the book, but for the time being please bear with me and just go along with the notion that some end time events will indeed happen before the rapture. The rapture is not the event that will trigger their beginning.
    In studying the writings of those who knew what John, the writer of Revelation, taught, we really do not get any specific starting point that we could pinpoint in real life as to when the Revelation verses will begin. The only one who refers to the Daniel 9:27 verse at all is Hippolytus, in his

"Treatise On Christ And AntiChrist." And all that Hippolytus says about that verse is,

> "By one week, therefore, he meant the last week which is to be at the end of the whole world; of which week the two prophets Enoch and Elijah will take up the half. For they will preach 1,260 days clothed in sackcloth, proclaiming repentance to the people and to all the nations."
> Number 43, "Treatise On Christ And AntiChrist." By Hippolytus.

As an aside, notice that he tells us who the two witnesses will be, Enoch and Elijah. That makes perfect sense because they are the only two people in history who were caught up to heaven without dying. Hebrews 9:27 tells us *"people are destined to die once,"* and Enoch and Elijah have not done that yet. As the two witnesses, they will die at the end of their three and a half year mission.

How often have you read or heard about the ongoing debate regarding who the two witnesses will be? More often that not "scholars" will make all sorts of arguments that Moses must be one of those witnesses since it was Moses and Elijah who met with Jesus on the Mountain of Transfiguration. Some, of course will say that the two must be Caleb and Joshua since they were the only two who came out of Egypt and lived to enter the Promised Land. And then we hear that the two witnesses will be the Old and New Testaments. Or we occasionally hear other "scholarly" ideas on the subject.

Had all the "scholars" only taken the time to read from our church Fathers, there would be no needless discussion on the topic. Polycarp, Irenaeus, and Hippolytus repeat exactly, to the letter, what the beloved Apostle John taught after he penned the Revelation of Jesus. This is the same John referred to in the story of the Last Supper in which the Bible says in John 13:23, *"Now there was leaning on Jesus' bosom one of His disciples, whom Jesus loved."* Can we not assume that this dearly beloved apostle and friend of Jesus would have more of an inside track than our modern "Biblical scholars" do pertaining to the events in the Revelation Jesus gave him to write down for us to read? I'll put my money on what John taught.

Getting back to the question of what we could look for to begin the events of Revelation, Hippolytus uses the Daniel 9:27 verse to tell us that the two witnesses, Enoch and Elijah, will preach for the first half of the Tribulation week. These same two witnesses are not introduced in the book of Revelation until chapter eleven, after which the antichrist is introduced; who Hippolytus later in his treatise says will reign and pretend he is God for the second half of the tribulation.

It seems, therefore, that the Revelation events that we read about before the introduction of the two witnesses in Revelation 11 will happen prior to the actual seven year period of the Tribulation, which will begin with the three and a half years of the witnesses' mission. It also appears that we have no clue as to how long those pre Tribulation events might take. This leads us to the possibility that we will explore next, that those Revelation events may have already begun. Yes, you and I may already be in the end times spoken of in Revelation, and we didn't even know it. We may well be in the end times we were never taught.

# End Time Prophecies

Many people consider the phrase "end times" to only include the final seven years of the Tribulation when, as we saw, Enoch and Elijah will preach to the nations for the first half, and the antichrist will be in full control and attempting to make the world worship him as a god during the second half. However, the "end times" include much more time than just that seven year period, and that time is filled with miraculous fulfillments of prophecies, especially in the land God gave Abraham's offspring. Dr. Charles Dyer took the picture below from the exact spot of oak of Moreh at Shechem, Abraham's first stop in the Promised Land.

The hill to the left on the horizon is Mount Gerizim, and the one to the right is Mount Ebal. The town in between is modern-day Nablus. That's where the ancient city of Shechem stood. This is where God appeared and said, *"To your offspring I will give this land"* Genesis 12:7. And it's also the first spot where Abraham built an altar to the Lord.

Of course, the main modern prophecy fulfillment that we are all familiar with is the reestablishment of Israel as a nation. God had boldly said,

*"I will take the Israelites out of the nations where they have gone. I will gather them from all around and bring them back into their own land. I will make them one nation in the land, on the mountains of Israel."* Ezekiel 37:20.

No other nation in history had ever been destroyed and scattered, and then come back together to form a nation. But God orchestrated that incredible event and we are witnesses to it.

Additionally, no other dead language had ever come alive again like we have seen happen with the Hebrew language. No one speaks the ancient languages of the dissolved empires. Even Latin is not spoken anywhere in every day life. But when Israel became a nation in 1948 and the people began to come back from the seventy nations they had been scattered in, a common language had to be found.

God had prophesied,

*"For then will I turn to the people a pure language, that they may call upon the name of the Lord, to serve Him with one consent."* Zephaniah 3:9.

In order for the Hebrew language to come alive again, new words even had to be added. Remember, when it died there were no words for airplane or internet or refrigerator. Now, after two thousand years as an extinct language, Hebrew is again taught to school children, and about seven million Jews use it as their common language. What an incredible story that is.

There is even a lot more to the rebirth of Israel that God foretold, such as where the Jews would come from. For instance, God said,

*"From beyond the rivers of Ethiopia my suppliants, even the daughter of my dispersed, shall bring mine offering."* Zephaniah 3:10.

Only God could know that His *"dispersed"* would even end up in Ethiopia, no less return from there, but about 1990 twenty five thousand black Jews returned to their homeland, Israel.

God also said in Isaiah 43:6,

*"I will say to the north, Give up; and to the south, Keep not back: bring my sons from afar, and my daughters from the ends of the earth."*

The north obviously is a reference to Russia, where Jews to this day are coming from in mass to their Promised Land. And they are arriving daily from the ends of the earth by boat, plane, and car. We are witnessing the fulfillment of prophecy, "end time" prophecy.

Other predictions for this renewed Israel are coming true right before our eyes. For example, speaking of the time after the return, God said,

*"Be glad then, Children of Zion, and rejoice in the Lord your God: for He hath given you the former rain moderately, and He will cause for you to come down rain, the former rain and the latter rain in the first month."*
Joel 2:23.

We need to remember what the land that we now know as Israel was like. It was an arid desert. Rain was a very seldomly seen commodity for centuries and centuries. Unusual as it is, however, the rainfall in Israel keeps increasing at a rate of 10% per year. Obviously God is doing something behind the scenes.

He told His people twenty seven hundred years ago,

*"Water will gush forth in the wilderness and streams in the desert. The burning sand will become a pool, the thirsty ground bubbling springs. In the haunts where jackals once lay, grass and reeds and papyrus will grow."*
Isaiah 35:6-7.

Today, that is exactly what is happening. One of the most desolate areas on earth was the land from south of the Dead Sea to the Gulf of Acaba. But today springs are literally gushing forth from rocks. In that spot there is now one of the most beautiful crystal clear, spring fed pools in the entire world. It did not exist at all only twenty years ago. All around it grows lush grass and *"reeds and papyrus."* And this pool, called Sapphire, which really is a small lake, is being used to irrigate the land around it to grow some of the most beautiful vegetables and flowers imaginable. Actually, God said,

*"In the days to come Jacob will take root, Israel will bud and blossom and fill all the world with fruit."*   Isaiah 27:6.

We are seeing that happening today in incredible ways. The United Nations says that Israel is now the most agriculturally efficient land in the world. Ninety percent of their flowers are now exported, primarily to Europe. Speaking of Europe, ninety percent of the citrus eaten there comes from

Israel, which only a few years ago was totally barren desert. God had said this all would happen when He foretold,

*"The desert and the parched land will be glad; the wilderness will rejoice and blossom. Like the crocus, it will burst into bloom; it will rejoice greatly and shout for joy. The glory of Lebanon will be given to it, the splendor of **Carmel** and Sharon; they will see the glory of the lord, the splendor of our God."* Isaiah 35:2.

An ironic side note is that one of the largest packing companies of the fruits, vegetables, and flowers that now are exported worldwide is the Carmel Packing Company in Israel.

God even got very specific as to locations in Israel that would produce different things in this time. For example, He prophesied,

*"There I will give her back her vineyards, and will make the Valley of Achor a door of hope."* Hosea 2:15.

We need to understand that the Valley of Achor, which lies between Jericho and Qumran, where the famous Dead Sea scrolls were found, was one of the least likely places in the world to see vineyards less than twenty years ago. To understate it, there was no water. It was sand and rock, and nothing else. The only thing that could grow there was your thirst.

Today it is literally mile after mile of the most beautiful grape vineyards you could ever hope to see. The entire area is a place of beauty. And the grapes are some of the most luscious on earth. But on top of the lush grape vineyards, a traveler will also see quite a few herds of healthy sheep in the area. That shouldn't be surprising, however, because God told us it would happen,

*"Sharon will become a pasture for flocks, and the Valley of Achor a resting place for herds."* Isaiah 65:10.

I find it extremely interesting that for centuries Biblical scholars thought that these "end time" prophecies about Israel being reborn as a nation, its language being restored, and the land dramatically changing from desert wasteland to a lush, productive garden, would come true, but only in heaven. They naturally supposed that these things were beyond the possible. People who spoke against the existence of God even pointed to these prophecies as places where the Bible obviously was in error. The chances of them being fulfilled seemed outlandish at best. They just didn't understand that,

    *"Nothing is impossible with God."*    Luke 1:37.

All of these foretellings are indeed part of what I classify as "end time" prophecies. In reality, though, there are also quite a few "end time" prophecies that describe events immediately preceding the tribulation period that don't necessarily have to do with the rebirth of Israel. One of those deals with the Dead Sea separating, with one part coming to life and the other part remaining salt. This was one of those "impossible" predictions less than twenty years ago. Speaking of the Dead Sea separating in the end times, God said,

    *"But the swamps and marshes will not become fresh; they will be left for salt."*    Ezekiel 47:11.

In the past twenty years a land mass has incredibly popped up that has divided the Dead Sea into two separate bodies, and the southern part is drying up at a rate of three feet per year, leaving behind big boulders of pure salt. There are now trees growing in the area where the southern part of the Dead Sea was only twenty years ago, trees surrounded by the salt piles that were left.

These are truly phenomenal times to be alive. End times prophecies are being fulfilled before our eyes. But what about the events prophesied in Revelation?

# Opening Revelation

The book of Revelation, written by the Apostle John while in exile on the Island of Patmos, begins with:

*"The revelation of Jesus Christ, which God gave him to show his servants what must soon take place. He made it known by sending his angel to his servant John, who testifies to everything he saw—that is, the word of God and the testimony of Jesus Christ. Blessed is the one who reads the words of this prophecy, and blessed are those who hear it and take to heart what is written in it, because the time is near."* Revelation 1:1-3.

Following that prologue, John goes on in verse nine to say,

*"I, John, your brother and companion in the suffering and kingdom and patient endurance that are ours in Jesus, was on the island of Patmos because of the word of God and the testimony of Jesus. On the Lord's Day I was in the Spirit, and I heard behind me a loud voice like a trumpet, which said: 'Write on a scroll what you see and send it to the seven churches: to Ephesus, Smyrna, Pergamum, Thyatira, Sardis, Philadelphia and Laodicea.'*
*'I turned around to see the voice that was speaking to me. And when I turned I saw seven golden lampstands, and among the lampstands was someone 'like a son of man,' dressed in a robe reaching down to his feet and with a golden sash around his chest. His head and hair were white like wool, as white as snow, and his eyes were like blazing fire. His feet were like bronze glowing in a furnace, and his voice was like the sound of rushing waters. In his right hand he held seven stars, and out of his mouth came a sharp double-edged sword. His face was like the sun shining in all its brilliance.*
*When I saw him, I fell at his feet as though dead. Then he placed his right hand on me and said: 'Do not be afraid. I am the First and the Last. I am the Living One; I was dead, and behold I am alive for ever and ever! And I hold the keys of death and Hades.*
*'Write, therefore, what you have seen, what is now and what will take place later."* Revelation 1:9-19.

For the next two chapters Jesus dictates the seven letters to seven actual churches. Not only were those seven letters written to seven real churches, but they were also written to the seven definitively separate church ages:

| Church in letter | Church Age | Dates |
| --- | --- | --- |
| Ephesus | Apostolic Age | Before 100 AD |
| Smyrna | Age of Persecution | 100 AD to 313 AD |
| Pergamum | Imperial Church Age | 313 AD to 590 AD |
| Thyatira | Age of Papacy | 590 AD to 1517 AD |
| Sardis | Age of Reformation | 1517 AD to 1730 AD |
| Philadelphia | Age of Missions | 1730 AD to 1900 AD |
| Laodicea | Age of Apostasy | 1900 AD to   ? |

In all seven letters to those church ages, Jesus starts out by saying something about himself, which corresponds to that age. He then gives a commendation, a complaint, a correction, and a promise. One exception is that with Smyrna and Philadelphia He has no complaint at all. Imagine that. He found nothing bad at all to say about those two church ages. Wonderful.

Obviously, during the Age of Persecution, when His followers were being thrown to the lions and still refused to denounce Him, Jesus was pleased. That was era depicted by the Church of Smyrna. The other church to receive no complaint at all was the Church at Philadelphia, the Age of Missions, an age in which the need for real repentance was preached, and a striving for true holiness was not only taught but practiced. It was a time in which the "Christian" focus was on God and His desires, not "me" and "my" wants and needs.

In addition, however, to the two exceptions of the churches that received no complaints, unfortunately there were two church ages that received no commendation at all. Those churches that Jesus had nothing at all good to comment about were Sardis and Laodicea, our church age. Astonishingly, in the letter from Jesus to the Church of Laodicea, which represents our modern church, Jesus even made the following statement,

*"I am about to spit you out of my mouth."* Revelation 3:16.

That statement from Jesus to us has made a dramatic impact on my life, and much of this book came about as a result of that impact. You see, the thought that Jesus had nothing at all good to say about our modern church, and in fact thought so little of us and our actions and our belief systems that He is going to spit us out of His mouth was something I could not get out of my mind. I finally decided that I had better dig into the teachings from the two church ages that Jesus had nothing at all negative to talk about, the church ages from 100 AD to 313 AD and from 1730 AD to 1900 AD. And dig in I did. I read hundreds and hundreds of sermons, biographies and teachings from the giants of God who lived between 1730 and 1900, and I read virtually everything that is available from the church Fathers who lived in the second and third centuries.

The result was that I became amazed at how different our church is from those churches and how diametrically opposed the beliefs and teachings of their leaders often are to those of our modern church and the Christian leaders of our day. It is almost like two completely different religions. And in some ways, it is like two entirely different Gods are worshipped and studied.

The prevue of this book is not such that I am going to spend the time going into all those differences now; however, allow me to give you just a sampling of the type of Christian teaching that was common during the Age of Missions, from 1730 to 1900.

One of the great giants of faith of that day, Charles Finney, in his exceptional book, <u>Experiencing the Presence of God</u>, rightfully stated that all sin comes from selfishness, a trait that our current Christianity has elevated to an art form. The difference is so obvious, not only in the teaching of "prosperity" that is so prevalent today, but even in the more subtle teachings. To point out the beliefs of that day versus what we are taught, I'll actually quote a smidgeon from that book:

"The Gospel has not canceled or set aside the obligations of the moral law. It has set aside the claims of the ceremonial law, or Law of Moses. The ceremonial law was nothing but a set of types pointing to the savior and was set aside when the great Antitype appeared.

Some people maintain that the Gospel has set aside the moral law so that believers are under no obligation to obey it. Such was the doctrine of the Nicolaitans, who were severely rebuked by Christ. (see Romans 2:6,15) The antinomians, in the days of the apostles and since, believed that they were without obligation to obey the moral law. They held that Christ's righteousness was so imputed to believers, and He had so fulfilled the law for them, that they were under no obligation to obey the law themselves.

In modern times, Perfectionists have held that they are not under obligation to obey the law. They suppose that Christ has delivered them from the law and given them the Spirit. They believe the leadings of the Spirit are now their rule of life instead of God's law. …

All such ideas are radically wrong."
Experiencing the Presence of God by Charles Finney.

The difference in teaching then from now is stark. In fact, here is another short quote from Finney;

"True submission requires complete acceptance of the terms of the Gospel. They are repentance, holiness, faith, perfect trust, and confidence toward God. This leads you, without hesitation, to throw body and soul into His hands to do with as He thinks good." By Charles Finney.

The Church of Missions was an era in which the total focus of the Christian was on God and His desires, not on "me" and "my" wants and needs.

As an aside, it is said of Charles Finney that he once walked through a factory, not saying a word to anyone, most of whom had no idea who he was, and by the time he had crossed the entire factory floor every single worker was on his knees sobbing uncontrollably, convicted of their sins, and repenting before their Maker.

As I said, the reason for this book does not include going into all of the many differences between the Church of Philadelphia, the church age from 1730 to 1900, and our present church age, the Church of Laodicea. I might suggest, however, that you investigate those differences yourself. A good place to start may well be with Charles Finney and the book I cited above, although there are scores of other giants of that era such as Andrew Murray who will echo what Finney taught and give you even more insight into why Jesus might have written His letter to them without bringing up a single negative, while writing to our church era without finding a single positive with which to commend us, and in fact stating that He was going to spit us out of his mouth. Your Christian walk is far too important to treat haphazardly. Some day I may take on the project of writing a book that would shed light on the hundreds of large and small differences in their teaching and behavior versus ours, but for your own good, please do not wait on such a book.

    I can tell now you that a small part of those differences between them and us include the beliefs and teachings surrounding the end times and the book of Revelation. It seems that the second and third century leaders from the Church of Smyrna in 100 AD to 313 AD revered, studied, and taught the oral teaching of John, the writer of Revelation, as well they should have. And much of the thinking of the Church of Philadelphia mirrored their thoughts. Whereas, on the other hand, our church leaders either consciously or subconsciously have decided to throw that teaching out because they think they know better. The word "arrogant" does not come close to describing such an idea.

    With that as a background, I will tell you that, wherever possible, I am going to give you the interpretations of the Revelation scriptures as passed down orally by the author, John, himself. To the best of my ability, thousands of hours of research in this area are going to be condensed into the following pages.

    Some of what you read may not sit well with you because it is so drastically different from what you have been taught, but if that happens, stop for a moment and consider the two different sources; modern men using their own imaginations, versus the apostle who was with Jesus during His entire ministry, and was at the cross when He died, walking away from that cross having been given the responsibility by Jesus Himself to look after the devoted mother who bore Him, the friend of Jesus who He selected to give His revelation to, the beloved Apostle John. Personally, I decided to believe that John knew best.

# What John Witnessed

After John finished writing the seven letters that Jesus dictated, he says:

*"After this I looked, and there before me was a door standing open in heaven. And the voice I had first heard speaking to me like a trumpet said, 'Come up here, and I will show you what must take place after this.' At once I was in the Spirit, and there before me was a throne in heaven with someone sitting on it. And the one who sat there had the appearance of jasper and carnelian. A rainbow, resembling an emerald, encircled the throne. Surrounding the throne were twenty-four other thrones, and seated on them were twenty-four elders. They were dressed in white and had crowns of gold on their heads. From the throne came flashes of lightning, rumblings and peals of thunder. Before the throne, seven lamps were blazing. These are the seven spirits of God. Also before the throne there was what looked like a sea of glass, clear as crystal.*

*In the center, around the throne, were four living creatures, and they were covered with eyes, in front and in back. The first living creature was like a lion, the second was like an ox, the third had a face like a man, the fourth was like a flying eagle. Each of the four living creatures had six wings and was covered with eyes all around, even under his wings. Day and night they never stop saying:*

> *'Holy, holy, holy is the Lord God Almighty,*
> *who was, and is, and is to come.'*

*Whenever the living creatures give glory, honor and thanks to him who sits on the throne and who lives for ever and ever, the twenty-four elders fall down before him who sits on the throne, and worship him who lives for ever and ever. They lay their crowns before the throne and say:*

> *'You are worthy, our Lord and God, to receive glory*
> *and honor and power, for you created all things, and*
> *by your will they were created and have their being."*

Revelation 4:1-11.

Wow, what a sight. I can not begin to imagine how John must have felt to be transported to the physical throne room of God Himself. As glorious as it obviously was, were it me in that room, I doubt I could have even seen it clearly because of the emotional tears that would have been flooding out of my eyes. Fortunately for us, John kept his composure enough to later record for us what he saw. But to think that we will one day have the opportunity to see that sight completely blows me away. What a phenomenal future awaits us!

# The Scroll

Exciting to me is the solving of a gigantic **Old** Testament mystery that occurs next. It is one simple sentence that no one ever seems to see the true relevance of. But when the truth of it finally hit me, I was flabbergasted.

*"Then I saw in the right hand of him who sat on the throne a scroll with writing on both sides and sealed with seven seals."* Revelation 5:1.

Did you see it? Let's go back to the Old Testament book that is most closely associated with the book of Revelation, Daniel. As I am sure you know, much of the book of Daniel is spent on end time prophecy. In the last few chapters, Daniel is told by an angel a fairly detailed account of what will happen during the end times. And in the last chapter Daniel writes;

*"I heard, but I did not understand. So I asked, 'My lord, what will the outcome of all this be?' He replied, 'Go your way, Daniel, because the words are closed up and sealed until the time of the end."* Daniel 12:8-9.

The scroll *"in the right hand of him who sat on the throne"* that John saw in the above Revelation verse is that exact same scroll that the angel told Daniel was *"closed up and sealed until the time of the end."* It was the scroll containing the end time prophecy; the opening of it would cause the prophecy to be fulfilled. The mystery of what is in Daniel's scroll is about to be solved.

After seeing that "Daniel scroll," John tells us;

*" And I saw a mighty angel proclaiming in a loud voice, 'Who is worthy to break the seals and open the scroll?' But no one in heaven or on earth or under the earth could open the scroll or even look inside it. I wept and wept because no one was found who was worthy to open the scroll or look inside."* Revelation 5:2-4.

It is in those verses that virtually everyone today misses the big clue of the timing of end time events. Almost all scholars assume that John is looking at an event that will occur in the future, but they are totally wrong. Read those two verses again, *"no one in heaven or on earth or under the earth could open the scroll or even look inside it."*

John is seeing a time in which there is absolutely no one worthy to break the seals and look inside the scroll that was sealed in Daniel's day. Think about that. When was there never anyone worthy to look inside that scroll? The answer is the time before Jesus died on the cross for mankind. Until Jesus had fulfilled His mission on earth there was absolutely *"no one in heaven or on earth or under the earth could open the scroll or even look inside it."*

But then the glorious day came. Jesus fulfilled His mission. And He ascended to the Fathers throne room. John was there in the spirit when Jesus arrived.

*"Then one of the elders said to me, 'Do not weep! See, the Lion of the tribe of Judah, the Root of David, has triumphed. He is able to open the scroll and its seven seals.' Then I saw a Lamb, looking as if it had been slain, standing in the center of the throne, encircled by the four living creatures and the elders."* Revelation 5:5-6.

John was not looking at an event in the future. He was looking at a day about sixty years earlier when John, as a young man, had witnessed the earthly departure of his Lord, Jesus. He had watched in stunned silence as Jesus ascended into the clouds. It had to have been a breathtaking experience, one he probably thought about every day since.

But now he was seeing what was happening that very same day, but from the side of the other, unseen dimension. John was seeing Christ's arrival in heaven into the Father's throne room, a scene no one in our earthly dimension had ever seen. But fortunately, in reading John's description, you and I can be there, too, to witness the unforgettably awesome sight, the day all heaven had been waiting for.

What John saw, however, was a different Jesus than the one he watched enter the clouds, for John tells us about the Lord's appearance on His arrival, and what he saw is still quite mysterious to us to this day,

*"He had seven horns and seven eyes, which are the seven spirits of God sent out into all the earth."* Revelation 5:6.

And then, that very day of His arrival in heaven, Jesus was able to do what no one before Him was able to do, for,

> *"He came and took the scroll from the right hand of him who sat on the throne. And when he had taken it, the four living creatures and the twenty-four elders fell down before the Lamb. Each one had a harp and they were holding golden bowls full of incense, which are the prayers of the saints. And they sang a new song:*
>
>> *"You are worthy to take the scroll and to open its seals, because you were slain, and with your blood you purchased men for God from every tribe and language and people and nation. You have made them to be a kingdom and priests to serve our God, and they will reign on the earth."*
>>
>> Revelation 5:7-10.

And the long awaited heavenly celebration began,

> *"Then I looked and heard the voice of many angels, numbering thousands upon thousands, and ten thousand times ten thousand. They encircled the throne and the living creatures and the elders. In a loud voice they sang:*
>
>> *'Worthy is the Lamb, who was slain, to receive power and wealth and wisdom and strength and honor and glory and praise!'*
>
> *Then I heard every creature in heaven and on earth and under the earth and on the sea, and all that is in them, singing:*
>
>> *'To him who sits on the throne and to the Lamb be praise and honor and glory and power, for ever and ever!'*
>
> *The four living creatures said, 'Amen,' and the elders fell down and worshiped."*   Revelation 5:11-14.

And immediately John saw Jesus do what had been waited for and eagerly anticipated in heaven for so long, for John tells us:

*"I watched as the Lamb opened the first of the seven seals."*
Revelation 6:1.

Even if you know virtually nothing about end time prophecy, you know that there has been much debate and discussion about what are referred to as "The Four Horsemen of the Apocalypse." Millions upon millions of words have been penned trying to answer the questions about what they represent and when they will ride. It may be the single most anticipated "future" event.

But I am now going to boldly tell you that what everyone thinks is a "future" event, happened the day Jesus arrived in heaven, on the day of His ascension. Let's read John's account of what Jesus did, even as the heavenly celebration was taking place:

*"I watched as the Lamb opened the first of the seven seals. Then I heard one of the four living creatures say in a voice like thunder, 'Come!' I looked, and there before me was a white horse! Its rider held a bow, and he was given a crown, and he rode out as a conqueror bent on conquest.*

*When the Lamb opened the second seal, I heard the second living creature say, 'Come!' Then another horse came out, a fiery red one. Its rider was given power to take peace from the earth and to make men slay each other. To him was given a large sword.*

*When the Lamb opened the third seal, I heard the third living creature say, 'Come!' I looked, and there before me was a black horse! Its rider was holding a pair of scales in his hand. Then I heard what sounded like a voice among the four living creatures, saying, 'A quart of wheat for a day's wages, and three quarts of barley for a day's wages, and do not damage the oil and the wine!'*

*When the Lamb opened the fourth seal, I heard the voice of the fourth living creature say, 'Come!' I looked, and there before me was a pale horse! Its rider was named Death, and Hades was following close behind him. They were given power over a fourth of the earth to kill by sword, famine and plague, and by the wild beasts of the earth."*         Revelation 6:1-8.

Interestingly the Bible provides the explanation of the spirit realm horses. First, we must take one thing to heart,

*"Above all, you must understand that no prophecy of Scripture came about by the prophet's own interpretation."*     2 Peter 1:20.

Every word of the Bible was written by the Holy Spirit of God, and many of the things we look at as mysteries can actually be solved by searching the other scriptures for the answer. In the case of the four different colored horses, our search ends in Zechariah:

*"I looked up again - and there before me were four chariots coming out from between two mountains - mountains of bronze! The first chariot had red horses, the second black, the third white, and the fourth dappled - all of them powerful. I asked the angel who was speaking to me, 'What are these, my lord?'*
*The angel answered me, 'These are the four spirits of heaven, going out from standing in the presence of the Lord of the whole world.'"*     Zechariah 6:1-5.

Throughout the book of Zechariah, the prophet encounters beings and creatures from the spirit realm. As is often the case when a prophet encounters an angelic being or sight that is confusing, the Holy Spirit provides an angel to explain things for us. The chariots and their horses are spirits that stand before God. They are spirit realm beings manifesting as a chariot and horses when they come to Earth. And their appearance happens to correspond to the colors of the horses we saw in the first four seals of Revelation.

Earlier Zechariah also saw colored horses and inquired as to who they are and receives similar confirmation:

*"During the night I had a vision - and there before me was a man riding a red horse! He was standing among the myrtle trees in a ravine. Behind him were red, brown and white horses.*
*I asked, 'What are these, my lord?'*
*The angel who was talking with me answered, 'I will show you what they are.'*

*Then the man standing among the myrtle trees explained, 'They are the ones the Lord has sent to go throughout the earth.'*

*And they reported to the angel of the Lord, who was standing among the myrtle trees, 'We have gone throughout the earth and found the whole world at rest and in peace."*  Zechariah 1:8-11.

It is clear that these are spirit realm beings that carry out certain tasks on earth for God.

A big question that is often asked pertains to whether or not the first rider on the white horse that John saw is the antichrist.

*"I watched as the Lamb opened the first of the seven seals. Then I heard one of the four living creatures say in a voice like thunder, 'Come!' I looked, and there before me was a white horse! Its rider held a bow, and he was given a crown, and he rode out as a conqueror bent on conquest."*
Revelation 6:1-2.

People often think that since he has a bow with no arrow, indicating that he comes in peace, and that he rides a white horse and sent to conquer, he is the antichrist. This interpretation fails for several reasons:

The Bible never says this is the antichrist. At no place in scripture is this ever stated or even alluded to. The antichrist is described in Revelation 13 as a man, whereas In Zechariah we are told that the horses are spirit realm beings.

The antichrist comes from the bottomless pit. In Revelation we are told twice that the Beast Spirit which will indwell the antichrist comes from the bottomless pit, also known as the abyss in God's Word. We are told of the two witnesses:

*"Now when they have finished their testimony, the beast that comes up from the Abyss will attack them, and overpower and kill them."*
Revelation 11:7.

The antichrist, going just by scripture, is never in heaven. It is clear, that he comes from the pit or the abyss. Therefore, an interpretation that has him coming to earth from heaven contradicts the Bible.

Even more important is the fact that Jesus told us who the first rider is, as well as the other three. Incredibly, and seldom if ever noticed, the prophecies of Jesus in Matthew 24 line up with the seals of Revelation. Let's read that scripture:

*"Now as He sat on the Mount of Olives, the disciples came to Him privately, saying, 'Tell us, when will these things be? And what will be the sign of Your coming, and of the end of the age?'*

*And Jesus answered and said to them: 'Take heed that no one deceives you. For many will come in My name, saying, "I am the Christ," and will deceive many. And you will hear of wars and rumors of wars. See that you are not troubled; for all these things must come to pass, but the end is not yet. For nation will rise against nation, and kingdom against kingdom. And there will be famines, pestilences, and earthquakes in various places. All these are the beginning of sorrows.*

*'Then they will deliver you up to tribulation and kill you, and you will be hated by all nations for My name's sake."*        Matthew 24:3-9 (NKJV).

Let's pull out of that the first four things Jesus said will come:
     1 - *"For many will come in My name, saying, 'I am the Christ,' and will deceive many."* A picture of false religions.
     2 - *"And you will hear of wars and rumors of wars"*
     3 - *"And there will be famines"*
     4 - *"Pestilences"*

So, there we have the answer to what the four horsemen represent. The first is false religions, the second is war and rumors of war, the third is famine, and the fourth is pestilences.

Jesus confirms the first two in Mark and Luke, which also contained end-times prophecies:

*"Many will come in my name, claiming, 'I am he,' and will deceive many. When you hear of wars and rumors of wars, do not be alarmed. Such things must happen, but the end is still to come."*        Mark 13:6-7.

*"He replied: 'Watch out that you are not deceived. For many will come in my name, claiming, "I am he," and, "The time is near." Do not follow them. When you hear of wars and revolutions, do not be frightened. These things must happen first, but the end will not come right away."* Luke 21:8-9.

What is also emphasized is that when the horsemen are released onto the world, it is not yet the end times. This also harmonizes with what we see in Revelation, since John sees Jesus take the book right after His resurrection and Ascension. The scroll is opened right after Jesus reached the throne room, almost 2,000 years ago. No, these four horsemen, according to Jesus,

*"These are the beginning of birth pains."* Mark 13:8.

While the *"birth pains"* unleashed by these four spirits from heaven sound like an end-times scenario, and obviously have been playing out in greater and greater intensity, as birth pains do, we must pay attention to the words of Bible over any pre-existing notions or private interpretations. Jesus, in describing the first four seals of Revelation, goes out of His way to remind us that these judgments are not part of the tribulation period. These are tribulations indeed, but tribulations that lead up to what we think of as the tribulation, the Day of The Lord that is yet to come.

As to the fifth seal, John says,

*"When he opened the fifth seal, I saw under the altar the souls of those who had been slain because of the word of God and the testimony they had maintained. They called out in a loud voice, 'How long, Sovereign Lord, holy and true, until you judge the inhabitants of the earth and avenge our blood?' Then each of them was given a white robe, and they were told to wait a little longer, until the number of their fellow servants and brothers who were to be killed as they had been was completed."* Revelation 6:9-11.

The sixth and seventh seals correspond with the sixth and seventh trumpets that we will be looking at in greater detail later, so we will examine them all at that time. And we will see that it may be that getting a clearer picture of all that is yet to come might be almost as simple as we found with the first five seals of Revelation.

# A Prophecy from God?

We have seen what we call "end time" prophecies that have been fulfilled concerning Israel, and what Jesus described as "birth pains" in the first seals that were opened, but obviously they are not in the same category with the more detailed prophecies in Revelation of events that are suppose to occur prior to Enoch and Elijah beginning their preaching on repentance.

A big question now would be "is there anywhere that we can find a time span that we might look at in which all of those more detailed and seemingly frightening things might happen?"

To answer the question we need to remember that the Bible tells us,

*"Surely the Sovereign Lord does nothing without revealing his plan to his servants the prophets."*                                        Amos 3:7.

OK. But that poses another question, "who is God's true prophet?"
God tells us,

*"You may say to yourselves, "How can we know when a message has not been spoken by the Lord?" If what a prophet proclaims in the name of the Lord does not take place or come true, that is a message the Lord has not spoken. That prophet has spoken presumptuously, so do not be alarmed."*
                                                                                      Deuteronomy 18:21-22.

So, the answer is that the prophet must be totally accurate. If he is ever wrong, he is not speaking God's prophecy. I mention this in order to introduce what could be a prophecy from God. We can't know for a fact that this prophecy is really from God because we don't have a lot of this man's prophecies to go on. But for that matter there are prophets in the Bible such as Obadiah, Nahum, Habakkuk, and Haggai who did not give us numerous prophecies to examine either, however, they were obviously true prophets of God. The man I am talking about is Judah Ben Samuel, a German rabbi of the 12th century.

Rabbi Judah Ben Samuel's predictions deal in time increments called jubilees. God described for us exactly what a jubilee is,

*"Count off seven sabbath years—seven times seven years—so that the seven sabbath years amount to a period of forty-nine years. Then have the trumpet sounded everywhere on the tenth day of the seventh month; on the Day of Atonement sound the trumpet throughout your land. Consecrate the fiftieth year and proclaim liberty throughout the land to all its inhabitants. It shall be a jubilee for you; each of you is to return to your family property and to your own clan. The fiftieth year shall be a jubilee for you; do not sow and do not reap what grows of itself or harvest the untended vines. For it is a jubilee and is to be holy for you; eat only what is taken directly from the fields. In this Year of Jubilee everyone is to return to their own property."*

Leviticus 25:8-13.

A jubilee, therefore, consists of fifty years, and the prophecies of Rabbi Ben Samuel talk about things that would happen concerning Jerusalem in time frames of fifty year periods. The rabbi actually made four predictions, of which we will look at three now and examine the fourth one later. His first three said:

1 - The Ottomans (Turks) will conquer Jerusalem and rule over it for eight jubilees, or four hundred years.
2 - Jerusalem will become a no-man's land for one jubilee, which would also signify the beginning of the Messianic end time.
3 - Then in the ninth jubilee, Jerusalem will once again come back into the possession of the Jewish nation.

Remember, Rabbi Judah Ben Samuel lived in the 12$^{th}$ century, from 1140 AD to 1217 AD. Not until 300 years after his death, in 1517, did the Ottoman Turks conquer Jerusalem. They ruled over Jerusalem for eight jubilees (8 x 50 = 400 years), so they were in Jerusalem for 400 years. Exactly 400 years later, in 1917, the Ottoman Turks were conquered by the British. The League of Nations conferred the Mandate for the Holy Land and Jerusalem to the British. Thus, from 1917, under international law, Jerusalem was no-man's land. And in 1967, one jubilee later, Jerusalem again came into possession of the new Jewish nation, a nation that could not have even been conceived of in Rabbi Ben Samuel's day.

All of the first three of Rabbi Judah Ben Samuel's timed prophecies came true exactly as he said they would, and all three could not possibly have been predicted by any human foreknowledge. No human could have foreseen by human wisdom, three hundred years in advance, that the Ottomans would conquer Israel in 1517. No human in 1200 AD could obviously see seven hundred years into the future and know that Jerusalem would be a no man's land from 1917 to 1967. And it was unthinkable then to even consider that Israel would again become a Jewish nation since the Jews had been scattered for more than a millennia. So, to predict that such a nation would not only be in existence, but would recapture Jerusalem in exactly 1967, in my opinion takes his prophecies way out of the realm of anything but divine knowledge.

It seems to me a whole lot more than plausible that Rabbi Judah Ben Samuel may indeed have been speaking for God. And if so, the part about 1917 being a start date for the Messianic end times may well be worth making note of. Yes, we may be in the realm of speculation, but I for one, considering the rabbi's record, believe we can live with that in this situation.

So, what was going on in 1917? If memory serves, WWI was still going strong, and would continue until November of 1918. Is there anything about that gigantic event that might relate to any of the prophetic events in Revelation that are supposed to occur prior to Enoch and Elijah beginning their preaching on repentance?

We will examine the answer to that, and as we do your beliefs about the prophecies in Revelation, like mine, may dramatically change. Yes, my friend, we are going to delve deeply into the end times we were never taught. And we will be in for some pretty big surprises.

# Fathers Know Best

In looking in depth into the events foretold in Revelation you will find that I will continually go back to the writings of our very first church fathers to see what they have to say about each topic. And you will be amazed as we go along at how different their beliefs about what the Revelation scriptures really mean are from what we are taught today in our modern church. That probably should not surprise us because in many ways their church and our church are so completely different as to be completely unrecognizable as worshipping the same God. So many traditions and ceremonies and beliefs have been added that I am sad to say that if Paul or one of the other Apostles were to enter our church today they may feel the need to start preaching the true gospel to us, having the impression that we don't know the same Jesus they know. An in depth book should probably be written about that subject.

Our focus, however, is on the end time events and how they will actually play out. And in staying in that arena, when we go back to the early church teachings we will primarily concern ourselves with what Irenaeus and Hippolytus had to say about those future events because they were the two from that time period who wrote the most about that subject. That being the case, it will be wise for us to discuss their system of instruction.

Before we get to them, however, let's look at their mentor, Polycarp, who was born in 69 AD and was mentored by none other than the beloved Apostle, John. In fact, Polycarp took the reins from John as the bishop of the church in Smyrna, possibly even before John died in 96 AD in Ephesus, near Smyrna. It is known that Polycarp was totally consumed with his Lord, Jesus, and lived every moment for Him. At the end, according to his student, Irenaeus, Polycarp was burned at the stake. Incredibly, though, the fire would not burn him, so they had to stab him to death through the fire. One of the places Irenaeus mentions his mentor says,

"But Polycarp also was not only instructed by apostles, and conversed with many who had seen Christ, but was also, by apostles in Asia, appointed bishop of the Church in Smyrna, whom I also saw in my early youth, for he tarried [on earth] a very long time, and, when a very old man, gloriously and most nobly suffering martyrdom, departed this life, having always taught the things which **he had learned from the apostles, and which the Church has handed down, and which alone are true.**" Against Heresies, III, 4, Irenaeus.

In order to understand Polycarp better, I think it might be important to take the time to read a letter he wrote to the Philippian church. It may seem a little long to you, but feel privileged as you read it. Very few of your Christian brothers or sisters will ever have the chance to read this important document. In fact, I dare say that if you asked a hundred Christians you know if they have ever read what you are going to get to read, not a single one will be able to say that they have. And amazingly, this is the only letter we have that was written by someone mentored directly by one of the Apostles of Jesus.

This translation, the first one into English (translated in 1885), includes the scripture chapters and verses that Polycarp quotes. What is fascinating is that he quoted from every single one of the 27 New Testament books, showing that the earliest church used exactly the same books that we have, long before the Roman church formally adopted those same 27 books. Take note of how Polycarp almost talks in New Testament quotes. It is obvious that all 27 books were extremely important to him.

Be blessed and edified by the below writing. You are one of the few fortunate ones who will ever read it. It contains a lot of meat. As an aside, "presbyters" in the below letter is the word used for "elders."

### Polycarp's Letter to the Philippians: An Annotated Version

"Polycarp, and the presbyters with him, to the Church of God sojourning at Philippi: Mercy to you, and peace from God Almighty, and from the Lord Jesus Christ, our Savior, be multiplied.

Chapter I – Praise of the Philippians.

I have greatly rejoiced with you in our Lord Jesus Christ, because you have followed the example of true love [as displayed by God], and have accompanied, as became you, those who were bound in chains, the fitting ornaments of saints, and which are indeed the diadems of the true elect of

God (Colossians 3:12) and our Lord; and because the strong root of your faith, spoken of in days long gone by (Philemon 5), endureth even until now, and bringeth forth fruit to our Lord Jesus Christ (John 15:8), who for our sins suffered even unto death (1 Corinthians 15:3), [but] "whom God raised from the dead, having loosed the bands of the grave" (Acts 2:24). "In whom, though now you see Him not, you believe, and believing, rejoice with joy unspeakable and full of glory" (1 Peter 1:8); into which joy many desire to enter (Matthew 13:17; 1 Peter 4:13), knowing that "by grace you are saved," (Ephesians 2:8-9) by the will of God through Jesus Christ (Ephesians 2:8-10).

Chapter II – An Exhortation to virtue.

"Wherefore, girding up your loins" (Ephesians 6:14;1 Peter 1:13), "serve the Lord in fear" (Hebrews 12:28) and truth, as those who have forsaken the vain, empty talk and error of the multitude, and "believed in Him who raised up our Lord Jesus Christ from the dead, and gave Him glory" (1 Peter 1:21) and a throne at His right hand. To Him all things in heaven and on earth are subject (1 Peter 3:22; Philippians 2:10). Him every spirit serves. He comes as the Judge of the living and the dead (Acts 10:42; 2 Timothy 4:1; 1 Peter 4:5). His blood will God require of those who do not believe in Him (Luke 11:50). But He who raised Him up from the dead will raise up us also (1 Corinthians 6:14; 2 Corinthians 4:14; Romans 8:11), if we do His will, and walk in His commandments (2 John 6; Revelation 22:14-15), and love what He loved, keeping ourselves from all unrighteousness (John 7:18), covetousness, love of money, evil speaking, false witness; "not rendering evil for evil, or railing for railing" (1 Peter 3:9), or blow for blow, or cursing for cursing, but being mindful of what the Lord said in His teaching : "Judge not, that you be not judged; forgive, and it shall be forgiven unto you; be merciful, that you may obtain mercy; with what measure you mete, it shall be measured to you again; and once more" (Matthew 7:1-2, Matthew 6:12,14; Luke 6:36-38), "Blessed are the poor, and those that are persecuted for righteousness' sake, for theirs is the kingdom of God" (Luke 6:20; Matthew 5:3,10).

Chapter III – Expressions or Personal Unworthiness.

These things, brethren, I write to you concerning righteousness, not because I take anything upon myself, but because you have invited me to do so. For neither I, nor any other such one, can come up to the wisdom (2 Peter 3:15) of the blessed and glorified Paul. He, when among you, accurately and stedfastly taught the word of truth (Ephesians 1:13) in the presence of those who were then alive (Acts 16:13). And when absent from you, he wrote you a letter (Philippians), which, if you carefully study, you will find to be the means of building you up in that faith which has been given you, and which, being followed by hope, and preceded by love towards God, and Christ, and our neighbour, "is the mother of us all" (Galatians 4:26). For if any one be inwardly possessed of these graces, he hath fulfilled the command of righteousness, since he that hath love is far from all sin ( James 2:8-9).

Chapter IV – Various exhortations.

"But the love of money is the root of all evils" (1 Timothy 6:10). Knowing, therefore, that "as we brought nothing into the world, so we can carry nothing out" (1 Timothy 6:7), let us arm ourselves with the armor of righteousness (2 Corinthians 6:7; Ephesians 6:11); and let us teach, first of all, ourselves to walk in the commandments of the Lord (John 14:15). Next, [teach] your wives [to walk] in the faith given to them, and in love and purity tenderly loving their own husbands in all truth, and loving all [others] equally in all chastity (Titus 2:4,5); and to train up their children in the knowledge and fear of God. Teach the widows to be discreet as respects the faith of the Lord, praying continually (1 Thessalonians 5:17) for all (1 Timothy 5:5), being far from all slandering, evil-speaking, false-witnessing, love of money, and every kind of evil; knowing that they are the altar is of God, that He clearly perceives all things, and that nothing is hid from Him, neither reasonings, nor reflections, nor any one of the secret things of the heart (1 Corinthians 14:25).

Chapter V – The duties of deacons, youths, and virgins.

Knowing, then, that "God is not mocked" (Galatians 6:7), we ought to walk worthy of His commandment (2 John 6) and glory (2 Peter 1:3). In like manner should the deacons be blameless before the face of His righteousness, as being the servants of God and Christ, and not of men (1 Timothy 3:2-10). They must not be slanderers, double-tongued (1 Timothy 3:8), or lovers of money (1 Timothy 3:8), but temperate in all things (1 Timothy 3:8), compassionate, industrious, walking according to the truth of the Lord (3 John 4), who was the servant of all (Matthew 20:28; Mark 9:35; John 13:14-16). If we please Him in this present world, we shall receive also the future world, according as He has promised to us that He will raise us again from the dead, and that if we live worthily of Him (Philippians 1:27), "we shall also reign together with Him" (2 Timothy 2:12), provided only we believe. In like manner, let the young men also be blameless in all things, being especially careful to preserve purity, and keeping themselves in, as with a bridle, from every kind of evil (Titus 2:6-8). For it is well that they should be cut off from the lusts that are in the world, since "every lust warreth against the spirit" (1 Peter 2:11); and "neither fornicators, nor effeminate, nor abusers of themselves with mankind, shall inherit the kingdom of God" (I Corinthians 6:9,10; Revelation 22:15), nor those who do things inconsistent and unbecoming (Ephesians 5:4). Wherefore, it is needful to abstain from all these things, being subject to the presbyters and deacons, as unto God and Christ (Ephesians 4:11-12). The virgins also must walk in a blameless and pure conscience (Titus 2:4-8).

Chapter VI – The duties of presbyters and others.

And let the presbyters be compassionate and merciful to all, bringing back those that wander, visiting all the sick, and not neglecting the widow, the orphan, or the poor, but always "providing for that which is becoming in the sight of God and man" (2 Corinthians 8:21; Romans 12:17); abstaining from all wrath (Galatians 5:19-20; 1 Peter 2:11), respect of persons, and unjust judgment; keeping far off from all covetousness, not quickly crediting [an evil report] against any one, not severe in judgment, as knowing that we are all under a debt of sin. If then we entreat the Lord to forgive us, we ought also ourselves to forgive (Matthew 6:14-15); for we are before the eyes of our Lord and God, and "we must all appear at the judgment-seat of Christ, and must every one give an account of himself" (Romans 14:10,12). Let us then serve Him in fear, and with all reverence (Hebrews 12:28), even as He Himself has commanded us, and as the apostles who preached the Gospel unto us, and the prophets who proclaimed beforehand the coming of the Lord [have alike taught us]. Let us be zealous in the pursuit of that which is good (Galatians 4:18), keeping ourselves from causes of offence (Matthew 17:27), from false brethren (2 Timothy 3:5), and from those who in hypocrisy bear the name of the Lord (1 Timothy 4:1-2), and draw away vain men into error.

Chapter VII – Persevere in fasting and prayer.

"For whosoever does not confess that Jesus Christ has come in the flesh, is antichrist"(1 John 4:3), and whosoever does not confess the testimony of the cross, is of the devil; and whosoever perverts the oracles of the Lord to his own lusts, and says that there is neither a resurrection nor a judgment, he is the first-born of Satan. Wherefore, forsaking the vanity of many, and their false doctrines, let us return to the word which has been handed down to us from the beginning (cf. Jude 3); "watching unto prayer" (1 Peter 4:7), and persevering in fasting; beseeching in our supplications the all-seeing God "not to lead us into temptation" (Matthew 6:13) as the Lord has said: "The spirit truly is willing, but the flesh is weak" (Matthew 26:41; Mark 14:38).

Chapter VIII – Persevere in hope and patience.

Let us then continually persevere in our hope, and the earnest of our righteousness, which is Jesus Christ, "who bore our sins in His own body on the tree" (1 Peter 2:24), "who did no sin, neither was guile found in His mouth" (1 Peter 2:22), but endured all things for us, that we might live in Him (1 John 4:9). Let us then be imitators of His patience (James 5:10); and if we suffer for His name's sake, let us glorify Him (Acts 5:41; Romans 8:17; 1 Peter 4:16). For He has set us this example in Himself, and we have believed that such is the case (1 Peter 2:21).

Chapter IX – Patience inculcated.

I exhort you all, therefore, to yield obedience to the word of righteousness, and to exercise all patience, such as you have seen [set] before your eyes, not only in the case of the blessed Ignatius, and Zosimus, and Rufus, but also in others among yourselves, and in Paul himself, and the rest of the apostles. [This do] in the assurance that all these have not run in vain (Philippians 2:16; Galatians 2:2), but in faith and righteousness, and that they are [now] in their due place in the presence of the Lord, with whom also they suffered. For they loved not this present world (1 John 2:15; 2 Timothy 4:10), but Him who died for us, and for our sakes was raised again by God from the dead.

### Chapter X – Exhortation to the practice of virtue.

Stand fast, therefore, in these things, and follow the example of the Lord, being firm and unchangeable in the faith (1 Corinthians 10:1; Jude 3), loving the brotherhood (1 Peter 2:17), and being attached to one another (1 Peter 3:8), joined together in the truth, exhibiting the meekness of the Lord in your intercourse with one another (2 Corinthians 10:1), and despising no one. When you can do good, defer it not (Galatians 6:10), because alms delivers from death. Be all of you subject one to another (1 Peter 5:5) "having your conduct blameless among the Gentiles," (1 Peter 2:12) that you may both receive praise for your good works, and the Lord may not be blasphemed through you. But woe to him by whom the name of the Lord is blasphemed (2 Peter 2:1-2)! Teach, therefore, sobriety to all, and manifest it also in your own conduct.

### Chapter XI – Expression of grief on account of Valens.

I am greatly grieved for Valens, who was once a presbyter among you, because he so little understands the place that was given him [in the Church]. I exhort you, therefore, that you abstain from covetousness (Hebrews 13:5; Titus 2:12), and that you be chaste (Titus 2:5) and truthful. "Abstain from every form of evil" (1 Thessalonians 5:22). For if a man cannot govern himself in such matters, how shall he enjoin them on others? If a man does not keep himself from covetousness, he shall be defiled by idolatry, and shall be judged as one of the heathen (Colossians 3:5-6). But who of us are ignorant of the judgment of the Lord? "Do we not know that the saints shall judge the world?" as Paul teaches (1 Corinthians 6:2). But I have neither seen nor heard of any such thing among you, in the midst of whom the blessed Paul labored, and who are commended in the beginning of his Epistle (Philippians 1:1-6). For he boasts of you in all those Churches which alone then knew the Lord; but we [of Smyrna] had not yet known Him. I am deeply grieved, therefore, brethren, for him (Valens) and his wife; to whom may the Lord grant true repentance (2 Timothy 2:24-25)! And be you then moderate in regard to this matter, and "do not count such as enemies" (2 Thessalonians 3:15), but call them back as suffering and straying members, that you may save your whole body. For by so acting you shall edify yourselves.

Chapter XII – Exhortation to various graces.

For I trust that you are well versed in the Sacred Scriptures, and that nothing is hid from you; but to me this privilege is not yet granted. It is declared then in these Scriptures, "Be you angry, and sin not," and, "Let not the sun go down upon your wrath" (Ephesians 4:26). Happy is he who remembers this, which I believe to be the case with you. But may the God and Father of our Lord Jesus Christ, and Jesus Christ Himself, who is the Son of God (Mark 1:1), and our everlasting High Priest (Hebrews 3:1), build you up in faith and truth, and in all meekness, gentleness, patience, long-suffering, forbearance, and purity; and may He bestow on you a lot and portion among His saints (Revelation 14:12), and on us with you, and on all that are under heaven, who shall believe in our Lord and God Jesus Christ, and in His Father, who "raised Him from the dead" (Galatians 1:1). Pray for all the saints (Ephesians 6:18,23). Pray also for kings, and potentates, and princes (1 Timothy 2:1-2), and for those that persecute and hate you (Matthew 5:44), and for the enemies of the cross (Philippians 3:18), that your fruit may be manifest to all, and that you may be perfect in Him.

Chapter XIII – Concerning the transmission of epistles.

Both you and Ignatius wrote to me, that if any one went [from this] into Syria, he should carry your letter with him; which request I will attend to if I find a fitting opportunity, either personally, or through some other acting for me, that your desire may be fulfilled. The Epistles of Ignatius written by him to us, and all the rest [of his Epistles] which we have by us, we have sent to you, as you requested. They are subjoined to this Epistle, and by them you may be greatly profited; for they treat of faith and patience, and all things that tend to edification in our Lord. Any more certain information you may have obtained respecting both Ignatius himself, and those that were with him, have the goodness to make known to us.

Chapter XIV – Conclusion.

These things I have written to you by Crescens, whom up to the present time I have recommended unto you, and do now recommend. For he has acted blamelessly among us, and I believe also among you. Moreover, you will hold his sister in esteem when she comes to you. Be you safe in the Lord Jesus Christ. Grace be with you all (Philemon 3). Amen."
Letter to the Philippians, by Polycarp.

What a letter! As I mentioned, we can see that Polycarp had studied what would later become our Bible so much that he actually talked in scriptures. Would that every Christian today would spend so much time in God's Word that he could converse naturally with quotes of verses.

There was a time in my life that I was so very privileged as to be with one of God's generals from the twentieth century for the last five months of his life. That man was Dr. Alfred B. Smith, known far and wide as the Dean of Gospel Music. He himself had written over fifty hymns that were standards in our churches, and in fact, he was Billy Graham's first minister of music and traveled with the Reverend Graham during his early days of evangelizing. To this day I still often repeat stories he told me with the exact same words he used, never varying a word he told me.

If I don't change any of Dr. Smith's words in the stories he told me, can we imagine how sacred the teachings of John were to Polycarp. He knew that he was being trained by a close friend and apostle of Jesus Himself. A friend who had walked with Jesus by the Sea of Galilee, had slept under the stars with Him, had sat beside Him at the Lord's Supper, had watched Him agonizingly die on the cross, and had then spent time with Him for forty days after He arose. And finally, this personal teacher of his had been taken to heaven by Jesus Himself to see the throne of God and witness the end times and Tribulation unfold sometime in the future, in order to be able to write the sacred Revelation. Whatever John told Polycarp obviously was memorized word for word. And more than that, he insisted that his student, Irenaeus, did the same and taught his future student, Hippolytus, to utter only the exact words of John as well. This oral teaching became as revered as the teaching of the scriptures, and any deviation of it at all was considered heresy.

Polycarp had so trained Irenaeus of the importance of teaching only the words that John spoke, that Irenaeus wrote a lengthy treatise titled "<u>Against Heresies</u>." He was quite upset when he saw others begin to add a little here and take away something else over there. He knew that everyone needed to be taught exactly the same thing or problems would naturally be encountered. In that work Irenaeus wrote,

"As a matter of course, these heretics, since they are blind to the truth, and deviate from the right way, will walk in various roads, and therefore the footsteps of their doctrines are scattered here and there without agreement or connection. But the path of those belonging to the Church circumscribes the whole world, as possessing the sure tradition from the apostles, and gives unto us to see that the faith of all is one and the same."

"<u>Against Heresies</u>," chapter XX, 1, by Irenaeus.

Unfortunately, human nature took over. By the third century some of the church leaders found that they would look bigger in folks eyes if they could become known as having added something to what was then known as the Apostolic Oral Teaching, so little details either were added or subtracted.

By the fourth century the church had grown to the point that there were some big name church "stars," such as today. And some of those "stars" felt that they were a lot smarter than the teaching of The Apostolic Oral Teaching. Things got more and more screwed up as time went on and more and more "stars" felt the need to add their own two cents into the mix. The result is the end time teaching that you and I learned that quite frankly is nothing like what John taught Polycarp.

The question for us today is whether or not we want to keep lopping off the end of the roast because someone tells us we should, or look closely at what John shared with Polycarp, and was guarded closely as "truth" by Irenaeus and Hippolytus. The answer for me is simple. John was taught by God Himself. He lived with Him, slept with Him, watched Him on the cross, learned directly from Him both before and after He arose from the grave, and was taken to Heaven and appointed to be the one to pen the final book of God's Word. John had the inside track of all inside tracks. The comparison for me is nonexistent between the validity of the information that came from

John's mouth, who personally received it from our Lord, versus the validity of some church "star" who came up with some nifty idea a hundred, or five hundred years ago, and had it passed down to me like the lopping off of the end of the roast was passed down from Grandma. And that is why I will give you John's teaching via Irenaeus and Hippolytus as often as I can pertaining to any of the future events we will now be talking about.

Finally, before we delve into these matters, let me be emphatic that everything we will be discussing from here on in will be speculation. If we can dig into the teaching of Irenaeus or Hippolytus, I feel that the speculative nature will be greatly reduced to a bare minimum. But even with that, interpreting prophetic details is speculative, not only in what you are going to read in the following chapters, but in every book you may ever pick up on the end times, by any author. The big things, such as Jesus coming back as King of kings, we can take to the bank. But the little details surrounding those big parts are a little trickier.

All that being said, let's get back to Rabbi Judah Ben Samuel, 1917, and World War I, and check out what the future might hold in store. I think you may be greatly surprised. We are now going to examine the end times we were never taught.

# Have Trumpets Been Blowing?

As we learned earlier, about the only thing that Hippolytus told us in reference to the Daniel 9:27 verse was that the seven year tribulation period mentioned by Daniel would begin with the two witnesses who he said would be Enoch and Elijah. And since those witnesses are introduced **after** the first six trumpets in Revelation, it makes sense to assume that those six trumpets would happen before Enoch and Elijah appear on the scene.

Then, if we give credibility to Rabbi Judah Ben Samuel's prophecy, which we have seen was incredibly correct in all other aspects, the beginning of the Revelation events could well have started in 1917.

### First Trumpet

*"The first angel sounded his trumpet, and there came hail and fire mixed with blood, and it was hurled down upon the earth. **A third of the earth was burned up**, a third of the trees were burned up, and all the green grass was burned up."* Revelation 8:7.

Could John have been seeing World War I? The intriguing thing to me was his mention that a third of the earth and trees were burned up along with the grass. That strikes me because World War I was notorious for the use of what is known as "the scorched earth policy" by virtually all the nations that were involved. This tactic simply meant that as an army left an area they would set everything in that area on fire so that the enemy could get no use from crops, buildings, or machinery, etc. The Russian troops, retreating along a front of more than 600 miles, burned anything that might be of use to their enemy, including crops, houses, railways and entire cities. Following the Russians lead, the German Army adopted the scorched earth policy in February, 1917, during their successful retreat to the Hindenburg Line, leaving everything ablaze as they retreated. Not to be outdone, the British liberally used their matches and torched thousands and thousands of acres. I can see how John would have been taken by the sight of so many million trees, etc., being put to the torch. He definitely would have seen fire mixed with the blood of war.

## Second Trumpet

We then read John's description of what he saw when the second trumpet was blown,

*"The second angel sounded his trumpet, and something like **a huge mountain, all ablaze, was thrown into the sea**. A third of the sea turned into blood, a third of the living creatures in the sea died, and **a third of the ships were destroyed.**"*                                               Revelation 8:8-9.

Let's jump ahead to World War II and you, like me, might find this statistic startling: a total of about 105,000 ships were involved in that war, and a little over 36,000 of them were sunk. That is almost exactly a third of the ships being destroyed. Kind of uncanny, isn't it, since John said *"and a third of the ships were destroyed."*

Now, let's look at a picture John might have described as:

*"something like a huge mountain, all ablaze, was thrown into the sea."*

The mushroom cloud over Nagasaki shortly after the bombing on August 9.

Are you, as I was, beginning to see some things that give you a funny feeling? Things that might be a touch beyond coincidence?

We need to remember that John was trying his best to explain what he saw occurring at least two thousand years prior to the events actually taking place. Nothing in his lifetime would have prepared him for being able to paint a word picture of the sight of an atomic blast. John was a normal first century man trying his best to explain to other first century men what to him was the unexplainable.

## Third Trumpet

*"The third angel sounded his trumpet, and a great star, blazing like a torch, fell from the sky on a third of the rivers and on the springs of water—the name of the star is Wormwood. A third of the waters turned bitter, and many people died from the waters that had become bitter."* Revelation 8:10.

We need to fast forward to April 26, 1986, and look at the catastrophic nuclear accident that occurred at the Chernobyl Nuclear Power Plant in the Ukraine. An explosion and fire released large quantities of radioactive contamination into the atmosphere, which spread over much of Western USSR and Europe.

According to UNSCEAR, up to the year 2005 more than 6000 cases of thyroid cancer were reported in children and adolescents exposed at the time of the accident, a number that is expected to increase. The disaster is widely considered to have been the worst nuclear power plant accident in history, and is one of only two classified as a level 7 event on the International Nuclear Event Scale, the other being the Fukushima Daiichi nuclear disaster in 2011.

The battle to contain the contamination from Chernobyl and avert a greater catastrophe has so far involved over 500,000 people. The official Soviet casualty count of 31 deaths has been widely disputed and is probably way lower than it actually was. Worse, though, the long-term effects such as death by cancers and deformities are still being accounted for.

The problem was that the wind carried the radiation for hundreds of miles and filled the European rivers with it, killing thousands of cattle among other types of animals, plus people. Greenpeace claims that 200,000 premature deaths have already occurred, and predicts 270,000 more cancer cases. Countless others will eventually suffer disease and premature deaths.

When Chernobyl exploded it caused a radioactive graphite fire that contaminated the surrounding area and spread a cloud of radioactivity around the world. As we mentioned, thirty one workers and firefighters were killed immediately. Because of faulty measurement equipment it was initially assumed the reactor had not lost containment. Most of the casualties were plant workers who stayed, most without radiation protection, to try to get water to the containment facility. They all died within three weeks since radiation levels were some 10,000 times higher than lethal levels.

Surrounding areas were also contaminated by the blasts and resulting fires, killing everything including the forests. More than a quarter of a million people were evacuated, never to return.

Today Chernobyl still radiates. In 2011 the Ukrainian Government was asking for a billion dollars in foreign aid with a plan to "seal" Chernobyl for 100 years. Still under construction, a 105-meter domed roof is being constructed with the hope that this dome will be rolled into place by 2014 to "seal in" the disaster a quarter of a century after the event. The U.S. has already donated $182 million to the cause.

Now, here is the kicker, Chernobyl is Russian for "Wormwood," as in the above verse that says, *"the name of the star is **Wormwood**."*

Every single thing about that third trumpet is wrapped up tightly in the Chernobyl disaster. The only thing John could have done to make this more clear would have been to give the longitude and latitude of Chernobyl. With only his first century experiences to draw from, I'd say that he did an excellent job of describing what he saw.

### Fourth Trumpet

*"The fourth angel sounded his trumpet, and a third of the sun was struck, a third of the moon, and a third of the stars, so that a third of them turned dark. A third of the day was without light, and also a third of the night."* Revelation 8:12.

We can move up a few more years to the invasion of Kuwait by Iraqi troops that began August 2, 1990. This, of course, was followed by Desert Storm, a war waged in 1991 by a coalition force from 34 nations led by the United States against Iraq in response to that invasion of Kuwait. Let's consider the seven hundred oil wells that the Iraqi troops set on fire. It was literally impossible to see much of anything from the ground looking up. The sun and sky were almost completely darkened.

Can we not imagine John looking at Kuwait and seeing what appeared to be the ground opening up and smoke rising from it?

**Fifth trumpet**

The fifth trumpet encompasses a lot of things happening, and rather than abbreviating it we would be wise to read the entirety of the scriptures that describe it.

*"The fifth angel sounded his trumpet, and I saw a star that had fallen from the sky to the earth. The star was given the key to the shaft of the Abyss. When he opened the Abyss, smoke rose from it like the smoke from a gigantic furnace. The sun and sky were darkened by the smoke from the Abyss. And out of the smoke locusts came down upon the earth and were given power like that of scorpions of the earth. They were told not to harm the grass of the earth or any plant or tree, but only those people who did not have the seal of God on their foreheads. They were not given power to kill*

them, but only to torture them for five months. And the agony they suffered was like that of the sting of a scorpion when it strikes a man. During those days men will seek death, but will not find it; they will long to die, but death will elude them.

The locusts looked like horses prepared for battle. On their heads they wore something like crowns of gold, and their faces resembled human faces. Their hair was like women's hair, and their teeth were like lions' teeth. They had breastplates like breastplates of iron, and the sound of their wings was like the thundering of many horses and chariots rushing into battle. They had tails and stings like scorpions, and in their tails they had power to torment people for five months.  They had as king over them the angel of the Abyss, whose name in Hebrew is Abaddon, and in Greek, Apollyon."

*Revelation 9:1-11.*

Let's consider the gulf wars.
We start with a star, which is an angel, opening the ground and,

*"smoke rose from it like the smoke from a gigantic furnace. The sun and sky were darkened by the smoke from the Abyss."*

Most people forget that at the very beginning of "Operation Iraqi Freedom," the second gulf war, Saddam was up to his old tricks and the first thing he did was set some of his own oil fields on fire, just like he had done in Kuwait twelve years earlier. His plan was to make an even bigger disaster than was encountered when his troops retreated from Kuwait, but as was reported by the US Department of State,

"U.S. and British troops are moving quickly to extinguish fires at a number of Iraqi oil wells and prevent the destruction by Iraqi troops of strategic oil fields that will be vitally important in ensuring Iraq's future economic recovery and prosperity."     March 23, 2003, Washington File.

So, if John was seeing oil well fires darkening the sky as he had in Trumpet number four, it is very likely that he would have again written, *"smoke rose from it like the smoke from a gigantic furnace. The sun and sky were darkened by the smoke from the Abyss."*

The next thing John sees coming out of the smoke are locusts. But we must keep in mind that John was of the first century. The only things that flew at that time were birds and some bugs, including locusts. If indeed he was witnessing events in Iraq, he may well have described what he saw in the skies as locusts. *"The sound of their wings was like the thundering of many horses and chariots rushing into battle."*

Actually, the full description John gives quite accurately portrays helicopters in battle formation:

*"The locusts looked like horses prepared for battle. On their heads they wore something like crowns of gold, and their faces resembled human faces. Their hair was like women's hair, and their teeth were like lions' teeth. They had breastplates like breastplates of iron, and the sound of their wings was like the thundering of many horses and chariots rushing into battle."*

John tells us also,

*"And out of the smoke locusts came down upon the earth and were given power like that of scorpions of the earth. They were told not to harm the grass of the earth or any plant or tree, but only those people who did not have the seal of God on their foreheads. They were not given power to kill them, but only to torture them for five months."*

If John was actually seeing helicopters, the scripture tells us they were not allowed to kill anyone who had the seal of God on their foreheads. That makes sense when we think about the fact that the Iraqis could not have had that seal because they were Muslim.

As to the reference to five months, if we combine the two gulf wars we find that the total duration was five months. I can understand how John could have been seeing what we consider two wars because in many ways the second gulf war was just a continuation of the first one.

What seems to be the most telling aspect to me, however, is that John says,

*"They had as king over them the angel of the Abyss, whose name in Hebrew is Abaddon, and in Greek, Apollyon."*

Abaddon and Apollyon each mean "The Destroyer." I hope you are sitting down for this because amazingly, the name Saddam means "The Destroyer."

Saddam, Apollyon, and Abaddon are one and the same. Incredible!

This is like Chernobyl being Russian for *"Wormwood."* Everything just fits like a glove. After a while the coincidences stop appearing to be coincidences.

Let's read that last sentence from the scripture again,

*"They had as king over them the angel of the Abyss, whose name in Hebrew is Abaddon, and in Greek, Apollyon."*

A thought on this last sentence is that if John started witnessing this conflict by looking at the hundreds of oil fields burning, and described that as smoke rising from the Abyss, and if God allowed him to watch until the end, John would have seen Saddam crawling out of that hole in the ground with hair all disheveled, appearing to John to be,

*"king over them, the angel of the Abyss, whose name in Hebrew is Abaddon, and in Greek, Apollyon."*

My hunch is that there may be something to this theory of the first five trumpets, beginning in 1917, the year Rabbi Judah Ben Samuel predicted. But again, that is only speculation. I doubt, however, that Irenaeus would label me as a heretic for saying that, because I suspect John never even talked about the subject of the first five trumpets in his oral teaching. It could well be that the only things John knew about them were what he astonishingly witnessed; and he wrote down exactly what he saw, probably with his hand shaking.

I don't doubt that Polycarp probably asked John about what he saw, but I imagine John would have said something like, "I wrote down what I saw and I don't know any more about it than that."

In the end, though, we won't be certain that those five trumpets revealed to John the exact five events we just read about until trumpet number six begins. However, if what we just looked at is indeed the first five trumpets, an interesting thing is unfolding for us, that being that the events that we read in Revelation that seem so unearthly, so eerie, and in many ways so mystical, are truly just events that we now look at as normal. In many ways that makes sense.

Consider for a moment if God had allowed another man to see into the future as John did. Now let's imagine that the first scene he sees is the terrible battle at Gettysburg. Might he have written that he saw what appeared to be the world at battle and a representative of God was standing on a hill and collecting the souls of the people to be kept forever? He might add that the souls were to remain forever small and flat but in the likeness of the men they had been. Of course, what the man would have been seeing was one of the early photographers on the hill overlooking the battle, taking pictures with one of the first cameras.

Or then we can pretend that God took the man into your house and showed you typing an e-mail to a friend in Europe. Is it possible that he might have written that he saw men's thoughts being captured by a demon and instantly given to foreigners thousands of miles away?

Think even of that man being given the task of explaining telephones, or jets, or microwaves, or the internet, or any of a myriad of things that we look at as normal. Could not his descriptions sound supernatural or even ethereal? If we were to read his descriptions today we might not even recognize what he saw, and we might even consider the things he described to be mystical, and interpret them in all kinds of unearthly ways.

So, if John saw a few flashes of the Gulf Wars, in his mind he would have seen the ground open up and out of the abyss smoke rising, *"from it like the smoke from a gigantic furnace. The sun and sky were darkened by the smoke from the Abyss."*

And then John saw the helicopters flying in a squadron like locusts. He would try to describe what he saw by saying *"The locusts looked like horses prepared for battle. On their heads they wore something like crowns of gold, and their faces resembled human faces. Their hair was like women's hair, and their teeth were like lions' teeth. They had breastplates like breastplates of iron, and the sound of their wings was like the thundering of many horses and chariots rushing into battle. They had tails and stings like scorpions."*

And then John was shown the end, with that terrible looking image of Saddam Hussein crawling out of that pit where he had hidden for days to escape capture. And, of course, John heard his name, Saddam, *"whose name in Hebrew is Abaddon, and in Greek, Apollyon."* We can easily imagine that John would have assumed, having been told that he was seeing the leader, that he was *"king over them, the angel of the Abyss."*

As I said, it all makes so much sense. These could be normal events described in unusual ways. But the most interesting thing to me is that the more I studied, being led by the truths I was uncovering instead of the teaching that I had heard in the past, the more I got the feeling that the same could be true not only of the rest of the Revelation scriptures that deal with the Tribulation, but also the descriptions of the Millennial reign of our Lord, and even heaven. Those things are going to be glorious, and far better than we can even imagine, but they may not be quite as unnatural or unfamiliar as we may have expected. Yes, our world and the unseen world are going to merge, but when they do, the results may not be as startling as we have thought. What I have uncovered in my digging has turned out to be a great comfort to me, and I hope that when you have seen the future I now envision, you will be comforted greatly as well.

I'm not trying to underplay the horrific nature of much of what will transpire in the Tribulation. As we have seen with just the first five trumpets, if the events we described were indeed what John saw, they were terrible. And trumpet number six will make them seem like child's play in comparison. To be sure, if that event happens to occur while we are still alive, we will definitely know that it is trumpet number six blasting away. Trumpet number six will be that gigantic. We can bank on that.

# Trumpet Six Is Deafening

Although the bloodshed and carnage that the world suffered in those first five trumpet events were horrific, all of it will pale in comparison to what will take place in trumpet number six. In fact, the way I see it, trumpet number six may result in more devastation and tragedy throughout the earth than we can imagine.

As it was with the first five trumpets, I think John wrote down all that he knew about number six when he penned Revelation, so the Apostolic Oral Teaching is of no help to us. The early church Fathers were completely mum on the subject. Therefore, let's just read what John recorded in Revelation:

*"The sixth angel sounded his trumpet, and I heard a voice coming from the horns of the golden altar that is before God. It said to the sixth angel who had the trumpet, 'Release the four angels who are bound at the great river Euphrates.' And the four angels who had been kept ready for this very hour and day and month and year were released to kill a third of mankind. The number of the mounted troops was two hundred million. I heard their number.*

*The horses and riders I saw in my vision looked like this: Their breastplates were fiery red, dark blue, and yellow as sulfur. The heads of the horses resembled the heads of lions, and out of their mouths came fire, smoke and sulfur. A third of mankind was killed by the three plagues of fire, smoke and sulfur that came out of their mouths. The power of the horses was in their mouths and in their tails; for their tails were like snakes, having heads with which they inflict injury.*

*The rest of mankind that were not killed by these plagues still did not repent of the work of their hands; they did not stop worshiping demons, and idols of gold, silver, bronze, stone and wood—idols that cannot see or hear or walk. Nor did they repent of their murders, their magic arts, their sexual immorality or their thefts."* Revelation 9:13-21.

## Islam's Involvement

Much of end time teaching these days is gravitating toward the theory that Islam will be a gigantic factor during the seven year Tribulation, and in the thought that the antichrist will be the Mahdi of Muslim prophecy. There are many arguments that seem at face value to validate that position, and of course, due to radical Islamist terrorism, the Muslim religion is not only continually in the news, but often is on our minds.

First of all, let's get one thing straight, the god worshipped by Islam is not the God of Christianity. Sadly, often even high profile ministers state that they are the same deities. In fact, there is a fairly strong movement afoot to try to bring Christianity and Islam together in what is called Chrislam. It is stunning but true that there are Baptist, Methodist, Presbyterian, Episcopal, Lutheran, Catholic, and charismatic churches that have embraced this apostasy. It seems that since Muslims trace their heritage to Abraham, and assume that they are worshipping the same God of Abraham, many Christians take that claim at face value without even looking into it at all. In fact, Pope Francis I, in his second week as the head of the Catholic Church washed the feet of a twelve year old Muslim girl. This act got the Catholic traditionalists up in arms because it was against Catholic law for a priest to wash the feet of a female because none of the twelve apostles of Jesus were female, but for me the fact that it was a Muslim was even more telling of a coming change. As it was, Pope Francis I is a big believer in bringing Islam and Christianity together, often referring to Muslims as his brothers and sisters.

The fact is, more and more I feel like Mark 1:3's description of John the Baptist as *"a voice of one calling in the wilderness,"* because either due to fear, political correctness, or just plain ignorance, more and more "Christian" leaders are subscribing to the false notion that Christianity and Islam both worship the same God; however the Quran clearly states in "The Women 4.171" that the belief of Islam is that God has no son. That section, which talks directly to Christians, says,

"O followers of the Book! do not exceed the limits in your religion, and do not speak (lies) against Allah, but (speak) the truth; the Messiah, Isa son of Marium is only an apostle of Allah and His Word which He communicated to Marium and a spirit from Him; believe therefore in Allah and His apostles, and say not, Three. Desist, it is better for you; Allah is only one God; far be It from His glory that He should have a son."

In sharp contrast, we all know by heart John 3:16 in the infallible Word of God, which declares that God does have a Son,

*"For God so loved the world that he gave his only begotten Son, that whosoever believeth in him should not perish, but have everlasting life."*

The Quran, however, even goes as far as to claim that Jesus never died, nor was He crucified. Read the Quran's blasphemy for yourself,

"And [for] their saying, 'Indeed, we have killed the Messiah, Jesus, the son of Mary, the messenger of Allah.' And they did not kill him, nor did they crucify him; but [another] was made to resemble him to them. And indeed, those who differ over it are in doubt about it. They have no knowledge of it except the following of assumption. And they did not kill him, for certain,"
(Quran 4:157).

Quite frankly, I could probably write an entire book about the gigantic differences between the God of Christianity and Judaism, and the god of Islam, however, there is no need to go that far afield of the purpose of this book. Just please know that Christianity and Islam are diametrically opposed to each other, and the main difference is that the God of Christianity and Judaism is real. He is alive. He is the one true God of everything. The god of Islam does not even exist. He is only as real as a pagan god made out of wood. Interestingly, a little known fact is that the earliest mention of Allah worship can be traced to Babylon, approximately 1700 B.C., in the "Epic of Atrahasis." In that story told on stone tablets, a portion of the legend talks about a god named Alla, who is described as a god of "violence and revolution." I guess things pretty much stay the same, don't they?

As an aside, the Arabs, from whom we get Islam, consider themselves to be descended from Ishmael, Abraham's son by Hagar in Genesis, where it says of Ishmael,

*"He will be a wild donkey of a man; his hand will be against everyone and everyone's hand against him, and he will live in hostility toward all his brothers."* Genesis 16:12.

Possibly a more fascinating and important point for us is that Ishmael's mother, Hagar, was Egyptian, which would probably make Ishmael a Hamite, rather than a Shemite (Semite). In studying the lineage of the Nephilim we found that it was through Ham, the wicked son of Noah, that the Nephilim gene survived. Could it be that Islam is the product of the Nephilim mindset, which is, like Islam, diametrically opposed to the one true God?

God teaches us,

*"Who is the liar? It is the man who denies that Jesus is the Christ. Such a man is the antichrist—he denies the Father and the Son."* 1 John 2:22.

And the Father wants us also to learn,

*"This is how you can recognize the Spirit of God: Every spirit that acknowledges that Jesus Christ has come in the flesh is from God, but every spirit that does not acknowledge Jesus is not from God. This is the spirit of the antichrist, which you have heard is coming and even now is already in the world."* 1 John 4:2-3.

The creator of Islam was obviously *"not from God"* since he denied the divinity of Jesus. And if *"not from God,"* the way I see it there is only one other choice possible as to who he was from, and that choice is Satan. If the assumption is true, that the Nephilim gene survived beyond Goliath and his brothers, and I believe that to be the case, a connection between the evil Nephilim gene and Islam actually may make very good sense. It would explain a lot.

Am I saying that I think all Muslims contain the Nephilim gene? Absolutely not. I do, though, believe that Islam is an evil religion created by Satan as an attempt to be the exact antithesis of the religion of the one true God. The followers, however, are all too often people who were born into it, indoctrinated as children, and have had no chance at all to learn the truth.

Interestingly, however, Jesus Himself is appearing to Muslims in greater and greater frequency, and the testimony from those people is wonderful. Jesus loves the Muslims and we need to remember to pray for their salvation. There obviously is a difference between Islam and the people blindly trapped in it. Having cleared that up, let's examine the possibility of the antichrist and the Islamic Mahdi being one and the same person.

As to the antichrist presented in the Bible being the Islamic Mahdi; they definitely are described in a similar manner in the Bible and the Quran. There are two things, however, that are somewhat troubling to me about that being the case. First, as you may know, there are over 8,350 prophetic verses in the Bible. Over 6,000 of those prophetic verses have already literally been fulfilled, exactly as God said they would. The remaining ones deal with the end times and most certainly will be fulfilled the same as the first 6,000 were. On the other hand, of all the other holy books on earth, from all the other religions, not a single prophecy has ever been fulfilled. Not one. That is beyond incredible. We would readily assume that at least some of those religions would have fulfilled prophecies, if for no other reason than random chance. But that is not the case. The score on fulfilled prophecies thus far is over 6,000 for the God of the Bible, and zero for all the other gods combined.

It seems reasonable to assume that God has had a hand in that situation. We can understand why God would have wanted to make sure that no other religion ever had a fulfilled prophecy because fulfilled prophecies are so extremely important to Him. God stated emphatically,

*"I am God, and there is none like me. I make known the end from the beginning, from ancient times, what is still to come."*     Isaiah 46:10.

In fact, my contention is that God told us that it was by His fulfilled prophecies that we could prove His existence. It was by them that we could prove to others that there truly is a God, outside our time limitation. Only the Sovereign God of everything could predict the future and be accurate over six thousand times in a row. To say otherwise is beyond ludicrous. God even put out a challenge to anyone who thought they could prophesy like He can:

*"Present your case,' the Lord God says. 'Bring forth your strong arguments,' the King of Jacob says. 'Let them declare to us what is going to take place; as for the former events, declare what they were, that we may*

*consider them, and know their outcome; or announce to us what is coming. Declare the things that are going to come afterward, so that we may know that you are gods."* Isaiah 41:21-23 NASB.

And it is because God is so adamant in His feeling about fulfilled prophecy that I believe He has not allowed any other religion to have a single one in their holy book, including Islam. Of course, it could well be that the Muslims believing the person who comes on the scene as the antichrist would not actually be a fulfillment of their prophecy because he in truth will not be their savior.

Another thing that is somewhat troubling to me about the Mahdi being the antichrist is that, unlike what is normally taught, the antichrist will actually be Jewish. I heard you gasp when you read that statement. I did, too, when I first was convinced that was the case. We will discuss the particulars of it in detail in a later chapter, and I am confident that once you see the facts you will understand completely; however, prior to getting to that astonishing discussion please just assume for a moment that I am correct that the antichrist will be a Jew. Could you imagine the Muslim world ever following such a man? Obviously that would be absolutely unthinkable. And if a Jewish world leader were to head up a "one world government," there would be somewhere between one and a half billion to a little over two billion people in total revolt. (Religiouspopulation.com estimates there are currently 2.1 billion Muslims.) Although, if the Muslims fall for Chrislam like many of the Christian leaders have, maybe they can change their mind about some other things, too. And since the antichrist will pursue the persecution and eradication of Christians and believing Jews, like the Muslims believe the Mahdi will when he arrives, maybe they will overlook his tribe of Dan Heritage

There are, as I say, a few situations that give me pause as far as jumping totally into the belief that the Mahdi and the antichrist will be one and the same. Another is the fact that there must be a new temple built on Mount Zion in order for the antichrist to commit what Jesus and Daniel both called *"the abomination of desolation."* Some people believe that since there is room for both the Dome of the Rock and a new temple on Mount Zion, that will be the solution. But as long as the Muslim world is as it is today, I can't see that happening. Muslims around the world would become incensed at just the suggestion of such a thing being planned; but then again, things can change.

Of course, there are several prophetic verses in the Bible that talk about wars between Israel and its neighbors, such as Psalm 83, Isaiah 17, and the famous Gog and Magog war in Ezekiel 38 and 39, so it is possible that the Islamic world may be greatly reduced before the sixth trumpet sounds. But it is also possible that one or two or possibly all three of those scriptural wars refer to the exact same war. We won't stop now to get into all the arguments for and against these wars mentioned in other scriptures being different wars or the same, but as we've discussed before, so many things can change in the world that speculation is only guessing, and normally that is wrong.

## The Sixth Trumpet War

Let's look at the first part of the sixth trumpet scripture again,

*"The sixth angel sounded his trumpet, and I heard a voice coming from the horns of the golden altar that is before God. It said to the sixth angel who had the trumpet, 'Release the four angels who are bound at the great river Euphrates."* Revelation 9:13-14.

First, we see from those verses that the war will begin at the Euphrates River, a 1700 mile long river that begins in Turkey and flows through Syria and Iraq, emptying in the Persian Gulf. The entire region is almost totally Islamic.

*"And the four angels who had been kept ready for this very hour and day and month and year were released to kill a third of mankind."*
Revelation 9:15.

This is the utterly astounding part of this trumpet. Think about what you just read. Fully a third of all mankind will be killed in this war. That is a figure that is almost beyond our comprehension. If we take today's population of roughly seven billion people, that verse just told us that about two and a third billion people are going to die in that one war. That is more people than have died in all the wars of the entire history of the planet. The devastation we are talking about will be more horrible than we can even imagine. Think about even trying to bury 2.3 billion people at one time. The tragedy described in that one verse is so utterly mind boggling that most of us who read it just mentally skip over the words. The thoughts of the vast number of parents who will watch their children die, or the reverse, resulting in millions and millions of babies and young ones who will be instantly left with no parent to care for them, means weeping will be everywhere.

However, although that verse intimates that the entire world will suffer human carnage on a massive scale because Revelation 9:15 told us *"a third of mankind"* will be killed, from what I see, the most concentrated area of death will be within the Muslim nations. As we saw, much of the Islamic world can be traced back to Ishmael, and his descendants will be hard hit to be sure; but the prophecy of the Lord is even grimmer for the other predominant portion of the Muslims who trace their heritage to Esau. We see that as the case when we study the tiny book of Obadiah:

*"In that day,' declares the Lord, 'will I not destroy the wise men of Edom, those of understanding in the mountains of Esau? Your warriors, Teman, will be terrified, and everyone in Esau's mountains will be cut down in the slaughter. Because of the violence against your brother Jacob, you will be covered with shame; you will be destroyed forever."* Obadiah 1:8-10.

*"As you have done, it will be done to you; your deeds will return upon your own head. Just as you drank on my holy hill, so all the nations will drink continually; they will drink and drink and be as if they had never been.*

*But on Mount Zion will be deliverance; it will be holy, and Jacob will possess his inheritance. Jacob will be a fire and Joseph a flame; Esau will be stubble, and they will set him on fire and destroy him. There will be no survivors from Esau.' The Lord has spoken."* Obadiah 1:15-18.

Did you notice that in the last sentence God said there will be *"no survivors"* of the descendants of Esau? Wow! Many scholars feel that these verses deal with the final battle of Armageddon at the very end of the seven year tribulation, and they may. However, those verses containing God's pronouncement of the entire annihilation of Esau's lineage obviously must deal with a gigantic world war, and since one third of mankind will die in the sixth trumpet war, we may well be looking at that war and not Armageddon. We can not be certain either way at this point in time.

But getting back to John's description of what he witnessed when the sixth trumpet was blown, we read,

*"The number of the mounted troops was two hundred million. I heard their number."* Revelation 9:16.

As we have reiterated, the only thing that makes sense is that although the war may have started out regionally, in order to kill a third of the population of the entire world it probably will become an all out world war the likes of which have never even seriously been contemplated. That being the case, envisioning two hundred million military personnel being involved does not sound at all unreasonable.

*"The horses and riders I saw in my vision looked like this: Their breastplates were fiery red, dark blue, and yellow as sulfur. The heads of the horses resembled the heads of lions, and out of their mouths came fire, smoke and sulfur. A third of mankind was killed by the three plagues of fire, smoke and sulfur that came out of their mouths. The power of the horses was in their mouths and in their tails; for their tails were like snakes, having heads with which they inflict injury."* Revelation 9:17-19.

This description sounds very similar to the way John described what he saw in earlier trumpet visions when he was trying to describe modern warfare. What is obvious from the results is that this is going to be nuclear.

*"The rest of mankind who were not killed by these plagues still did not repent of the work of their hands; they did not stop worshiping demons, and idols of gold, silver, bronze, stone and wood—idols that cannot see or hear or walk. Nor did they repent of their murders, their magic arts, their sexual immorality or their thefts."* Revelation 9:20-21.

Unfortunately, the world that remains after the dust clears, and the enormity of the toll in lives is felt, will not turn to God. And since God knows *"the end from the beginning, from ancient times, what is still to come,"* He will not be at all surprised. And quite frankly, you, like me, are probably not surprised either. In our lifetimes we have seen wars, natural disasters of all kinds, and terror throughout the world, and we have witnessed no gigantic revival of faith. In fact, what we do see year after year is more shunning of the God of all creation. So, even after this trumpet blast that surpasses all the rest has been blown, the world will not repent of its ways and turn to God; therefore the tribulation must begin and then be played out to its conclusion. And interestingly, although our initial impression of the devastation caused by the sixth trumpet will be that it was senseless and of no value, those terrible events will result in making the tribulation and what comes after that possible. We will find out why in chapters coming up. All the pieces will come together.

# The Timing of the Tribulation

     Of course, we are still in the realm of speculation in thinking that the first five trumpets have already sounded. But the question naturally arises in our minds; if the first five actually have sounded, and trumpet number six is next to blow, can we come up with any plausible answer as to when the Great Tribulation might begin?

     Obviously the Middle East seems to be in constant turmoil, and as you read these words there may have been articles in your morning newspaper today that lead you to believe that the final eruption could occur any day. That seems to have been the case since Israel became a nation in 1948. So, are there any other indicators we can look at besides the instability in the Middle East? God's Word does not seem to set a date for it.

     Of course, since Jesus ascended in the clouds, people have been trying to ascertain the date of His return. Even Isaac Newton, the seventeenth century scientist, who many credit as being the greatest scientist of all time, spent the better part of fifty years trying to determine the time when Jesus would return to set up His earthly Kingdom. Newton finally settled on the year 2060 as being that glorious year. For him that year was not a prophecy; it was a result of his logical mind and many calculations. Was he correct? Who knows?

     Rabbi Judah Ben Samuel's prophecy that gave us a start date for the trumpets we looked at in previous chapters gives us a date of 2017 as being the beginning of the jubilee that will see the return of Christ. But since a jubilee is fifty years long, that means that his prophecy only gives us a time frame of from 2017 to 2067 for seeing Jesus sit on His earthly throne.

     And then there are Biblical parallels that are fascinating in this regard. For instance, Persian King Artaxerxes issued a decree to restore and rebuild Jerusalem in the spring of the twentieth year of his reign, 445 BC. On the 483rd anniversary of this decree Jesus rode into Jerusalem on a donkey on what we know as the first Palm Sunday. This was the first coming of Jesus. Later, in 70 AD the city was destroyed again, this time by the Romans. The fascinating part is that like Artaxerxes, Suleiman, in the twentieth year of his reign, ordered the walls of Jerusalem to be rebuilt. This occurred in 1535 AD. If the same 483 years applies, which corresponds to Daniel's sixty seven year prophecy relating to the Messiah's first coming, we would be looking at the year 2018. Is this meaningful? Again, who knows?

There is a prophecy that I think gives us a clue. It is Saint Malachy's prophecy. In case you are not familiar with it, allow me to quote what I wrote about it in Unlocking God's Secrets,

"This prophecy comes from a very Godly Irish priest who became the Archbishop of Armage in 1132 AD. Sainthood was conferred on him following his death and he is known today as Saint Malachy. Many miracles were attributed to him because of specific prayers he prayed, and he was known to have the gift of prophecy, even predicting the hour and date of his own death.

In 1139 Malachy had a vision in which he was given a long list of popes that would head the Catholic Church until the last pope. Malachy wrote down the list and in the following year personally gave it to Pope Innocent II. It remained in the Vatican until 1590 when it was printed by the church historian, Arnold Wion.

The 1913 edition of the Catholic Encyclopedia says of these prophecies, 'These short prophetic announcements ... indicate some noticeable trait of all future popes from Celestine II, who was elected in the year 1130, until the end of the world. They are enunciated under mystical titles. Those who have undertaken to interpret and explain these symbolic prophecies have succeeded in discovering some trait, allusion, point or similitude in their application to the individual popes, either as to their country, their name, their coat of arms or insignia, their birthplace, talent or learning, the title of their cardinalate, or the dignities which they held. There is something more than coincidence in the designations given to ... popes so many hundreds of years before their time.'

Malachy listed 112 popes in the list he said God gave him in his vision, and the list has proven to be extremely accurate. We won't take the time to go through all 112 of them here, but let's at least look at Malachy's designations and the actual popes of the past fifty years by Malachy's pope number:

105 - "Pastor and Marine" - Pope John XXII was from Venice, a marine city.

106 - "Flower of Flowers" - Pope Paul VI's coat of arms was three lilies.

108, plus 109, & 110 were then lumped together and designated - "The year of three popes." - In 1978 we saw three popes in the same year, Popes Paul VI, John Paul I and John Paul II.

109 -"of the half of the moon" - Pope John Paul I died a month after he was elected. He was elected during a half moon and died during a half moon.

110 - "of the eclipse of the sun" - Pope John Paul II was born may 18, 1920, during a solar eclipse, and was buried April 8, 2005, also during solar eclipse.

111 - "the glory of the olive" - Joseph Ratzinger, the current Pope Benedict XVI came from the order known as Olivetans.

112 - "Peter the Roman" - According to Malachy this would be the last pope in world history. Interesting is the fact that since the apostle Peter was the first pope, no other pope has had the audacity to call himself Peter."

Saint Malachy's exact quote concerning the pope he numbered 112 is,

"Peter the Roman, who will nourish the sheep in many tribulations; when they are finished, the city of seven hills will be destroyed, and the dreadful judge will judge his people. The end."

From Unlocking God's Secrets by Bob Morley.

As you know, since I wrote that section several years ago for the book, Unlocking God's Secrets, Pope Benedict XVI, the number 111 in Saint Malachy's list, resigned. We now have Pope Francis 1 as the head of the Catholic Church. He is number 112. Many have said that he fits the St. Malachy description exactly since his father was an Italian immigrant, and since he came from Buenos Aires, Argentina, which has been labeled the "Rome of the New World" because of its large Italian population. And as to the name Peter, many say that all popes are the representative of Peter, who the Catholics look at as being the very first pope. More significant, however, is that he named himself after Francis of Assisi; a Roman priest whose original name was Francesco di Pietro (Peter) di Bernardone, literally, "Peter the Roman." But, whether or not Pope Francis 1 is in fact "Peter the Roman" of St. Malachy's prophecy, the pope who will be alive at the time of the Great tribulation, only time will tell. I will say, however, that St. Malachy was correct 111 out of 111 times, so I would be a little bit startled if he missed on the last one, number 112. We shall see.

Therefore, my best guess for the start of the tribulation is some year prior to 2067, and depending on how long Pope Francis 1 lives, if we assume St. Malachy batted a thousand, it naturally could be quite a bit sooner. I understand that is quite a wimpy answer, especially since there are so many other authors who will not only give you an anticipated year, but also the month and day. Talk about radical speculation! My only suggestion is to not bet the farm on them being right. You just might find that you need a new farm house to live in when their guaranteed date comes and goes.

# The Source of Teaching

In the latter part of this book, when we actually get into digging out what John the Revelator taught his student, Polycarp, concerning how he interpreted the things he wrote about in Revelation, you may wonder how our modern church got so far afield from his teaching. I'm talking about such things as who the antichrist would be, what the mark of the beast really is, who the woman with the child is, the head wound being healed, and many other critical topics pertaining to the tribulation, including the true reason for it all. I have a theory as to both the why and the how of such radical discrepancies having occurred.

The Protestant Reformation came about primarily because the reformers rightly believed that Satan had manipulated some of the thinking within the church, and as result such anti Biblical traditions as buying indulgences came into being. The problem today, as I see it, is that the modern church must think that Satan stopped trying to infiltrate the church with his lies when the Reformation was over. Personally, I think Satan is a lot more persistent than that. I don't think the Reformation slowed down Satan one bit.

So, when new ideas are instituted in theological thinking that contradict the beliefs of the early church and the teaching of the church founders like the Apostle John, we should be very wary. Unfortunately that has not been the case. For example, let's look at the man whose unique new ideas regarding the book of Revelation and end time events have completely taken over today's church. I'm referring to someone you may have never heard of, but, by proxy of your minister, is your mentor, the same as he was my invisible mentor for several years. The man is:

### John Nelson Darby

You might be surprised to learn that what we have been taught about the book of Revelation in our modern church can virtually all be traced back to John Darby, with almost none of it being subscribed to or even heard of prior to him coming on the scene.

Reading what we have talked about with the first six trumpets possibly made you feel uncomfortable because chances are you may have learned that all the things described in the Revelation scriptures had to be taken literally. A third of the earth being burned up meant exactly that. A huge mountain all ablaze being thrown into the sea meant what it said. References to the moon, sun, and stars turning dark talked about those things actually happening. All of the descriptions would come to pass exactly as John wrote them, and to believe otherwise was heresy. The reality is that prior to John Darby coming on the scene, very little in Revelation was taken literally.

The first and second century church founders like Polycarp, Irenaeus, and Hippolytus knew that most of the things in Revelation were allegorical and some were literal. Revelation is, of course, the Revelation of Jesus, Who although He taught with parables in the four Gospels, also occasionally spoke directly, as he did in the Sermon on the Mount. But Darby, in his own "wisdom," decided that Revelation, as well as all of the rest of the Bible, should be taken literally. And that was just one of the many things he changed. In fact, the entirety of the Revelation message was replaced by brand new ideas at the whim of one man, John Darby. So, who was he?

I must tell you that I have read volumes about and by John Darby, and the result is that in many ways I am befuddled by him. I've studied commentaries about him written by both his critics and his loyal friends, and in doing so I felt I was reading about two distinctly different people. Some of his critics wondered if his conversion to Christianity was actually real; however, after reading many of his own writings and letters I felt strongly that his love for Jesus was real, and a driving force in his life, especially in his later years. Much of his life was spent in Christian service that should humble most of us, and his devotion to the scriptures was second to none. He was a true fundamentalist where the Bible was concerned, but at the same time he invented new meanings for verses that would have made the Apostle John scream and pull his hair out. To me, Darby's life, beliefs, and actions are a complete contradiction.

John Nelson Darby was born in Westminster, London, to a fairly wealthy Anglo-Irish family on March 3, 1801. His training as a lawyer was completed in 1819 and as far as we know he had no theological education at all. However, by 1825, at the tender age of 24 he had decided not to be an attorney and instead was ordained as a deacon of the established Church of Ireland. The following year he was made a priest of a parish of peasants in Calary, near Enniskerry, County Wicklow, Ireland. He worked hard in this new capacity and later claimed to have won hundreds of converts to the

Church of Ireland, taking them away from the Church of England. The conversions ended, however, when William Magee, the Archbishop of Dublin, ruled that converts were obliged to swear allegiance to George IV as rightful king of Ireland. This was such a blow to Darby that he resigned his curacy in protest. And it seems that Darby, following this action by the Archbishop that he perceived as a personal slap in his face, became totally bitter at all formal Christianity.

In looking at his early life we can see that Darby grew up in an upper class home. His middle name, Nelson, came from his godfather and family friend, Lord Nelson. Schooling came very easy for him and he was even given the Classical Gold Medalist award at Trinity College. It appears that what Darby considered a slap in the face by the Archbishop of Dublin may have been the first time he had not gotten his way, and possibly Darby did not know how to handle it; the result being a gigantic overreaction. Inwardly he wanted to lash out at the offending party, William Magee, but instead he went after the church establishment as a whole. Remember, Darby was still only in his early 20's when appointed to his position as priest in the Church of Ireland, and it may be that he was just too young and immature for such a position. From what I can gather, it was the first job of responsibility he had ever had. In that position he felt he had done a superior job, but as a result, instead of being praised, he received what he took to be an unfair reprimand.

During the next few years Darby met some like minded young men who for one reason or another were also disillusioned with the traditional church, including A. N. Groves, Edward Cronin, J. G. Bellett and Francis Hutchinson. These men started meeting to "break bread" together in Dublin. By 1832, this group had grown and began to identify themselves as a distinct Christian assembly. They traveled around Ireland and England recruiting other like minded souls and forming the movement now known as the Plymouth Brethren.

It was during this time that Darby developed the principles of what he called his "mature theology," which included his conviction that the very notion of a clergyman was a sin against the Holy Spirit because it limited the recognition that the Holy Spirit could speak through any member of the church. We must remember that John Darby felt betrayed by the established clergy in the Church of Ireland and we can look at this "conviction" that being a clergyman was a sin as a way to strike back at them, and for that matter at all of established religion. But Darby was not satisfied with that.

Still relatively young, and I believe somewhat immature, it seems he wanted to prove them to be wrong in their belief system as well. And this desire gave birth to what most Christians believe today regarding many things.

At the Powerscourt Conference, an annual meeting of Bible students organized by his friend, the wealthy widow Lady Powerscourt, Darby announced that he had had a "revelation," a whole new way of thinking about Christianity that would develop into what is known today as Dispensationalism, a system of thinking that is far removed from what the beloved Apostle John taught Polycarp, but a system of thinking that has taken over our modern church.

As I said, from his writings it is very obvious that Darby was a true fundamentalist, so I find it surprising that he would come up with brand new ideas that he knew were completely contradictory to the teaching of the Apostle John as painstakingly preserved by Polycarp, Irenaeus, and Hippolytus. But in <u>The Collected writings of J.N. Darby</u>, edited by W. Kelly (volume 14, page 68) we read Darby's own words about those church fathers,

"None are more untrustworthy on every fundamental subject than the mass of primitive Fathers."

You can see why studying Darby has been baffling to me. Such a statement, which was the same as saying, "I know better than those taught by the Apostle John" doesn't seem to gel with the obvious reverence for early church tradition I found in other of his writings. Granted, though, statements such as the one above were made by Darby in his early years.

But let's read on in Darby's own words what he had to say specifically about Polycarp, Irenaeus, and Hippolytus, who he called the Millenarians,

"For my own part, if I were bound to receive all that has been said by the Millenarians, I would reject the whole system, but **their views and statements weigh with me not one feather.** But this does not hinder me from inquiring by the teaching of the same Spirit … **what God has with infinite graciousness revealed to me concerning His dealing with the Church.**" From "Reflections upon the Prophetic Inquiry and the Views Advanced in It." J.N. Darby.

The phrase about the early church Fathers that their **"views and statements weigh with me not one feather"** seems excessively harsh to me. I will admit that I have pondered whether the spirit Darby was listening to was the same Spirit working with Polycarp, Irenaeus, and Hippolytus, and unfortunately I feel that the spirit Darby was hearing was the same one who had been trying to get his lies into the church for centuries.

So, what was included in Darby's new system that changed the teaching John passed down? First, as we mentioned, Darby said every word in Revelation <u>must</u> be taken literally, no exceptions.

Next, whereas all the new teaching from Darby maintained that the persecution of the antichrist would be against the Jews, all teaching from the Apostle John, and for the next eighteen hundred years, taught that it would be the church that would be the target of persecution. For instance, among many, many references Irenaeus wrote, we find him saying:

"They [the ten kings of Rev. 17:1-13] shall ...give their kingdom to the beast [Antichrist], and put the **Church to flight**"   <u>Against Heresies</u> V, 26, 1.

Irenaeus also said:

"but he [the Apostle John] indicates the number of the name [666 of Antichrist] now, that when this man comes **we** may avoid him, being aware who he is"   <u>Against Heresies</u> V, 30, 4.

And then there is Justin Martyr, another church Father who lived from 100 A.D. to 167 A.D., who wrote,

"the man of apostasy [Antichrist] ...shall venture to do unlawful deeds on earth against **us** the **Christians**"   Trypho cx.

Plus Tertullian, who lived from 150 A.D. to 220 A.D., said the tribulation situation will be such,

"that the beast Antichrist with his false prophet may wage war on the **Church of God**"   On the Resurrection of the Flesh xxv.

Then we have Hippolytus, the direct student of Irenaeus, saying,

"... the one thousand two hundred and three score days (the half of the week) during which the tyrant is to reign and persecute the **Church** ..."
Treatise on Christ and Antichrist, 61.

And from just a little later we have Saint Augustine (AD 354-430),

"... the kingdom of Antichrist shall fiercely, though for a short time, assail the **Church**... "  <u>The City of God</u>, XX, 23.

I could go on and on for several pages with quotes from early church Fathers that say the same thing, the antichrist will persecute the church, but I think you get the idea. And as I said, this was the teaching all the way up to Darby. For example, looking at the Reformers we find Martin Luther:

"[The book of Revelation] is intended as a revelation of things that are to happen in the future, and especially of tribulations and disasters for the **Church**.... "  <u>Works of Martin Luther</u>, VI, p. 481.

And John Knox (AD 1515-1572) wrote:

"the great love of God towards his **Church**, whom he pleased to forewarn of dangers to come ... to wit, The man of sin, The Antichrist... "
<u>The History of the Reformation, etc.</u>, 1, p. 76.

Not until John Nelson Darby did anyone in Christianity teach that the Jews, and not the church, would be the target of the antichrist's persecution. In fact, a brief list of famous Bible teachers in church history that I have encountered who taught that the church would encounter the persecution of the antichrist here on earth before the Second Coming include the following names you are probably familiar with:

John Calvin, Martin Luther, John Knox, John Bunyan, Isaac Newton, George Whitefield, Charles Spurgeon, Charles Hodge, Henry Alford, J.Sidlow Baxter, F.F. Bruce, Thomas Chalmers, Adam Clarke, Jonathan Edwards, Jim Elliott, W.J. Erdman, Robert Gundry, Carl F. Henry, Matthew

Henry, John Huss, Orson Jones, C.S. Lovett, J.Gresham Machen, Peter Marshall, Walter Martin, Gary Matsdorf, G.Campbell Morgan, Leon Morris, George Mueller, Ian Murray, B.W. Newton, John Newton, H.J. Ockenga, Bernard Ramm, Alexander Reese, A. Saphir, Demos Shakarian, Oswald J. Smith, Jim Spillman, R.C. Sproul, Charles Spurgeon, Corrie TenBoom, S.P. Tragelles, William Tyndale, B.B. Warfield, and Charles Wesley.

Obviously John Darby handily dismissed all of these giants of Christian thinking like he did Polycarp and Irenaeus with the same thought, **"their views and statements weigh with me not one feather."**

Don't get me wrong, I'm not saying that Covenant Theology, the seemingly only alternate teaching today, which basically teaches that God is totally through with the Jews, is correct either. The Jews are still the apple of God's eye, and they are still Israel, unlike what Covenant Theology teaches. But our goal here is to get to what the Apostle John had to say about the end times in the oral teaching passed down to Irenaeus and Hippolytus, and I don't want us to get bogged down too much on Dispensationalism versus Covenant Theology. However, since probably 95% of the Protestant churches today have fallen in line with Darby's radical ideas that he claimed were revealed to him as a young man, we need to get to the heart of his "revelations" before we can move on.

As an aside, the time that Darby lived in was ripe for all sorts of new and strange ideas coming into Christianity, for at the same time we had the beginnings of such things as Mormonism, with "revelations" that God came from another planet and that Jesus and Lucifer were brothers, and we saw the birth of the very way out ideas of Jehovah's Witnesses. So lots of other folks were also getting "revelations," from "some" spirit.

There are many other parts to Darby's teaching, such as the thought that the Jews will receive an earthly kingdom and remain on the earth for eternity, while the church will go to heaven and receive a heavenly kingdom. However, for our purposes we do not need to get into all of the details of all his revelations. It may be important, though, to see how Darby's brand new ideas so rapidly became the norm in the modern church as a whole, and are taught today in virtually all modern Christian TV programming.

Within a few years of its beginning, there was a split within the Plymouth Brethren and Darby formed the "Exclusive" Brethren, as opposed to the "Open" Brethren. The Exclusive Brethren became known as the "Darbyite" Brethren. What made his branch so exclusive was that anyone who disagreed with Darby on any point was kicked out. In fact, any Darbyite who was caught even associating with anyone from the Open Brethren was no longer allowed in any Darbyite Brethren congregational meetings.

Darby was driven to get his positions accepted by the whole world, at least the Christian world, and in this pursuit he became one of the most prolific Christian writers and logged thousands of miles in traveling. Additionally he encouraged others in the Brethren to write and do extra speaking as well. And the work paid off.

One of the first big converts was James Brookes, who from 1864 to 1897 pastored two large Presbyterian churches in St. Louis, Missouri. Brookes also published a hugely read monthly periodical called "The Truth." Darby not only preached his new doctrine in Brookes' pulpit, but he and other Brethren found an audience for their writings in "The Truth." I seriously doubt that he told James Brookes of his conviction that Brookes was a sinner because he was a clergyman. Darby needed Brooks to get his ideas into America.

In 1879 a young lawyer named Cyrus Ingersoll Scofield became a Christian in Brookes' church, and Brookes developed an instant liking to him, personally mentoring him in Darby's ideas. In just three short years, in 1882, the year Darby died, Scofield became the pastor of a Congregational church in Dallas, Texas, and stayed there until 1895. During this time he came up with the notion of publishing a Bible commentary and calling it a Bible. With financing from two Brethren businessmen, the Scofield Bible became reality, filled from front to back with Darby's new "religious truths."

Scofield, being a lawyer like Darby, used his "interpretive" skills as a "Bible commentator" to interpret gobs of scriptures to "prove" Darby's ideas to be gospel truth, even though those scriptures had never in all church history been interpreted as having that same meaning Darby had given them. Truckloads of the Scofield Bibles went out to laymen and ministers alike, in all denominations. And with Scofield's personal friendships with big name people like D.L. Moody, Dispensationalism spread like crazy.

Strange as it is to me, by the end of the nineteenth century, evolution had already gained a foothold in many of the traditional seminaries in America. This was disturbing to the evangelicals like A.B. Simpson who opened his own Bible Institute. That idea caught on and two year Bible institutes began to flourish, all using the Scofield Bible, indoctrinating all who read it on John Darby's new doctrine. Soon, even traditional seminaries followed like sheep, and today, if you are a church member in America, you are probably being taught the ideas of John Darby, ideas that would cause another John, the beloved Apostle, to turn over in his grave if he heard them. That's right, most of us have had as a mentor a person who as a young man, whether consciously or unconsciously, wanted to strike back at the establishment that he felt had treated him wrong, leading to ideas that were totally opposite of what the church had held since its inception. And since everyone else around us accepted this new doctrine at face value, most of us have believed his teaching without ever even thinking to question it.

Of course, as mentioned earlier, we take most of the traditions in our modern church, including actions and dogma, as being good things, not having a clue as to where they came from, even sometimes falsely assuming they were practiced or taught in the first century church. For instance, it may be surprising to you to find out that the "altar call" that has become so common in the modern church was first introduced by Billy Sunday in the early 1900's. It was then used as a standard by Billy Graham in the 1950's. Reverend Graham then came up with what is now known as the sinners' prayer, which has become almost an automatic part of the salvation process in most Christians' thinking. I have the greatest respect for both evangelists and see nothing disparaging about either the altar call or the sinners' prayer, but I give those only as examples of things we see practiced today that many might believe were practiced by the Apostle John himself.

The problem is that very few people have the time to research what they learn in their church to find out who first "lopped off the end of the roast," and more importantly, why it was originally lopped off. Most of us are left hoping our church leaders will do that research for us, but unfortunately they seldom do either, which leaves room for the enemy to institute his plans without being caught. The only solid defense against our being taken in is for us to daily spend time in God's Word alone, without the assistance of study guides, etc., that may themselves be erroneous without our knowing it. We also must continually work on developing a close personal relationship with Jesus, asking often in prayer for the Holy Spirit to guide us in what we do and believe. Trusting blindly any information, including what is in this book, can be a recipe for disaster.

In two thousand years since Jesus taught his disciples and they taught their students, a whole lot of stuff has come into our church teaching that was not there originally. And we had better be very aware that some of it came from Satan. Knowing that, we had better also be aware that of the 600,000 listed church leaders in America alone, some of them, although extremely persuasive, likable, and seemingly knowledgeable, have not done the personal research that they should have to earn your blind trust. If they depend solely on their seminary training, we may be being led down the wide road Jesus warned us about, instead of the very narrow road that truly leads to eternity with Him. Many, many trusting souls sitting in church pews every Sunday may be in for a big surprise. What we believe truly does matter, and the stakes are gigantic.

# Timing of the Rapture

We know the rapture will occur because the Bible is very clear about it:

*"... the dead in Christ will rise first. After that, we who are still alive and are left will be caught up together with them in the clouds to meet the Lord in the air. And so we will be with the Lord forever. Therefore encourage yourselves with these words."*          1 Thessalonians 4:16-17.

The vast majority of us Christians believe that this rapture, or catching away, will occur before the tribulation begins. Some, however, believe that the rapture will occur in the middle of the tribulation. And a small percentage of folks, about 5%, see it as happening at the very end. My position has always been that since our belief as to the timing of the rapture did not affect our entrance into heaven one way or the other, it didn't really matter. To me, it was just a point to ponder. However, our belief in this area may matter.

As you have gathered by now, I have chosen to spend most of my research time in studying the teachings of the giants of the faith from years past, from the first century church Fathers who studied directly under John the Revelator, up to the wonderful Biblical scholars and Godly teachers who lived through the 1800's. One thing I have found odd is that never do I find any of them teaching that Christians, or the church as a whole, will be taken off the earth in order to not have to go through the tribulation. In fact, very, very rarely do I even encounter anything written in the late 1800's or early 1900's that mentions anything about a pre-tribulation rapture.

Of course, skeptics of the whole idea of the rapture use this as one of their strong points for discarding the teaching altogether. Their argument is that the concept of the rapture was first put forward by Margaret McDonald who was a self proclaimed prophetess of questionable note in the Irvingite sect of the Catholic Apostolic Church. It seems that in 1830 she had a dream in which she saw Christians being taken off the earth immediately prior to the start of the tribulation. Many visited her home to discuss her dream, including the same John Darby of the Brethren who we just finished discussing. Within a few months of Darby's visit with Margaret McDonald an issue of the Exclusive Brethren's *The Morning Watch* published the new "pre-tribulation doctrine" in Plymouth, England.

I had known that story for years, but had discredited the skeptics' argument that a pre-tribulation rapture was a new idea because one of my favorite prophecy "scholars" supposedly found proof that the doctrine was actually not new. His proof was a line in a 373 AD text by Ephraem the Syrian, who wrote Christian hymns, poems, and sermons, that showed that he believed in a pre-tribulation rapture of the church. Even after I later learned that good old Ephraem did not actually write the text, I was not swayed away from my thinking because other "scholars" claimed that the text was at least written prior to 700AD, and that was good enough for me.

To be honest, I had written, taught, and debated on the side of pre tribulation thinking, and being human, I admit that I probably wanted to believe I had been not been wrong to teach it. And besides, it was much more pleasant to believe that I would be snatched out of here before the really bad stuff started to happen. However, I will also admit that this obvious absence of early teaching on the rapture did sometimes beg the question for me, "If the doctrine of a pre-tribulation rapture was Biblical, why, in almost two thousand years of Christian writing, did only one of the great Christian thinkers ever mention it? And that one text was extremely questionable at best."

The more I started really questioning our Christian traditions, the more I was forced to truly examine the rapture. Could it be that the entire doctrine was a "lopping off of the end of the roast?" Quite frankly, I didn't want to consider it. As you might imagine, I didn't want to be confronted with the possibility that I had taught good people something that was really not accurate. But if the whole idea of the rapture and my belief in the timing of it were incorrect, I had to find out for myself. I could not simply trust anyone else's word in the matter. I owed it to myself, and to you, to find out the truth.

As I said, validity of the rapture was easy and quick. The Bible is extremely clear in saying,

*"... the dead in Christ will rise first. After that, we who are still alive and are left will be caught up together with them in the clouds to meet the Lord in the air. And so we will be with the Lord forever. Therefore encourage yourselves with these words."*     1 Thessalonians 4:16-17.

The question for me then became, when will this rapture occur? Fortunately, or unfortunately for my ego, when I allowed my eyes to be opened, the answer was starring me right in the face. It had been there all along, but I had been blinded by "tradition." I had let myself be led astray by not questioning the traditional teaching of most of the modern day church leaders and scholars.

Look again at the above defining verse of the rapture. Read it slowly. Do it with open eyes, as if reading that verse for the very first time. As you read it, ask yourself, "When will the rapture happen?" If your eyes are truly open you will see it, like I finally did. *"... **the dead in Christ will rise first. After that**, we who are still alive and are left will be caught up ..."* The unnerving answer is that the rapture of those still alive will occur immediately following the raising of the Christian dead. It is as plain as day. There can be no rapture until the dead in Christ are resurrected.

The question then becomes, "When will the dead in Christ arise?"

If we are truly honest with ourselves, the answer to that is also easy. They arise at the end of the tribulation, since the Bible again tells us plainly,

*"I saw the thrones on which were seated those who had been given authority to judge. And I saw the souls of those who had been beheaded because of their testimony for Jesus and because of the word of God."*
Revelation 20:4.

These are not just those who were saved in the tribulation and died.

*"They came to life and reigned with Christ a thousand years. (The rest of the dead did not come to life until the thousand years were ended.)* **This is the first resurrection.**" Revelation 20:4-5.

None of the *"dead in Christ"* had been resurrected at any time earlier, other than the ones who arose the same day Jesus did. We are told that the resurrection at the end of the tribulation *"is the **first** resurrection."* There is not another resurrection before this one that occurs prior to or in the middle of the tribulation so that the church could be raptured. No, God is emphatic:

*"This is the **first** resurrection."* Revelation 20:5.

When I was honest with myself, it was easy to see. I had been wrong. I had been swayed by tradition. If those who are alive, those raptured, must wait until the dead in Christ arise first, this was the very first chance for the rapture to occur. This was the **first** resurrection. There was not one before it.

But I wanted very much to dig deeper. This was a hard pill for me to swallow. So dig I did. I went back and truly examined:

*"... the dead in Christ will rise first. After that, we who are still alive and are left will be caught up together with them in the clouds to meet the Lord in the air. And so we will be with the Lord forever. Therefore encourage yourselves with these words."*         1 Thessalonians 4:16-17.

In searching out the matter, I now knew that the rapture needed always to be coupled with the raising of the dead, thus making the true doctrine a "resurrection/rapture" combination, not just a "rapture."

Even more clarification for me came when I learned that the meaning of the Greek "eis apantesin" (to meet, as in '*to meet the Lord in the air*') actually means,

**"to meet an incoming official such as a newly appointed governor, with honor and praise, in order to escort him into the city,"**

This revelation gave me a whole new understanding of what the rapture will be all about. It is not meant for us to escape hard times. That has nothing to do with it. In reality, it is a part of the holy event of Jesus coming to earth to claim His Kingdom once and for all. Those who are raptured will, with those who had died in Christ in the past, make up the committee who will usher the new Ruler into His earthly realm. We will do it with honor and praise. We will go up in order to escort Him to His throne on earth.

The Common Greek for this verse is "epeita hemeis oi zontes hoi perileipomenoi ama sun autois arpagesometha en nephelais eis apantesin tou kuriou eis aera; kai houtos pantote sun kurio esometha." In the Greek, it is "eis apantesin" that is the important phrase, which simply is translated in English with the phrase "to meet." Unfortunately "to meet" does not adequately describe the full meaning of "eis apantesin." We need to remember that God directed Alexander the Great in the formulation of common Greek because it was the most complex language and could describe things in the New Testament writings that even the complex Hebrew could not. Our English language occasionally falls woefully short in translating common Greek.

The Greek "to meet," as expressed by the words, "eis apantesin," is not simply encountering someone. Rather, it refers to "the action of going out to meet an arrival, especially as a mark of honor." Evidently, when a dignitary came to visit a city in those days, the inhabitants would pay him tribute by going out of the city to meet him at the proper time and they would then accompany him back to the city which he was planning to enter. This is what happened in John 12:13, when the crowd on Palm Sunday came out of Jerusalem to meet Jesus and to accompany him back in to the city.

Also, the Olivet Discourse contains the metaphor of a ruler coming to the city, which he enters *"when you see all these things: know that he is near, right at the gates."* Matthew 24:33.

What makes Paul's language in 1 Thessalonians 4:17 unusual is that he turns the normal action of the dignitary's approach, reception and entrance into a gated city into an "up and down" action: when Christ comes, he "descends" to his domain, and his subjects "ascend to the clouds, to the air," as befits his honor and glory.

Based on this conventional usage of this Greek phrase then, Paul is actually saying that Jesus will come to the air, and first the resurrected believers and then those believers who are still alive, will together ascend to honor Him. Then they will immediately accompany him back to the earth. It is pretty similar to the thought that says,

*"when He comes on that Day to receive glory from all His people and honor from all who believe."*                                         2 Thessalonians 1:10.

In addition to the true meaning of the words that are translated as "to meet," something else jumped out at me as I studied the 1 Thessalonians 4:17 verse more in depth. What Paul is doing in the verses before and after it, is trying to give comfort to the readers about loved ones who have died. When looking at verse 17 in context, as we are always suppose to do, it makes no sense that Paul would pop a brand new concept as important as a pre-tribulation or mid-tribulation rapture into what he was trying to accomplish, and then leave his readers dangling. No, when we look at those eighteen verses as a whole, we can see that what he was trying to tell them was that when their loved ones arise from the dead at the first resurrection, they will get to be reunited with them, and along with them they will rise in the air to escort the Lord to His new domain. In other words, Paul was telling the Thessalonians that they need not grieve over the loss of their loved ones because they would see them again on that glorious day when Jesus will return.

Leaving the study of 1 Thessalonians 4:17 and turning to the other main verse we ascribe as talking about the rapture, I Corinthians 15:51, I found that the transformation at the first resurrection also fits perfectly. That verse reads,

*"Listen, I tell you a mystery: we will not all sleep, but we will all be changed – in a flash, in the twinkling of an eye, at the last trumpet. For the trumpet will sound, the dead will be raised imperishable, and we will be changed. For the perishable must clothe itself with the imperishable, and the mortal with immortality."* 1 Corinthians 15:51-52.

The context of that total section from verse 35 to the end of chapter 15 has to do with our bodies changing from the natural to the spiritual. Again, it was not a brand new concept we call the pre-trib or mid-trib rapture being popped into the middle of that discussion. Yes, the change from our natural bodies to our spiritual bodies will happen in the twinkling of an eye, at the last trumpet. And the timing of this event is also very clear, *"For the trumpet will sound, the dead will be raised imperishable, and we will be changed."* And we have seen that *"the dead will be raised imperishable"* at *"the first resurrection,"* which Revelation 20:4 tells us occurs at the end of the tribulation, not at the beginning or in the middle of it.

But what about the passages that refer to the church being kept from God's wrath? Everything is still in line. First, The wrath of God is not actually displayed until Jesus returns to put an end to the tribulation period, and those raptured will return with Jesus at that time, having gone up to escort him back to earth, as we saw the true meaning of "to meet" really is. The deeper look into that question also reveals that the persecution during the tribulation comes from the antichrist and Satan, not God.

Once my eyes were opened as to what the rapture was really all about, I could see that the wrath talked about in those verses is not the bad things that will happen during the tribulation, but being thrown in the lake of fire, the epitome of wrath. Of course, the best thing for us to do is look at God's Word once more, for we will find in it the definition of the wrath God will save those in Christ's church from. The Bible talks about anyone who takes the mark of the beast, saying,

*"He, too, will drink of the cup of God's fury, which has been poured full strength into the cup of His wrath. He will be tormented with burning sulfur in the presence of the holy angels and of the Lamb. And the smoke of their torment rises for ever and ever."* Revelation 14:10-11.

Obviously this is talking about destruction in the lake of fire being God's wrath that our salvation through Christ saves us from. It is not the troubles and woes poured out during the tribulation, as I had always thought when I believed in a pre-tribulation rapture. This definition of the wrath we will be saved from being the lake of fire destruction, even makes more sense when we look at the "shadow of the rapture" in the story of Lot being taken out of Sodom and Gomorrah. Those cities were totally destroyed, more closely paralleling what will happen to those whose names are not written in the book of life.

Another one of the questions I personally had to deal with concerned the "traditional" teaching I had held on to that says that the church is not in the book of Revelation after the seven letters to the seven churches. But once our thinking changes and our eyes are opened, verses that talk about the church are seen to be throughout Revelation. How I had missed them before I have no idea, other than that I was blinded by tradition.

Verses like the following now jumped out at me,

*"Then the dragon was enraged at the woman and went off to make war against the rest of her offspring - those who obey God's commandments and hold to the testimony of Jesus."* Revelation 12:17.

This is the church that *"holds to the testimony of Jesus."* These are not just the new believers in the tribulation. This is the church.

And again in verse 13:7, *"He was given power to make war against the saints ..."* The saints is referring to the church. How was I so blinded?

Also in verse 13:10, *"this calls for patient endurance and faithfulness on the part of the saints."* Once again, obviously the church.

And verse 14:12, *"This calls for patient endurance on the part of the saints who obey God's commandments and remain faithful to Jesus."* And again, this is talking about the church.

I had been lopping off the end of the roast, following the tradition that said that the church was not mentioned after the seven letters, solely because some man somewhere in the past 180 years said it was so, and the teaching caught on. God certainly did not teach it in His Word.

And it is the church that is harvested a few verses later when we read that the angel was told, *"Take your sickle and reap, because the time to reap has come, for the harvest of the earth is ripe."* Revelation 14:15. And those members of Christ's church who are harvested are seen in a few verses later in 15:2 as having been *"victorious."*

It is the very next chapter, in Revelation 16:15 when Jesus says *"Behold, I come ..."* The saints have gone up to greet the incoming King of kings, to honor and praise Him, and escort him back to earth. (eis apantesin). Call it a pre-wrath rapture if we want. And immediately after that is when we are told that, *"This is the **first resurrection**."* Revelation 20:5.

The semantics don't matter. What does matter is that we all have been taught to not to be concerned about the tribulation because we will be snatched out of here. We have made the cute little saying that "Christ would not slap His bride around immediately prior to the marriage." He isn't slapping us around, but He is testing our *"patient endurance and faithfulness."*

It may be tough to admit we were wrong, and most "Bible scholars and teachers" won't do it for anything in the world, because they have written and preached over and over about the pre-trib rapture and they think they will look foolish. But as I see it now, Revelation was written as a program for Christ's followers to study in order to be prepared to go through it if necessary, with *"patient endurance and faithfulness."*

On top of all of the above overwhelming proof that the tribulation occurs at the end of the tribulation and not the beginning, we now also have the words of the Apostle John himself, as written down by Irenaeus and Hippolytus. If you recall in the discussion in the last chapter, we read the quote by Irenaeus that said plainly,

"they [the ten kings of Rev. 17:1-13] shall ...give their kingdom to the beast [Antichrist], and put the **Church** to flight"   Against Heresies V, 26, 1

Obviously Irenaeus is telling us that the church will be the object of the persecution of the antichrist, not the Jews. So the truth is as plain as the nose on our face. The church will not be raptured prior to the tribulation. And that is only one of the places that Irenaeus is clear about it. For example, he also wrote:

"but he [the Apostle John] indicates the number of the name [666 of Antichrist] now, that when this man comes we may avoid him, being aware who he is"       Against Heresies, V, 30, 4, Irenaeus.

And we also saw that Justin Martyr, another highly regarded church Father, who lived from 100 A.D. to 167 A.D. and wrote,

"the man of apostasy [Antichrist] ...shall venture to do unlawful deeds on earth against us the **Christians**"       Trypho cx, Justin Martyr.

Plus Tertullian, who said the tribulation situation will be such,

"that the beast Antichrist with his false prophet may wage war on the **Church of God**"       On the Resurrection of the Flesh xxv, Tertullian.

We even have quotes from Hippolytus, who we know wrote without variance what the Apostle John taught Polycarp about the end times,

"... the one thousand two hundred and three score days (the half of the week) during which the tyrant is to reign and persecute the **Church** …"
       Treatise on Christ and Antichrist, 61, by Hippolytus.

And then from Saint Augustine,

"... the kingdom of Antichrist shall fiercely, though for a short time, assail the **Church**... "       The City of God, XX, 23, Augustine.

Yes, once we blink our eyes and get man's "tradition" out of our line of sight, the church is seen all through the book of Revelation and all of the church leaders knew it. And since Irenaeus and Hippolytus wrote about it we can know that the Apostle John taught it.

At this point I unfortunately need to warn you about a piece of paper that is passed out in many churches that claims to show that early church leaders did believe in a pre-tribulation rapture. You may have seen it or been told about it already. It purportedly lists quotes from the second and third centuries by The Shepherd Of Hermas, The Epistle of Barnabus, The Didache, Cyprian, Victorinus and even Hippolytus. As I said, these quotes supposedly show that the pre-tribulation rapture theory was believed and taught. I will not take the time here to go through each one of these quotes, but I can assure you I have personally researched the claims, and that each and every one of the quotes is either taken out of a context that shows the exact opposite or the quotes were deliberately misquoted in order to try to defend the undefendable. Although I will not give the name, I got to the bottom of the matter and now know who originally came up with these false quotes. I was saddened to find that a famous "scholar" would stoop to such tactics just to keep from admitting that he had been so wrong for so many years in what he had taught and written about. I was and still am troubled by it, and am grieved that I would even need to mention such a thing, but it is important that you not be deceived.

But what about Jesus Himself? Did He say anything concerning the timing of the rapture? He sure did, but virtually no one today evidently cares. Below are the words of Jesus:

*"Immediately **after** the distress of those days 'the sun will be darkened, and the moon will not give its light; the stars will fall from the sky, and the heavenly bodies will be shaken.' Then will appear the sign of the Son of Man in heaven. And then all the peoples of the earth will mourn when they see the Son of Man coming on the clouds of heaven, with power and great glory.* **And he will send his angels with a loud trumpet call, and they will gather his elect from the four winds, from one end of the heavens to the other."**
Matthew 24:29-31.

How could we miss that? Jesus is clear. What he talks about happens,

*"**Immediately after** the distress of those days ..."*

That is **immediately after** the great tribulation, at the time of His second coming. It occurs in Revelation 20:4 when the **first resurrection** occurs.

In that last sentence of that quote when Jesus says,

*"And he will send his angels with a loud trumpet call, and they will gather his elect from the four winds, from one end of the heavens to the other."*

*"from the four winds"* actually means "from all parts of the earth." Kind of like we say today, "from the four corners of the earth." And then the last phrase says, *"from one end of the heavens to the other,"* which is referring to the dead in Christ who are already in heaven.

In other words,

*"... the dead in Christ will rise first. After that, we who are still alive and are left will be caught up together with them in the clouds to meet the Lord in the air. And so we will be with the Lord forever. Therefore encourage yourselves with these words."* 1 Thessalonians 4:16-17.

So, in summary we not only have the writings of the early church Fathers stating over and over and over that it is the church that will be persecuted by the antichrist and not the Jews, totally disproving John Darby's pre-tribulation rapture theory, but we also have that long list of Christian leaders through the centuries up to John Darby that we listed in the last chapter stating the same thing. Additionally we have the scriptures showing exactly when the timing of the rapture will be, which is when *"the dead in Christ rise first,"* and we know that the time of that event, the first resurrection, is clearly noted in Revelation 20:4 as being at the end of the tribulation, immediately prior to Christ's second coming. We also have all the scriptures in Revelation that talk about the saints being on earth during the tribulation. Additionally, we have the real meaning of the idea of "to meet" Jesus in the air. And finally, we have the words of Jesus Himself telling us that the rapture will occur *"Immediately after the distress of those days ...,"* with *"those days"* referring to the three and a half year great tribulation.

I have spent a lot of time and space in this book refuting John Darby's ideas for three reasons. First, in order to understand "the end times we were never taught" but which were taught by the Apostle John to Polycarp and described for us by Irenaeus and Hippolytus, we must be on the same page they were. We need to be fully ingrained in the facts that the persecution of the antichrist will be directed toward the Christian church and not the Jews, and that there will be no pre-tribulation rapture.

Second, one of the great regrets in my life has been that I personally defended Darby's ideas in my earlier teaching and writings, specifically in two of my first books. Having taken part in that false teaching has caused me time with God in true repentance, with tears in my eyes. I am so very sorry for having written about a pre-tribulation rapture, and I have vowed to do everything in my power to research everything I write even more fully than ever before.

And third, with every fiber of my being I honestly believe that these ideas that John Darby came up with as a young man wanting to lash out at the established church of his day, were ideas whispered in his mind by Satan himself. I believe that the pre-tribulation teaching is one of the things that Satan has successfully maneuvered into church teaching that has caused our modern church as a whole to become the Church of Laodicea which was written to by Jesus in Revelation 3:16, when He said, *"because you are lukewarm—neither hot nor cold—I am about to spit you out of my mouth."* Additionally, I feel that it may be one of the ideas that could play a part in the "great delusion" that Jesus warns us about in Matthew 24 and Mark 13 that could *"deceive, if possible, even the elect."* Matthew 24:16.

No longer do I believe that our beliefs in regards to these things are not all that important. I now understand that what we believe in this area is of critical importance. And I earnestly pray that you will not fall for what I am one hundred per cent convinced is doctrine straight from Satan, delivered through an unsuspecting young man who tried hard during much of his life to live a Godly life for Jesus, but who also spent his entire life promoting and defending those lies from our enemy, as did his organization, the Brethren, which incidentally also has done much good and developed many true saints along the way. Of course, anyone who believes Satan stopped trying to get false doctrines into the church after the Reformation would never believe that. However, as I've been repeating over and over, I believe Satan has been working harder than ever to infiltrate Christ's church with his lies.

Irenaeus fought hard to keep that infiltration by Satan from happening in his time. It was Irenaeus, the most highly esteemed of the church Fathers, who first put forward the word "heresy" to be something negative. Until he came along the word only meant "school of thought," and was commonly used to describe different Greek philosophical schools of thought. Irenaeus purposefully gave it a negative meaning in the Christian sense because He knew that the Apostolic Oral Teaching was <u>divinely</u> revealed to the Apostles, so it was not the product of "human thought process."

Please make sure you understand that statement. Irenaeus knew that the oral teaching handed down from John through Polycarp to him came directly from God, and was in no way just interpretations of things that John came up with on his own. It was not a "school of thought." It was from God.

So anyone who taught anything at all different from that of the "Apostolic Oral Teaching," using their own "school of thought," was a heretic, and not a true Christian. Transport Irenaeus to today in a time machine and he would not hesitate in labeling John Darby a heretic, and his pre-tribulation "school of thought" pure heresy. Yet it is taught throughout our modern Church of Laodicea with no hesitation. Totally unbelievable!

The rapture will happen, but it would be better named a "resurrection/rapture" or a "pre-wrath rapture." And the purpose for the rapture is not to keep us from harms way, as if we were somehow better than all those who have been persecuted and martyred from the days of Christians being thrown to lions in Rome in the first century to today, when more Christians are being martyred world wide every year than at any time in history. No, the reason for the resurrection/rapture is for the saints to escort our God, our King, our Savior, Jesus, to His kingdom on earth.

So, here we go. Hang on tight. It is time to learn about "the end times we were never taught." Remember as we do, God has our backs. He loves us very, very much. That love will result for us in unimaginable joy.

# Antichrist

The main thing we need to remember is that Satan will be trying to duplicate the Holy Trinity of God the Father, Son, and Holy Spirit. In his version, the "unholy trinity," Satan will try to take the role of the Father, with the antichrist being like the Son, Jesus, and the false prophet playing the part of the Holy Spirit. We start with Hippolytus telling us of this copycat behavior of the antichrist:

"Now, as our Lord Jesus Christ, who is also God, was prophesied of under the figure of a lion, on account of His royalty and glory, in the same way have the Scriptures also aforetime spoken of Antichrist as a lion, on account of his tyranny and violence. For the deceiver seeks to liken himself in all things to the Son of God.
1) Christ is a lion, so Antichrist is also a lion;
2) Christ is a king, so Antichrist is also a king.
3) The Savior was manifested as a lamb; so he too, in like manner, will appear as a lamb, though within he is a wolf.
4) The Savior came into the World in the circumcision, and he will come in the same manner.
5) The Lord sent apostles among all the nations, and he in like manner will send false apostles.
6) The Savior gathered together the sheep that were scattered abroad, and he in like manner will bring together a people that is scattered abroad.
7) The Lord gave a seal to those who believed on Him, and he will give one like manner.
8) The Savior appeared in the form of man, and he too will come in the form of a man.
9) The Savior raised up and showed His holy flesh like a temple, and he will raise a temple of stone in Jerusalem."   Hippolytus.

When we look at number three on Hippolytus's list, we see that the antichrist will start out as a lamb, even though deep down he is a wolf. Let's look at how the antichrist will start out according to the Bible:

*"And there was given unto him a mouth speaking great things."*
Revelation 13:5.
*"He will act deceitfully."* Daniel 11:23.

Of course, both of those verses could sound like many modern politicians, great orators whose lies come off their lips like honey, and people don't know the truth at the beginning.

The antichrist is often called the Peacemaker because of several Biblical verses such as,

*"He shall come in peaceably."* Daniel 11:21.

Most politicians do start out that way. In fact, we saw one recent US president who was given the Nobel Peace Prize for doing nothing but talking about peace in his first campaign for president. The antichrist will start out the same way, as Hippolytus says, he "will appear as a lamb, though within he is a wolf."

Then we find in the scriptures,

*"He will distribute plunder, loot and wealth among his followers."*
Daniel 11:24

So, this guy will be big into wealth distribution, a system as we know that generates lots and lots of eager followers who love the wealth spreader.

*"With flattery he will corrupt those who have violated the covenant, but the people who know their God will firmly resist him."* Daniel 11:32.

Of course, as we discussed earlier, most Christians don't even know God's covenants, but even if they do, flattery can go a long way toward easing any guilt they might have had anyway.

Some Christians will see through the charade, though, for God's Word says,

*"Those who are wise will instruct many, though for a time they will fall by the sword or be burned or captured or plundered. When they fall, they*

*will receive a little help, and many who are not sincere will join them. Some of the wise will stumble, so that they may be refined, purified and made spotless until the time of the end, for it will still come at the appointed time."*
Daniel 11:33-35.

So, some of the Christians who are on top of things will try to show their brothers the truth, but I can imagine a situation in which someone falls for this smooth talking, flattering, wealth distributor. He tells his Christian brother what a wonderful person and super leader the smooth talker is, only to be told that maybe he had best hold his praise because the guy just may in fact turn out to be the antichrist. The first person, the adorer of the flatterer responds with, "That's not possible because the Christians have not been raptured yet."

Because that person has been indoctrinated for years by his church, Christian radio and TV, and all the best selling books he has read by all the big name Christian prophecy "scholars," He is so entrenched in his belief in a pre-tribulation rapture that he is absolutely certain beyond a shadow of a doubt that the smooth talking, flattering, wealth distributor could not possibly be the antichrist. So he laughs his friend off with an air of arrogance because he *knows* that he knows best, feeling sorry for his ignorant friend who hasn't learned enough prophecy to realize that the rapture must come before the antichrist and the tribulation.

Of course, then we learn from the Bible about the antichrist:

*"The king will do as he pleases. He will exalt and magnify himself above every god and will say unheard-of things against the God of gods. He will be successful until the time of wrath is completed, for what has been determined must take place."* Daniel 11:36.

That's right, he will proclaim himself to be the Messiah. By this time, our pre-trib friend will be so enamored by the antichrist, and such a devout follower of him, that he may even believe the antichrist when he says either that the rapture did occur four years earlier but only 144,000 were taken, or that the rapture was an inward, emotional feeling that the followers had, or some other such deceiving lie.

Do you see the big trap that could await the believers in Darby's pre-tribulation rapture? It could be gigantic. In fact, could it be the big delusion that Jesus warned us would happen?

*"For false Christs and false prophets will appear and perform signs and miracles to deceive the elect—if that were possible. So be on your guard; I have told you everything ahead of time."* Mark 13:22-23.

Paul makes it even clearer:

*"They perish because they refused to love the truth and so be saved. For this reason God sends them a powerful delusion so that they will believe the lie and so that all will be condemned who have not believed the truth but have delighted in wickedness."* 2 Thessalonians 2:10-12.

The truth that if we are alive then we might have to suffer the persecution of the antichrist is not pleasant, and in my personal life I have tried to explain the fallacies of Darby's pre-tribulation rapture theory to some who flat out *"refused to love the truth."* If you get nothing else from this book, I beg you to heed my warnings on this subject. Do not believe the lie Satan put in Darby's head. The masses are dead wrong on this one, and it could lead some to be eternally dead wrong. It is that critical.

Getting back to the list Hippolytus gave us about the antichrist, notice in number four of that list that he says, "The Savior came into the World in the circumcision, and he will come in the same manner." In other words, he is telling us that the antichrist will be a Jew. Not a gentile, not the Muslim Mahdi that is currently so in vogue to believe, but a Jew.

Irenaeus tells us the exact tribe the antichrist will come from:

"He who shall come claiming the kingdom for himself, and shall terrify those men of whom we have been speaking, having a name containing the aforesaid number, is truly the abomination of desolation. This, too, the apostle affirms:
'When they shall say, Peace and safety, then sudden destruction shall come upon them.' 1 Thessalonians 5:3.

And Jeremiah does not merely point out his sudden coming, but he even indicates the tribe from which he shall come, where he says,

'We shall hear the voice of his swift horses from **Dan**; the whole earth shall be moved by the voice of the neighing of his galloping horses: he shall also come and devour the earth, and the fullness thereof, the city also, and they that dwell therein.' Jeremiah 8:16

This, too, is the reason that this tribe is not reckoned in the Apocalypse along with those which are saved." 30:2, Irenaeus.

We probably should have figured this out long ago, because even Jacob, the father of Dan, the patriarch of that tribe said,

*"Dan will be a serpent by the roadside, a viper along the path."*
Genesis 49:17.

We know of Satan as the serpent in the Garden of Eden, and even in Revelation we read about,

*"the dragon, that ancient **serpent**, who is the devil, or Satan."*
Revelation 20:2.

The tribal emblem of the Danites was even a snake with a serpent in its claws.

That the antichrist will come from the tribe of Dan is also forcefully put forward by Hippolytus:

"We find it written regarding Antichrist; Moses speaks thus: 'Dan is a lion's whelp, and he shall leap from Bashan.' But that no one may err by supposing that this is said of the Savior, let him attend carefully to the matter. 'Dan,' he says, 'is a lion's whelp;' and in naming the tribe of Dan, he declared clearly the tribe from which Antichrist is destined to spring. For as Christ springs from the tribe of Judah, so Antichrist is to spring from the tribe of Dan. And that the case stands thus, we see also from the words of Jacob: 'Let Dan be a serpent, lying upon the ground, biting the horse's heel.' What, then, is meant by the serpent but Antichrist, that deceiver who is mentioned in Genesis, who deceived Eve and supplanted Adam (bruised

Adam's heel)? But since it is necessary to prove this assertion by sufficient testimony, we shall not shrink from the task.

That it is in reality out of the tribe of Dan, then, that that tyrant and king, that dread judge, that son of the devil, is destined to spring and arise, the prophet testifies when he says, 'Dan shall judge his people, as (he is) also one tribe in Israel.' But some one may say that this refers to Samson, who sprang from the tribe of Dan, and judged the people twenty years. Well, the prophecy had its partial fulfillment in Samson, but its complete fulfillment is reserved for Antichrist. For Jeremiah also speaks to this effect: 'From Dan we are to hear the sound of the swiftness of his horses: the whole land trembled at the sound of the neighing, of the driving of his horses.' And another prophet says: 'He shall gather together all his strength, from the east even to the west. They whom he calls, and they whom he calls not, shall go with him. He shall make the sea white with the sails of his ships, and the plain black with the shields of his armaments. And whosoever shall oppose him in war shall fall by the sword.' That these things, then, are said of no one else but that tyrant, and shameless one, and adversary of God."

14 and 15, Hippolytus.

Dan was the son of Rachel's handmaid Bilhah in Genesis 35:25, so he started out life much as Ishmael had, whose mother was Hagar, Sarah's handmaid. So Dan can be better compared to Ishmael instead of the blessed Isaac. The shadows in that fact may well allude to the difference between the true Christ, Jesus, the legitimate Son of God, and Satan, the illegitimate pretender.

But why would the antichrist come from the tribe of Dan? Part of the answer may be contained in the book of Judges. There is a strange story that most of us shake our heads over when we read it. Many have never even read it, but since this will end up being a critical part of who the antichrist is, I think it is important enough that we read it now:

*"Now a man named Micah from the hill country of Ephraim said to his mother, 'The eleven hundred shekels of silver that were taken from you and about which I heard you utter a curse—I have that silver with me; I took it.'*
*Then his mother said, 'The Lord bless you, my son!'*

When he returned the eleven hundred shekels of silver to his mother, she said, 'I solemnly consecrate my silver to the Lord for my son to make a carved image and a cast idol. I will give it back to you.'

So he returned the silver to his mother, and she took two hundred shekels of silver and gave them to a silversmith, who made them into the image and the idol. And they were put in Micah's house.

Now this man Micah had a shrine, and he made an ephod and some idols and installed one of his sons as his priest. In those days Israel had no king; everyone did as he saw fit.

A young Levite from Bethlehem in Judah, who had been living within the clan of Judah, left that town in search of some other place to stay. On his way he came to Micah's house in the hill country of Ephraim.

Micah asked him, 'Where are you from?'

'I'm a Levite from Bethlehem in Judah,' he said, 'and I'm looking for a place to stay.'

Then Micah said to him, 'Live with me and be my father and priest, and I'll give you ten shekels of silver a year, your clothes and your food.' So the Levite agreed to live with him, and the young man was to him like one of his sons. Then Micah installed the Levite, and the young man became his priest and lived in his house. And Micah said, 'Now I know that the Lord will be good to me, since this Levite has become my priest.'

In those days Israel had no king.

And in those days the tribe of the Danites was seeking a place of their own where they might settle, because they had not yet come into an inheritance among the tribes of Israel. So the Danites sent five warriors from Zorah and Eshtaol to spy out the land and explore it. These men represented all their clans. They told them, 'Go, explore the land.'

The men entered the hill country of Ephraim and came to the house of Micah, where they spent the night. When they were near Micah's house, they recognized the voice of the young Levite; so they turned in there and asked him, 'Who brought you here? What are you doing in this place? Why are you here?'

He told them what Micah had done for him, and said, 'He has hired me and I am his priest.'

Then they said to him, 'Please inquire of God to learn whether our journey will be successful.'

*The priest answered them, 'Go in peace. Your journey has the Lord's approval.'*

So the five men left and came to Laish, where they saw that the people were living in safety, like the Sidonians, unsuspecting and secure. And since their land lacked nothing, they were prosperous. Also, they lived a long way from the Sidonians and had no relationship with anyone else.

When they returned to Zorah and Eshtaol, their brothers asked them, 'How did you find things?'

They answered, 'Come on, let's attack them! We have seen that the land is very good. Aren't you going to do something? Don't hesitate to go there and take it over. When you get there, you will find an unsuspecting people and a spacious land that God has put into your hands, a land that lacks nothing whatever.'

Then six hundred men from the clan of the Danites, armed for battle, set out from Zorah and Eshtaol. On their way they set up camp near Kiriath Jearim in Judah. This is why the place west of Kiriath Jearim is called Mahaneh Dan to this day. From there they went on to the hill country of Ephraim and came to Micah's house.

Then the five men who had spied out the land of Laish said to their brothers, 'Do you know that one of these houses has an ephod, other household gods, a carved image and a cast idol? Now you know what to do.' So they turned in there and went to the house of the young Levite at Micah's place and greeted him. The six hundred Danites, armed for battle, stood at the entrance to the gate. The five men who had spied out the land went inside and took the carved image, the ephod, the other household gods and the cast idol while the priest and the six hundred armed men stood at the entrance to the gate.

When these men went into Micah's house and took the carved image, the ephod, the other household gods and the cast idol, the priest said to them, 'What are you doing?'

They answered him, 'Be quiet! Don't say a word. Come with us, and be our father and priest. Isn't it better that you serve a tribe and clan in Israel as priest rather than just one man's household?' Then the priest was glad. He took the ephod, the other household gods and the carved image and went along with the people. Putting their little children, their livestock and their possessions in front of them, they turned away and left.

*When they had gone some distance from Micah's house, the men who lived near Micah were called together and overtook the Danites. As they shouted after them, the Danites turned and said to Micah, 'What's the matter with you that you called out your men to fight?'*

*He replied, 'You took the gods I made, and my priest, and went away. What else do I have? How can you ask, "What's the matter with you?"*

*The Danites answered, 'Don't argue with us, or some hot-tempered men will attack you, and you and your family will lose your lives.' So the Danites went their way, and Micah, seeing that they were too strong for him, turned around and went back home.*

*Then they took what Micah had made, and his priest, and went on to Laish, against a peaceful and unsuspecting people. They attacked them with the sword and burned down their city. There was no one to rescue them because they lived a long way from Sidon and had no relationship with anyone else. The city was in a valley near Beth Rehob.*

*The Danites rebuilt the city and settled there. They named it Dan after their forefather Dan, who was born to Israel—though the city used to be called Laish. There the Danites set up for themselves the idols, and Jonathan son of Gershom, the son of Moses, and his sons were priests for the tribe of Dan until the time of the captivity of the land. They continued to use the idols Micah had made, all the time the house of God was in Shiloh."* Judges 17&18

In that strange story in Judges 17 and 18, we find that it was through the tribe of Dan that idolatry was first introduced into the land of Israel. For this reason the tribe of Dan is left out of the 144,000 listed in Revelation, with 12,000 coming from each of the other tribes. Joseph's second son's tribe is listed in place of the Danites. The tribe of Dan will not receive God's protective seal. But God is merciful, and the faithful from the tribe of Dan will survive. We know this because at the beginning of the Millennial Kingdom, following the tribulation, when the land is carved up for the twelve tribes, Dan's descendants will receive the first share according to god's Word:

*"This is what the Sovereign Lord says: "These are the boundaries by which you are to divide the land for an inheritance among the twelve tribes of Israel, with two portions for Joseph. You are to divide it equally among*

*them. Because I swore with uplifted hand to give it to your forefathers, this land will become your inheritance."*            Ezekiel 47:13-14.

*"These are the tribes, listed by name: At the northern frontier, Dan will have one portion; it will follow the Hethlon road to Lebo[a] Hamath; Hazar Enan and the northern border of Damascus next to Hamath will be part of its border from the east side to the west side."*           Ezekiel 48:1.

So, what happened to the tribe of Dan? History reveals some fascinating facts about the powerful tribe of Dan and their migrations in ancient times, as well as where they are located today.

In the downfall of the northern kingdom of Israel in 718-721 B.C., the inland portion of the tribe of Dan was carried into captivity with the other northern Kingdom tribes. This portion of Dan was taken into captivity beyond the Euphrates River, into Assyria, and when the Assyrian Empire fell in the seventh century B.C., they migrated through the Caucasian Pass, just north of the Caucasus, and continued onward through what is now Europe, ending up primarily in modern day Ireland.

Interestingly, they named many of the things they came across on their journey after their father. Since there are no vowels in the Hebrew language, Dan is spelled DN, or its Hebrew equivalent. Thus words like Dan, Din, Don, Dun, Den, or Dn, correspond to the name of Dan. We see the tribes movement, therefore, with names of rivers such as DN-iper, DN-ister, and the DON, plus of course the DAN-ube River. We also see Mace-DON-ia, and the Dar-DAN-elles, etc. DEN-mark, the name of the modern country in Europe north of Germany, in the Scan-DIN-avian peninsula, means literally "Dan's mark."

However, the other portion of Danites, those who actually spent their lives on and lived aboard ships, and who associated themselves with the sea peoples of Tyre and Sidon, fled westward through the Mediterranean when northern Israel fell and their tribal brothers and sisters were carried off to Assyria. Those Danites migrated through Sar-DIN-ia, leaving their trail along the sea-coasts of the Mediterranean, ending up as well in what is today Ireland, where historians explain that the early settlers were known as the "Tuatha de Danaan," literally the "tribe of Dan."

In Ireland, today, we find their customary evidence, their place names in abundance. Such names as Dans-Lough, Dan-Sower, Dan-Monism, Dundalke, Dun-drum, Don-egal Bay, Don-egal City, Dun-glow and Lon-donderry, as well as Din-gle, Dun-garven and Duns-more, which means "More Dans." It is plain that the country of Ireland is filled with names which derive from the ancient patriarch of the Hebrews, Dan, the son of Jacob. Therefore, both portions of the ancient Danites, those inland and those on the coast, ended up settling in Ireland, and most of them dwell in that land, today.

Somewhere in the world, the future antichrist is probably humming,

> "Oh, Danny boy, the pipes, the pipes are calling
> From glen to glen, and down the mountain side
> The summer's gone, and all the flow'rs are dying
> 'Tis you, 'tis you must go and I must bide."

In number five on his list, Hippolytus tells us of the antichrist that since "The Lord sent apostles among all the nations, and he in like manner will send false apostles." Of course, this could just mean that he has under him something like our State Department from which he will send out delegates or ambassadors to parrot his talking points.

When we come to number six on the list we find Hippolytus explain to us that "The Savior gathered together the sheep that were scattered abroad, and he (the antichrist) in like manner will bring together a people that is scattered abroad."

Some Christians hold to a view that is known as "Replacement Theology," which teaches that the church has replaced the Jews because they did not accept Jesus as their messiah when He came the first time. The theology states. "We believe that the international Church has superseded for all times national Israel as the institution for the administration of divine blessing to the world." (Kenneth Gentry).

Replacement theologians base their case on scriptures such:

*"If you belong to Christ, then you are Abraham's seed, and heirs according to the promise."*  Galatians 3:29.

and:

> *"It was not through law that Abraham and his offspring received the promise that he would be heir of the world, but through the righteousness that comes by faith."* Romans 4:13.

and:

> *"A man is not a Jew if he is only one outwardly, nor is circumcision merely outward and physical. No, a man is a Jew if he is one inwardly; and circumcision is circumcision of the heart, by the Spirit, not by the written code. Such a man's praise is not from men, but from God."* Romans 2:28-29.

and:

> *"Therefore I tell you that the kingdom of God will be taken away from you and given to a people who will produce its fruit."* Matthew 21:43.

I will not take the time to go through a complete rebuttal of Replacement Theology here, such as how in that last verse Jesus was talking to the Pharisees and leaders of Judaism in that day and not the nation of Israel as a whole, but I will point out an important truth from God's Word that the Replacementists conveniently forget:

> *"I do not want you to be ignorant of this mystery, brothers, so that you may not be conceited: Israel has experienced a hardening in part until the full number of the Gentiles has come in. And so all Israel will be saved, as it is written:*
>
> *'The deliverer will come from Zion;*
>   *he will turn godlessness away from Jacob.*
> *And this is my covenant with them*
>   *when I take away their sins.'*
>
> *As far as the gospel is concerned, they are enemies on your account; but as far as election is concerned, they are loved on account of the patriarchs, for God's gifts and his call are irrevocable."* Romans 11:25-29.

In other words, very plainly God is saying that He made a promise to each of the Patriarchs (Abraham, Isaac, and Jacob) and His promises are irrevocable. They can not be broken. Israel is still the apple of His Eye.

I mention all of this to say that Replacement Theology would say that in regards to number six on Hippolytus' list, it is Satan who is bringing the Jews back to Israel, not God. My somewhat less than dignified response to that is: "Hog wash."

In the first place, earlier we looked at a slew of miracles God has caused to occur in the creation of Israel "in only one day," and the bringing back of the Jews to the land He promised the Patriarchs. Satan is not God. He could not accomplish those miracles. Secondly, Hippolytus is saying about the antichrist, not Satan, "in like manner (the antichrist) will bring together a people that is scattered abroad." Hippolytus is saying that the antichrist will bring (some) people who are currently scattered from where they once lived.

So, other than the Jews, what people group is currently scattered who the antichrist might bring together? Although this is just an educated guess, could it be the people group known as the Palestinians who are still sitting in refuge camps, forced to stay there by their Muslim brothers?

Let me take a side trip with you and explain something I think you may find fascinating. After many hours of digging into areas of history, weather archives, and the Bible, I stumbled onto a discovery that I found awesome. A discovery so important, that the implications of the conclusion it brought me to, are so far reaching that I believe it is quite relevant to this discussion of number six on Hippolytus' list.

First, a little history. As you know, the Romans, under Titus, destroyed Jerusalem in 70 AD, even tearing down the temple stone by stone to get at the gold that melted into the stones when they set it on fire. About a million Jews were slaughtered, and most of the rest were taken into captivity as slaves. The few that remained seemed to make a comeback, and sixty years later, in 130 AD, Caesar Hadrian visited the city and said that he would rebuild the city as a gift to the remnant of Jews still there. However, as politicians seem in the habit of doing, he changed his mind and even outlawed circumcision. The Jews became enraged, and led by Simon Bar Koseba, once again rose up against Rome. There were even Christians in the community who pledged to fight along side the Jews. However, when the Jewish spiritual leader, Rabbi Akiva, declared Simon Bar Koseba to be the Messiah the Jews were waiting for, the Christians, knowing that Jesus was the true Messiah, left the Jews to fend for themselves against the Roman legions. By 135 AD the rebellion had been totally suppressed and Caesar Hadrian had had enough of the Jews and all things Jewish. He changed the name of the land from Judea to Syria Palestina, built a temple to Zeus on the Temple Mount, and changed the name of Jerusalem to Aelia Capitolina. He even banished all Jews from the city, declaring immediate death to any who dared to ever return.

Hadrian even salted the land so that nothing would grow. It seemed that the curse of the fig tree, which Jesus foreshadowed that represented Israel, had truly begun in earnest. In fact, it seemed like God was behind it, because the rains even stopped about the same time. As we can tell from both the Old Testament and the New Testament, as well as other sources, up until that time the land of Israel was fairly fertile. Just think of all the scriptures that make mention of vineyards, orchards, and gardens throughout the land of Israel. It obviously rained there. Israel was even described as the "land of milk and honey" because it was so lush. But from what we can ascertain, the rains seemed to rapidly reduce about 70 AD, and dried up to almost nothing about the same time the Jews were banished under penalty of certain death in 135 AD. And the drought remained.

Rabbi Menachem Kohen of Brooklyn wrote, "Israel suffered an unprecedented, severe and inexplicable (by anything other than supernatural explanations) drought that lasted from the first century until the 20th - a period of 1800 years coinciding with the forced dispersion of the Jews." Rabbi Kohen looked at the drought as being a result of a curse from God, and he has a point, for God says of the land of Israel,

*"The sky over your head will be bronze, the ground beneath you iron. The LORD will turn the rain of your country into dust and powder; it will come down from the skies until you are destroyed."* Deuteronomy 28:23-24.

In speaking about Israel in my book, Unlocking God's Secrets, I wrote,

"It was an arid desert. Rain was a very seldom seen commodity for centuries and centuries. When Mark Twain traveled there he stated that it was the most barren land he had ever seen, with nothing growing at all. He called it a complete wasteland. In Innocents Abroad, written in 1867, Twain called it "desolate and unlovely. It is a hopeless, dreary, heartbroken land."

And what normally happens to deserts? They continue to expand and take over more land each year, such as the case with the Sahara."     Bob Morley.

Nationally syndicated columnist and founder of WND, Joseph Farah, later discovered that only after the Jews returned did the rain begin to come. Farah wrote,

"For 1800 years, it hardly ever rained in Israel. This was the barren land discovered by Mark Twain. So-called Palestine was a wasteland - nobody lived there. There was no indigenous Arab population to speak of. It only came after the Jews came back. Beginning in AD 70 and lasting until the early 1900's - about 660,000 days - no rain."

Now, hold on to your hat. The rains seemed to begin in the early 1900's and all of a sudden there were record rainfalls in 1948 and 1967, the year Israel became a nation and the year Israel recaptured Jerusalem. Think hard about what you just read; **for 1800 years the land of Israel was in total drought conditions and then the year Israel became a nation, 1948, the land experienced downpours of rain, only to be exceeded again in 1967 when Israel finally took back Jerusalem in the Six Day War against the surrounding Muslim nations**. This may be one of the most incredible things you have ever read. And you won't learn about it from the liberal, anti-Semitic media.

Was this phenomenal miracle the result of the lifting of the curse in Deuteronomy 28:23-24? Probably partially. But allow me to put forward the conclusion I believe that makes me quiver. I believe God turned the land of Israel into a desolate wasteland that no one would want to live in primarily so that indeed no one would live there. Think about this. Had the land remained a pleasant place to live, cities would have flourished and the population would have exploded, especially along the coastline in places like where Tel Aviv now exists. Why not? With the Jews gone, the Arabs would have found the sea port areas to be fabulously inviting for trade and commerce. By 1948 there would have been several cities along the coast with multimillion populations. The Jews would have had no homeland to return to.

The truth is the land of Israel was given to the Jews through the covenants God made to Abraham, Isaac, and Jacob. And God does not break a promise. He is such a phenomenal God that even though the Jews were dispersed, He made sure that no one would want to move to Israel, saving the land for over 1800 years for his chosen people. To me, this may be one of the most awesome miracles of all time. The implications are numerous. It proves to me that the Jews are God's people and everyone had better come to grips with that fact. Also, the miracle itself should even make atheists stand up and pay attention and rethink their position about the existence of God. And it says to me that God's promise to the Israelites will last. The more we ponder the ramifications of this 660,000 day drought, and the dramatic timing in which it ended, the more we all should stand in awe of our mighty God.

There is a post script, however, that may be worth musing over. As we all know, Israel has been pushed to give up even more land to create a new state for the so-called Palestinians. This push seemed to escalate toward the end of the Bush administration. It was as though George W. Bush was obsessed with leaving a legacy as the president who succeeded in creating the "desired" two state solution, and doing it with land that God had given Israel. That did not happen, and of course, Obama has pushed even harder.

Interesting is the fact that Netenyahu has gone along with the rhetoric, like his predecessors before him. But even more interesting to me is that when Bush started his big push at the end of his term in office another drought in Israel began.

Finally, after being snubbed, belittled, and treated like an enemy by Obama, Netenyahu pushed back hard at the end of 2011. Prior to Netenyahu standing tall, the lack of rain persisted in Israel for three and a half years, resulting in the largest forest fire in Israel's history. Then Netenyahu basically said to the world, "Get lost." The result: January 2012, broke all Israeli records as the rainiest month ever. There were 29 days with some rain during the month of January, which broke the previous record of 25 wet days in January 1947.

Yes, our God is a mighty God. He shut the heavens and kept it from raining for 1800 years in order to keep the land of Israel unpopulated for the return of the Jews, the apple of His eye. I find that to be out of this world miraculous!

I brought this up to make a big point and give you some untold truth in the next few sentences. The vast majority of the people group known as the Palestinians did not live in what is now Israel before God stopped the draught and formed the nation of Israel in 1948. After that happened, and the draught stopped, Muslims from places like Jordan moved into the area because it was then inhabitable.

Then, when the Muslim nations were planning to invade Israel, the Muslims put out the propaganda that when they did invade, the Jews would kill the Muslims who lived among them, so those Muslims living in Israel had better get out before the invasion. The Jews told their Muslim neighbors that they had nothing to fear and should remain in their homes, but most fled anyway, ending up in refuge camps in places like Jordan, where they had originally come from.

Starting with the murderous terrorist, Yasser Arafat, a decision was reached whereby the refuges would be kept in squalor in those camps for propaganda reasons in order to induce world hatred toward the Jews and cause the Jews to have to give up their land in order to have a new state of Palestine created. There you have it. I have given you the truth of the Palestinian situation; a truth the liberal media will never tell, and a true history that has been rewritten and is no longer even believed by most of the world.

But getting back to Hippolytus and his number six on his list, that the antichrist would return a scattered people; let's watch and see what world leader forces the Jews to back down and hand over more of their land for a new Palestinian state. That man will probably be the antichrist.

Number seven on the list tells us, "The Lord gave a seal to those who believed on Him, and he (the antichrist) will give one like manner." We'll just have to see how this plays out in real life.

"The Savior appeared in the form of man, and he too will come in the form of a man" is the eighth on the list. There is not much new here; however, even though the antichrist will "appear in the form of a man," we will see in a moment that he will most probably have the Nephilim seed that we discussed earlier.

Finally, when we read in number nine that "The Savior raised up and showed His holy flesh like a temple, and he (the antichrist) will raise a temple of stone in Jerusalem" we can know that the antichrist will indeed build an actual temple in Jerusalem, thus ending the debate among prophecy "scholars" pertaining to that.

Hippolytus summarizes the antichrist by saying:

"He will make himself like the Son of God, and set himself forward as king" 49.

Let's leave Hippolytus and go to the words of his mentor, Irenaeus, who you will remember was taught directly by Polycarp after Polycarp had learned the truth at the feet of none other that the Apostle John. Remember as you read these exact words of Irenaeus that when he uses the term "saints" he is referring to the church, the followers of Jesus:

"By means of the events which shall occur in the time of Antichrist is it shown that he, being an apostate and a robber, is anxious to be adored as God; and that, although a mere slave, he wishes himself to be proclaimed as a king. For he (Antichrist) being endued with all the power of the devil, shall come, not as a righteous king, nor as a legitimate king, [i.e., one] in subjection to God, but an impious, unjust, and lawless one; as an apostate, iniquitous and murderous; as a robber, concentrating in himself [all] satanic apostasy, and setting aside idols to persuade [men] that he himself is God, raising up himself as the only idol, having in himself the multifarious errors of the other idols. This he does, in order that they who do [now] worship the devil by means of many abominations, may serve himself by this one idol, of whom the apostle thus speaks in the second Epistle to the Thessalonians:

*'Unless there shall come a failing away first, and the man of sin shall be revealed, the son of perdition, who opposes and exalts himself above all that is called God, or that is worshipped; so that he sits in the temple of God, showing himself as if he were God."* Thessalonians 2:2-3.

The apostle therefore clearly points out his apostasy, and that he is lifted up above all that is called God, or that is worshipped— that is, above every idol — for these are indeed so called by men, but are not [really] gods; and that he will endeavor in a tyrannical manner to set himself forth as God.

Moreover, he (the apostle) has also pointed out this which I have shown in many ways, that the temple in Jerusalem was made by the direction of the true God. For the apostle himself, speaking in his own person, distinctly called it the temple of God. Now I have shown in the third book, that no one is termed God by the apostles when speaking for themselves, except Him who truly is God, the Father of our Lord, by whose directions the temple which is at Jerusalem was constructed for those purposes which I have already mentioned; in which [temple] the enemy shall sit, endeavoring to show himself as Christ, as the Lord also declares:

*'But when you shall see the abomination of desolation, which has been spoken of by Daniel the prophet, standing in the holy place (let him that reads understand), then let those who are in Judea flee into the mountains; and he who is upon the house-top, let him not come down to take anything out of his house: for there shall then be great hardship, such as has not been from the beginning of the world until now, nor ever shall be.'*
Matthew 24:15-21

Daniel too, looking forward to the end of the last kingdom, i.e., the ten last kings, among whom the kingdom of those men shall be partitioned, and upon whom the son of perdition shall come, declares that ten horns shall spring from the beast, and that another little horn shall arise in the midst of them, and that three of the former shall be rooted up before his face. He says:

*'And, behold, eyes were in this horn as the eyes of a man, and a mouth speaking great things, and his look was more stout than his fellows. I was looking, and this horn made war against the saints, and prevailed against them, until the Ancient of days came and gave judgment to the saints of the most high God, and the time came, and the saints obtained the kingdom.'*
Daniel 7:8, 21-22.

Then, further on, in the interpretation of the vision, there was said to him:

*'The fourth beast shall be the fourth kingdom upon earth, which shall excel all other kingdoms, and devour the whole earth, and tread it down, and cut it in pieces. And its ten horns are ten kings which shall arise; and after them shall arise another, who shall surpass in evil deeds all that were before him, and shall overthrow three kings; and he shall speak words against the*

*most high God, and wear out the saints of the most high God, and shall purpose to change times and laws; and [everything] shall be given into his hand until a time of times and a half time.'* Daniel 7:23-29.

That is, for three years and six months, during which time, when he comes, he shall reign over the earth. Of whom also the Apostle Paul again, speaking in the second [Epistle] to the Thessalonians, and at the same time proclaiming the cause of his advent, thus says:

*'And then shall the wicked one be revealed, whom the Lord Jesus shall slay with the spirit of His mouth, and destroy by the presence of His coming; whose coming [i.e., the wicked one's] is after the working of Satan, in all power, and signs, and portents of lies, and with all deceivableness of wickedness for those who perish; because they did not receive the love of the truth, that they might be saved. And therefore God will send them the working of error, that they may believe a lie; that they all may be judged who did not believe the truth, but gave consent to iniquity.'* 2 Thessalonians 2:8-12

The Lord also spoke as follows to those who did not believe in Him:

*'I have come in my Father's name, and you have not received Me: when another shall come in his own name, him you will receive.'* John 5:43.

calling Antichrist the other, because he is alienated from the Lord. This is also the unjust judge, whom the Lord mentioned as one who feared not God, neither regarded man, (Luke 18) to whom the widow fled in her forgetfulness of God—that is, the earthly Jerusalem,— to be avenged of her adversary. Which also he shall do in the time of his kingdom: he shall remove his kingdom into that [city], and shall sit in the temple of God, leading astray those who worship him, as if he were Christ. To this purpose Daniel says again:

*'And he shall desolate the holy place; and sin has been given for a sacrifice, and righteousness been cast away in the earth, and he has been active and gone on prosperously.'* Daniel 8:12.

And the angel Gabriel, when explaining his vision, states with regard to this person:

*'And towards the end of their kingdom a king of a most fierce countenance shall arise, one understanding [dark] questions, and exceedingly powerful, full of wonders; and he shall corrupt, direct, influence, and put strong men down, the holy people likewise; and his yoke shall be directed as a wreath [round their neck]; deceit shall be in his hand, and he shall be lifted up in his heart: he shall also ruin many by deceit, and lead many to perdition, bruising them in his hand like eggs.'*     Daniel 8:23-25.

And then he points out the time that his tyranny shall last, during which **the saints shall be put to flight**."
Against Heresies, Book V, Chapter XXV, by Irenaeus.

As we have discussed, the church Fathers never waivered in their stance that it would be the church that would be persecuted by the antichrist, again totally refuting Darby's notion of a pre-tribulation rapture. The last sentence above uses the word "saints," referring to individual Christians, but in many other places Irenaeus says, "and put the **church to flight**," such as in Chapter XXVI.

In chapter XXIX there is a paragraph that you will find interesting. In it Irenaeus is talking about the antichrist as the beast, and he says:

"And there is therefore in this beast, when he comes, a recapitulation made of all sorts of iniquity and of every deceit, in order that all apostate power, flowing into and being shut up in him, may be sent into the furnace of fire. Fittingly, therefore, shall his name possess the number six hundred and sixty-six, since **he sums up in his own person all the commixture of wickedness which took place previous to the deluge, due to the apostasy of the angels.** For Noah was six hundred years old when the deluge came upon the earth, sweeping away the rebellious world, for the sake of that most infamous generation which lived in the times of Noah."

As we can see by that paragraph, it was common knowledge that the flood was caused by "the apostasy of the angels," which was the taking of women by angels that resulted in the Nephilim. But moreover, this is the first actual time Irenaeus tells us the antichrist will contain the Nephilim seed. It makes so much sense, though. Jesus, the true Christ, was a result on earth of a union between a woman and God's "holy seed," as brought about by the Holy Spirit. Therefore, in trying to create his unholy trinity, Satan will want his seed to be in the antichrist, and the only way he can do that is by utilizing the Nephilim seed.

Since Irenaeus, the father of teaching about heresies, taught that the antichrist "sums up in his own person all the commixture of wickedness which took place previous to the deluge, due to the apostasy of the angels," we can know for a certainty that his having the Nephilim seed is not speculation, or a mere "school of thought." We can be sure without a shadow of a doubt that Irenaeus only taught what John taught, and as we saw earlier, "he knew that the Apostolic Oral Teaching was divinely revealed to the Apostles, so it was not the product of human thought process. Irenaeus knew that the oral teaching handed down from John through Polycarp to him came directly from God, and was in no way just interpretations of things that John came up with on his own. It was not a 'school of thought.' It was from God."

For this reason we spent so much time early on discussing the Nephilim, being confident that those chapters were not mere speculation. That the antichrist is the end product of "the apostasy of the angels" is obviously important, but not nearly as important as will be our understanding of what the true Millennial Kingdom will be like, as we will discuss in later chapters. That understanding, which will totally surprise you, could not be possible without having a complete knowledge of what transpired prior to Noah, as well as afterward, in respect to the Nephilim.

We will be finding out much more about the antichrist as we look at more information from the Oral Teaching of John. In fact, as we investigate his teaching about his own vision in Revelation, it will be almost unbelievable to see some big differences from John's teaching as opposed to the end times we are taught today. To see that dramatically revealed we will now continue on with our study of Revelation events.

# The Little Scroll

Immediately following the description of the first six trumpets, John writes:

*"Then I saw another mighty angel coming down from heaven. He was robed in a cloud, with a rainbow above his head; his face was like the sun, and his legs were like fiery pillars. He was holding a little scroll, which lay open in his hand. He planted his right foot on the sea and his left foot on the land, and he gave a loud shout like the roar of a lion. When he shouted, the voices of the seven thunders spoke. And when the seven thunders spoke, I was about to write; but I heard a voice from heaven say, 'Seal up what the seven thunders have said and do not write it down.'*

*Then the angel I had seen standing on the sea and on the land raised his right hand to heaven. And he swore by him who lives for ever and ever, who created the heavens and all that is in them, the earth and all that is in it, and the sea and all that is in it, and said, 'There will be no more delay! But in the days when the seventh angel is about to sound his trumpet, the mystery of God will be accomplished, just as he announced to his servants the prophets.'*

*Then the voice that I had heard from heaven spoke to me once more: 'Go, take the scroll that lies open in the hand of the angel who is standing on the sea and on the land.'*

*So I went to the angel and asked him to give me the little scroll. He said to me, 'Take it and eat it. It will turn your stomach sour, but in your mouth it will be as sweet as honey.' I took the little scroll from the angel's hand and ate it. It tasted as sweet as honey in my mouth, but when I had eaten it, my stomach turned sour. Then I was told, 'You must prophesy again about many peoples, nations, languages and kings."*   Revelation 10.

We have no teaching from the church Fathers that discuss these verses that I am aware of, but it seems that when the angel says, *"There will be no more delay! But in the days when the seventh angel is about to sound his trumpet, the mystery of God will be accomplished,"* we are being told that after the sixth trumpet, the tribulation will begin.

We have seen that, just like Jesus told us, the end time events speed up and grow more intense, just like birth pains do. The seven seals started when Jesus arrived in heaven after His ascension, and cover about two thousand years from then until His return. The seven trumpets, if we assume that Rabbi Judah Ben Samuel was right, and I believe he was, started in 1917. And they also will continue until the second return of Christ.

One thing I might mention concerning the seals and trumpets we looked at is that I believe that when John sees things that are happening on earth, they may well be indicators of things that happen in the spiritual world at the same time. For example, if what we looked at as a possibility of the fifth trumpet events that John saw was correct, including helicopters that he referred to as locusts, my belief is that at the same time that actually happened on earth, swarms of demons were also unleashed in the spiritual realm. Of course, that is pure speculation on my part, but think back; does it seem to you that the world has become exponentially more evil since the gulf wars? It sure does to me.

Evil has always been among us, but in the years since those wars I see things in the newspaper and on the TV news that are far beyond anything I can remember happening prior to those times. I'm not saying that there weren't horrific things in years past, but now I see things like representatives of Planned Parenthood openly and calmly talking about the need to kill babies that somehow survived abortions as if those living, breathing, innocent infants were inanimate objects. And children killing children. And parents killing their own children almost daily. The list goes on and on.

My point is that John's visions in which events seemed to escalate from trumpet to trumpet could very well have been shadows of events actually escalating in the unseen world, events leading up to the actual tribulation years that will be filled with atrocities that are more hideous that we can now even imagine. We must remember that behind the scenes are the evil Satan and his horde of demons, the souls of the Nephilim, working night and day for what they erroneously believe is a real showdown with God that could change the course of their futures. And now in our study we are entering those final evil days.

Therefore, the little scroll that John was just handed by the angel will cover the time of the actual tribulation period. So John is told, *"You must prophesy again about many peoples, nations, languages and kings."* And he begins this final prophecy by telling us about the two witnesses.

# The Two Witnesses

*"And I will give power to my two witnesses, and they will prophesy for 1,260 days, clothed in sackcloth." These are the two olive trees and the two lampstands that stand before the Lord of the earth."*     Revelation 11:3-4.

We have already learned from Hippolytus that these two will be Enoch and Elijah, the two Old Testament prophets who have not yet died.

"Now Daniel will set forth this subject to us. For he says, 'And one week will make a covenant with many, and it shall be that in the midst (half) of the week my sacrifice and oblation shall cease.' By one week, therefore, he meant the last week which is to be at the end of the whole world of which week the two prophets Enoch and Elias will take up the half. For they will preach 1,260 days clothed in sackcloth, proclaiming repentance to the people and to all the nations."     <u>Treatise on Christ and Antichrist</u>, 43, Hippolytus.

After three and a half years of listening to Enoch and Elijah preach the truth, the antichrist will be so fed up with them that he will have them killed:

*"Now when they have finished their testimony, the beast that comes up from the Abyss will attack them, and overpower and kill them. Their bodies will lie in the street of the great city, which is figuratively called Sodom and Egypt, where also their Lord was crucified. For three and a half days men from every people, tribe, language and nation will gaze on their bodies and refuse them burial. The inhabitants of the earth will gloat over them and will celebrate by sending each other gifts, because these two prophets had tormented those who live on the earth.*

*But after the three and a half days a breath of life from God entered them, and they stood on their feet, and terror struck those who saw them. Then they heard a loud voice from heaven saying to them, 'Come up here.' And they went up to heaven in a cloud, while their enemies looked on. ...*

*The second woe has passed; the third woe is coming soon."*
Revelation 11:7-14.

The three and a half year Great Tribulation will now begin.

# The Woman and the Dragon

I must tell you that I am amazed at the enormous difference in our modern church's interpretation of the gigantically important topics such as the woman and the dragon, and two beasts in Revelation, versus what the church Fathers knew to be the truth. You may be familiar with the woman and the dragon; however, so that we won't miss anything, let's read what John wrote in Revelation:

*"A great and wondrous sign appeared in heaven: a woman clothed with the sun, with the moon under her feet and a crown of twelve stars on her head. She was pregnant and cried out in pain as she was about to give birth. Then another sign appeared in heaven: an enormous red dragon with seven heads and ten horns and seven crowns on his heads. His tail swept a third of the stars out of the sky and flung them to the earth. The dragon stood in front of the woman who was about to give birth, so that he might devour her child the moment it was born. She gave birth to a son, a male child, who will rule all the nations with an iron scepter. And her child was snatched up to God and to his throne. The woman fled into the desert to a place prepared for her by God, where she might be taken care of for 1,260 days."* Revelation 12:1-6.

If you have taken any course on Revelation in any Protestant church you no doubt learned that the woman represents Israel and that Israel will flee to a desert location to be kept away from the persecution from the antichrist. We are even told specifically that the place in the desert Israel will go to hide will in all probability be Petra, in the southern part of Jordan. It makes for a very convincing story. But is any of it correct?

To find out, we need to read the truth John taught Polycarp, as explained by Hippolytus:

"By '*the woman then clothed with the sun,*' he meant most manifestly the Church, endued with the Father's word, whose brightness is above the sun. And by the '*moon under her feet*' he referred to her being adorned, like the moon, with heavenly glory. And the words, '*upon her head a crown of twelve stars,*' refer to the twelve apostles by whom the Church was founded.

And those, *'she, being with child, cries, travailing in birth, and pained to be delivered,'* mean that the Church will not cease to bear from her heart the Word that is persecuted by the unbelieving in the world. *'And she brought forth,'* he says, *'a man-child, who is to rule all the nations;'* by which is meant that the Church, always bringing forth Christ, the perfect man-child of God, who is declared to be God and man, becomes the instructor of all the nations.

And the words, *'her child was caught up unto God and to His throne,'* signify that He who is always born of her is a heavenly King, and not an earthly; even as David also declared of old when he said,

> *'The Lord said unto my Lord, Sit Thou at my right hand, until I make Thine enemies Thy footstool.'* Psalm 110:1.

John says,

> *'And the dragon saw and persecuted the woman which brought forth the man-child. And to the woman were given two wings of the great eagle, that she might fly into the wilderness, where she is nourished for a time, and times, and half a time, from the face of the serpent.'* Revelation 12:13-14.

That refers to the one thousand two hundred and threescore days (the half of the week) during which the tyrant is to reign and persecute the Church, which flees from city to city, and seeks concealment in the wilderness among the mountains, possessed of no other defense than the two wings of the great eagle, that is to say, the faith of Jesus Christ, who, in stretching forth His holy hands on the holy tree, unfolded two wings, the right and the left, and called to Him all who believed upon Him, and covered them as a hen her chickens. For by the mouth of Malachi also He speaks thus:

> *"And unto you that fear my name shall the Sun of righteousness arise with healing in His wings."* Malachi 4:2.

<u>Treatise on Christ and Antichrist</u>, 61, by Hippolytus.

Wow. The difference between the above Apostolic Oral Teaching and what we are currently taught about the Revelation scripture on the woman and the dragon is staggering.

First, instead of the woman being Israel as we are currently taught, we now find the truth, *"By the woman then clothed with the sun,'* **he meant most manifestly the Church**, endued with the Father's word, whose brightness is above the sun. And by the *'moon under her feet'* he referred to her being adorned, *"like the moon, with heavenly glory."* By Hippolytus telling us that the woman is the church, John Darby's Dispensationalism is totally shattered and shown to be the heresy that it really is.

This has been the big stumbling block for our modern church. We all thought that since Jesus was born as a Jew, the *"she, being with child, cries, travailing in birth, and pained to be delivered,"* had to refer to Israel. The early church Fathers, having been taught by John through the Apostolic Oral Tradition, however, knew very well that the *"she"* was the church. They understood such scripture as Isaiah 54 so much better than we do. Let's read from that chapter in which God talks to today's Israel:

*"Sing, O barren woman, you who never bore a child; burst into song, shout for joy, you who were never in labor; because more are the children of the desolate woman than of her who has a husband,' says the Lord.*

*'Enlarge the place of your tent, stretch your tent curtains wide, do not hold back; lengthen your cords, strengthen your stakes. For you will spread*

*out to the right and to the left; your descendants will dispossess nations and settle in their desolate cities.*

*Do not be afraid, you will not suffer shame. Do not fear disgrace, you will not be humiliated. You will forget the shame of your youth and remember no more the reproach of your widowhood.*

*For your Maker is your husband, the Lord Almighty is his name, the Holy One of Israel is your Redeemer; he is called the God of all the earth.*

*The Lord will call you back as if you were a wife deserted and distressed in spirit - a wife who married young, only to be rejected,' says your God.*

*'For a brief moment I abandoned you, but with deep compassion I will bring you back. In a surge of anger I hid my face from you for a moment, but with everlasting kindness I will have compassion on you,' says the Lord your Redeemer."* Isaiah 54:1-8.

In the very first paragraph we just read, God calls Israel a *"barren woman, you who never bore a child."* The reason for that is that Israel never *"bore"* her messiah, her savior. Yes, Jesus was born a Jew, but He was not acknowledged as Israel's savior. It was the church that did that. In the second part of that first sentence God says,

*"More are the children of the desolate woman than of her who has a husband."* Isaiah 54:1.

The desolate woman is the church, primarily the gentiles. Although the church is the bride of Christ Jesus, Israel's husband was and is God the Father. We can read:

*"Return, faithless people,' declares the Lord, 'for I am your husband."*
Jeremiah 3:14.

God went on to say,

*"The Lord will call you back as if you were a wife deserted and distressed in spirit - a wife who married young, only to be rejected,' says your God. 'For a brief moment I abandoned you, but with deep compassion I will bring you back."* Isaiah 54:6-7.

We can see by that scripture that Israel could never have been the woman with the dragon in Revelation. Israel was barren. The woman in Revelation is the church. The early church Fathers had such a better grasp of God's Word than we do today.

Next we learned that "the words, *'upon her head a crown of twelve stars,'* refer to the twelve apostles by whom the Church was founded," not the patriarchs of the twelve tribes as is commonly thought today.

Then Hippolytus taught us, "And those, *'she, being with child, cries, travailing in birth, and pained to be delivered,'* mean that the Church will not cease to bear from her heart the Word that is persecuted by the unbelieving in the world. *'And she brought forth,'* he says, *'a man-child, who is to rule all the nations;'* by which is meant that the Church, always bringing forth Christ, the perfect man-child of God, who is declared to be God and man, becomes the instructor of all the nations."

Next, we are all familiar with the verse,

*"And to the woman were given two wings of the great eagle, that she might fly into the wilderness, where she is nourished for a time, and times, and half a time, from the face of the serpent."*           Revelation 12:14.

It is at that point in our modern teaching that we are normally told that John was seeing airplanes taking the Jews out of harms way, and normally the instructor or author goes into a short discussion about whether or not those are American planes because of the "great eagle" reference, or maybe because he doesn't see America in any prophecy he might propose that they are British airplanes that come to the rescue of the Jews. Sometimes a full half hour TV program is devoted to that debate, or several pages in the latest prophecy book, or a complete weekly church study session is used up on it.

But now we find Hippolytus telling us that **God told John** to teach that the *"two wings of the great eagle"* refers to "the faith of Jesus Christ, who, in stretching forth His holy hands on the holy tree, unfolded two wings, the right and the left, and called to Him all who believed upon Him, and covered them as a hen her chickens. For by the mouth of Malachi also He speaks thus: *'And unto you that fear my name shall the Sun of righteousness arise with healing in His wings."*           Malachi 4:2.

In other words, there will be no airplanes from America or England coming to rescue the persecuted, who are not even Jews as we are taught, but Christians. No, the truth, which according to Irenaeus came to John from God Himself, is that Christians will be the group the antichrist will persecute, and they, as all who have been persecuted before them, will rely on their faith in Jesus.

The scenarios made possible by the heretic "school of John Darby's thought" play well on the movie screen, and make for lively and exciting debate in study groups, but they are all fantasy. Had the church only paid attention to Irenaeus when he wrote his extensive and inspired masterpiece, <u>Against Heresies</u>, we would not be involved in the foolishness that masquerades as prophetic Bible study today. Had the church held strictly to the truth from God, found in the sacred Holy Bible and the Apostolic Oral Teaching, our modern church might not be looking forward to being spit out of the Lord's mouth. How sad it is that instead of the truth, we continue to spread the man made ideas of the most titillating "school of thought" of the day. A price will be paid.

Soon in our study of Revelation we will be looking at the two beasts, one coming from the sea and the other from the land. The surprise we have in store for us concerning who or what those two beasts represent will be shocking. But before we can look at the truth, as told to us by our church Fathers, we need to take a little side trip in order to be able to fully understand and grasp the magnitude of that truth.

# Parables, Allegory, and Swine

Jesus taught with parables, a form of allegory. We all know that. And we are told that He did so because it made the lessons stand out so much for His listeners. There is something to that logic, but that is not the main reason He used that device. Dr. Charles Stanley wrote an article that will give us a touch more insight:

"Before a certain point in His ministry, Jesus had employed many graphic analogies using common things that would be familiar to everyone (salt, bread, sheep, etc.) and their meaning was fairly clear in the context of His teaching. Parables required more explanation, and at one point in His ministry, Jesus began to teach using parables exclusively.

The question is why Jesus would let most people wonder about the meaning of His parables. The first instance of this is in His telling the parable of the seed and the soils. Before He interpreted this parable, He drew His disciples away from the crowd. They said to Him,

*"Why do You speak to them in parables?' Jesus answered them, '***To you it has been granted to know the mysteries of the kingdom of heaven, but to them it has not been granted***. For whoever has, to him more shall be given, and he will have an abundance; but whoever does not have, even what he has shall be taken away from him. Therefore I speak to them in parables; because while seeing they do not see, and while hearing they do not hear, nor do they understand. In their case the prophecy of Isaiah is being fulfilled, which says,*

*"Hearing you will hear and shall not understand, And seeing you will see and not perceive; For the hearts of this people have grown dull. Their ears are hard of hearing, And their eyes they have closed, Lest they should see with their eyes and hear with their ears, Lest they should understand with their hearts and turn, So that I should heal them." But blessed are your eyes, because they see; and your ears, because they hear. For truly I say to you that many prophets and righteous men desired to see what you see, and did not see it, and to hear what you hear, and did not hear it."* Matthew 13:10-17.

From this point on in Jesus' ministry, when He spoke in parables, He explained them only to His disciples. But those who had continually rejected His message were left in their spiritual blindness to wonder as to His meaning. He made a clear distinction between those who had been given *'ears to hear'* and those who persisted in unbelief - ever hearing, but never actually perceiving and *'always learning but never able to acknowledge the truth.'* (2 Timothy 3:7). The disciples had been given the gift of spiritual discernment by which things of the spirit were made clear to them. Because they accepted truth from Jesus, they were given more and more truth."

From "Why did Jesus teach in parables?" By Dr. Charles Stanley.

Yes, Jesus taught in parables. They are found in all four gospels. But let's take a look at the list of parables of Jesus in chronological order with the Bible book and verse beside them and see if something jumps out at us:

1. New Cloth on an Old Coat — Matthew 9:16, Mark 2:21, Luke 5:36
2. New Wine in Old Wineskins — Matthew 9:17, Mark 2:22, Luke 5:37-38
3. Lamp on a Stand — Matthew 5:14-15, Mark 4:21-22, Luke 8:16, Luke 11:33
4. Wise and Foolish Builders — Matthew 7:24-27
5. Moneylender Forgives Debts — Luke 7:41-43
6. The Rich Fool — Luke 12:16-21
7. The Watchful Servant — Luke 12:35-40, Mark 13:35-37
8. The Faithful Servant — Luke 12:42-48, Matthew 24:45-51
9. Unfruitful Fig Tree — Luke 13:6-9
10. Sower and Types of Soil — Matthew 13:3-8, Mark 4:3-8, Luke 8:5-8
11. Wheat and — Matthew 13:24-30
12. Growing — Mark 4:26-29
13. Mustard — Matthew 13:31-32, Mark 4:30-32, Luke 13:18-19
14. Yeast — Matthew 13:33
15. Hidden Treasure — Matthew 13:44
16. Valuable Pearl — Matthew 13:45-46
17. Fishing Net — Matthew 13:47-50
18. Owner of a House — Matthew 18:12-13, Luke 15:4-7
20. **The Good Shepherd** — **John 10:1-18**
21. Master and His Servant — Luke 17:7-10
22. Unmerciful Servant — Matthew 18:23-34
23. Good Samaritan — Luke 10:30-37

| | |
|---|---|
| 24. Friend in Need | Luke 11:5-8 |
| 25. Lowest Seat at the Feast | Luke 14:7-14 |
| 26. Invitation to Banquet | Luke 14:16-24 |
| 27. Cost of Discipleship | Luke 14:28-33 |
| 28. Lost Coin | Luke 15:8-10 |
| 29. Prodigal Son | Luke 15:11-32 |
| 30. The Unjust Steward | Luke 16:1-8 |
| 31. Rich Man and Lazarus | Luke 16:19-31 |
| 32. Workers in the Vineyard | Matthew 20:1-16 |
| 33. Persistent Widow | Luke 18:2-8 |
| 34. Pharisee and Tax Collector | Luke 18:10-14 |
| 35. Ruler and Servants | Luke 19:12-27 |
| 36. Two Sons | Matthew 21:28-32 |
| 37. Wicked Tenants | Matthew21:33-44,Mark12:1-11,Luke20:9-18 |
| 38. Wedding Banquet | Matthew 22:2-14 |
| 39. Signs of Fig Tree | Matthew24:32-35,Mark13:28-29,Luke21:29-31 |
| 40. Wise and Foolish Virgins | Matthew 25:1-13 |
| 41. The Talents | Matthew 25:14-30 |
| 42. Sheep and Goats | Matthew 25:31-46 |

I tried to make it a little easier for the big exception to jump off the page at you. And yes, you got it. There is only one parable in the entire book of John. In fact, The Greek word "parabolē" is used a total of fifty times in the New Testament: thirteen times in Mark, seventeen in Matthew, eighteen in Luke, and twice in Hebrews, but not once in John. Does that strike you as somewhat peculiar? Do you think that it might be wise to delve into this apparent oddity a little? Could it be that maybe there is a reason for this that may be important to us?

Let's start with something else that you, like me, may have found to be a little bit strange in John's writing; the fact that he continually called himself *"the disciple whom Jesus loved,"* or *"the Beloved Disciple."* In examining this, let's start with a few excerpts from a sermon given by one of the giants of the faith in the Church of Missions era of 1730 to 1900, the Church of Philadelphia in the letters Jesus wrote in Revelation. I'm referring to C.H. Spurgeon who gave a sermon in 1880, aptly titled "The Disciple Whom Jesus Loved." Next is a taste of that sermon:

"Our Lord loved all His disciples—*'having loved His own which were in the world, He loved them unto the end.'* He said to all the Apostles, *'I call you not servants; for the servant knows not what his Lord does: but I have called you Friends; for all things that I have heard of My Father I have made known unto you.'* And yet within that circle of love there was an innermost place in which the beloved John was favored to dwell. Upon the mountain of the Savior's love there was a knoll a little higher than the rest of the mountain and there John was made to stand, nearest to his Lord. Let us not, because John was specially loved, think less, even in the slightest degree, of the love which Jesus Christ gave forth to the rest of His chosen. I take it, Brothers and Sisters, that those who display an extraordinary love to one are all the more capable of great affection to many and, therefore, because Jesus loved John most, I have an enhanced estimate of His love to the other disciples.

It is not for a moment to be supposed that any one suffered from His supreme friendship for John. John was raised and they were not lowered, but raised with him. All Believers are the dear objects of the Savior's choice, the purchase of His blood, His portion and inheritance, the jewels of His crown.

Some men go two ways, or they tack about, or they go towards their objective in an indirect manner. But John steams straight forward with the fires blazing and the engine working at full speed. His whole soul was engaged in his Lord's cause, for he was a deep thinker, a silent student and then a forceful actor. He was not impetuous with the haste of Peter, but yet he was determined and thorough-going and all on fire with zeal.

He was exceedingly livid in his beliefs and believed to the utmost what he had learned of his Lord. Read his Epistle through and see how many times he says 'we know,' 'we know,' 'we know.'

Let us now view him in his relation to his Lord. The name he takes to himself is, *'the disciple whom Jesus loved.'* Jesus loved him as a disciple. What sort of disciples do masters love? You that have ever been teachers of youth know that if teachers had their choice, certain persons would be selected before others. If we teach, we love teachable people! Such was John. He was a man quick to learn. He was not like Thomas who was slow, argumentative, cautious. But having once assured himself that he had a true Teacher, he gave himself right up to Jesus and was willing to receive what He had to reveal. He was a disciple of a very keen eye, seeing into the soul of his Instructor's teaching. His emblem in the early church was the eagle - the eagle which soars, but also the eagle which sees from afar.

John saw the spiritual meaning of types and emblems. He did not stop at the outward symbols, as some of the disciples did, but his penetrating soul read into the depths of the Truth of God. You can see this both in his Gospel and in his Epistles. He is a spiritually-minded man. He stays not in the letter, but he dives beneath the surface. He pierces through the shell and reaches the inner teaching." "The Disciple Whom Jesus Loved." 1880, C Spurgeon.

I am sure you will agree that if you were to spend three years with a group of twelve other folks, one of them would stand out to you. And the two of you would form a closer bond than you would with the others. We all have friends, but we also have best friends. We can be certain this was the case with Jesus and John. It was only John who stayed with Jesus until the very painful end. The others all scattered. And it was John who Jesus chose to take care of his widowed mother. Not only was John in the inner circle of the twelve, along with Peter and James, but John was Jesus' best friend.

But could it be that there was even more to it than that? Could it be that of all the disciples, John was the one who understood best what Jesus was trying to teach? Spurgeon said in his sermon we just read:

"If we teach, we love teachable people! Such was John. He was a man quick to learn. He was not like Thomas who was slow, argumentative, cautious. But having once assured himself that he had a true Teacher, he gave himself right up to Jesus and was willing to receive what He had to reveal. He was a disciple of a very keen eye, seeing into the soul of his Instructor's teaching." C. H. Spurgeon.

If that is the case, that John was the most teachable, we might assume that John was the one disciple above all the others who fully and completely grasped those words of Jesus that Dr. Charles Stanley quoted in his article we read at the beginning of this chapter:

*"To you it has been granted to know the mysteries of the kingdom of heaven,* **but to them it has not been granted.** *For whoever has, to him more shall be given, and he will have an abundance; but whoever does not have, even what he has shall be taken away from him."* Matthew 13:11-12.

Jesus, through his parables, was not "granting" some people the truth. One of the main reasons Jesus came the first time was to prepare the world for His coming kingdom. After Jesus was baptized and spent forty days in the wilderness being tempted by Satan, but even before He started selecting His disciples, Jesus began to preach. We are told about the first sermon He preached"

*"Jesus went into Galilee, proclaiming the good news of God. 'The time has come,' he said. 'The kingdom of God is near. Repent and believe the good news!"* Mark 1:14-15.

Matthew describes that same time:

*"From that time on Jesus began to preach, 'Repent, for the kingdom of heaven is near."* Matthew 4:17.

What Jesus knew was that everyone would not repent. All who heard Him preach would not make it into the kingdom of heaven. Therefore, disclosing the truths He told to people who would not ever be a part of His kingdom would have been absolute foolishness, and possibly harmful to those who would be in His kingdom. For that reason, Jesus increasingly used parables and allegory.

Evidently John understood this very well, along with the reason for it, and he kept some things very close to the vest when he wrote his Gospel and Epistles. He knew that there were some individuals who should not be taught the truth behind some parables and scriptural allegory. By the time John wrote his first Epistle, he obviously had seen deep truths passed on to some who should not have been given them, for he says in that letter:

*"Dear children, this is the last hour; and as you have heard that the antichrist is coming, even now many antichrists have come. This is how we know it is the last hour. They went out from us, but they did not really belong to us. For if they had belonged to us, they would have remained with us; but their going showed that none of them belonged to us."* 1 John 2:18-19.

We can almost hear the regret in John's words about those who had really not belonged being taught things they should not have heard. John knew there were two camps of people in this world, for then John says:

*"He who does what is sinful is of the devil, because the devil has been sinning from the beginning. The reason the Son of God appeared was to destroy the devil's work. No one who is born of God will continue to sin, because God's seed remains in him; he cannot go on sinning, because he has been born of God. This is how we know who the children of God are and who the children of the devil are:"*                         1 John 3:8-10.

As an aside, the phrase *"God's **seed** remains in him,"* as opposed to Satan's seed obviously being in other people, continues to make my hair stand on end due to what we studied at the beginning of this book. Hebrews 4:12 tells us *"The word of God is alive and active."* And the more I study the Bible the truer that becomes to me. Years ago I read that phrase *"God's seed"* numerous times, but I just kind of skimmed over it. You may have, too. I am now seeing that God's Word contains so very much, but it unveils certain things to us when we are at the correct time in our understanding to grasp the significance or meaning of those things.

At any rate, John evidently was the one disciple who understood the best that when a parable or an allegory was given to someone who understood the hidden meaning or interpretation, that person was suppose to be selective with regards to who they in turn passed the precious information on to. Thus, the only parable from Jesus that John passed on in his Gospel was one in which Jesus Himself divulged the meaning to the entire throng of listeners. Let's read John's one and only account of Jesus' use of a parable:

*"I tell you the truth, the man who does not enter the sheep pen by the gate, but climbs in by some other way, is a thief and a robber. The man who enters by the gate is the shepherd of his sheep. The watchman opens the gate for him, and the sheep listen to his voice. He calls his own sheep by name and leads them out. When he has brought out all his own, he goes on ahead of them, and his sheep follow him because they know his voice. But they will never follow a stranger; in fact, they will run away from him because they do not recognize a stranger's voice.'*

Jesus used this figure of speech, but they did not understand what he was telling them. Therefore Jesus said again,

'I tell you the truth, I am the gate for the sheep. All who ever came before me were thieves and robbers, but the sheep did not listen to them. I am the gate; whoever enters through me will be saved. He will come in and go out, and find pasture. The thief comes only to steal and kill and destroy; I have come that they may have life, and have it to the full.

I am the good shepherd. The good shepherd lays down his life for the sheep. The hired hand is not the shepherd who owns the sheep. So when he sees the wolf coming, he abandons the sheep and runs away. Then the wolf attacks the flock and scatters it. The man runs away because he is a hired hand and cares nothing for the sheep.

I am the good shepherd; I know my sheep and my sheep know me— just as the Father knows me and I know the Father—and I lay down my life for the sheep. I have other sheep that are not of this sheep pen. I must bring them also. They too will listen to my voice, and there shall be one flock and one shepherd. The reason my Father loves me is that I lay down my life only to take it up again. No one takes it from me, but I lay it down of my own accord. I have authority to lay it down and authority to take it up again. This command I received from my Father."    John 10:1-18.

The understanding that the meanings and hidden truths in parables and allegories was of such importance to John that late in his life, after he had written Revelation, he obviously passed his understanding on as a strict commandment to his trusted student, Polycarp. He made sure Polycarp understood that he was not to pass certain truths to individuals who were never going to become fellow kingdom citizens. Polycarp then passed the same order on to Irenaeus, who likewise strictly instructed Hippolytus. We can see that all three were diligent in keeping that instruction when we read the following words of Hippolytus, who obviously had had that instruction drummed into him by his mentor, Irenaeus. The opening lines of Hippolytus' <u>Treatise on Christ and AntiChrist</u>, which was written to his student, Theophilus, gave extremely terse warnings to Theophilus about passing the information on to just anybody and everybody who might want it:

"As it was your desire, my beloved brother Theophilus, to be thoroughly informed on those topics which I put summarily before you, I have thought it right to set these matters of inquiry clearly forth to your view. … For this will be as a sure supply furnished you by us for your journey in this present life, so that by ready argument applying things ill understood and apprehended by most, you may sow them in the ground of your heart, as in a rich and clean soil. By these, too, you will be able to silence those who oppose and gainsay the word of salvation. **Only see that you do not give these things over to unbelieving and blasphemous tongues, for that is no common danger. But impart them to pious and faithful men, who desire to live holily and righteously with fear.** For it is not to no purpose that the blessed apostle exhorts Timothy, and says,

'Thou therefore, my son, be strong in the grace that is in Christ Jesus. **And the things that thou hast heard of me in many exhortations, the same commit thou to faithful men, who shall be able to teach others also.**" 2 Timothy 2:1-2.

**If, then, the blessed (apostle) delivered these things with a pious caution, which could be easily known by all, as he perceived in the spirit that 'all men have not faith,' how much greater will be our danger, if, rashly and without thought, we commit the revelations of God to profane and unworthy men?"** Treatise on Christ and Antichrist, 1.

Jesus did not want the whole truth, His revelations, told to every individual on the planet. John understood that, and chose his students well. And that understanding was handed down in the Apostolic Oral Teaching to Polycarp, Irenaeus, Hippolytus, and at least to Theophilus. Therefore, we can know for a certainty that what we read from Irenaeus and Hippolytus is the truth. We also know that there is only one truth, as we read earlier when introducing Polycarp:

"But Polycarp also was not only instructed by apostles, and conversed with many who had seen Christ, but was also, by apostles in Asia, appointed bishop of the Church in Smyrna, whom I also saw in my early youth, for he tarried [on earth] a very long time, and, when a very old man, gloriously and most nobly suffering martyrdom, departed this life, having always taught the things which he had learned from the apostles, and which the Church has handed down, and **which alone are true.**" Against Heresies, III, 4, Irenaeus.

Therefore, when weighing the correctness of end time interpretation of the allegory in Revelation between our current Bible teaching versus the teaching of The Apostolic Oral Teaching, the latter wins hands down. There are no ifs, ands, or buts in the determination. It is solely the Apostolic Oral Teaching **which alone is true**. As Irenaeus has taught us, any argument to the contrary is pure heresy, plain and simple. There was and is only one truth concerning the interpretations of the images in Revelation, and those true interpretations were passed down from John through Hippolytus, and then to his student, Theophilus. Any different interpretation, coming from John Darby, or any of the myriad of today's Biblical prophecy "scholars," is flat out wrong. The modern teaching is a false teaching, probably proposed by well meaning men, but a false teaching just the same.

There is only one truth, and John was given it by Jesus. Think about it, they were best friends. Jesus trusted John more than anyone. Can we not see clearly that John and Jesus communicated for hours every day, not only while Jesus was here on earth, but also after He went to heaven? John obviously spent lots and lots of time in prayer with Jesus after he had written down in Revelation what Jesus had wanted him to write.

Jesus had made the images in Revelation even harder to understand than any of His parables had been. He did not want the wrong individuals to see the truths of the end times. But Jesus would have made sure that John, the one He trusted most, did indeed know the true interpretations so that he could pass them along to his students. This is the Apostolic Oral Teaching. This is the truth all were not suppose to hear.

So, who were those individuals who were not suppose to hear the truth? Are there innocent people who will not be saved because of this? Not at all. Hippolytus answered that question very plainly for his student Theophilus,

"And by those who live by faith He is easily found; and to those of pure eye and holy heart, who desire to knock at the door, He opens immediately. For He casts away none of His servants as unworthy of the divine mysteries. He does not esteem the rich man more highly than the poor, nor does He despise the poor man for his poverty. He does not disdain the barbarian, nor does He set the eunuch aside as no man. He does not hate the female on account of the woman's act of disobedience in the beginning, nor does He reject the male on account of the man's transgression. But He seeks all, and desires to save all, wishing to make all the children of God, and calling all the saints unto one perfect man."          Treatise on Christ and AntiChrist,1.

    The truth about the absolute and unequivocal requirement for true repentance, what Jesus did on the cross, and the unchanging path to salvation, were never hidden from anyone due to Biblical parabolic or allegorical language. Those important issues were always made crystal clear and repeated over and over; at least until just recently when the need for the true repentance of sin appears to have faded rapidly from the discourse in many modern churches, replaced by the notion that man's sole requirement in the salvation process is nonexistent, except for a mental assent of what Jesus did on the cross. Any mention of true repentance has often disappeared completely. But again, that was never hidden in the Holy Scriptures. This modern trend of the avoidance of teaching repentance has mushroomed in the last decade or so, and should be a worrisome omen. Perhaps our church leaders should be paying more attention to the words of Jesus in his letter to the Church of Laodicea, our church age:

    *"So, because you are lukewarm—neither hot nor cold—I am about to spit you out of my mouth. You say, 'I am rich; I have acquired wealth and do not need a thing.' But you do not realize that you are wretched, pitiful, poor, blind and naked. I counsel you to buy from me gold refined in the fire, so you can become rich; and white clothes to wear* (the sign of righteousness), *so you can cover your shameful nakedness; and salve to put on your eyes, so you can see. Those whom I love I rebuke and discipline. So be earnest and repent."*          Revelation 3:16-19.

    To repeat the question, though, by the use of allegory in Revelation, exactly who was the end times truth hidden from? Let's try to see things from God's perspective. He sees the big picture. And to God there are no dimensions. No unseen and seen world. No natural and supernatural. God created everything, and He sees everything as one creation, moving along in His plan, on His timetable. And there is not a battle between God and Satan. Satan and his demons are pawns being used by God for His purposes. Satan may think there is a battle going on, but there isn't. The minute Satan is of no more use to God's plan, he is toast. The same for the demons. God is in control. And possibly the individual He controls the most is Satan. Satan may be called the prince of this world, but the King is still King, and always will be. Remember Job? At the beginning of that book we eavesdrop on a conversation:

> "Then the Lord said to Satan, 'Have you considered my servant Job? There is no one on earth like him; he is blameless and upright, a man who fears God and shuns evil.'
> 'Does Job fear God for nothing?' Satan replied. 'Have you not put a hedge around him and his household and everything he has? You have blessed the work of his hands, so that his flocks and herds are spread throughout the land. But stretch out your hand and strike everything he has, and he will surely curse you to your face.'
> The Lord said to Satan, 'Very well, then, everything he has is in your hands, but on the man himself do not lay a finger.'" Job 1:8-12.

We think Satan did a job on Job (excuse me for that), but in reality God was always totally in control. God wanted to teach Job even more, and through His puppet, Satan, He did. Then He rewarded Job for passing the test with twice as much as everything he had before. Job's later life, due to those trials God allowed, became the epitome of righteousness. In fact, God Himself mentioned Job as one of His top three examples of righteousness. We see that in a statement God made in a passage in which God is talking to Ezekiel about sending judgment on Israel. In those verses Ezekiel says,

> "The word of the Lord came to me: 'Son of man, if a country sins against me by being unfaithful and I stretch out my hand against it to cut off its food supply and send a famine upon it and kill its men and their animals, even if these three - Noah, Daniel, and **Job** - were in it, they could save only themselves by their righteousness, declares the Sovereign Lord."
> Ezekiel 14:12-14.

And through all of the purification process Job endured that led to the attaining of that righteousness that put Job on God's top three list, God kept a tight rein on the hapless Satan. Nothing has changed. Satan is still God's puppet, a puppet that will be discarded before the final acts of God's plan play out.

As to the truth about the meanings of the Revelation images being hidden from some individuals and then seemingly lost for centuries, God is in charge of all of that, too. Satan may have thought he was winning some big skirmishes in his fantasy war against God when he whispered to some second and third century church "stars" and had them add or subtract from the Apostolic Oral Teaching, muddying the water, but God was watching closely. He knew what was going on, had seen it all in advance, and had planned it all. The intelligence of God is beyond anyone's comprehension, especially it would seem, Satan's.

So, when John Darby came out with an entirely new and different "school of thought" about the end times, do we think for a minute that God had let his guard down and Satan had finally landed a punch? Not on your life. It was all in God's master plan, thought up and put in motion at the creation of everything. When God spoke and there was a big bang, every single detail of the history of everything had all been planned out to the minutest part. God has left nothing to chance. And when you hear Darby's crazy ideas being preached in our churches, God's hand is in that as well.

I suppose it is natural for most of us to believe that even if we can't, those in the unseen world have the ability to see into the future. Unfortunately our perception of God is so limited that we truly don't envision how far superior He is to all of His creation. We tend to think, for instance, that angelic beings are just a few notches below Him, but the truth is that nothing at all is remotely comparable to the Creator of all. No words even come close to any semblance of a description of the Almighty God. There is a verse in Job that we might look at that pertains to Him:

*"He spreads out the northern skies over empty space; He suspends the earth over nothing."* Job 26:7.

A simple verse at first reading, but that simplicity flies out the window if we let our limited brainpower try to imagine what it is really telling us. There was God. That was it. There was nothing else at all. There wasn't even a vacuum for Him to be in. There was nothing. Period. Nothing but the same God Who is in control of everything today. At that time, He was it. God was the full extent of all that existed. But then, He thought. He decided. And it was done. *"He spread out the northern skies over empty space; He suspended the earth over nothing."* Only an entity that neither we nor the angels can even begin to comprehend could create from nothing. There are no words.

Yet we somehow kind of lump the whole unseen dimension together, including the angels and the demonic forces as being only a few pegs below God. Nothing is further from the truth. The individuals in the unseen world, like us in our world, have virtually no intelligence compared to The One Supreme Being, God.

And so it is with seeing into the future. Only God can do that. This is why I have harped over and over in all of my writing that this ability to see the future that only God has is the easiest and surest way to prove His existence. With over six thousand fulfilled Biblical prophecies to date, God has more than proved His existence. And if you are ever in a discussion with an atheist, this is the path you should trod. There is no rebuttal to it. I can attest to that from actual experience; both from conversions by atheists who either were readers I heard from or who I discussed God with face to face. Only God can predict the future with one hundred per cent accuracy. This truth is borne out by this:

"We are told in 1 Peter 1:12 that *'Even angels long to look into these things'* that have been told to us by those who preach the gospel. And then we find in Ephesians 3:10 an extremely interesting but unheralded scripture that says, '*... to the extent that now the manifold wisdom of God might be made known by the church to the principalities and powers in the heavenly places.*'

The *'principalities and powers'* referred to in that verse are angels. Notice how they now learn about *"the manifold wisdom of God."* It is *'by the church.'*

W.A. Criswell said, 'Just the idea of it is astonishing: that the angels in heaven are taught the manifold wisdom of God by the church. What an amazing discovery!'

So next Sunday, when you are in church, you can ponder the Biblical fact that there are angels sitting there with you, probably listening even more intently than you are. It truly is an amazing discovery."

From <u>Musings from Me and My Master</u>, by Bob Morley.

No, angels can not see the future. Satan can not see the future. And lowly demons, the souls of Nephilim, certainly can not see the future. Yes, they can read the Bible. That helps. But the allegory in Revelation is as treacherous a road for them to try to interpret as it is for normal men. When they were still alive before the flood we know that they were smarter than those around them in some ways, primarily in ways dealing with things that were wicked and evil. But as to demons being wise, we can see that they are far from it. Consider the following from an earlier book of mine:

"There is an episode in the life of Jesus that puts a grin on my face whenever I read it. You're probably familiar with the story. It is the one in which Jesus met a man who had been demon possessed and lived in the tombs. The man was such a mess that he lived naked and had been driven by the demons to live in solitary places. When he met Jesus he started shouting,

*'What do you want with me, Jesus, Son of the Most high God? I beg you, don't torture me!" For Jesus had commanded the evil spirit to come out of the man.'*
*Jesus asked him, "What is your name?"*
*"Legion," he replied, because many demons had gone into him. And they begged Him repeatedly not to order them into the abyss.*
*A large herd of pigs was feeding there on the hillside. The demons begged Jesus to let them go into them, and He gave them permission. When the demons came out of the man, they went into the pigs, and the herd rushed down the steep bank into the lake and was drowned.'* Luke 8:30-33.

So, why does that make me grin? Is it because Jesus played a joke on the demons? Kind of, but it is funnier than just that. Think for a moment with me. Obviously those pigs were in no way used by Jews. Pigs were disgusting in the Jewish culture. They would never eat them. They had no use for them. So, what were those pigs there for?

This is where searching out the matter can result in fun and surprises. The fact is that Jesus was in the region of the Gerasenes. This was not Jewish countryside. The people in that region worshiped idols made of wood and stone. And the way they worshiped these worthless gods was to sacrifice pigs to the idols. Yes, Jesus sent the demons into the lake, but at the same time He destroyed months and maybe years of pig production that was meant for the sacrifices to false gods. If it had been possible, I suppose some stone idols had pouty faces for a long time to come.

I'll bet Jesus had a grin on His face when He went to sleep that night. Talk about a practical joke! That one ranks as one of the best of all time."

From <u>Musings from Me and My Master</u>, by Bob Morley.

No, demons are not as brilliant as we might think. So, they peer into church windows and listen to sermons in the hope that someone has gotten a divine revelation. They want to plan for the "time of their lives," the time that will tell if they will even have future lives or instead will be totally destroyed. They want an edge going into the upcoming seven year tribulation period. And so they listen to our church for clues. That may be one of the reasons the end times in Revelation are presented so allegorically.

There are, however, some things in Revelation that are extremely apparent, and even the demons are aware of them. And they are plotting and planning, in the hope that their dark world, and their master, Satan, will be in control of end time events. We will see that in play in the next chapter.

# There are Two Sides to Everything

It took me a while after I was born again before I finally became a believer that demons actually did occasionally talk with people. I think deep down I still disliked even thinking about the dark side of the unseen world, so I concentrated on this earthly world or the more pleasant world in which the Father, Jesus, and the good angels resided. But I did believe every word in the Bible. So I had to believe there was a reason God commanded us to not communicate with the deceased, and it had to be because if we ever got an answer, it would probably not be our loved one talking, but a demon. In fact, let's look at a few verses that in the past I kind of skipped over, and maybe you have, too.

*"Do not turn to mediums or seek out spiritists, for you will be defiled by them. I am the Lord your God."* Leviticus 19:31.

*"A man or woman who is a medium or spiritist among you must be put to death."* Leviticus 20:27.

*"Let no one be found among you who sacrifices his son or daughter in the fire, who practices divination or sorcery, interprets omens, engages in witchcraft, or casts spells, or who is a medium or spiritist or who consults the dead. Anyone who does these things is detestable to the Lord."* Deuteronomy 18:10-12.

*"Saul died because he was unfaithful to the Lord; he did not keep the word of the Lord and even consulted a medium for guidance, and did not inquire of the Lord. So the Lord put him to death and turned the kingdom over to David son of Jesse."* 1 Chronicles 10:13-14.

*"He* (King Manasseh) *sacrificed his sons in the fire in the Valley of Ben Hinnom, practiced sorcery, divination and witchcraft, and consulted mediums and spiritists. He did much evil in the eyes of the Lord, provoking him to anger."* 2 Chronicles 33:6.

*"Satan himself masquerades as an angel of light. It is not surprising, then, if his servants masquerade as servants of righteousness. Their end will be what their actions deserve."*                        2 Corinthians 11:14-15.

*"The Spirit clearly says that in later times some will abandon the faith and follow deceiving spirits and things taught by demons."*     1 Timothy 4:1.

*"You cannot drink the cup of the Lord and the cup of demons too; you cannot have a part in both the Lord's table and the table of demons."*
<br>                                                                                    1 Corinthians 10:21.

*"The coming of the lawless one* (antichrist) *will be in accordance with the work of Satan displayed in all kinds of counterfeit miracles, signs and wonders, and in every sort of evil that deceives those who are perishing. They perish because they refused to love the truth and so be saved."*
<br>                                                                                     2 Thessalonians 2:9-10.

After a while I finally allowed myself to take off my blinders and truly come to grips with the fact that there really is a dark side of the unseen world, and it can and does occasionally come into play in our world. And the fact is that demons from that dark side do sometimes even talk with those in our world. Sometimes they even are so brash as to talk to Christians. The example of that fact that has stayed with me for years since I read it was a description of an event that happened in the life of Fred Stone, Perry Stone's Godly father and true giant of the faith. His account of it, from his early years as an evangelist, will stay with you forever:

"While I was away from home conducting revivals, Mom gave birth to a baby boy, Kenny Edgar, who was named after two of my brothers-in-law. When he was born, there didn't appear to be anything wrong with him. But when he was about six months old, he would often tremble and scream as he clutched his chest.

Doctors at Grace Hospital X-rayed him and checked everything they could possibly check. They could find nothing wrong with him, so they could not explain why he suffered like this every day.

By this time, Mom and Dad had moved to a larger, two bedroom house. When I came home from revivals, I usually slept on a cot in the corner of the second bedroom. During one visit home, Kenny had been crying from pain for quite a while, so I asked Mom if I could hold him and care for him while she and Dad tried to get some sleep.

Mom said, "Well, he does stop crying when you hold him. I don't understand that. As long as you are holding him, he won't cry. And if he is crying, he stops when you pick him up. He doesn't do that for anybody else."

I lay on the cot and held Kenny, patting him on the back. I prayed for him silently and asked the Lord to show me what was wrong with him. Suddenly, at the foot of my cot I saw a creature that was about four and a half feet tall. It was a battleship gray color, and even its teeth, hair, and fingernails were a dull gray. It had a vicious, ugly, perverse-looking face.

This creature snarled at the baby and thrust its hands toward Kenny. The fingers of this creature disappeared into Kenny's chest and, when they did, Kenny doubled up in pain. I was shocked when I realized that, in the spirit realm, I was seeing a demonic being. I rose up in bed and threw my hand toward the demon. I rebuked the demonic spirit in the name of Jesus and commanded it to leave the baby alone and to leave the house immediately.

When I spoke those words, the creature backed up three steps and threw his hands out toward the baby. By that time I was so angry that I was ready to lay the baby down and leap toward the demonic spirit. This creature said to me with a snarl, "I can't torment him while you're here. I can't get back in this house while you're here. But you're going to leave in three days. When you leave, I'll come back in this house and I'll torment this kid and do what I want to with him. And you won't be here to stop me." Then he vanished.

I was furious that a demonic spirit was able to torture my baby brother. All I could do was pray and ask the Lord what could be done to stop this.

During the night I had a dream. God showed me that my parents' lives were unclean. He spoke to me in the dream and said, "While your mother is fixing breakfast in the morning, I want you to tell your parents that I showed you what is wrong with Kenny Edgar. I will not allow this child to be raised up in a sinful environment. I want him to be raised right. I gave your parents this little boy to be a blessing to them and to care for them in their old age. But if they are not going to live for me, I will take him while he is a baby. Tell them that, if they do not repent, I will take this child home to be with me."

You can imagine how shook up I was. I was almost afraid to tell them what the Lord had spoken. Since they were not serving God, I had no idea how they would react. But the next morning during breakfast, I told them what happened the night before, and I told them about the dream and the message the Lord had spoken. "You need to repent now," I told them.

Dad cursed and said, "I can't live for God in this hellhole. Before it's over with, I might kill some of these moonshiners."

Mom said, "Well Fred, if your Dad can't live right, then I know I can't."

And that is the way I had to leave them three days later and go to my next revival.

About two weeks after that incident, I was preaching a revival and staying in the pastor's home. He received a phone call and said to me, "Brother Stone, come to the telephone. Brother McDonald from War is on the phone and your dad is there at the house. I think it has something to do with your little brother."

Sure enough, it was Dad on the phone, telling me that Kenny Edgar had died. I left the next day for the funeral. We buried him in a homemade casket on the Stone farm in Johnny Cake Hollow.

After Kenny's death, Mom was so distraught that she had a nervous breakdown. Dad suffered a permanent disability, and things became so bad in their lives that they finally realized God was the only solution to their problems. They repented; but by that time, it was too late for Kenny Edgar."

From <u>Fire on the Altar</u>, page 81-83, by Perry Fred Stone, Sr.

What a chilling, and for me, life altering, story. As an aside, did you notice God's requirement of the need for repentance and the absolute turning away from sin for Fred's parents? This was not an admonition from Biblical times. These were words from God given in my lifetime. That many of the leaders of our Church of Laodicea no longer emphasize true repentance as an essential requirement, as did the Church of Philadelphia or the earlier Church of Smyrna eras, saddens me greatly. By the way, I spent hundreds of hours listening to Fred Stone when he was alive, and his Godly son, Perry Stone, and I know both to be honorable and completely honest men of God. The above story is true.

Demons are not just something we theorize about. They are not an intellectual concept. They are real. They may not be brilliant, but they are mean, vicious, cunning creatures who hate you and me with everything that is in them. They abhor the true God and worship Satan, knowing that their only chance for ultimate survival is in helping their master do anything that can be done to try to prove the ending text of Revelation wrong and defeat God. They probably understand how hopeless their cause is, which makes them even more desperate and dangerous.

Instructional information our Almighty Father gave us says,

*"Every spirit that does not acknowledge Jesus is not from God. This is the spirit of the antichrist, which you have heard is coming."*     I John 4:3.

The spirits of every religion in the world are in this category, with the two striking exceptions being Christianity and Judaism. Judaism because we know there are over 333 prophecies in the Old Testament, the foundation of Judaism, that point to Christ's first coming, plus upwards of a thousand which point to His second coming. That the current Jews do not recognize that Jesus is that Messiah spoken of is due right now to the blinding of their eyes and the hardening of their hearts by God, which gave us gentiles the opportunity for salvation, too. For God's Word tells us:

*"I do not want you to be ignorant of this mystery, brothers and sisters, so that you may not be conceited: Israel has experienced a hardening in part until the full number of the Gentiles has come in, and in this way all Israel will be saved. As it is written:*

> *"The deliverer will come from Zion;*
> *he will turn godlessness away from Jacob.*
> *And this is my covenant with them*
> *when I take away their sins."*

*As far as the gospel is concerned, they are enemies for your sake; but as far as election is concerned, they are loved on account of the patriarchs, for God's gifts and his call are irrevocable. Just as you who were at one time disobedient to God have now received mercy as a result of their disobedience, so they too have now become disobedient in order that they too may now receive mercy as a result of God's mercy to you. For God has bound everyone over to disobedience so that he may have mercy on them all."* Romans 11:25-32.

Obviously, if all religions of the world, with the exception of Judaism and Christianity, are *"not from God"* because they *"do not acknowledge Jesus,"* they were formed by *"the spirit of the antichrist, which you have heard is coming,"* then Islam and New Age religion both fall into this category. They were both created by Satan. Yes, both New Age and Islam speak of Jesus as a prophet, but they both deny that He is God. Neither one *"acknowledge Jesus"* in the Biblical sense, as being God.

I imagine that Satan is quite pleased with himself because of both of those religions. But Satan must really love his New Age religion because he often gets to use absolute and direct demonic control over the individuals in New Age by having his demons converse directly with these gullible souls. But from those conversations we can get some clues as to the demonic planning that is going on these days.

In reality, the New Age movement consists of over 10,000 different groups who share several common beliefs. Although not an official organization, put together these 10,000 groups make up a religion, and they share the same "bibles," which are either The Aquarian Gospel of Jesus the Christ, My Truth, the Lord Himself, or My Peace, the Lord Himself.

About New Age, Dr. Chuck Missler summed up the religion quite well by saying:

"Although the New Age movement is a loose network of independent organizations, they share a number of common doctrines including: The belief in a central spirit being known as 'the source' or 'the God of Force.' The belief in the god within, the divinity of man, the law of rebirth (reincarnation), the belief that Jesus and the Christ consciousness are two separate entities and that the Christ is an office rather than a man.

They share a belief in evolution, the perfectability of man, the belief in the law of Avatars, which teaches that at the start of every new age the supreme being known as 'the Solar Logos' sends the Christ consciousness who overshadows a human being. This Avatar then imparts to the world 'new revelation' to help mankind through the coming new age.

New Age groups share the belief in the interconnectedness of all things, and many groups share a deep hatred of Judaism, Catholicism, and fundamental Christianity. Finally, they share the belief that Jesus, Buddha, Mohammed, and the great religious teachers of Earth are part of a hierarchy of 'Capital Masters' originating from an extraterrestrial environment.

The goals of the New Age movement can be summarized as follows: They share the goal of creating world peace through unification in a one-world spiritual system and a one-world government through a one-world leader of their choosing. Their covert goals are to abolish all systems based on the Bible."  <u>Alien Encounters</u> by Dr. Chuck Missler and Mark Eastman.

The anti-Christian goals of New Age have been a prominent part since its inception almost 150 years ago. One of the founders of the movement, Helena Blavatski (1836-1891), wrote in an early brochure in 1875 put out by her group, the Theosophical Society, that the goals of the society and the New Age movement were:

"To oppose the materialism of science and every form of dogmatic theology, especially the Christian, which the chiefs of the society regard as particularly pernicious; to make known among Western nations the long suppressed facts about Oriental religious philosophies, their ethics, chronology, esoterism, symbolism; to counteract, as far as possible, the efforts of missionaries to delude the so called 'Heathens' and 'Pagans' as to the real origins of Christianity."     Helena Blavatski.

In the past fifty years New Age has become more and more ingrained in the belief that UFO's are from other friendly solar systems and are inhabited by beings from other planets of far away stars who are our mentors and guides, and that these guides lead us toward perfection and fulfillment of "Earth Mother's" plan for our race and our planet though channeling messages that are given to us for our wellbeing.

Within New Age religion there are possibly thousands of people who may seem like the folks next door but who are involved with this channeling. Some of it is nonsense; they are probably "channeling" their own thoughts. However, some actually are channeling other beings who they think are from other planets. The truth I found in pouring over many, many transcripts of the messages was that the messages came directly from demons.

Part of what you are about to read is the result of some of the most troubling research hours I have ever spent on any subject. I really and truly hated doing it. I consider myself to be a strong Christian, and I believe that I have a very close walk with my Savior, but I was not immune to the effects of the communications I was reading. The darkness and evil that seemed to invade my office as I read these messages was almost unbearable. I knew without a shadow of a doubt that just by reading these communiqués I was putting myself in the presence of real living demons. I truly wanted to end the project several times but I felt that in order to competently explain this part of the puzzle to you I had to go on. But I will tell you that it was one of the more disturbing experiences of my life. The darkness and foreboding evil I encountered was indescribable. My only escape was to quickly leave my office at times and almost run to my normal place of intense prayer and get on my knees, into the presence of Jesus. A few moments with Him and I was cleansed anew, able to continue.

I will tell you, though, that I will never put myself in that position again. And, although I normally encourage readers to look up for themself anything that I write about, I strongly encourage you to take my word for my findings in these paragraphs. I urge you to not explore for yourself the myriad of writings that are available from these demonic creatures within published transcripts of channeling sessions. Had it not been for the strong feeling I had that it was important to discuss this subject with you, I would not have put myself that close to pure evil. Fortunately, you don't have to, because I will very briefly uncover what I found without having to expose you to such darkness.

As an aside, but in the same vein, allow me to once again warn you not to talk to your departed loved ones, as it can very easily lead you into unknowingly communicating with demons. As we saw earlier, God instructs us in Leviticus 19:31, *"Do not turn to mediums or seek out spiritualists, for you will be defiled by them. I am the Lord your God."* May I suggest that if you feel the desire to tell a departed loved one that you love them, or some bit of earthly news, ask Jesus while you are in prayer to pass along a message. I feel confident that He will. If you feel you need their advice, Jesus is the one to ask instead. He is the ultimate answer to any need you might have anyway.

Getting back to our subject, in my research I often found statements I thought to be absurd and even almost comical. For instance, a New Age channeler named Roberta Margerot channels a "guide" by the name of Songee, who starts out by saying, "Welcome to the sanctuary of the Holy Breath, the home of Songee, the energy of Earth Mother." To me, a line like that would be directly out of an old "B" movie. Obviously, though, thousands upon thousands of people are hoodwinked into such ridiculous tripe. In fact, sadly, New Age religion is the fastest growing religion of our day. Of course, with celebrities like Oprah Winfrey pushing it over the air waves, movies like Avatar sweeping the theater box offices, and our educational system condoning what seems to me to be a reverence for "Earth Mother," there are an inordinate amount of tentacles pulling in the unaware masses. Satan must be toasting himself every night over this New Age creation of his.

We can even find the New Age movement in what is thought of as Christian settings, even including churches. Consider Ebenezer Lutheran Church in San Francisco, in hosting their fifth annual Faith and Feminism Conference, had for the theme of the conference, "The Feminine Face of God/dess – Paradigm for justice and empowerment." Among the workshops being offered are:

Sacred Hiking with Kristen Hansen
Kundalini Yoga with Instructor Alison Newvine
Talking to Goddess, Powerful Voices from Many Traditions
Women Body Modifications as spirituality?   By Artist Sybil Erden
Drumming Circle - Drumming Priestess Dionne Kohler
Chanting with Musician and Isis Priestess Katie Ketchum
The Unconscious Mind by Design by Priestess Shmana Cea Heart

One of the participants in the conference, Loreon Vigne, who claims to be high priestess of Isis Oasis, said,

"I personally see Isis as Mother Nature, and that she encompasses everything with her wings. She's a winged goddess. She encompasses any other goddess from any culture. Guided meditation is where the audience closes their eyes and you take them on a little journey.  I've taken people to their past lives in Egypt, as [that culture] had all the secrets. They're the ones that knew. Their main concept is to know thyself, know thy heart, know thy soul and know thy purpose. It's kind of like a Ten Commandments, but all done in a positive concept. 'I shalt not kill,' [is rendered as] 'I honor all lives as sacred."

What these New Age converts are buying into is exciting to them, especially the channeling part, because they think it gives them answers from super intelligent beings as to where we came from and where we are going. For instance, New Age channeler and teacher, Jeana Lake, supposedly gives her readers the secrets of our beginning by quoting Theodore, a supposed extraterrestrial being that she is in constant contact with through channeling,

"Human beings did not evolve naturally on Earth; they evolved from genetic engineering of ape-like primates by beings visiting your Earth millions of years ago. These extraterrestrials were the first intelligent species to discover the Earth besides one former colony of extraterrestrials that had landed here and left when your extraterrestrial forefathers/mothers arrived. That extraterrestrials altered the DNA of certain primates on Earth to create the human species is understandably shocking, and yet, your scientists are beginning to play with that same technology - like father, like son."
The Extraterrestrial Vision by Jeana Lake.

And in another book, a New Age channeler relates even more about our supposed beginning from her guide, who she believes is an extraterrestrial from Pleiades,

"Where have you come from? Who are your creator parents? Who conceived you, then made you? The Sumerians understood the visitors from the stars, who for hundreds of thousands of years influenced and played with experiments of life on each continent.... Ancient myths and legends hundreds of thousands of years old tell of the serpents, dragons, and reptilian visitors from the skies. The reptilian race, or Lizzies as we affectionately call them, is an integral part of your ancestral line.... Understand that the reptilian energies are creator gods. They are master geneticists.... They were some of the prime instigators of putting together the human species on this planet."
Earth, Pleiadian Keys to the Living Library by Barbara Marcinaik.

I could go on and on with examples of this outlandish drivel. If you are like me, you must be wondering how in the world otherwise intelligent people could be lured into believing such ridiculous nonsense. The answer lies in what God said,

*"My people are destroyed from lack of knowledge."* Hosea 4:6.

New Agers might respond to our thinking by saying that the Bible has hard to believe passages a well. Unfortunately, they have never seen what we have seen, the reality we discussed earlier that the true God and Creator of everything unequivocally proved His existence, plus He proved the fact that the Bible is His true communication to mankind. God showed us these things by prophesying in over 6,000 verses future events that have already come to pass exactly as He said they would. That is the real test, fulfilled prophecy, and our God passed it with flying colors. Not once did He predict something that did not actually happen as He said it would, other than the over 2,000 prophecies that are still to come to pass in the end times. No other holy book, including the so called bibles of the New Agers, can lay hold to such a claim. None of them have even had one prophetic event come to pass. Not one. Our Father has an uninterrupted string of over 6,000 fulfilled prophecies. He told us,

*"I am God and there is none like Me. I make known the end from the beginning, from ancient times, what is still to come."* Isaiah 46:9-10.

God even threw out a challenge to any being that might try to usurp His divinity and power when He said,

*"Present your case,' the Lord God says. 'Bring forth your strong arguments,' the King of Jacob says. 'Let them declare to us what is going to take place; as for the former events, declare what they were, that we may consider them, and know their outcome; or announce to us what is coming. Declare the things that are going to come afterward, so that we may know that you are gods."* Isaiah 41:21-23, NASB.

These supposed extraterrestrial beings obviously can't take that challenge, but the New Agers don't even have a clue that fulfilled prophecy is the litmus test for proving who is God and who is not. As always, God was right when He said,

*"My people are destroyed from lack of knowledge."*            Hosea 4:6.

The sad fact is that millions and millions are being duped by the channeled demons of New Age religion. The important thing for our current study is what exactly the demons are saying that are being channeled right now. In my research I found that two distinct messages seem to be urgently given today by demons to the leaders of the New Age movement.

The first important message that the New Agers are getting in their channelings has been a consistent message for many years. That message is that the New Agers should be working hard to bring about a one world government. That is understandable because Satan knows that when he makes his big move and brings forth his antichrist, there needs to be a one world government for him to lead. Individual nations such as exist today would create a problem for the antichrist to overcome in his bid to control the minds and souls of the entire world population. Through channeling, the message is being delivered more strongly than ever that Satan's unsuspecting minions, the New Agers, must intensify their effort to push forward a one world agenda.

With major financial backing from such proponents as George Soros, the one world government movement does seem to be gaining steam. We even have heard a US Treasury Secretary talk about a global currency in a positive light, which would have been completely unthinkable to all previous people in his position. Just ponder how often globalization is being bandied around in the news these days by people like Al Gore, to business and political leaders. Globalization is no longer a dirty word. In fact, it seems to be an "in" word, even outside the circles of the elite.

The second dominant message to come through New Age channeling is that "Earth Mother" is having some extremely big problems right now. Vibrations from old time thinkers are creating a catastrophic crisis for her, and in order for "Earth Mother" to survive she must soon cleanse herself from the menace of these bad vibrations. As you might expect, the terrible vibrations that are causing "Earth Mother" such harm are emanating from one source, and one source alone, Christians. That's right; you and I are the problem. In order for "Earth Mother" to survive she must remove the Christians from planet Earth.

You will be pleased to find out that according to the entities being channeled, the cleansing will be a good thing not only for "Earth Mother," but also for us Christians who must be removed. New Age channeler and author, Kay Wheeler, who is more commonly known by her spiritual name, Ozmana, brings us this good news. She channels many beings she calls the "Souls of Light," who she has been told are a group of extraterrestrial beings from the "Seventh Celestial Plane of Life." Messages from these beings are similar to what multitudes of other channelers are hearing today,

"The Mother is desperately fighting for her life. Many of her vortexes have been drained. She is in critical condition at this time and must turn her thoughts to herself if she is to survive."     Ozmana.

And of the Christians on Earth, Ozmana says,

"Many of these beings have appointments to be removed at this time.... Your Earth is a fourth-dimensional being at this time. She has moved into this energy pattern, and those upon Earth who plan to stay must be of this vibration.... Many of the beings who must be removed from this planet at this time have completed that which they came to do. ... Do not feel sad about their leaving. They are going home. Many are waiting to be with them again... Many beings must move on, for their thought patterns are of the past. They hold on to these thoughts that keep Earth held back."     Ozmana.

Exactly the number of us who "have completed that which they came to do" seems up for question for these guides, but the number evidently is fairly significant. For instance, the estimate of the number of us who will be somehow removed was given to channeler John Price by his spirit guide, Asher, who told him that "over two billion people will be wiped off the face of the Earth during the coming cleansing."

It seems pretty obvious to me that Asher has read what we read about the Sixth Trumpet in Revelation which told us, *"And the four angels who had been kept ready for this very hour and day and month and year were released to kill a third of mankind."* Rev. 9:15.

As we saw, since we already have an earthly population of over seven billion, their two billion figure aligns well with the Sixth Trumpet verses. We can assume that the spiritual world of darkness is trying to get folks prepared to believe that the gigantic mortality figures that will be seen on earth from the sixth trumpet war plus the persecution of the Christians during the tribulation will only be a result of "Mother Earth" cleansing herself. The dark powers won't want people to even consider God in the equation when the death toll mounts.

Yes, all of what is to come is being portrayed as being quite necessary to save Mother Earth. And boy, is good old Mother Earth being played up a lot for our children in school. Don't be uninformed, the earth days, etc., are not pure and innocent. Evil is behind them. And it obviously is not only pushed in our schools. In fact, I recently was struck by something I saw in my morning Daytona Beach News-Journal newspaper. Here is what the article said, with the caption in big bold letters that read:

### "Write a Love Letter to the Earth"

Do you love the earth and all her fantastic wonders? If so, participate in writing a 'love letter to the earth.' People of all ages are asked to write letters (try to write your letter on recycled paper) of no more than one page to the Earth they love so much.

Mail letters to Washington Oaks Gardens State Park, 6400 N. Oceanshore Blvd, Palm Coast, FL 32137.

The "Love Letters to the Earth" will be displayed at the Friends of Washington Oaks Gardens State Park on April 21-22."

Ask yourself, how many of these innocent sounding things do you see? I'll bet it is a lot more than you know or pay attention to. If you are not seeing many, go into one of our public schools. I am telling you that our children are being indoctrinated by some of the brightest demons around, and virtually no one is paying attention. Nice little old Christian school teachers are involved in this evil and don't even have a clue that they are the hands of demons. Mother Earth and Father Satan!

What is so plain to me is that what we call New Age is nothing more than a method Satan is using to prepare the world for what he knows is coming. Just like Ashtar, Satan can read the Bible. He knows what is in the future. He has been quoting scripture for ages, like he did with Jesus while our Savior was in the wilderness for forty days immediately following His baptism by John the Baptist. Satan understands God's plan for the end times, but he is still an optimist. He still has hope that he can defeat God.

Satan must believe that times are drawing to a climax, and that if he has any chance to succeed he must get the world to move into a one-world government system, and he must come up with plausible explanations of the massive death and destruction of World War III, his coming persecution and eradication of the Christians, and the monumental natural disasters that Revelation says will occur so that the world population won't totally freak out and turn to God to save them. So far he has duped millions. How many more could he dupe with the signs and miracles that will be done by the false prophet and the antichrist as prophesied in Revelation?

If this is the first time you have ever been exposed to some of this, it might seem extremely bizarre and beyond the realm of belief. And you may well be totally skeptical of any or all of it, as I certainly was with my first exposure to any of this. My mind couldn't, or at least didn't want to, give any of it any credibility. I guess I could not grasp the idea of demons sitting around planning for the end times. Now, however, I see things more clearly.

There is a little book that I often recommend folks read that I will mention. It is the Christian classic, <u>The Screwtape Letters</u>. It is a lighthearted and fun little book written by C.S. Lewis about an imaginary middle management demon named Screwtape who writes letters to a rookie demon named Wormwood, who also happens to be his nephew, about how to proceed in keeping his "patient" away from God. The letters are sometimes hilarious, but in what Lewis is showing us there may well be more truth than we might suspect as regards to the goings on in the unseen world. Here is a quick tidbit from one of Screwtape's letters:

"My Dear Wormwood,

You mentioned in your last letter that your patient has continued to attend one church, and one only, since he was converted, and that he is not wholly pleased with it. May I ask what you are about? Why have I no report on the causes of his fidelity to the parish church? Do you realize that unless it is due to indifference it is a very bad thing? Surely you know that if a man can't be cured of churchgoing, the next best thing is to send him all over the neighborhood looking for the church that 'suits' him until he becomes a taster or connoisseur of churches." <u>The Screwtape Letters</u> by C.S. Lewis.

Unlike God, Satan can only be in one place at a time. As an aside, the place he probably is normally at is his home base, which was a few miles north west of Bergama, Turkey, the site of the ancient city of Pergamum, the location of the church that Jesus wrote His third letter to in Revelation, for He said of that church, *"I know where you live - where Satan has his throne."* Revelation 2:13.

It was in Pergamum that the great temple of the Egyptian gods Isis and/or Serapis was located, known today as the "Red Basilica." The beloved Apostle John ordained Saint Antipas as the first bishop of Pergamum, who in 92 AD was burned alive inside a Brazen Bull incense burner, which represented the bull god Apis and was called The Great Altar of Pergamon, believed to have been dedicated to Zeus. Kaiser Wilhelm II had that altar moved to Berlin, Germany, where it now sits in the Pergamon Museum. The base of this altar, however, remains on the upper part of the Acropolis in old Pergamum. There are intricate carvings on Satan's Throne of giants depicted as half human and half serpent. These are obviously the Nephilim.

The history of that altar after it arrived in Germany is quite interesting. Hitler's architect, Albert Speer, used the Pergamon Altar with Satan's Throne as the model for the Zeppelintribüne. The Führer's pulpit and the Pergamon Throne were in the center of the tribune, which was completed in 1937. Hitler would actually sit on this throne as he reviewed the troops at Zeppelin Field, and it was from this ancient throne that he began World War II in 1939. At the conclusion of World War II, the Soviets took the Pergamon Altar and Throne to Leningrad, Russia, in 1948 as spoils, the same year Israel became a nation. Satan's Throne was later returned to Germany in 1958. It seemed Kruschev was spooked by some strange paranormal anomalies around the "Throne."

Strangely enough, candidate Barak Obama was invited to Berlin in 2008 and was given a private audience at the Pergamon Altar. Then, incredibly, the stage set up for Barack Obama at the Democratic National Convention held back in August, 2008, in Denver Colorado was artistically designed based upon this very same Altar of Zeus. Interesting.

# John's Teaching

It is time to get into the meat of John's teaching that was given to him by our Lord, and then was passed down to Polycarp, Irenaeus, and Hippolytus. It is here that you will initially be shocked at how different our modern teaching of the end times is; but then your eyes, like mine, will be opened as to how much sense not only Revelation, but the entire Bible will make. You will see all of God's Word unfold for you as never before, and if the revelation of the simplicity of it affects you as it did me, it will give you a much greater understanding of the entirety of our future, which in turn will provide you with a true sense of calm and peace about that future. And I am talking about both your short term and your eternal future. All of a sudden, when everything clicks in your mind and you inwardly say "aha, I've got it," not only will a kind of serenity flood over you because for the first time you will truly *know* what lies ahead, but that future will almost fit like comfortable shoes; and you will be able to mentally relax in your Father's divine plan.

Cliff Claven, the mail man on the TV comedy, "Cheers," was absolutely correct in the last episode. Before his turn came, the others, Norm, Carla, and Sam had come up with profound things like friendship or love as being the meaning of life. Then Cliff spoke and announced that the true meaning of life is comfortable shoes. And ridiculous old Cliff may have stumbled onto something. It is the feeling that comfortable shoes bring when you slip them on; like the feeling you will get when John's teaching sinks in, a feeling that will cause you to inwardly purr "ahhhh" like a kitten.

When last we looked at John's teaching we delved into the meaning of the section of Revelation that talks about "The Woman and the Dragon." And we found out that the woman was the church and the dragon, of course, was Satan. We will now go into the next chapter, number thirteen, and learn the real truth about "The Beast out of the Sea" and "The beast out of the Earth." Let's read it:

*"And I saw a beast coming out of the sea. He had ten horns and seven heads, with ten crowns on his horns, and on each head a blasphemous name.*

*The beast I saw resembled a leopard, but had feet like those of a bear and a mouth like that of a lion. The dragon gave the beast his power and his throne and great authority. One of the heads of the beast seemed to have had a fatal wound, but the fatal wound had been healed. The whole world was astonished and followed the beast. Men worshiped the dragon because he had given authority to the beast, and they also worshiped the beast and asked, 'Who is like the beast? Who can make war against him?'*

*The beast was given a mouth to utter proud words and blasphemies and to exercise his authority for forty-two months. He opened his mouth to blaspheme God, and to slander his name and his dwelling place and those who live in heaven. He was given power to make war against the saints and to conquer them. And he was given authority over every tribe, people, language and nation. All inhabitants of the earth will worship the beast - all whose names have not been written in the book of life belonging to the Lamb that was slain from the creation of the world.*

*He who has an ear, let him hear.*

> *If anyone is to go into captivity,*
> *   into captivity he will go.*
> *If anyone is to be killed with the sword,*
> *   with the sword he will be killed.*

This calls for patient endurance and faithfulness on the part of the saints.
   Then I saw another beast, coming out of the earth. He had two horns like a lamb, but he spoke like a dragon. He exercised all the authority of the first beast on his behalf, and made the earth and its inhabitants worship the first beast, whose fatal wound had been healed. And he performed great and miraculous signs, even causing fire to come down from heaven to earth in full view of men. Because of the signs he was given power to do on behalf of the first beast, he deceived the inhabitants of the earth. He ordered them to set up an image in honor of the beast who was wounded by the sword and yet lived. He was given power to give breath to the image of the first beast, so that it could speak and cause all who refused to worship the image to be killed. He also forced everyone, small and great, rich and poor, free and slave, to receive a mark on his right hand or on his forehead, so that no one could buy or sell unless he had the mark, which is the name of the beast or the number of his name.

*This calls for wisdom. If anyone has insight, let him calculate the number of the beast, for it is man's number. His number is 666."*

Revelation 13:1-18.

It is here that we have been taught that the first beast in these verses is the antichrist, and he will receive a fatal wound and be miraculously brought back to life, and the second beast is the false prophet. But is that how Jesus explained it to John? We can find out by reading what Hippolytus said, as he starts out explaining the second beast and in that explanation goes back and explains the first beast:

"By the beast, then, coming up out of the earth, he means the kingdom of Antichrist; and by the two horns he means him and the false prophet after him. And in speaking of *'the horns being like a lamb,'* he means that he will make himself like the Son of God, and set himself forward as king. And the terms, *'he spake like a dragon,'* mean that he is a deceiver, and not truthful. And the words, *'he exercised all the power of the first beast before him, and caused the earth and them which dwell therein to worship the first beast, whose deadly wound was healed,'* signify that, after the manner of the law of Augustus, by whom the empire of Rome was established, he too will rule and govern, sanctioning everything by it, and taking greater glory to himself.

For this is the fourth beast (of Daniel 7:7), whose head was wounded and healed again, in its being broken up or even dishonored, and partitioned into four crowns; and he then (Antichrist) shall with knavish skill heal it, as it were, and restore it. For this is what is meant by the prophet when he says, *'He will give life unto the image, and the image of the beast will speak.'* For he will act with vigor again, and prove strong by reason of the laws established by him; and he will cause all those who will not worship the image of the beast to be put to death. Here the faith and the patience of the saints will appear, for he says: *'And he will cause all, both small and great, rich and poor, free and bond, to receive a mark in their right hand or in their forehead; that no man might buy or sell, save he that had the mark, the name of the beast, or the number of his name.'* For, being full of guile, and exalting himself against the servants of God, with the wish to afflict them and persecute them out of the world, because they give not glory to him, he will order incense-pans to be set up by all everywhere, that no man among the saints may be able to buy or sell without first sacrificing; for this is what is meant by the mark received upon the right hand. And the word—*'in their forehead'*--indicates that all are crowned, and put on a crown of fire, and not of life, but of death.

But now we shall speak of what is before us. For such measures will he, too, devise, seeking to afflict the saints in every way. For the prophet and apostle says: *'Here is wisdom, Let him that hath understanding count the number of the beast; for it is the number of a man, and his number is six hundred threescore and six.'* With respect to his name, it is not in our power to explain it exactly, as the blessed John understood it and **was instructed about it,** but only to give a conjectural account of it; for when he appears, the blessed one will show us what we seek to know."

Treatise on Christ and Antichrist, 49-50, Hippolytus.

Wow! There is a lot of information in what Hippolytus just told us. And we will examine it. First, however, did you notice in the last paragraph the phrase I put in bold print about John, that he "was instructed about it?" Obviously there was no one who could instruct the Apostle John about the meaning of the images in Revelation except Jesus. Once again I will reiterate that what we are reading from Irenaeus and Hippolytus that came to them in the Apostolic Oral Teaching is **the** definitive interpretation, because it was given to John by God Himself. Never, ever lose sight of that gigantically important fact. That being emphasized yet again, we can now dissect the meaning of those two beasts from Christ's standpoint.

The first beast, the one coming from the sea, is definitely not the antichrist because we learned that the antichrist is one of the horns on the second beast, the one coming from the earth. Boy, that sure throws a monkey wrench in everything we see and hear these days. I mean, seriously, how many chapters in the Left Behind series were taken up with the antichrist having a fatal head wound and then coming back to life? And what about the books and movies about the big image to the antichrist being made that speaks, and the world worshipping it or being killed? And how many dramatic scenes in end time movies revolve around those phenomenal events? Oh well, the Bourne movies and the Rocky movies have no basis in reality either, but we have enjoyed them for what they are. And that is what we have been dealing with as far as all the modern end time teaching is concerned. Fantasy. But it is time we start giving the same amount of credence to today's Revelation teaching as we do to any other fantasy. None.

All right, if the first beast isn't the antichrist, what is it. Since Hippolytus equates it to the fourth beast in Daniel we probably should examine that beast. In actuality, the chapter in which those four beasts are mentioned may well be the most informative chapter in the Bible pertaining to what will happen in the tribulation period, so in order to get the full impact of it we need to read it in its entirety. May I suggest you slow down your reading so as to fully comprehend what God is explaining to us:

*"In the first year of Belshazzar king of Babylon, Daniel had a dream, and visions passed through his mind as he was lying on his bed. He wrote down the substance of his dream.*

*Daniel said: 'In my vision at night I looked, and there before me were the four winds of heaven churning up the great sea. Four great beasts, each different from the others, came up out of the sea.*

*The first was like a lion, and it had the wings of an eagle. I watched until its wings were torn off and it was lifted from the ground so that it stood on two feet like a man, and the heart of a man was given to it.*

*And there before me was a second beast, which looked like a bear. It was raised up on one of its sides, and it had three ribs in its mouth between its teeth. It was told, "Get up and eat your fill of flesh!"*

*After that, I looked, and there before me was another beast, one that looked like a leopard. And on its back it had four wings like those of a bird. This beast had four heads, and it was given authority to rule.*

*After that, in my vision at night I looked, and there before me was a fourth beast—terrifying and frightening and very powerful. It had large iron teeth; it crushed and devoured its victims and trampled underfoot whatever was left. It was different from all the former beasts, and it had ten horns.*

*While I was thinking about the horns, there before me was another horn, a little one, which came up among them; and three of the first horns were uprooted before it. This horn had eyes like the eyes of a man and a mouth that spoke boastfully.*

*As I looked,*

*thrones were set in place, and the Ancient of Days took his seat. His clothing was as white as snow; the hair of his head was white like wool.*

*His throne was flaming with fire, and its wheels were all ablaze.*

*A river of fire was flowing, coming out from before him.*

*Thousands upon thousands attended him; ten thousand times ten thousand stood before him.*
*The court was seated, and the books were opened.*

*Then I continued to watch because of the boastful words the horn was speaking. I kept looking until the beast was slain and its body destroyed and thrown into the blazing fire. (The other beasts had been stripped of their authority, but were allowed to live for a period of time.)*
*In my vision at night I looked, and there before me was one like a son of man, coming with the clouds of heaven. He approached the Ancient of Days and was led into his presence. He was given authority, glory and sovereign power; all peoples, nations and men of every language worshiped him. His dominion is an everlasting dominion that will not pass away, and his kingdom is one that will never be destroyed.*

*The Interpretation of the Dream*
*I, Daniel, was troubled in spirit, and the visions that passed through my mind disturbed me. I approached one of those standing there and asked him the true meaning of all this.*
*So he told me and gave me the interpretation of these things: "The four great beasts are four kingdoms that will rise from the earth. But the saints of the Most High will receive the kingdom and will possess it forever—yes, for ever and ever."*
*Then I wanted to know the true meaning of the fourth beast, which was different from all the others and most terrifying, with its iron teeth and bronze claws—the beast that crushed and devoured its victims and trampled underfoot whatever was left. I also wanted to know about the ten horns on its head and about the other horn that came up, before which three of them fell—the horn that looked more imposing than the others and that had eyes and a mouth that spoke boastfully. As I watched, this horn was waging war against the **saints** and defeating them, until the Ancient of Days came and pronounced judgment in favor of the saints of the Most High, and the time came when they possessed the kingdom.*
*He gave me this explanation: "The fourth beast is a fourth kingdom that will appear on earth. It will be different from all the other kingdoms and will devour the whole earth, trampling it down and crushing it. The ten horns are ten kings who will come from this kingdom. After them another king will*

*arise, different from the earlier ones; he will subdue three kings. He will speak against the Most High and oppress his saints and try to change the set times and the laws. The saints will be handed over to him for a time, times and half a time.*

*But the court will sit, and his power will be taken away and completely destroyed forever. Then the sovereignty, power and greatness of the kingdoms under the whole heaven will be handed over to the saints, the people of the Most High. His kingdom will be an everlasting kingdom, and all rulers will worship and obey him."*

*This is the end of the matter. I, Daniel, was deeply troubled by my thoughts, and my face turned pale, but I kept the matter to myself."* Daniel 7.

First, Daniel says:

*"In my vision at night I looked, and there before me were the four winds of heaven churning up the great sea. Four great beasts, each different from the others, came up out of the sea."* Daniel 2:2.

Those four winds of heaven are the four spirits of God. They are the "Four Horseman of the Apocalypse" that Jesus released when He opened the first four seals the day He arrived in heaven after He ascended from earth. The four beasts are empires or kingdoms that will be on the earth after those four Horsemen are released.

Earlier in the book of Daniel, King Nebuchadnezzar had been troubled by a dream and Daniel was able to interpret it for him. Concerning that, God's Word tells us Daniel said to the king:

*"You looked, O king, and there before you stood a large statue—an enormous, dazzling statue, awesome in appearance. The head of the statue was made of pure gold, its chest and arms of silver, its belly and thighs of bronze, its legs of iron, its feet partly of iron and partly of baked clay."*
Daniel 2:31-33.

In the interpretation of that dream, the head of gold turns out to be the Assyrian or Babylonian Empire, the silver chest is the Medo-Persian Empire, the belly of bronze is the Greek empire, The legs of iron is the Roman Empire, and the toes are an empire in the future.

Some people think that this statue depicts the same thing as the four beasts, but that can not be because if we reread those verses the angel tells Daniel:

*"The four great beasts are four kingdoms that **will rise** from the earth."*
Daniel 7:17.

When Daniel was alive the Assyrian Empire was already alive and prospering. No, the four beasts are four entities that will exist at the time of the end. A popular theory holds that the first beast of a lion with wings of an eagle that were ripped off represent Great Britain and the United States, the second beast, the bear stands for Russia, the third beast of the leopard with a fowl on its back is Germany and France since Germany is often associated with the Leopard and France's symbol is a rooster, and the terrifying and frightening fourth beast is a coming one world government.

I could agree with those interpretations because they make sense, but even though they do, any interpretation is mere speculation. Nobody knows what the world will look like then, even if it is only a few years away. Remember, before that time the earth will have gone through World War III, the sixth trumpet, in which a third of the people of the world will have been destroyed. After such a war occurs, the landscape may have drastically changed. Israel may be the super power of that new world. And what about China or India? Who knows, the US may have been annihilated but Australia may have become a world leader after World War III. Or the South American nations may be the only ones not hit by devastating nuclear bombs. Or African nations. Or Canada may be one of the few thriving economies left in the world. The possibilities of the situation following a gigantic world wide nuclear war are endless.

There are way too many things that could have happened to be able to pinpoint today's governments as being those future beasts. Any Biblical scholar who tells you that he knows for sure is one you had better not pay attention to. Consider this, who would have thought that a mere fifty years after the devastating Civil War, the US would become such a world power as it became in World War I? Only God can predict the details of what he is telling us, and although some predictions may seem to make a whole lot of sense today, tomorrow they may be looked at as having been utterly ridiculous. I use to fall for this stuff, but no more. And the truth is that the exact details don't even matter, as long as we have the big picture, or as long as not knowing a specific detail could lead us down a path we should not go.

I will say that the United States being depicted by those wings on the lion in the first beast is a pleasant thought, because that would tell us that our nation would have survived the sixth trumpet war. And even more important, since we were told in the Daniel account of the four beasts that *"the other beasts had been stripped of their authority, but were allowed to live for a period of time,"* it would mean that we would be allowed to remain as a nation for a period of time after the forth beast was destroyed by God, which would mean into the coming Millennial Kingdom. We will explore that more fully later.

However, as much as I would like the above modern day interpretation to be correct for our nation's sake, we are still only dealing in total speculation, which is a fairly dangerous thing to do with regard to God's unfulfilled prophecies. As He has shown time and time again through His fulfilled prophecies, He is full of surprises.

What we do know for sure, however, is the truth from the Apostle John we read in the Hippolytus explanation, so let's get back to it. In speaking of the first beast that came from the sea, the Apostolic Oral Teaching as relayed to us by Hippolytus said in the first paragraph:

"And the words, 'he exercised all the power of the first beast before him, and caused the earth and them which dwell therein to worship the first beast, whose deadly wound was healed,' signify that, after the manner of the law of Augustus, by whom the empire of Rome was established, he too will rule and govern, sanctioning everything by it, and taking greater glory to himself."

So, what in the world did he mean by "after the manner of the law of Augustus, by whom the empire of Rome was established, he too will rule and govern, sanctioning everything by it, and taking greater glory to himself."

Writers say that Rome had an empire before it had an emperor. It had gone through various transitions from the city of the early kings to a republic. In January 27 B.C. the title "Augustus" was bestowed upon Octavian by the Roman Senate. Later in 27 B.C. he reformed the Praetorian Guard, once used to guard generals, in order to protect himself. The Praetorian Guard was made up of nine "cohorts" consisting each of 480 men. This personal body guard of about 4,500 soldiers gave Augustus clout no one had ever had in Rome. In 30 B.C. Augustus was granted powers of a tribune which gave him power and control over assemblies. After the death of Lepidus he received the title Pontifex Maximus (Chief Priest), which meant he then also had control over the state religion. Augustus had total control over everything. So with that statement Hippolytus is explaining to us that the antichrist will turn that new world governing body, the first beast, into a true dictatorship with himself in stern control of everything. Prior to that, it may have been something more closely resembling a confederation of sorts.

Next, Hippolytus wrote:

"For this is the fourth beast (of Daniel 7:7), whose head was wounded and healed again, in its being broken up or even dishonored, and partitioned into four crowns; and he then (Antichrist) shall with knavish skill heal it, as it were, and restore it. For this is what is meant by the prophet when he says, 'He will give life unto the image, and the image of the beast will speak.' For he will act with vigor again, and prove strong by reason of the laws established by him."

So, not only is the antichrist not the one with the fatal wound, but it will be the antichrist that will heal the wound, whatever that is, of the governmental confederation or organization he takes over. Again, we can't speculate as to details, but from what Hippolytus wrote, the organization had been in existence, but for some reason had been broken up into four separate parts. Maybe it had just become a useless organization prior to the sixth trumpet war, but then was seen as something that could help put the world back in order after such a calamity. At any rate, the antichrist will restore it, and obviously strengthen it mightily.

Now, here is another big difference I see between the truth from John and our normal modern fantasy. We keep hearing over and over how the antichrist will have an image of himself made, something like a great big statue, and the statue will miraculously start to actually speak. Sincere men behind hundreds of thousands of pulpits preach this without ever realizing not only how duped they have been, but how duped they are making their congregants. How sad. Yes, Revelation says, *"He will give life unto the image, and the image of the beast will speak,"* but we are shown that this just means that the antichrist will restore the governing body he takes over (think something like UN or League of Nations) not only back to what it had been, but make it such a force in the world that the world will truly pay attention to it. So, instead of the old advertisement that said, "When E.F. Hutton speaks, people listen," we will now have, "When XYZ governing body, headed up by the antichrist, speaks, the world will listen."

The first beast, we now know, is an organization that previously existed, and that evidently had fallen out of favor before the sixth trumpet. Maybe it will have just served out its usefulness. We don't know. But after World War III, things will have changed.

Our main reason for looking at the New Age religion was to see what was going on in the minds of the demons, and one of the main things was their focus on getting folks to establish a one world government and a one world religion that the antichrist could walk into and be the head of. The idea behind that, as currently proposed by the elitists of the world, does not carry that evil intent, and quite frankly, is a noble concept.

The thinking is that all wars throughout history have been caused by nation fighting against nation or religion fighting against religion. And in a nutshell, that is right. If everyone lived in the same nation, and if everyone held the same religious beliefs, wars would immediately end. Even wars that are economically motivated would stop. It makes very good sense, doesn't it? And thoughtful, noble people have pushed for it. Of course, also through the years there have been individuals and groups who have pushed the idea because with it they think they can gain power and wealth. Mankind can mess up the purest of things.

Although you may not know much about them because of their past secrecy, you probably have heard of groups such as the Bilderbergers, the Club of Rome, the Illuminati, the Freemasons, the Council on Foreign Relations, the Trilateral Committee, and others whose sole goal seems to be to gain control of the world by being in the hidden background of the establishment of a one world government. The same is true of more open concepts such as socialism, communism, and secular humanism.

And then there are individuals who on their own have been driving forces in pushing the one world government, or new world order agenda. Some folks like George Soros come from the monetary arena, whereas others like Mikhail Gorbachev come from the political side of things. And the lines can get pretty blurry. Gorbachev, for instance, is currently working with the Council on Foreign Relations, the Bilderbergers, and the Trilateral

Commission, plus he is a member of the Club of Rome, and quite naturally is a communist, having been a former dictator of the USSR and a lifelong member of the KGB.

In the past few decades numerous books and exposés have come out showing not only that the above organizations are extremely intertwined, but they are also based in the demonic realm. For example, the Freemasons and the Illuminati have been extremely close, with most 32nd and 33rd degree members also being members of the Illuminati, and up until just a few years ago the Freemasons incredibly published the New Age magazine. Wow! Due to the outing of upper degree Freemason satanic secrets, their membership, which was largely made up of unsuspecting regular folks, has dropped to about a third of what it was in 1980.

Although demons have put a lot of effort into getting the new world order established, the reluctance of the masses to give up their national sovereignties has been a big stumbling block. The demons have made big strides, but the closest they have come has been the United Nations, which so far is long way from an actual one world government. Following the massive destruction and the unbelievable loss of life of well over two billion people that will occur during World War III, the world's population may well say "enough is enough." They may be willing to finally give up their national sovereignty for the safety and security of the world peace they will then believe a one world government would bring about. And it will be at that point that an organization like the UN or something similar may be used as the chassis for the new world order. And a smooth talking upstart, likeable, politically attractive leader might be the obvious choice. Then we will see the appearance of the antichrist.

One thing I hope is coming through loud and clear is that the things in Revelation are not really as supernatural and spooky as we might have thought. Throughout history God has used the world as He created it to accomplish His purposes, and the same will be true with the future tribulation period, and as we will see, even beyond that. When God destroyed Sodom and Gomorrah with "fire and brimstone," it was with a volcano. When he punished the Israelites for worshipping idols, it was with the armies of the surrounding nations. I don't know about you, but not only does this make things much more understandable, but I am a lot more comfortable with it. Old comfortable shoes. Cliff Claven on "Cheers" was right. The meaning of life just may well be comfortable shoes.

Yes, it seems to me that in His incredible foresight God created everything He was going to need in the first chapter of Genesis for what Jesus called "this age". For instance, when God disbursed the Jews throughout the world as a punishment, He knew that it was only temporary. He knew, and He prophesied, that He would bring them back to the land He had promised to Abraham and his descendants. So, God needed to make sure the land would be available to them when the time was right. But did He have big strong angels with flaming swords stationed every ten feet around the borders? Maybe that would have been exciting for the movies, but instead, God held up the rain which caused the land to be such that no one could raise crops there. He made it the uninhabitable wasteland that Mark Twain encountered when he crossed it in the late 1890's. And when it was time to bring them back, God just let it start raining again. And so it has been with what we have seen thus far in the Revelation story. The antichrist won't be miraculously healed from a fatal head wound, and there won't be a towering statue of the antichrist that will mysteriously speak like a human, and that everyone must bow down to or be killed. So, let's see what else is true, and what has been only spectacular speculation.

Getting back to the scriptures, we read of the second beast:

*"Then I saw another beast, coming out of the earth. He had two horns like a lamb, but he spoke like a dragon. He exercised all the authority of the first beast on his behalf, and made the earth and its inhabitants worship the first beast, whose fatal wound had been healed."* Revelation 13:11-12.

The truth in the Apostolic Oral Teaching of these two verses was given to us by Hippolytus when he said:

"By the beast, then, coming up out of the earth, he means the kingdom of Antichrist; and by the two horns he means him and the false prophet after him. And in speaking of 'the horns being like a lamb,' he means that he will make himself like the Son of God, and set himself forward as king. And the terms, 'he spoke like a dragon,' mean that he is a deceiver, and not truthful."

Therefore, the antichrist is not the first beast but only one of the two horns of the second beast, with the other horn being the false prophet, the sidekick of the antichrist. And it is in those verses that we first see that the antichrist will try to set himself up as Jesus, the Son of God.

As an aside, we need to understand the words "sea" and "land" in the Bible. Sea often refers to the domain of Satan. The Canaanite word for sea is Yam, which was the Ugaritic god of chaos from the Canaanite religion which was worshipped in the day of Nimrod. That religion came down to Nimrod from before the flood, as we will discuss in a later chapter, and we know that it was the religion of the Nephilim. In that Ugaritic religion the gods cast out Yam from the heavenly mountain Sappan, and the serpent is frequently used to describe him. Yam's palace is in the abyss associated with the depths, or Biblical "tehwom," of the oceans. Yam wished to become the lord god in his place, and in Ugaritic texts we will later delve into, Yam's special enemy Hadad is also known as the "king of heaven" and the "first born son" of El, the supreme god, the father of humankind and all creatures and the husband of the goddess Asherah. Kind of spooky, isn't it?

Once we understand that, we can start seeing the truths contained in places like when God parted the sea so the Israelites could cross over, and Jesus calming the storm on the Sea of Galilee, and then even walking on it. These actual events are also shadows showing God's dominance of Satan and his satanic realm. There is so much to the Bible that completely blows me away the more I understand what is truly being told to us. In the end of Revelation, we learn something very interesting in what John writes:

*"Then I saw 'a new heaven and a new earth,' for the first heaven and the first earth had passed away, and there was no longer any **sea**."*
Revelation 21:1.

The meaning is obvious, once we understand what the "sea" in that verse is really talking about; in *"a new heaven and a new earth,"* Satan will be gone.

So when we see the first beast coming out of the *"sea,"* John is telling us that the first beast, the empire that the antichrist will control, comes from Satan.

As to the words "the land" or "the earth," they normally refer only to the land of Israel, what was once the combined land of Judah and Israel. It makes sense then, that this second beast would come from the earth, probably getting back to the fact that the antichrist will be Jewish from the tribe of Dan. This may also tell us that the false prophet will also be Jewish. Of course, that is just me speculating about that and not Hippolytus telling us that as the sure truth.

Hippolytus then went on to tell us of the antichrist, one of the horns of the second beast:

"this is what is meant by the prophet when he says, *'He will give life unto the image, and the image of the beast will speak.'* For he will act with vigor again, and prove strong by reason of the laws established by him; and he will cause all those who will not worship the image of the beast to be put to death. Here the faith and the patience of the saints will appear, for he says: *'And he will cause all, both small and great, rich and poor, free and bond, to receive a mark in their right hand or in their forehead; that no man might buy or sell, save he that had the mark, the name of the beast, or the number of his name.'* For, being full of guile, and exalting himself against the servants of God, with the wish to afflict them and persecute them out of the world, because they give not glory to him, he will order incense-pans to be set up by all everywhere, that no man among the saints may be able to buy or sell without first sacrificing; for this is what is meant by the mark received upon the right hand. And the word—*'in their forehead'*--indicates that all are crowned, and put on a crown of fire, and not of life, but of death."

Here we have another big difference from what we have been taught about the end times. We can see that Hippolytus says the antichrist will begin by trying to get folks to "worship" the first beast, the organization he will head up, but then the worship he is seeking will be of himself, which brings us to the truth about the well known and frightening "Mark of the Beast."

The truth is that the dreaded "Mark of the Beast" does not exist. The mark on the right hand only means "to worship" or "to offer sacrifices to," and to quote Hippolytus, "And the word, 'in their forehead,' indicates that all are crowned, and put on a crown of fire, and not of life, but of death."

In reality, the old Hebrew phase of "a mark on the right hand and forehead" basically meant "to worship in action and thought," with the right hand signifying action and the forehead signifying thought. Hippolytus' use of the phrase, incense-pans, by the way, refers to the pans or dishes incense was put in to burn during worship services. Occasionally priests would get burned on their hand while doing this, which may have been the origin of the "mark on the right hand."

But here we go again. I have actually seen a two hour presentation with pictures and graphs on how the mark of the beast will be microchips that people must have implanted beneath their skin that will be scanned before a person can buy anything. And naturally, anyone with a microchip will never be able to enter heaven.

We need to remember that folks in Biblical times had figures of speech just as we do today. A "mark" by a deity simply signified that the person worshipped that deity and had been accepted by the deity. The word "seal" was used in the same way. If you recall when we were looking at the fifth trumpet, the scorpions were told in Revelation 9:4 they could harm people, *"but only those people who did not have the* **seal of God on their foreheads.** *"* The seal of God was not a physical seal, just like the mark of the beast is not a physical mark or a physical thing at all. It just means that someone is a worshipper.

So don't worry about your children being tricked into "taking the mark of the beast" without understanding what it was, and then being excluded from heaven for all of eternity. Outlandish tales like this are based on a fantasy that is so far from reality as to be a real head scratcher when we learn the truth from John's teaching that was given to us in the Apostolic Oral Teaching. What we have been listening to that we thought was "Bible study" when we attended classes on Revelation were more closely related to studying old "B" class science fiction movies from the 1950's. The fact is that there was probably more truth and important information in the old Buck Rogers serials that played at the movies on Saturday afternoons years ago than there is in most of the "end times" study that passes as "Bible study" these days. What a gullible lot we humans are.

Another figure of speech used in Revelation that causes much needless conversation is found in Revelation 14:20, *"They were trampled in the winepress outside the city, and blood flowed out of the press, rising as high as the* **horses' bridles** *for a distance of 1,600 stadia."* Blood rising as high as a horses bridle simply meant a bloody battle or event. We run across that phrase in other places, such as the Book of Enoch, where it says (in XCIX, C.3) about another event, "And the horse shall walk up to the breast in the blood of sinners, and the chariot shall be submerged to its height." Once again, though, I have seen people go through hours of calculations trying to figure out how many people will die to fill 1,600 stadia (180 miles) with blood as high as a horses bridle, using the amount of blood in a normal person and guessing at the width of the path. The word "ridiculous" does not come close to describing today's Christian when it comes to such things. Can we not use some common sense anymore? "Raining dogs and cats" means a downpour of water, otherwise the poor dogs and cats would get hurt or killed when they hit the ground. And the mark of the beast is not a microchip implanted in unsuspecting innocent people who will then lose their salvation. Fortunately God has common sense, even if we humans don't.

As to the requirement for the buying or selling, everything we might say would just be speculation. I'm not saying that a person may not need to pledge allegiance in some way to the new world order run by the antichrist, or something like that, but there is no literal "Mark of the Beast." Of course, if you are a professed Christian during that time, you very well may not be allowed to buy or sell. You will be on a black list of some sort because the warning of the persecution of the saints is real. A Christian will not be welcomed around the antichrist. I have no doubt at all about that.

There is one more item brought up in the Revelation chapter about the two beasts. We are told that the number for the antichrist is 666. Pertaining to that, Hippolytus said,

"For such measures will he, too, devise, seeking to afflict the saints in every way. For the prophet and apostle says: *'Here is wisdom, Let him that hath understanding count the number of the beast; for it is the number of a man, and his number is six hundred threescore and six.'* With respect to his name, it is not in our power to explain it exactly, as the blessed John understood it and was instructed about it, but only to give a conjectural account of it; for when he appears, the blessed one will show us what we seek to know."                                                                Hippolytus.

Was that as refreshing for you as it was for me? Hippolytus followed his mentor's instruction to the letter. He was told to teach his students the words of God's Word and of the Apostolic Oral Teaching, and to go beyond that was heresy. So, since Hippolytus had not been told by either the scriptures or John's oral teaching what the number 666 meant, he did not give us a bunch of pure speculation. And we are to follow that example. Concerning that number, when it is time, "the blessed one will show us what we seek to know." So, when the next TV preacher starts giving you his guesswork on 666, you are now allowed to change the channel and watch that ball game you really wanted to see, or "Antiques Roadshow." See how much valuable time this book has already saved you.

Seriously, though, ascertaining the meaning of even fulfilled prophecies is not as easy a task as we might imagine. We sometimes wonder why the Jews did not recognize their Messiah when He came the first time. They literally had at least 333 prophecies to go by that foretold all sorts of things about the birth, life, message, death, and resurrection of Jesus. How in the world could they have been so uninformed as to not see that He was indeed the Savior they had waited so long for? It seems incredible. Incredible, that is, until we put ourselves in their shoes.

Sure, Bethlehem was mentioned in prophecy. That should have been a gigantic key. But so was Nazareth. Which one would He be born in? Or was either one to be His birth place? Maybe He would only live or teach in both. Or maybe His mother or father would come from one of them. The fact is that until the final piece to the puzzle is completed, nothing is truly as obvious as we may think.

Plus, God makes things even more difficult by spreading the prophecies around. For instance, in <u>Unlocking God's Secrets</u> I listed 332 prophecies that were fulfilled by Jesus. I did not discover the $333^{rd}$ one concerning how God had prophesied that His name would be Jesus until after that book was in print, and I later wrote about that one in <u>Musings from Me and My Master</u>. The point is that in checking those 333 prophecies I realized that they were spread out over twenty two of the thirty nine Old Testament books. If someone concentrated on one hundred of the prophecies, he might not realize that one of the other 233 prophetic scriptures in the other Biblical books he was not researching may have clarified the meaning of some of the hundred he was looking at in such a way as to completely change what he was expecting.

Earlier we examined some of the fulfilled end time prophecies concerning Israel, but I can assure you that as obvious as they are to us today, until 1948 when Israel became a nation again, being one hundred per cent sure of any of the things we looked at as being the actual fulfillment of a specific prophecy would have been impossible.

We also looked at the opening of the seals and the blowing of the first five trumpets and gave quite plausible fulfillment events that have already occurred. We even had Rabbi Samuel ben Judah's date of 1917 as being the beginning of the trumpets, which gives a lot of additional credibility to the events listed as being the actual events John saw in his vision. But are those events we talked about really the ones John saw? We can't be sure at all until the rest of the pieces to the end times puzzle are put in place. There could well be five more sequential events that occur twenty five years from now that might match even closer to what John saw in the first five trumpets. Quite honestly, although we were given Rabbi ben Judah's prophecy to give us a starting date, a prophecy that has been so uncannily accurate so far, the main reason I presented that scenario was to make the point that what is being taught today as being the gospel truth about the end times is just guesswork; and that the only thing we should take to the bank is what the Bible tells us, plus what the Apostle John passed on to Polycarp in the Apostolic Oral Teaching, because those are the only two things we can count on as being divinely inspired.

So, if correctly identifying specifics in prophecies that have already been fulfilled is that hard, can we even begin to realize how unbelievably difficult and unreliable it is to predict specifics about future prophecies. The Bible warns us,

*"Now listen, you who say, 'Today or tomorrow we will go to this or that city, spend a year there, carry on business and make money.' Why, you do not even know what will happen tomorrow."* James 4:13-14.

James is absolutely right. We don't even have a guaranteed understanding on our own "tomorrow." So, how can we see into the world's future with any semblance of accuracy? The answer is that we can't. Not without divine knowledge.

Even John's divine knowledge about what he wrote in Revelation does not help us with specifics. Evidently he only interpreted for Polycarp the big picture items; like the beasts, the antichrist, Mystery Babylon, the mark of the beast, etc. He did not get into specific events at all.

Today, however, every event of the end times is laid out for us as if there is absolute certainty as to how it will play out. We are told that the rapture will happen first. Then the seven year peace treaty between the antichrist and Israel. They tell us the antichrist will come from Europe and will head up a revised Roman Empire and that that empire most likely will be the European Union. And the list goes on and on and on, right down to how the microchips will be put under the skin of our right hands. We are told that New York will be Mystery Babylon, although there is some debate about that one. In most protestant teaching we learn that the Pope will be the antichrist, and how he will miraculously heal the fatal head wound of the antichrist and then build a giant statue of him that will begin to speak. Of course, in those same protestant churches we also find out that the Harlot on the Beast is the Catholic Church. Etc., etc., etc. As I said, the list goes on and on and on, in the minutest detail. Surely you know the drill. But as we have seen, all of those things we are taught are absolutely wrong.

And we learn all about the War of Gog and Magog because every Sunday School student needs to know that Russia is the head of that war time confederacy. The exception is what the few "scholars" say who are just as certain that the end time prophecies only deal with Israel. And these teachers have just as many details to awe us with as the revised Roman Empire teachers. They are just as confident, by the way, that Magog is Turkey.

As an aside, Russia being Magog was never even thought of until the Cold War. And interestingly, in studying that subject I came across the fact that two giants named Gog and Magog are the "patron saints" or "protectors" of the City of London and every year, on the second Saturday in November, they are paraded through the streets of the City. That's right; two satanic giants, Gog and Magog, are a big part of the annual Lord Mayor's Procession in the City of London. This parade is one of the oldest in the world, going back to the 13th century, but the giants Gog and Magog were not introduced until the reign of King Henry V, which was from 1413 to 1422. Back then, Gog was considered to be Satan and Magog was looked at as representing the giants of the Bible, the Nephilim. Those folks may have been more correct in their interpretation than we might imagine.

Yes, explaining specifics of unfilled prophecy is close to being a ludicrous endeavor. In doing so we will be more often wrong than right. Although I must say that we are all going to continue to do it. We humans are a curious lot. We wonder about the future. God made us that way. I doubt any animals have that trait. So, it is not wrong to speculate about how things might play out. But if we come up with what we think might happen, we should not teach it as if it were the gospel truth. And in our imagining things, we should at least start with the big picture that John taught Polycarp. The big problem today is that the church as a whole uses as a starting point a big picture that was invented by John Darby; a big picture that claims that the church will not even be part of the tribulation years because it will have been raptured before those years even start.

I will say, however, that if I sound sarcastic toward those who teach the fantasy that we are taught about the end times, I should apologize. It is the teaching I am critical of, not the teachers of it. They are only doing what they were taught to do. The teachers today were not taught, as Polycarp, Irenaeus and Hippolytus were, that to go beyond what the Bible and John's Apostolic Oral Teaching taught, would be heresy. So it is not today's teachers who are to blame, as much as it is the entire Christian interpretive system that encourages folks to try to come up with what looks to be the most plausible explanation for Biblical allegory, and to then teach it as if the ideas were actually fact. And this system has been in place since the time of the St. Augustine, who was the founder of this ridiculous system; a system which was taken to a new level by Darby.

So, if I offend any of today's teachers, I sincerely apologize. Please remember that I was once as guilty of teaching the same things, and even inventing possible scenarios myself, and teaching them without pointing out how speculative they were. I loved the Lord then, as I do now, and I honestly thought I was teaching the way I was suppose to. And I know that those who continue to teach such things today in that manner love Jesus, too, and are trying very hard to do the best they know how to serve Him. It is the teaching that is absurd, not the teachers. Their service to Jesus is to be commended.

At any rate, we will be going into more of what should be being taught; interpretation of allegory as explained to us by the Bible or the Apostolic Oral Teaching of John. And in doing that we will find out the much debated answer to the big question, "What really is Mystery Babylon?"

But first, let's visit the heavens.

# The Heavens

Since we all know that several end time prophecies deal with things happening in the heavens, I thought we might explore that subject briefly. Today was the day for me to begin typing regarding that topic. I sat down at my computer to get started and decided to first of all scan over some of the things that had come in my e-mail. Then a funny thing happened. Coincidently there were two very timely articles in the newsletters that I had received. When that type of thing happens I am always reminded of the saying, "A 'coincidence' is something that happens when God decides to remain anonymous." That statement being probably more insightful than we may think, I decided to share some of each of the articles with you.

The first comes from World Net Daily (WND). Of all the free "newsy" newsletters that I have subscribed to through the years, WND is by far the best. If you are not signed up for it, I highly recommend that you do. Whereas I believe that most of the news contributors today for most of the media outlets are whispered to by old Screwtape or one of his colleagues, I find that the WND contributors are Christian and their reporting is more factual than most. In other words, I trust WND far more than any of the completely secular media. So, that is my unsolicited advertisement for WND.

At any rate, one of the articles in WND today was written by Alex Newman and entitled, "What are the heavens telling us?" Quoting directly from that article:

"February was packed with celestial events – notably the meteor that exploded over Russia – and some theological leaders and experts are convinced that God is trying to send a message.

Citing biblical passages about signs and wonders in the heavens, more than a few have been talking about whether biblical prophecies in Scripture are being fulfilled.

One incident that received widespread coverage, for example, was a lightning bolt that struck St. Peter's Basilica just hours after Pope Benedict XVI announced his resignation.

The meteor that shook Russia, along with numerous other meteors documented over the last month, also have believers and non-believers alike wondering where this all may be going.

A seeming surge in recent UFO sightings, corresponding with a deluge of coverage in the media and the entertainment industry over the last few years, plays a role as well, experts told WND.

Rabbi Jonathan Cahn, author of the New York Times bestseller 'The Harbinger' as well as its DVD version, 'The Isaiah 9:10 Judgment,' the No. 1 faith video in the world, told WND he has been deluged with inquiries from people around the world as to what lies ahead.

'We know we're in the last days,' Cahn said. 'The signs are evident – Israel's return to the land, the world's focus on the Middle East, the increase in man's powers, including that of self-destruction, the increase in immorality and a massive worldwide apostasy.'

Cahn, who also serves as president of Hope of the World ministries and the senior pastor and messianic rabbi of the Jerusalem Center/Beth Israel in New Jersey, said the evidence is becoming clear.

'In addition, there are very precise signs of biblical warning and judgment which have been manifesting, particularly in America,' he warned.

'These signs, recorded in "The Harbinger," are distinct warnings given to a nation in defiance and departure from God. Thus, we're in a critical time of transition,' Cahn concluded. 'As we watch the spiritual and physical decline of America, it only further sets the stage for what the Bible foretells of the last days.'

### Signs and wonders in the Bible

As Bible readers know, there are numerous references to signs and wonders in the heavens found throughout Scripture.

Luke 21:25-26, for example, states: *'And there will be signs in sun and moon and stars, and on the earth distress of nations in perplexity because of the roaring of the sea and the waves, people fainting with fear and with foreboding of what is coming on the world. For the powers of the heavens will be shaken.'*

In the Old Testament, Joel 2:30-31 says: *'And I will show wonders in the heavens and in the earth, blood, and fire, and pillars of smoke. The sun shall be turned into darkness, and the moon into blood, before the great and the terrible day of the LORD come.'*

The book of Revelation is known for its numerous references to signs and wonders in the heavens preceding the end of days.

Many other prophecies in both the New and Old testaments contain similar passages.

### Russian meteor: A message from God?

On Feb. 15, the same day that a large asteroid passed some 18,000 miles from the Earth's surface, an unrelated explosion above the Chelyabinsk region of Russian released an estimated 500 kilotons of energy – the force of about 30 Hiroshima atomic bombs, according to news reports.

The impact was detected by sensors operated by the nuclear-watchdog International Monitoring System as far as Antarctica, over 9,000 miles away. Contrary to early reports of a meteor shower, Russian officials and scientists said the blast – the largest infrasound event recorded in history – was caused by a single 10,000-ton meteor burning up in the lower atmosphere.

After the massive explosion over the Ural Mountains region, at least 1,000 injuries were reported. Thousands of buildings were also reported damaged.

Despite the magnitude of the explosion, the event was not the first of its kind. More than a century ago, a suspected asteroid leveled almost 1,000 square miles of forest in remote Siberia in what eventually became known as the Tunguska event. Indeed, over the last 4,000 years, scientists say tens of thousands of meteorites have hit the earth.

Still, Russians were suspicious of the official explanation.

A poll of readers published by the Noviye Izvestia newspaper found that just half of respondents believed the government's account.

Some thought it was a UFO or an alien invasion, while others, including a Russian politician, claimed it was some sort of secret U.S. government weapon.

'Our people remember the Soviet past, when news of disasters was concealed or lied about,' Deputy Director Alexei Grazhdankin of the independent Moscow polling agency Levada Center told reporters. 'A lot of our people just prefer not to accept the safe explanations they were taught at school,' Grazhdankin added. 'Even when all necessary information is available, they don't want to believe it.'

Despite all the talk of UFOs, alien invasions and U.S. weapons, a Christian leader had a different explanation: The spectacular blast was a message from God.

The Russian Orthodox bishop of Chelyabinsk and Zlatoust, Metropolitan Feofan, urged locals 'not to lose the strength of will.' He added that the narrow escape from devastation should spark reflection on how often people pray, as well as a reassessment of people's lives through the prism of Scripture.

'The Holy Bible says that God sends us signs and warnings through natural calamities,' the Christian cleric said in a widely quoted statement. 'The meteor shower seen last night was a reminder for residents of the Urals and the rest of the world that we all live in a fragile and unpredictable world.'

'We must be happy that God has saved us from a more severe aftermath, and we must thank Him for this favor,' Metropolitan Feofan said.

'A natural phenomenon must not incite panic or despondency,' he concluded. 'No natural disaster, sickness or even death can separate us from God. The only real evil in the world is sin.'

The Orthodox bishop was hardly alone in seeing the hand of God behind the meteor.

### Other meteors dazzle

On Feb. 16, the Associated Press, citing state-run media outlets, reported that Cuba experienced a similar, albeit smaller, meteor that also shook buildings and left residents bewildered.

'On Tuesday we left home to fish around five in the afternoon, and around 8:00 we saw a light in the heavens and then a big ball of fire, bigger than the sun,' a local man said in the video cited by the AP.

A woman quoted in the report said her home "shook completely" and that she 'had never heard such a strange thing.'

Another major event happened over the skies of Southern California on Feb. 22, when a giant streak of light prompted dozens of eyewitness to file reports with the American Meteor Society.

Residents were apparently so concerned that government officials even responded to the event.

A few days before that, numerous witnesses reported a meteor over Florida's Eastern coast, according to press reports. Video of the event captured by startled onlookers was run by local media outlets.

'I was like, "Wow! That's weird," West Palm Beach resident Amanda Mayer, who obtained footage of the event, told the local NBC affiliate. 'I just started videotaping, and that's when it happened. I was pretty sure it was a meteor because of everything else that's been happening.'

Operations Manager Mike Hankey with the American Meteor Society told WND that he has been asked a lot recently about whether or not the number of meteors has been increasing.

However, it is a hard question to answer, particularly since the U.S. Department of Defense stopped sharing its data about the phenomena with scientists in 2008.

'The number of meteor sightings filed with the AMS has been increasing over the last few years and also the last few months,' Hankey said, adding, however, that this could be due to a number of factors unrelated to the actual frequency of events.

'At this point, we cannot in any way conclude that there is any real increase in fireball rates,' he explained. 'We can only conclude that more people are filling out reports on our site.'

AMS is currently working on a statistical analysis of the data to try to explain the increase, Hankey said, offering links to information provided by other experts.

Starting Feb. 1, however, when a bright fireball soared over the Dallas, Texas, area, NASA made some interesting conclusions.

'This month, some big space rocks have been hitting Earth's atmosphere,' Bill Cooke with NASA's Meteoroid Environment Office said on the agency's website. 'There have been five or six notable fireballs that might have dropped meteorites around the United States.'

What really has scientists and researches baffled, NASA said, is the extraordinary appearance and trajectory of the recent meteor events.

'These fireballs are particularly slow and penetrating,' explained meteor expert and University of Western Ontario physics Professor Peter Brown.

'They hit the top of the atmosphere moving slower than 15 kilometers per second, decelerate rapidly, and make it to within 50 kilometers of Earth's surface,' he added.

Senior Pastor Carl Gallups with Hickory Hammock Baptist Church, also a best-selling author and popular conservative talk-radio host, cautioned against drawing any biblical conclusions based on a particular incident or series of events.

'There is always a danger when we point to a specific thing and say that this is a definitive sign from God — especially some type of natural event,' the widely respect Christian leader told WND in a phone interview.

'However, it cannot be denied that we are living in biblically prophetic times – some of the major signs being the fulfillment of Daniel chapter 12; the increase in transportation and communication technology over the last days; the prophecies of Ezekiel 38 and 39; Israel being surrounded by enemies that are conspiring and plotting against them; the prophecy of Israel being restored to the land in the last days, which was fulfilled in 1948; the prophecy in Mathew 24:14 where Jesus declares that this Gospel of the Kingdom shall be preached to all the earth and then the end shall come,' Gallups said.

'When Jesus uttered those words, the Gospel had not yet been completed – He had not gone to the Cross, there was no empty tomb, the whole world had not been discovered, and the technology to take the Gospel to the whole world had not yet been invented,' he added. 'We're the only generation to see that fulfillment, so when you look at the clear biblical signs, then you add to it the seemingly increased activity of the heavenly signs and wonders, then you could certainly say that these might very well be harbingers of last-day prophetic events.'

Gallups noted that he would not consider the meteor in Russia, for example, as proof to the world that the end times have arrived—after all, meteors have always fallen. The same holds true for tsunamis and earthquakes, which have also been around throughout human history.

'On the other hand, Jesus said that the very last days would be accompanied by signs in the heavens and rumblings on the earth,' he explained. 'When you add all of these things together... I don't think it can be denied that we are getting very close to the return of the Lord.'

## Unidentified Flying Object sightings

Pastor Gallups also offered WND his thoughts on the UFO phenomenon, which appears to have become increasingly prominent in recent years and especially over the last few weeks.

In Mexico, which has become a hot spot for these types of events in recent years, at least two UFO sightings were documented in February over the Popocatepetl volcano outside of the capital.

On Feb. 21 at around 2 a.m., a 'cigar-shaped' UFO can be seen clearly in video footage posted online that is making waves among researchers.

Before that, on Feb. 7, multiple strange lights were also caught on camera over the same volcano.

Analysts and researchers dealing with the subject claimed that video shows UFOs as well.

Also during the month of February, the Huffington Post and other major media outlets tracked a number of seemingly credible UFO reports out of Oregon, Florida and even Australia.

The same day as the blast over Russia, for example, two residents of Grants Pass in Oregon caught what they believe was a UFO on camera.

'At first I was like what's wrong with that star? I thought, whoa, that's kind of trippy. So I went to get him and he's like "whoa! What is that?" And it started moving,' one of the residents who captured the event on camera, Heather Scherffius, was quoted as saying in major media reports.

Gregory Soldner, who also witnessed the event, was amazed as well – even though he does not believe in UFOs.

'It looked like a metal disk of some sort. I'm not sure, but it was metal and the way it moved was weird,' he said. 'I mean, I don't believe in flying saucers, but I've never seen anything quite like this.'

A local news station added a special light filter to the video footage, which helped reveal the bizarre phenomenon more clearly.

The Federal Aviation Administration said it was investigating the incident.

On Feb. 11, the Huffington Post and the International Business Times also reported an alleged UFO sighting over Melbourne, Australia, that was caught on video as well.

The bright lights in the sky are seen buzzing around and aligning in a variety of formations. At one point, one of the objects speeds off at a remarkable speed.

Countless other, similar reports around the world have emerged over the last few weeks.

UFO researchers say the vast majority have a simple explanation: birds, drones, airplanes, hot air balloons or natural phenomena. Many are hoaxes.

More than a few analysts believe government tests explain most, if not all, of the purported UFOs.

However, in recent years, the number of apparently unexplained UFO sightings documented by the mainstream media seems to have soared.

From Jerusalem and Moscow to Mexico City, Norway and all across China, the number of bizarre flying objects and celestial events dazzling witnesses without rational explanation is seemingly exploding.

The phenomenon has been getting quite a bit of attention in major media, too, with Fox News, CNN, and Russia Today offering coverage.

## Government also is taking notice.

In September of 2010, for instance, the United Nations appointed a so-called 'alien ambassador' to be charged with coordinating Earth's response to a potential encounter with extraterrestrial life.

The entertainment industry, meanwhile, has also been focusing a lot more attention on UFOs and fictional alien invasions, with more than a few major shows and movies in recent years dealing with the subject.

Some Christian leaders who spoke with WND are suspicious about the widespread, global interest in purported unexplained aerial phenomena.

Many suspect that, if real, the UFOs are not actually space craft operated by extraterrestrial beings, despite the media hype.

Instead, more than a few experts who have studied the matter say the UFO phenomenon is more likely inter-dimensional.

Some Christian researchers believe UFOs and supposed 'alien abductions' are related to demons and fallen angels – possibly a part of Satan's great deception foretold in the Scriptures.

In this line of thinking, authorities may try to deceive the public into believing absurdities and heresies related to UFOs and 'aliens.'

'I think these UFO appearances are demonically related,' Senior Pastor Gallups told WND, citing scientific and biblical research.

'Why would these supposed aliens come here for the sole purpose of performing so-called sexual experiments, kidnappings, possessions, and trashing the Gospel of Jesus Christ?' he wondered. 'Every time you talk to somebody who says they've had contact with an alien being, that's what it's about.'

Like virtually every Christian researcher who has studied the UFO phenomena, Gallups believes the devil is hard at work trying to deceive the nations.

'My estimation is that this is all part of the last days deceptions — the signs and wonders from the heavens,' he said, adding that Satan and the Anti-Christ would likely use the phenomenon as part of their effort to deceive the world with lies.

'I think the bottom line is that this is demonic,' continued Gallups, who served as a law enforcement officer and continues to serve on the Board of Regents for University of Mobile. 'The whole thing is demonic and we're watching an outpouring of demonic appearances, demonic manifestations, and demonic activity, because I think we're living in the last days. Without putting a date on what I mean by the last days, I think we're living in the last days,' he noted, echoing an increasingly widespread belief among Christians of all denominations. The only rational explanation is that this is a part of that demonic outpouring — that delusion, that deception of the last days, part of the signs and wonders in the heavens."

Other Christian experts in the field who spoke with WND had similar thoughts on the matter.

'These are signs preceding God's judgment of the world, as the Bible foretells,' said author Paradox Brown, who has written extensively on the issue, including two books, 'A Modern Guide to Demons and Fallen Angels' and 'The Bible, Physics, and the Abilities of Fallen Angels: The Alien Abduction Phenomenon.'

'The UFOs sightings and alien abduction reports today, in the case of paranormal events taking place, are being orchestrated by Satan and his fallen angels, as events leading up to this deception by Abaddon, as an Antichrist claiming to be humanity's god,' Brown told WND, citing multiple passages in Scripture.

'There is a strong delusion coming, and people best get right with God through Jesus Christ His Son now, before these events come to pass,' he concluded.

## More celestial events coming soon

As WND reported last month, there will be more events in the sky to watch for later this year, including Comet ISON, which is expected to pass near earth and put on spectacular heavenly show by autumn.

'While the world did not end with the end of the Mayan calendar last year, Comet ISON is considered by some to be another celestial sign of things to come,' wrote Koinonia Institute Executive Research Analyst Steve Elwart for WND, citing multiple passages from Scripture."

From "What are the heavens telling us?" by Alex Newman, WND.

Mr. Newman covered a lot of ground in that WND article, and interestingly he mentioned Comet ISON at the end. I say "interestingly" because the other e-mail that I received at the same time was another free newsletter I subscribe to from Tim McHyde, and this issue was entitled, "Comet ISON in 2013: Nibiru Doomsday or Omen of Christ's Return?" What a day for coincidences! So, to quote the beginning paragraphs from Mr. McHyde:

"If you have not heard much about the odd-named Comet "ISON" yet, you may become quite sick of it before 2013 is out. Comet C/2012 S1 (ISON) could become one of only ten comets in history to be visible during the daytime. It may even be as bright as the moon for a short time at its perihelion—or closest approach to the sun—on November 28, 2013 (Thanksgiving). After that, if the sun does not rip it apart (like it did to Comet Elenin in 2011), then it will swing back around and pass the earth in January, 2014.

Unlike much more common asteroids, comets are not made of metal or rock but of ice, dust and rocky material. The vaporization of the comet's dusty ice by the Sun is what gives comets their characteristic bright tails (or 'long hair' as the word comet or kometes means in Greek.)

As you can easily imagine, this comet is ripe for speculation. Comets already are viewed with suspicion, concern and fear among normal people due to their bright ominous appearance in the sky.

Comet ISON is expected to be at its brightest just one month before Christmas, 2013; one prophecy website has already suggested the following meaning of Comet ISON:

'Could this comet be the "sign" or "portent" of the glorious coming of the Messiah? This comet, if it lives up to its billing, certainly could point to the glorious soon coming of the Lord Jesus Christ from heaven!'

It does not help that the much-hyped four blood moons of 2014 and 2015 are happening so soon after Comet ISON passes. This will no doubt give some extra reason to speculate that this comet is a special sign or harbinger."     From "End Times Bible Prophecy" Newsletter, Tim McHyde.

## UFO's

One of the subjects brought up in the WND article that is also very closely related to New Age Religion was the UFO phenomenon. About half of the American population say they believe in UFO's. In the past I had definitely not been numbered in that population. But what about now? Have my beliefs changed? Before I get into my personal thoughts, even though thousands of books have been published on the subject, it is best that we examine the phenomenon at least briefly.

There have been numerous sightings worldwide that have been witnessed by over a thousand people at the same time. And in recent years these mass sightings have produced literally thousands and thousands of still photographs and videos. They have also attracted the attention of countless military and civil air traffic controllers. The numbers I have encountered in my research have been staggering to say the least.

Perhaps one of the most widely known occurrences in recent years in America happened in and around Phoenix, Arizona, on March 13, 1997. Even Governor Symington, the then governor of the state, was one of the eye witnesses of the event. The consensus was that the object was a huge V-shaped craft that, although it had lights in the front and rear, was somehow somewhat transparent. The striking thing to me about the episode is that it lasted for an incredible hour and forty six minutes. In that length of time, as you might expect, several thousand residents watched it, photographed it, and videotaped it. And as you can imagine, the story was later carried on ABC, NBC, CBS, and MSNBC.

In describing the object in the USA Today newspaper, the investigative reporter, Richard Price, wrote.

"Witnesses generally agree on three things. First, it was enormous. The most conservative estimate describes it as three football fields long. Computer analysis of the tapes puts it at 6,000 feet, or more than a mile. Second, it made no sound. Third, it moved slowly over Phoenix, cruising at 30 miles per hour. Several times it hovered in place in the sky."     R. Price.

Although, the US Air Force will not confirm, which seems typical in my research findings, it was common knowledge at the time that Luke Air Force base scrambled three F-16 Interceptors and it was when the jets approached that the object, according to one eye witness, "shot straight up and disappeared like a blink of an eye."

Interesting to me in reading the accounts of this almost two hour history of Arizona is the fact that of the hundreds of civilian reports that were filed, many were filed by scholarly university professors, respected business men and women, and professionals like doctors and lawyers. This was not one of those sightings that was reported by only Bubba and Wally after they claimed to have seen "something" as they stumbled out of Jimmy's Bar following a four hour exercise of throwing back pitchers of beer. And the reports from policemen and fire fighters can be found along with the above mentioned eyewitness report by the governor. It does make even a skeptic pause for a moment.

One of the things that got my attention in studying the entire UFO phenomenon for this section of this book was the number of reports that came from NASA. For example, Major Gordon Cooper, one of the original Mercury astronauts, reported numerous sightings during his distinguished career. His first sightings were in 1951 in West Germany while he was flying an F-86 Superjet. He said at that time that he saw several UFO's over a two day period that were metallic, saucer shaped, and flying at high altitudes. He also stated emphatically that they easily outmaneuvered his and other fighter jets. Six years later, Cooper and his colleagues actually photographed a "flying saucer" that landed near the base. The photograph and report were sent to his superiors for evaluation, but he never got a single reply.

Then in May, 1963, during his well documented 22 earth orbit Mercury flight, Cooper told the Australian tracking station that a glowing greenish UFO was approaching his space ship. The tracking station verified the object on their radar. NBC reported it as the event was actually taking place, but the press was not allowed to question Cooper about it upon his return. Years later, on July 14, 1978, Cooper met with the UN Secretary General, Kurt Waldheim, to encourage international research on the UFO phenomenon. Prior to Cooper's death in 2004, this heroic astronaut was still trying to get the government to release classified documents on the subject, but to no avail.

Gordon Cooper was not alone among the NASA community in his frustration with the secrecy of the US government regarding its knowledge. Respected Apollo astronaut Ed Mitchell stated in an interview in 1996, with Billy Cox, staff writer for Florida Today,

"The information is now being held by a body of semi- or quasi-private organizations that has spun off from the military organizations of the past. The dangerous part is that they're still operating under a black budget, which has been estimated at over $30 billion per year. And nobody knows what goes into black budgets. The prime requisite is security first and everything else second. Imagine an organization that has a black budget, an unquestionable amount of funds, reports to no one, and has the exotic technology that they can keep to themselves and play with."     Ed Mitchell.

Interestingly, Jimmy Carter, who himself filed two separate UFO sighting reports in 1969, prior to becoming governor of Georgia, stated while running for the presidency that he would get to the bottom of the UFO secrecy and open it up to the public. But after he became president, even he was thwarted in his efforts, and ended up leaving the White House without ever seeing the classified data or conclusions himself. It is still a point of contention and concern with him.

In my opinion one of the most hair raising statements to come out of the NASA community came from Dr. Brian O'Leary, an astronaut who received his Ph.D. in astronomy and since leaving NASA has served on the faculties of the University of California at Berkeley, Cornell, California Institute of Technology, and Princeton.

In a public statement on September 18, 1994, at the International Forum of New Science at Fort Collins, Colorado, Dr. O'Leary stated,

"For nearly fifty years the secrecy apparatus within the United States Government has kept from the public UFO and alien contact information.... We have contact with alien cultures.... The suppression of UFO and other extraterrestrial intelligence information for at least 47 years is probably being orchestrated by an elite band of men in the CIA, NSA, DIA, and their like. This small group appears able to keep these already-hard-to-believe secrets very well....Those who have investigated this hydra-headed beast believe that the Cosmic Watergate of UFO, alien, mind control, genetic engineering, free energy, anti-gravity propulsion, and other secrets will make Watergate or Irangate appear to be a kindergarten exercise." Dr. Brian O'Leary.

One person with senior insider knowledge has however opened up. Maurice Chatelain was the chief of NASA communications and as such was privy to everything that went on within NASA. In his book, Our Cosmic Ancestors, Chatelain opened up a can of worms by writing,

"All Apollo and Gemini flights were followed, both at a distance and sometimes also quite closely, by space vehicles of extraterrestrial origin - flying saucers, or UFO's, if you want to call them by that name. Every time it occurred the astronauts informed Mission Control, who then ordered absolute silence." From Our Cosmic Ancestors, by Maurice Chatelain.

Chatelain also spilled the beans in his book about NASA code names. He wrote,

"I think that Walter Schirra aboard Mercury 8 was the first of the Astronauts to use the code name 'Santa Claus' to indicate the presence of flying saucers next to space capsules. However, his announcements were barely noticed by the general public. It was a little different when James Lovell on board the Apollo command module came out from behind the moon and said for everybody to hear: 'PLEASE BE INFORMED THAT THERE IS A SANTA CLAUS." Maurice Chatelain.

Maurice Chatelain, moreover, backed up the claims made by another NASA insider, Otto Binder, who revealed NASA's policy of blocking sensitive transmissions by having them go through secret nonpublic frequencies. One of the most shocking of these was a message sent via this routing by Apollo 11 when it landed in the Sea of Tranquility on the moon. According to both Binder and Chatelain, the astronaut transmission sent in response to Mission Control's question concerning what they were seeing was,

"These babies are huge, Sir... enormous... Oh God, you wouldn't believe it! I'm telling you there are other space craft out there... lined up on the far side of the crater edge... they're on the moon watching us."

Please remember that the quotes I am giving you in this short examination are not from Bubba and Wally. These are trained scientists who are not prone to jump off the deep end with wild imaginations. And I could continue in this vein, filling page after page with quotes and documented reports of scores of similarly credible participants in this UFO mystery. But other than these accounts obviously lending credence to the fact that these things do exist, what are we learning about the unknown visitors?

In his excellently researched book, <u>Alien Encounters</u>, Dr. Chuck Missler wrote,

"UFO's have been tracked on radar traveling at over 25,000 miles per hour within our atmosphere. Yet unlike physical objects, they do not cause sonic booms and they do not burn up. They have been known to make right-angle turns at over 15,000 miles per hour, something no physical object could endure. And despite visual confirmation, UFO's often fail to show up on photographic film or radar devices."

<u>Alien Encounters</u>, by Dr. Chuck Missler.

Did we read that correctly? Is Dr. Missler stating that UFO's are not ordinary physical objects such as we might expect to come from a far off planet? Incredibly, the answer is yes. And he is far from alone. The vast majority of the truly credible researchers in the field hold the same view. These UFO's are not from outer space. They are from another dimension.

Dr. Missler continues,

"The bizarre physics of UFO's is further illustrated by the fact that many apparently reliable witnesses, including civilian and military pilots, have seen UFO's materialize and dematerialize instantaneously.... Furthermore, some have even reported metallic craft that change shape ('Morph'), breaking into multiple objects, or merge from multiple into one UFO."     Alien Encounters, by Dr. Chuck Missler.

Reliable examples of UFO characteristics that defy the physics of our universe are actually quite plentiful. One such illustration is shown on a video tape that scientists at the Atmospheric Sciences Department at Creighton University in Nebraska released. The footage shows the spherical UFO traveling at 1,860 miles per second, one hundredth of the speed of light, retaining its shape the entire time. Morris Pongratz, a scientist at Los Alamos National Laboratory, said of this particular UFO, "It is clearly something that does not have any mass; the angular speed is too fast to be anything at orbital velocity."

One of the best documented cases was a wave of UFO's that lasted an astonishing four months, from November, 1989 to March, 1990, in Belgium. It included over 26,000 sightings by policemen, civilians, military personnel, and NATO fighter pilots. As you might imagine the voluminous data on file is a plethora for true scientific researchers. Much of the data was gathered first hand by the military and scientists from the Belgium Society for the Study of Space Phenomena. Abnormally, the Belgium Minister of Defense authorized full cooperation between the military and scientific community.

The final nights of the wave, March 30 and 31 of 1990, were simultaneously tracked by two separate NATO radar installations and was meticulously detailed in the final report of Air Force Major Lambrechts of the Air Force General's staff in Brussels. The triangular objects were tracked by both radar installations and at one point were noted to change speed from 280 kilometers per hour to 1,800 kilometers per hour and drop from 3,000 meters altitude to 1,000 meters in only one second. That amounts to an acceleration of 40 G's, five times what a human could withstand in a G suit without blacking out. Astonishingly, the radar even tracked the objects dipping below ground level and reemerging seconds later, something no physical object could possibly do.

F-16s were sent out by the Air Force to engage the objects, and although they were unable to do so because of their inferior speed, they were able to lock onto the UFO's with their radar for over an hour. During this tracking, one UFO was observed to break into four separate parts that disappeared in four different directions. During the wave of UFO sightings, many credible eyewitnesses observed the triangular craft change shapes, materialize, and dematerialize.

Concerning this ability to materialize and dematerialize, researcher Brit Elders stated,

"Utilizing an Inovian PT53, which was specifically designed to analyze raw video data and is used for such by the U.S. Department of Defense, we have been able to determine that the objects have the ability to materialize or dematerialize in one frame of video, which is one-30th of a second. We have also learned that they appear to be solid objects, highly reflective. In short, they defy physics as we understand the term." Brit Elders.

Respected researcher Jacques Vallee stated further, after examining thousands of such cases on the subject,

"Consider what these sightings have in common. In each case the so-called spacecraft did not disappear by moving away, even at high speed. It simply vanished on the spot, or it slowly faded away like a Cheshire cat, sometimes leaving behind a whitish cloud, sometimes also producing the sound of an explosion. UFO's have been reported to enter the ground. I hardly need to point out that this behavior is contrary to what physical objects do." Jacques Vallee.

Vallee went on to say,

"I believe the UFO phenomena represents evidence for other dimensions beyond space-time; the UFO's may not come from ordinary space but from a multiverse which is all around us, and we have stubbornly refused to consider the disturbing reality in spite of the evidence available to us for centuries. ... I believe there is a system around us that transcends time and it transcends space. Other researchers have reached the same conclusion." Jacques Vallee.

## Branes, Worm Holes, and Israel

Of course, we Christians have always known there were other dimensions. We know them as the Spirit world, which includes at least two dimensions, heaven and hell. Science, however, with its new string theory is just now catching up to us. One of the ideas of string theory is that there are nine, now some say ten or eleven, parallel dimensions that those theorists call membranes, or branes. (As an aside, early rabbis are said to have discovered ten dimensions in the Torah, the first five books of the Old Testament.) According to this new mathematical and scientific theory, branes are flat universes, kind of like slices of bread in a loaf. In my book, Unlocking God's Secrets, I mentioned how that thought had helped to explain a Biblical verse that had always been a mystery to me. In that book I wrote:

"One phrase that mystified me is found in Hebrews, which says,

*'In the beginning, O Lord, You laid the foundations of the earth, and the heavens are the work of your hands. They will perish, but you remain; they will all wear out like a garment. You will roll them up like a robe; like a garment they will be changed. But You remain the same, and your years will never end.'* Hebrews 1:10-12.

What struck me so odd was the phrase, *'You will roll them up like a robe.'* It just didn't make sense to me at all. I knew there was universe in every direction from the earth. To me the entire universe must be like a ball. How in the world could God roll up the universe like a garment if it was a ball? It would have to be flat to do that. Can you see the problem I struggled with?

Now comes the hottest thing in science, string theory. It is only about fifteen years old and every new physicist and mathematician wants to specialize in it. Many string theory scientists believe it holds the answers to everything in the universe. It is the basis for all the popular Matrix movies, so it must be important stuff.

The basic thought of string theory is that everything taken to its base form is made up of energy that is in the shape of a string. The latest discovery in string theory physics is that these "strings" make up membranes, cleverly called 'branes'. These 'branes' can be infinitesimally small, or they can be gigantic. The newest suggestion coming out of 'brane' physics is that all of the universe exists on one 'brane,' a relatively flat surface, kind of like a piece of cloth, or would you believe, a 'robe'. If this theory is true, and scientists all seem to agree that it is, then God could truly roll the universe up like a robe. Some of the simplest statements in God's Word are turning out to be the most awesome."     From <u>Unlocking God's Secrets</u>, by Bob Morley.

Another part of string theory revolves around the notion that there are holes or access doors between these parallel universes. String theory scientists call these openings worm holes. If we Christians ponder such an idea, and believe it to be conceivable, we would likely come to the conclusion that the mother of all worm holes must be over the Biblical land of Israel. I mean, just think of all the things in the Bible that could be explained by the reality of a big opening between heaven and earth being directly over Israel. In speaking of these worm holes in my book I went on to say:

"String theory even talks about something it calls 'worm holes', which are actually tunnel like holes that exist between the parallel dimensions. In other words, these are tunnel like openings between the universes in which something could travel back and forth between the two. Does that sound to you like the tunnels constantly described by people who have had near death experiences. It does to me. It also sounds a lot like descriptions of things mentioned in the Bible, such as Jacob's ladder. I personally believe it all makes sense, and I also believe that there could well be the main 'worm hole' over Jerusalem. If so, that would explain so much that is in the Bible."
                      From <u>Unlocking God's Secrets</u>, by Bob Morley.

This idea of a tunnel or worm hole over Israel might even explain one of the strangest accounts in the Bible. Ezekiel tells us,

*"I looked and saw a windstorm coming out of the north - an immense cloud with flashing lightning and surrounded by brilliant light. The center of the fire looked like glowing metal."*              Ezekiel 1:4.

Could Ezekiel have been writing up his report on a UFO sighting? Quite frankly, I have never been satisfied by any of the myriad of commentaries I've read on this chapter by Biblical scholars. They always talk about the symbolism, which obviously is meaningful, but they never address what Ezekiel actually saw. He goes on to tell us about seeing four creatures. Each of these creatures was with a wheel. In fact, I'll let Ezekiel describe what he saw,

> "This was the appearance and structure of the wheels: they sparkled like chrysolite, and all four looked alike. Each appeared to be made like a wheel intersecting a wheel. As they moved, they would go in any one of the four directions the creatures faced, the wheels did not turn about as the creatures went. Their rims were high and awesome, and all four rims were full of eyes all around." Ezekiel 1:16-18.

I'll leave it to you to muse over whether Ezekiel could have seen what we refer to as a UFO.

Speaking of the area of Israel, though, even the modern history of that area is replete with reports of the clashing of our universe with what we think of as the spiritual dimension. Some of my most favorite stories come from occurrences in the Six Day War (1967) and the Yom Kippur War (1973).

In one instance five Israeli soldiers were on top of a hill overlooking a valley. Suddenly hundreds of Syrian soldiers appeared and stormed the hill. The five Israelis fired their rifles until each of them ran out of bullets. They waited for the onslaught that was to come, prepared to die for their country in hand to hand combat. Amazingly, just as the Syrian forces were almost to the top of the hill where the five had braced themselves, the hundreds of Syrian soldiers dropped their guns and fled. Later, when some of that Syrian company were captured by other Israeli troops, they all told the same story to their captors. They said they had run away because they saw "Father Abraham" in the sky above the five Israelis. Incidentally, the same thing happened in the Yom Kippur War with thousands of Egyptian soldiers.

That story is only one of hundreds of miracles that occurred in those two wars and it illustrates the point I was trying to make, that there does seem to be a fairly open doorway or tunnel over Israel into other dimensions. That being the case, it is fascinating to me that Israel may be the single hottest spot of UFO sightings in the entire world. And the forces behind the UFO's appearances in Israel seem to know exactly where they are. In fact, a journalist for the Jerusalem Report wrote, "Ufologists are at a loss to explain the lack of sightings in Israel's near neighbors - it is as if the aliens, unlike most earthlings, are aware of Israel's borders."

With Israel's fairly dense population, sightings are normally reported by hundreds, and many times thousands of eyewitnesses. Such was the case reported by the son of the deputy mayor of Eilat, Rafi Edri, who stated in his report,

"At 2:30 A.M., a group of fifty people stood and watched a UFO, like a giant tent full of lights, light up the sky over two residential districts. The UFO passed just over our heads at a height of not more that 100 to 200 meters. The event lasted close to ten minutes. Suddenly, without any advance warning, it disappeared." Edri.

In examining that particular mass sighting, Missler wrote,

"Other residents who observed the UFO stated that at first it was semicircle-shaped; afterward it split in two; then instantaneously disappeared. In a similar sighting in August 1996, the deputy editor of the local paper in Eilat reported an enormous red and purple boomerang-shaped UFO the size of 'half the city' which split in two, then floated above the city of Aqaba and disappeared above Jordan.

According to published reports, in September 1996, in the village of Netenya, an estimated 5,000 people were terrified when a UFO descended between a group of nearby buildings. That event was witnessed by numerous local officials including at least ten police and patrol cars.

On other occasions residents have reported disruptions of electrical appliances, burn marks on the ground, burnt out street lamps, 'crop circle' landing sites, cattle mutilations, close encounters with 'giant alien entities,' and yes, even alleged alien abductions."

<u>Alien Encounters</u> by Chuck Missler and Mark Eastman.

An interesting side note, though, to Jerusalem being the main "worm hole" to God's dimension is that the early people of Damascus had their own "worm hole." It was located atop what is, at 9,232 feet elevation, the highest mountain from the Euphrates in the north all the way south to Egypt and down to the center part of the Sinai peninsula. That mountain was Mount Hermon. It was the greatest of the sacred mountains of the Middle East and was considered the most holy mountain of the early Hittites, of all the Gentiles of Palestine, and even by the Greeks and Romans, for even in the Greek and Roman periods Mount Hermon's sanctity was recognized as the central worship of **all** the Gods of the world, no matter who they were.

At the bottom of Mount Hermon on the southwest side was a place called Panias by the Greeks after the time of Alexander the Great. It is the modern day, Banias, which was Caesarea Philippi in New Testament times. This place was devoted "to ALL the Gods of the whole world." In fact, the word "Panias" at the foot of Mount Hermon in Greek meant that the place was devoted as a divine sanctuary to "All the Gods." On the northeast section of this "divine mountain" was the principal city of the area, Damascus, whose people in ancient times looked directly toward their Mount Hermon as the center place of their religious beliefs, and it was believed by most early peoples on earth to be the most important of all mountains in the world.

The Book of Enoch tells us that when the *"Sons of God"* came to earth and had sex with the daughters of men, the place they entered into the earth's environment was at the top of Mount Hermon. Let's read it again,

"And it came to pass when the children of men had multiplied that in those days were born unto them beautiful and comely daughters. And the angels, the children of the heaven, saw and lusted after them, and said to one another: 'Come, let us choose us wives from among the children of men and beget us children.' And Semjaza, who was their leader, said unto them: 'I fear ye will not indeed agree to do this deed, and I alone shall have to pay the penalty of a great sin.' And they all answered him and said: 'Let us all swear an oath, and all bind ourselves by mutual imprecations not to abandon this plan but to do this thing.' Then swore they all together and bound themselves by mutual imprecations upon it. And they were in all two hundred; who descended in the days of Jared on the summit of **Mount Hermon**."

From Book of Enoch, Chapter 6:1-6.

This incident was thought by early people as meaning that the "Gate to Heaven" where divine beings could come to earth or return to heaven was at the top of Mount Hermon. This is why it became a "holy place" for all people on earth. (Although a few people have mentioned it as being the sight of the mountain where Jesus was transfigured, primarily due to its height, that is highly unlikely because it is so far from Jerusalem where Jesus was then.)

This means that Mount Hermon was considered an entrance to the heavenly domain even before the Tower of Babel was built by Nimrod, who we earlier learned was a Nephilim. We know that the Tower of Babel happened in the land of Shinar for we read:

*"Now the whole world had one language and a common speech. As people moved eastward, they found a plain in Shinar and settled there."*
(Genesis 11:1-9).

And, when God destroyed the influence of the "Tower of Babel" in Shinar, some people simply focused again their attention back to Mount Hermon as the holiest place on earth, and they made a connection with it to the "Tower of Babel" for the Bible says, *"Hermon is called Sirion by the Sidonians; the Amorites call it Senir."* calling it "Senir," a variant of "Shinar." Deuteronomy 3:9. So, the main group of Amorites simply used a variant of "Shinar" to religiously connect Hermon to Babylon and its Tower.

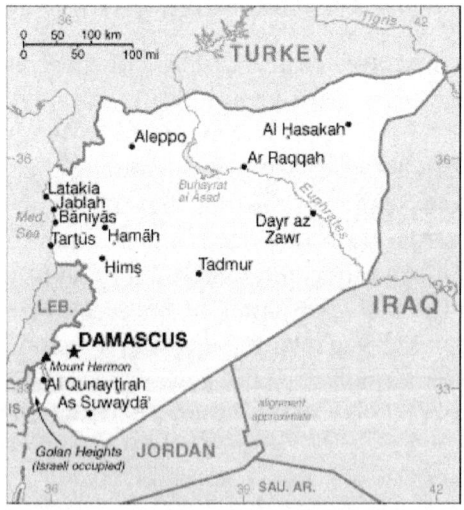

Above we can see how close Damascus is to Mount Harmon, and we are reminded of God's Word concerning the end time:

*"See, Damascus will no longer be a city*
 *but will become a heap of ruins."*  Isaiah 17:1.

Could it be that God will plug up that "worm hole;" a "worm hole" that evidently was an entrance to the dark dimension?

We know so little about the other dimensions.

## Abductions?

The word abductions was mentioned in that last quote by Chuck Missler, and although we do not have the vast amount of corroborated evidence, radar tracking, photographs, and video tapes, like we do with UFO sightings, we probably need to at least broach the subject somewhat.

You have probably surmised if you have read much of my writing that I am most comfortable with Biblical topics because I believe that rationally and logically I have indisputably proven both to myself and to the readers of both <u>Wonder No More</u> and <u>Unlocking God's Secrets</u> that God did in fact write every single word of our Bible. Likewise I am comfortable in making points on a topic when I have the back up of numerous quotes by credible people such as we discussed in the conversation of UFO's. In that section I was able to supply direct quotes from a myriad of scientists of note as well as NASA professionals like Gordon Cooper, Ed Mitchell, Dr. Brian O'Leary, Maurice Chatelain, etc.

The subject of alien abductions, however, does not lend itself to such unquestionable expert back up. By its very nature, alleged abductions are solitary events that must rely on hearsay from individuals. There are very rarely eyewitness accounts to what abductees say. That being said, I feel that I am a fairly well-grounded person who is not prone to flights of fancy in my thinking, and at age 68 my past life experiences help me from being as easily duped as I might have been in my younger years. Therefore, let's proceed with caution into this unusual area of study.

One thing I think that can be helpful is good, old fashioned, common sense. And in that regard, one statistic jumps out at me. Fully three percent of the population claims to have experienced an alien abduction. In America, that would amount to about nine million people. Common sense tells me that out of nine million people, some of them have got to be reliable, sane, intelligent individuals who have actually experienced something. This same common sense has led noted scientists to truly delve into this phenomenon that seems to go hand in hand with any UFO research.

In this light, a rather large scientific conference specifically to study alien abductions was recently hosted by and held at the prestigious Massachusetts Institute of Technology (MIT). Additionally, along with MIT, the distinctive body was hosted by Dr. John Mack, M.D., a cum laude graduate of Harvard Medical School, and head of the department of psychiatry at Cambridge Hospital, and author of over 150 peer reviewed scientific papers, as well as winner of the Pulitzer Prize, and MIT physicist David E. Pritchard. In attendance were scientific abduction researchers like Budd Hopkins and John Carpenter. According to C.D.B. Bryan, in discussing the individuals examined at this conference,

"... hundreds of individuals who, uncontaminated by exposure to any previous unidentified flying object lore or to each other, have so hesitatingly, reluctantly, timidly came forward with their utterly incredible accounts of having been abducted and examined in UFO's ..."  C.D.B. Bryan.

At this point I could quote Hundreds of reports from seemingly normal citizens who have been examined by individual researchers or at the MIT conference, but instead, since invariably the accounts are all extremely similar, I will just summarize what the participants, almost to a person, describe concerning what transpires during these UFO abductions.

First, the abductee describes being levitated into the spacecraft. During the entire encounter they are normally fully aware of what is happening, but cannot do anything about it. They cannot speak but are communicated with by their abductors through telepathic means. Then, almost unanimously the description becomes sexual or reproductive in nature. Men tell of embarrassing and intrusive examinations of their more private parts, as well as the harvesting of seed, and women relate similar procedures as well as forced sexual relations, followed by a second future abduction which includes the retrieval of an embryo. My mind, of course, flashes back to,

*"The Nephilim were on the earth in those days - and also afterward - when the sons of God went to the daughters of men and had children by them."*  Genesis 6:4.

Dr. John Mack, M.D., one of the hosts of the MIT conference, after studying thousands of abduction cases wrote:

"The idea that men, women, and children can be taken against their wills, from their homes, cars, and school yards by strange humanoid beings, lifted onto spacecraft, and subjected to intrusive and threatening procedures is so terrifying and yet so shattering to our notions of what is possible in our universe, that the actuality of the phenomenon has been largely rejected out of hand or bizarrely distorted in most media accounts. This is altogether understandable, given the disturbing nature of UFO abductions and our prevailing notions of reality. The fact remains, however, that for thirty years, and possibly longer, thousands of individuals who seem to be sincere and of sound mind and are seeking no personal benefit from their stories have been providing to those who will listen consistent reports of precisely such events."

John Mack, M.D., Forward to <u>Secret of Life</u> by David M. Jacobs.

In his own book on the subject, Dr. Mack gives his opinion on what is going on,

"The alien beings that appear to come to us from the sky in strange spacecraft ... seem to partake of properties belonging to both the spirit and the material worlds, bridging, as if effortlessly the division between these realms which have become increasingly sacred and unbreachable since science and religion went their separate ways in the 17th century. On the one hand these beings seem able to be seen by the abductees, who feel their bodies moved and find small lesions inflicted upon them. On the other hand these beings seem to come, like intermediaries from God or the devil, from a no embodied source, and they are able to open the consciousness of abductees to realms of being that do not exist in the physical world as we know it." <u>Abductions</u> by John Mack, M. D.

Interesting to me is the fact that in many of the reports the subjects state that they had the feeling that the new "realms of being" that Dr. Mack referred to seemed at the time to be "more real" than our normal physical world. Is the spiritual world "more real" than the world we live in? Quite frankly, my sense from God's Word is that that truly is the case. At any rate, the secular Dr. Mack continues,

"My own impression is that we may be witnessing something far more complex, namely an awkward joining of two species, engineered by an intelligence we are unable to fathom ..." <u>Abductions</u> by Dr. John Mack, M.D.

Noted researcher, Budd Hopkins, who has studied over 300,000 abduction cases writes,

"And what is the ultimate purpose of these abductions, these examinations and implants, these genetic attempts to produce hybrids, which have inevitably created emotional havoc among many innocent people?"
<u>Intruders</u> by Budd Hopkins.

"Everything I have learned in twenty years of research into the UFO abduction phenomenon leads me to conclude that the alien's central purpose ... points to their being here to carry out a complex breeding experiment in which they seem to be working to create a hybrid species, a mix of human and alien characteristics." <u>Witnessed</u> by Budd Hopkins.

The researchers all seem to be coming up with the same conclusions, including Jacques Vallee, who stated in his book, <u>Forbidden Science</u>, "The abduction experience, in my opinion, is real, traumatic and very complex." If they are correct, that the abductions do indeed happen, their problem in trying to figure out what to make of the event stems from their lack of knowledge of actual past events that are chronicled in God's Word. And, of course, the prophecy made by Jesus Himself of his second coming,

*"As it was in the days of Noah, so it will be at the coming of the Son of Man."* Matthew 24:37.

However, at this juncture we are still,

*"Looking through a glass, darkly."* 1 Corinthians 13:12.

I mentioned at the beginning of this section pertaining to UFO's that I would give you my current personal thoughts on the subject. As I told you, I started out my research as a complete and total unbeliever in any of it. I was convinced it was all totally loony.

As you may have guessed, I spend a whole lot of time in research prior to typing a single word of a book. And because of my initial high level of skepticism in this subject, I did what even for me was an abnormal amount of research. The result was that I could have filled several books with nothing but quotes from people who I deemed to be highly credible and sane. I discarded all of the "Wally and Bubba" stuff and concentrated on the likes of the people I quoted for you in the above discussion. To a man, they were all highly recognized and extremely credible leaders in their fields of study, or in the case of the astronauts, their occupation. And the quotes I gave you only scratched the surface of what I discovered.

The end result is that I now do indeed believe UFO's are real, and I truly believe they are demonic. I also do believe that abductions have been taking place. And I believe they may well have something to do with the breeding of Nephilim. Beyond that, I am at a loss to even guess what the future holds in regard to these things. Your ideas would be just as good as mine, so I will leave it to you to make your own conclusions as to the possibilities.

As to the overall message of this chapter, we do know that the Bible tells us that there will be things happening in the heavens in the end times:

> *"I will show wonders in the heavens and on the earth,*
> *blood and fire and billows of smoke.*
> *The sun will be turned to darkness and the moon to blood before*
> *the coming of the great and dreadful day of the Lord."*     Joel 2:30-31.

> *"There will be signs in the sun, moon and stars. On the earth, nations will be in anguish and perplexity at the roaring and tossing of the sea. People will faint from terror, apprehensive of what is coming on the world, for the heavenly bodies will be shaken."*     Luke 21:25-26.

Whether or not the seeming uptick in such things as meteors, lights, UFO's, etc., have anything to do with those Biblical prophecies, we don't know. And we won't know until the final pieces of the puzzle are put in place. I will say that the latest statistics on UFO reporting did seem quite unusual. For instance, the National UFO Reporting Center recently stated,

"Beginning in mid-June of 2012, the volume of seemingly credible reports rose dramatically, for reasons that we still do not understand."

And the United Nations UFO Panel announced that more people reported UFOs in the past year than in the last five years combined. They ended their report by saying,

"Over the past year, we've been averaging 1,071 sighting reports a month, compared to about 300 three years ago,"
UN-UFO director, Dr. David Schumacher.

There may be something to these things or there may not. You be the judge. But for now, let's get back to projections into the future that we can be totally confident of, those being the explanations given us by Irenaeus and Hippolytus, as passed down to them from the Apostle John through his personal student, Polycarp. And let's see if we can finally get to the bottom of the Mystery Babylon mystery. We'll start, however, with seeing where we stand in relation to the seals, trumpets, and bowls.

# Seals, Trumpets, and Bowls

Before we get further into the tribulation itself, I thought we would discuss ever so briefly the seven seals, seven trumpets, and seven bowls.

There are two basic thoughts concerning the seals, trumpets, and bowls. The first one holds that the three are sequential and successive, that there are twenty one different events that come one after the other; whereas the other position says that the seals, trumpets, and bowls are parallel and simultaneous.

The primary arguments for the sequential viewpoint are that the successive descriptions seem to increase in intensity. In other words, a case is made that God seems to keep trying harder to get folks' attention. Also, there is delineation made by John when he says things like "**then** I saw." In addition to these, there are differences in the description of each.

The parallel theory holds to the idea that the seals, trumpets and bowls are talking about the exact same things from different vantage points, like the four Gospels are all talking about the life and ministry of Jesus as viewed through four different people. God does, in fact, also show the same events in different ways to Daniel who has entirely different dreams or visions that prophecy the exact same future occurrence.

One perspective pertaining to the parallel way of thinking holds that the seals are the long story, ending with Jesus' return to earth. The trumpets are the short story, ending at the same place. And the bowls or vials are the very short story ending again at the same event, the second coming of Jesus.

I will say that the similarities are often striking, especially between the trumpets and bowls. For instance, the second trumpet states in Revelation 8:8 that *"a third of **the sea turned into blood**,"* while the second bowl states in Revelation 18:3, *"The second angel poured out his bowl on **the sea, and it turned into blood**."* They sure do sound like the same thing.

In Revelation 8:10 we read of the third trumpet, *"The third angel sounded his trumpet, and a great star, blazing like a torch, fell from the sky on a third of **the rivers and on the springs of water;**"* whereas, quite similarly the third bowl states, *"The third angel poured out his bowl on **the rivers and springs of water**."* Revelation 16:4.

Both the fourth trumpet and fourth bowl talk about the sun, as do the fifth of both, with very little change in the wording. The fifth trumpet verse in Revelation 9:2 says, *"The sun and sky were **darkened**,"* and we read of the fifth bowl, *"The fifth angel poured out his bowl on the throne of the beast, and his kingdom was plunged into **darkness**."* Revelation 16:10.

Revelation 9:14, *"It said to the sixth angel who had the trumpet, 'Release the four angels who are bound at **the great river Euphrates**,"* and as we might imagine by now *"The sixth angel poured out his bowl on **the great river Euphrates**."* Revelation 16:12.

There are similarities with the seals as well, although not quite as pronounced until we get to the seventh and final one of each. There we read of the seventh seal in Revelation 8:5, *"and there followed **peals of thunder and sounds and flashes of lightning and an earthquake**."* The seventh trumpet description is *"and there came **flashes of lightning**, rumblings, **peals of thunder, an earthquake** and a great hailstorm."* Revelation 11:13. And finally, the seventh bowl image includes *"And there were **flashes of lightning** and sounds and **peals of thunder**; and there was **a great earthquake**, such as there had not been since man came to be upon the earth, so great an earthquake was it, and so mighty."* Revelation 16:17.

Actually, I tend to partially agree with both. I think that in some places the seals, trumpets, and bowls are probably parallel, and in others they could be sequential, for as we speculatively laid things out, the seals started when Jesus first arrived in heaven, the trumpets started in 1917, and the bowls will cover the actual tribulation, with all three ending at the resurrection/rapture and Jesus' return. But until those last two events occur, there is absolutely no way we can be sure if we are correct or way off base. And since that is the case pertaining to events that might already be history, we won't even attempt to guess about the specifics of the events that will happen during the final tribulation.

I will tell you that the reason I surmise that the sixth trumpet and the tribulation will include nuclear warfare is that there are too many Biblical references to the final battles that seem to be undeniably nuclear. To give you two examples:

*"This is the plague with which the Lord will strike all the nations that fought against Jerusalem: Their flesh will rot while they are still standing on*

*their feet, their eyes will rot in their sockets, and their tongues will rot in their mouths."*                                                    Zechariah 14:12.

Does that not sound like scenes from the two WWII atomic blasts in Japan? And then we find a description of the aftermath:

*"For seven months the Israelites will be burying them in order to cleanse the land. All the people of the land will bury them, and the day I display my glory will be a memorable day for them, declares the Sovereign Lord. People will be continually employed in cleansing the land. They will spread out across the land and, along with others, they will bury any bodies that are lying on the ground.*

*After the seven months they will carry out a more detailed search. As they go through the land, anyone who sees a human bone will leave a marker beside it until the gravediggers bury it."*              Ezekiel 39:12-15.

That sure sounds to me like they are being careful of a radioactive site. So I think we are fairly safe in assuming that WWIII and any battles during the tribulation are more likely than not going to include nuclear bombs. Beyond that, however, we will not speculate.

Next, we will leave any and all speculation behind and delve once more into the things that John taught, things that we know to be absolutely certain. And we may well be very surprised.

# The Harlot and Babylon

We are coming into what truly is the meat of Revelation, what the end times are all about. I could say it in one or two sentences, but in order to understand it fully will require that we spend some time learning what John taught through Irenaeus and Hippolytus. This information will astound you, as it did me. And it will put to bed once and for all so much of the speculation that we have been bombarded with in our normal studies of the end times. This is crucial information that we need to fully comprehend in order to get past all the clutter and finally grasp the truth.

To begin, we are going to let Hippolytus impart to us from the Apostolic Oral Teaching. Immediately following his list of characteristics of the antichrist that we looked at earlier, Hippolytus quotes the entire chapters from Daniel that relate to both his vision of the four beasts as well as the statue with a golden head, shoulders and arms of silver, belly and thighs of brass, and legs of iron. He then explains how the beasts and parts of the statue represent empires. After talking about the legs of iron, Hippolytus writes:

"And mystically by the toes of the feet he meant the kings who are to arise from among them; as Daniel also says,

> 'While I was thinking about the horns, there before me was another horn, a little one, which came up among them; and three of the first horns were uprooted before it. This horn had eyes like the eyes of a human being and a mouth that spoke boastfully.' Daniel 7:8.

And under this was signified none other than Antichrist, who is also himself to raise the kingdom of the Jews. He says that three horns are plucked up by the root by him, the three kings of Egypt, and Libya, and Ethiopia, whom he cuts off in the array of battle. And he, after gaining terrible power over all, being nevertheless a tyrant, shall stir up tribulation and persecution against men, exalting himself against them. For Daniel says:

*'Then I continued to watch because of the boastful words the horn was speaking. I kept looking until the beast was slain and its body destroyed and thrown into the blazing fire.'*                     Daniel 7:11.

After a little space the stone will come from heaven which smites the image and breaks it in pieces, and subverts all the kingdoms, and gives the kingdom to the saints of the Most High. This is the stone which becomes a great **mountain**, and fills the whole earth, of which Daniel says:

*'In my vision at night I looked, and there before me was one like a son of man, coming with the clouds of heaven. He approached the Ancient of Days and was led into his presence. He was given authority, glory and sovereign power; all nations and peoples of every language worshiped him. His dominion is an everlasting dominion that will not pass away, and his kingdom is one that will never be destroyed.'*     Daniel 7:13-14.

He showed all power given by the Father to the Son, who is ordained Lord of things in heaven, and things on earth, and things under the earth, and Judge of all: of things in heaven, because He was born, the Word of God, before all (ages); and of things on earth, because He became man in the midst of men, to re-create our Adam through Himself; and of things under the earth, because He was also reckoned among the dead, preaching the Gospel, (and) by death overcoming death.

As these things, then, are in the future, and as the ten toes of the image are equivalent to (so many) democracies, and the ten horns of the fourth beast are distributed over ten kingdoms, let us look at the subject a little more closely, and consider these matters as in the clear light of a personal survey.

The golden head of the image and the lioness denoted the Babylonians; the shoulders and arms of silver, and the bear, represented the Persians and Medes; the belly and thighs of brass, and the leopard, meant the Greeks, who held the sovereignty from Alexander's time; the legs of iron, and the beast dreadful and terrible, expressed the Romans, who hold the sovereignty at present; the toes of the feet which were part clay and part iron, and the ten horns, were emblems of the kingdoms that are yet to rise; the other little horn that grows up among them meant the Antichrist in their midst; the stone that smites the earth and brings judgment upon the world was Christ.

Let us look, therefore, at the things which are to befall this **unclean harlot** in the last days; and (let us consider) what and what manner of tribulation is destined to visit her in the wrath of God before the judgment as an earnest of her doom.

Come, then, O blessed Isaiah; arise, tell us clearly what thou didst prophesy with respect to the mighty **Babylon**."

Treatise on Christ and Antichrist, By Hippolytus.

Did you see what Hippolytus just told us? He was talking about the different past and future empires of the world, and he labels them as both "this unclean harlot" and "Babylon." Is it possible that the woman on the beast (the Harlot), and Mystery Babylon are one and the same? It obviously is nothing that we have ever been taught. Surely there must be a mistake here somewhere. Let's just hold that thought and jump right into section thirty four of his teaching:

"But as the task before us was to speak of the **harlot**, be thou with us, O blessed Isaiah. Let us mark what thou sayest about **Babylon**." Hippolytus.

Oooops. There it is again. Hippolytus is using the Harlot and Babylon interchangeably. He must actually believe they are the same thing. Well, let's read that again and see what follows:

"But as the task before us was to speak of the **Harlot**, be thou with us, O blessed Isaiah. Let us mark what thou sayest about **Babylon**.

*'Go down, sit in the dust, Virgin Daughter Babylon;*
*sit on the ground without a throne, queen city of the Babylonians.*
*No more will you be called tender or delicate.*
    *Take millstones and grind flour; take off your veil.*
*Lift up your skirts, bare your legs, and wade through the streams.*
    *Your nakedness will be exposed and your shame uncovered.*
*I will take vengeance; I will spare no one.*

*Our Redeemer, the Lord Almighty is his name,*
*is the Holy One of Israel.*

*Sit in silence, go into darkness, queen city of the Babylonians;
no more will you be called queen of kingdoms.
I was angry with my people and desecrated my inheritance;
I gave them into your hand, and you showed them no mercy.
Even on the aged you laid a very heavy yoke.
You said, 'I am forever—the eternal queen!'
But you did not consider these things or reflect on what might happen.
Now then, listen, you lover of pleasure, lounging in your security
and saying to yourself, "I am, and there is none besides me.
I will never be a widow or suffer the loss of children."
Both of these will overtake you in a moment, on a single day:
loss of children and widowhood.*

*They will come upon you in full measure, in spite of your many sorceries and all your potent spells.*

*You have trusted in your wickedness and have said, "No one sees me."*

*Your wisdom and knowledge mislead you when you say to yourself, "I am, and there is none besides me."*

*Disaster will come upon you, and you will not know how to conjure it away. Calamity will fall upon you that you cannot ward off with a ransom; a catastrophe you cannot foresee will suddenly come upon you.*

*Keep on, then, with your magic spells and with your many sorceries, which you have labored at since childhood.*

*Perhaps you will succeed, perhaps you will cause terror.*

*All the counsel you have received has only worn you out!*

*Let your astrologers come forward, those stargazers who make predictions month by month, let them save you from what is coming upon you.*

*Surely they are like stubble; the fire will burn them up. They cannot even save themselves from the power of the flame. These are not coals for warmth; this is not a fire to sit by.*

*That is all they are to you— these you have dealt with and labored with since childhood. All of them go on in their error; there is not one that can save you.'* Isaiah 47:1-15.

These things does Isaiah prophesy for thee. Let us see now whether John has spoken to the same effect. For he sees, when in the isle Patmos, a revelation of awful mysteries, which he recounts freely, and makes known to others. Tell me, blessed John, apostle and disciple of the Lord, what didst thou see and hear concerning Babylon? Arise, and speak; for it sent thee also into banishment.

'One of the seven angels who had the seven bowls came and said to me, "Come, I will show you the punishment of the great prostitute, who sits by many waters. With her the kings of the earth committed adultery, and the inhabitants of the earth were intoxicated with the wine of her adulteries."

Then the angel carried me away in the Spirit into a wilderness. There I saw a woman sitting on a scarlet beast that was covered with blasphemous names and had seven heads and ten horns. The woman was dressed in purple and scarlet, and was glittering with gold, precious stones and pearls. She held a golden cup in her hand, filled with abominable things and the filth of her adulteries. The name written on her forehead was a mystery:

Babylon the great

the mother of prostitutes

and of the abominations of the earth.

I saw that the woman was drunk with the blood of God's holy people, the blood of those who bore testimony to Jesus.

When I saw her, I was greatly astonished. Then the angel said to me: "Why are you astonished? I will explain to you the mystery of the woman and of the beast she rides, which has the seven heads and ten horns. The beast, which you saw, once was, now is not, and yet will come up out of the Abyss and go to its destruction. The inhabitants of the earth whose names have not been written in the book of life from the creation of the world will be astonished when they see the beast, because it once was, now is not, and yet will come.
This calls for a mind with wisdom. The seven heads are seven hills on which the woman sits. They are also seven kings. Five have fallen, one is, the other has not yet come; but when he does come, he must remain for only a

little while. The beast who once was, and now is not, is an eighth king. He belongs to the seven and is going to his destruction.

The ten horns you saw are ten kings who have not yet received a kingdom, but who for one hour will receive authority as kings along with the beast. They have one purpose and will give their power and authority to the beast. They will wage war against the Lamb, but the Lamb will triumph over them because he is Lord of lords and King of kings—and with him will be his called, chosen and faithful followers."

Then the angel said to me, "The waters you saw, where the prostitute sits, are peoples, multitudes, nations and languages. The beast and the ten horns you saw will hate the prostitute. They will bring her to ruin and leave her naked; they will eat her flesh and burn her with fire. For God has put it into their hearts to accomplish his purpose by agreeing to hand over to the beast their royal authority, until God's words are fulfilled. The woman you saw is the great city that rules over the kings of the earth."

After this I saw another angel coming down from heaven. He had great authority, and the earth was illuminated by his splendor. With a mighty voice he shouted:

"Fallen! Fallen is Babylon the Great!'
  She has become a dwelling for demons
  and a haunt for every impure spirit,
  a haunt for every unclean bird,
  a haunt for every unclean and detestable animal.
For all the nations have drunk
  the maddening wine of her adulteries.
The kings of the earth committed adultery with her, and
the merchants of the earth grew rich from her excessive luxuries."

Then I heard another voice from heaven say:

"'Come out of her, my people,
  so that you will not share in her sins,
  so that you will not receive any of her plagues;
  for her sins are piled up to heaven,
  and God has remembered her crimes.

Give back to her as she has given;
   pay her back double for what she has done.
   Pour her a double portion from her own cup.
Give her as much torment and grief
   as the glory and luxury she gave herself.
In her heart she boasts,
   'I sit enthroned as queen.
I am not a widow
   I will never mourn.'
Therefore in one day her plagues will overtake her:
   death, mourning and famine.
She will be consumed by fire,
   for mighty is the Lord God who judges her.

When the kings of the earth who committed adultery with her and shared her luxury see the smoke of her burning, they will weep and mourn over her. Terrified at her torment, they will stand far off and cry:

'Woe! Woe to you, great city,
   you mighty city of Babylon!
In one hour your doom has come!'

The merchants of the earth will weep and mourn over her because no one buys their cargoes anymore— cargoes of gold, silver, precious stones and pearls; fine linen, purple, silk and scarlet cloth; every sort of citron wood, and articles of every kind made of ivory, costly wood, bronze, iron and marble; cargoes of cinnamon and spice, of incense, myrrh and frankincense, of wine and olive oil, of fine flour and wheat; cattle and sheep; horses and carriages; and human beings sold as slaves.

They will say, 'The fruit you longed for is gone from you. All your luxury and splendor have vanished, never to be recovered.' The merchants who sold these things and gained their wealth from her will stand far off, terrified at her torment. They will weep and mourn and cry out:

'Woe! Woe to you, great city,
   dressed in fine linen, purple and scarlet,
   and glittering with gold, precious stones and pearls!

*In one hour such great wealth has been brought to ruin!'*

*Every sea captain, and all who travel by ship, the sailors, and all who earn their living from the sea, will stand far off. When they see the smoke of her burning, they will exclaim, 'Was there ever a city like this great city?' They will throw dust on their heads, and with weeping and mourning cry out:*

> *'Woe! Woe to you, great city,*
> *where all who had ships on the sea*
> *became rich through her wealth!*
> *In one hour she has been brought to ruin!*
>
> *Rejoice over her, you heavens!*
> *Rejoice, you people of God!*
> *Rejoice, apostles and prophets!*
> *For God has judged her*
> *with the judgment she imposed on you.'*

*Then a mighty angel picked up a boulder the size of a large millstone and threw it into the sea, and said:*

> *'With such violence the great city of Babylon*
> *will be thrown down, never to be found again.*
> *The music of harpists and musicians, pipers and trumpeters,*
> *will never be heard in you again.*
> *No worker of any trade will ever be found in you again.*
> *The sound of a millstone will never be heard in you again.*
> *The light of a lamp will never shine in you again.*
> *The voice of bridegroom and bride*
> *will never be heard in you again.*
> *Your merchants were the world's important people.*
> *By your magic spell all the nations were led astray.*
> *In her was found the blood of prophets and of God's holy people,*
> *of all who have been slaughtered on the earth.'*

Revelation 17-18:24.

With respect, then, to the particular judgment in the torments that are to come upon it in the last times by the hand of the tyrants who shall arise then, the clearest statement has been given in these passages. But it becomes us further diligently to examine and set forth the period at which these things shall come to pass, and how the little horn shall spring up in their midst. For when the legs of iron have issued in the feet and toes, according to the similitude of the image and that of the terrible beast, as has been shown in the above, (then shall be the time) when the iron and the clay shall be mingled together. Now Daniel will set forth this subject to us. For he says, 'And one week will make a covenant with many, and it shall be that in the midst (half) of the week my sacrifice and oblation shall cease.' By one week, therefore, he meant the last week which is to be at the end of the whole world of which week the two prophets Enoch and Elias will take up the half. For they will preach 1,260 days clothed in sackcloth, proclaiming repentance to the people and to all the nations."

Treatise on Christ and Antichrist, by Hippolytus.


Confused yet? Let's simplify everything. Yes, Babylon, the Harlot, and Mystery Babylon are indeed all one and the same. They are interchangeable. They are the world system in its totality. The governing systems, the economic systems, and the false religious systems are all represented in Babylon, the Harlot, and Mystery Babylon.

The world system is the enemy of God. The Word of God states it clearly:

*"You adulterous people, don't you know that friendship with the world means enmity against God? Therefore, anyone who chooses to be a friend of the world becomes an enemy of God."*  James 4:4.

And everything is wrapped up in that word, "world." It is all of the religions that Satan and mankind have started. It is the economic systems. And it is the different governing systems. All three put together what is Babylon in Revelation. And the name Babylon is so fitting, for it was our Nephilim friend, Nimrod, who began the entire downward spiral of the world with his Tower of Babel.

God wanted the world to love and worship Him, not idols or satanically concocted religions like Islam, New Age, Hinduism, Buddhism, etc. He wanted the economic system to be based in trusting Him. And He wanted the governance to be His Kingdom, the Kingdom of God.

God punished his people over and over for worshipping anything other than Him.

He gave us the system of tithing so that He could prove to us His faithfulness in His economic system if we trusted Him even that small percentage. He even told us to test him in that:

*"Bring the whole tithe into the storehouse, that there may be food in my house. Test me in this," says the Lord Almighty, "and see if I will not throw open the floodgates of heaven and pour out so much blessing that there will not be room enough to store it."* Malachi 3:10.

It was the only thing He ever told mankind to test him about.

And He surely never wanted any governance except His Kingdom. Samuel had to argue and argue in order to get God to allow the Jews to have a king like their neighbors. And God reluctantly gave them Saul.

The world system of doing things. That is Babylon, the Harlot, and Mystery Babylon. They are interchangeable. And once we see it, everything in all of the above scripture makes perfect sense. So much sense that you will shake your head in wonder as you look at the hoop jumping that is done to make other things fit. We will be discussing this more a little later.

But since this is naturally totally new to you, there are probably still doubts and questions going though your head. For instance, you might be thinking "the Harlot has to be a false religion," or "the Harlot has to be Catholicism," or if you are a student of the most recent of the scholarly breed you might be inwardly saying, "the Harlot has to be Islam." Naturally these things come rushing to our minds. These are the things we have been taught, even though the angel in explaining the woman told us that the name written on her head was "Babylon the great."

## The Harlot as a Religion

Allow me to tell you a short story about how the majority of Protestant teaching on this scriptural section ended up being portrayed as the Catholic Church. I am going to have to mention a man's name who is still alive and at age 83 seems to be going strong, but please don't send me hate mail about how I besmirched a good man by doing so. Personally, I like him very much. I am confident that he loves the Lord Jesus with every fiber of his being. And he would be one of the very last people I would ever consider as being one who would break any of the Ten Commandments. Additionally, he has done a lot of good in his ministry and brought a lot of people to Jesus. But the story is extra relevant to this topic, and it is one I have heard him tell often.

Hal Lindsey became a born again believer in 1955, and in the 1960's he deservedly made an excellent name for himself nationwide with Campus Crusade for Christ. With the long hair and mustache that he had at the time, and his rebellious background from when he had been a young tug boat captain on the Mississippi River, Hal made inroads into the hippie dominated campuses that no one else could have. In Christian circles Hal won well earned recognition.

Hal's early years with Christ came at a time when virtually no one talked about end times prophecy. In those days, if a minister said anything about Revelation he would just say, "God wins." However, Hal happened to hear about a minister who was doing a study on the subject so he went to a meeting to check it out. Hal was immediately hooked on Biblical prophecy.

In 1970 he published his first book, The Late Great Planet Earth, which was a runaway success, selling tens of millions of copies.

During the early eighties, the New York Times gave Hal Lindsey the title, "The Jeremiah of Today". The New York Times also lauded Lindsey with being the best-selling non-fiction author in the world during the 1970's, after reporting only half of the books he had actually sold. He has also been called "the father of modern-day Bible prophecy." To date his books are approaching forty million copies sold and The Late Great Planet Earth was even made into a feature film in 1979, narrated by the famous Orson Welles.

Hal's own story that he loves to tell was about his early days of studying prophecy. He tells that he had been thinking about the "Woman on the Beast" passages, wondering what it described, when walking through the Houston airport he happened to see an advertising poster for travel to Rome.

The poster mentioned that wonderful tourist destination as being "the city on seven hills," and knowing that the harlot scriptures mentioned *"The seven heads are seven hills on which the woman sits,"* Hal immediately figured that God had sent him a sign that the Vatican was his answer.

That was it. That was the beginning of virtually every Protestant church today teaching that the false religion is Catholicism and the Pope will be the false prophet.

No one paid attention to the fact that hills and mountains in the Bible are images for nations and empires. Nobody cared that the very next sentence said, *"They are also seven kings. Five have fallen, one is, the other has not yet come; but when he does come, he must remain for only a little while."*

No, Hal Lindsey said it; the New York Times gave him the title "The Jeremiah of Today," so that was good enough for everybody else. Presto, the Catholic Church was the villain and a pope will be the false prophet. Remember Hal is called the father of modern-day Bible prophecy, and he is. Ironic that his first book was the best selling non fiction book of the decade, and it was really mainly fiction.

Interesting, I tuned into his TV program last night and he had two subjects to discuss. One pertained to the immigration debate and how the proposed identification cards would be the forerunner of the mark of the beast. The second subject was about the Catholic Church being the false religion and the pope would be the false prophet. I suppose if it works, don't fix it, especially since people have seemed to have forgotten that Hal also said in The Late, Great Planet Earth that the Soviet Union would play the role of antagonist during the end times. Of course the collapse of the Soviet Union in 1991 forced him to change his end times antagonist to radical Islam. Plus, folks evidently don't remember that he said the rapture would occur in 1981, which was then revised to 1988, neither of which dates turned out to see the mass pre-trib exodus of the Christians. What matters is that Hal's words got published and sold big time, and those words became golden.

We do need to note that Hal studied at the Dallas Theological Seminary following its deep immersion into Darby's "school of thought" about the pre-trib rapture, and this "school of thought" was adopted wholeheartedly by him. Yes, Hal Lindsey is the father of modern-day Bible prophecy, but John Darby is the grandfather. Virtually all of today's teaching still goes back to him. It's too bad Darby was not fortunate enough to have lived in the age of flight, and airports with depictions of Rome being the city on seven hills, or we might be able to say that **all** of today's teaching can be credited to him.

Seriously, Hal was initially indoctrinated into what by that time had become a complete system of Darbyism and dispensationalism taught in seminaries. Had Hal Lindsey been taught about the Apostolic Oral Teaching, today's teaching in our churches might be a whole lot different, for Hal would have learned that the church would in fact be present during the tribulation. He would have found out that Irenaeus had said of the antichrist:

"He shall remove his kingdom into that city (Jerusalem), and shall sit in the temple of God, **leading astray those who worship him, as if he were Christ**. To this purpose Daniel says again:

*'And he shall desolate the holy place; and sin has been given for a sacrifice, and righteousness been cast away in the earth, and he has been active, and gone on prosperously.'* Daniel 8:12.

And the angel Gabriel, when explaining his vision, states with regard to this person:

*'And towards the end of their kingdom a king of a most fierce countenance shall arise, one understanding [dark] questions, and exceedingly powerful, full of wonders; and he shall corrupt, direct, influence, and put strong men down, the holy people likewise; and his yoke shall be directed as a wreath [round their neck]; deceit shall be in his hand, and he shall be lifted up in his heart: he shall also ruin many by deceit, and lead many to perdition, bruising them in his hand like eggs.'* Daniel 8:23-25.

And then he points out the time that his tyranny shall last, during which **the saints shall be put to flight, they who offer a pure sacrifice unto God**:

*'And in the midst of the week,'*

he says,

*'the sacrifice and the libation shall be taken away, and the abomination of desolation [shall be brought] into the temple: even unto the consummation of the time shall the desolation be complete.'*          Daniel 9:27.

Now three years and six months constitute the half-week.

From all these passages are revealed to us, not merely the particulars of the apostasy, and [the doings] of him who concentrates in himself every satanic error, but also, that there is one and the same God the Father, who was declared by the prophets, but made manifest by Christ. For if what Daniel prophesied concerning the end has been confirmed by the Lord, when He said,

*'When you shall see the abomination of desolation, which has been spoken of by Daniel the prophet.'*          Matthew 24:15.

(and the angel Gabriel gave the interpretation of the visions to Daniel, and he is the archangel of the Creator, who also proclaimed to Mary the visible coming and the incarnation of Christ), then one and the same God is most manifestly pointed out, who sent the prophets, and made promise of the Son, and called us into His knowledge.

In a still clearer light has John, in the Apocalypse, indicated to the Lord's disciples what shall happen in the last times, and concerning the ten kings who shall then arise. He teaches us what the ten horns shall be which were seen by Daniel, telling us that thus it had been said to him:

*'And the ten horns which you saw are ten kings, who have received no kingdom as yet, but shall receive power as if kings one hour with the beast. These have one mind, and give their strength and power to the beast. These shall make war with the Lamb, and the Lamb shall overcome them, because He is the Lord of lords and the King of kings.'*          Revelation 17:12-14.

It is manifest, therefore, that of these [potentates], he who is to come shall slay three, and subject the remainder to his power, and that he shall be himself the eighth among them. **And they shall lay Babylon waste, and burn her with fire, and shall give their kingdom to the beast, and put the Church to flight.** After that they shall be destroyed by the coming of our

Lord. For that the kingdom must be divided, and thus come to ruin, the Lord [declares when He] says:

> 'Every kingdom divided against itself is brought to desolation, and every city or house divided against itself shall not stand.'   Matthew 12:25.

<u>Against Heresies</u>, book V, Chapters XXV, 4&5, and XXVI, 1, By Irenaeus.

Just by reading that little excerpt from Irenaeus, Hal would have seen that the antichrist will come as the Christ, leading many astray, and "**the saints shall be put to flight, they who offer a pure sacrifice unto God**," which can only be the church, not the Jews.

Furthermore he would have learned that it will be the antichrist and his seven remaining "potentates" that "**shall lay Babylon waste, and burn her with fire, and shall give their kingdom to the beast, and put the church to flight**," teaching him that it will be the antichrist that will destroy the world system, as we will see in more detail later. And if there were any question in Hal's mind about the church being present during this time, Irenaeus made it abundantly clear by using the word "church."

Even if he had been taught both Darbyism and Irenaeus, he would have had no problem choosing between the two because Irenaeus would have told him:

"Now all these **[heretics] are of much later date than the bishops to whom the apostles committed the Churches**; which fact I have in the third book taken all pains to demonstrate. It follows, then, as a matter of course, that these heretics aforementioned, since they are blind to the truth, and deviate from the [right] way, will walk in various roads; and therefore the footsteps of their doctrine are scattered here and there without agreement or connection."        <u>Against Heresies</u>, Book V, Chapter XX, 1, Irenaeus.

With this we all learn that heretics came **after** the Bishops like Polycarp. In other words, Polycarp was taught the truth by John. And he passed on that truth. And continuing, Irenaeus says:

"Those, therefore, who call in question the knowledge of the holy presbyters (The apostles and first Bishops), ... such are all the heretics, and those who imagine that they have hit upon something more beyond the truth, so that by following those things already mentioned, **proceeding on their way variously, inharmoniously, and foolishly, not keeping always to the same opinions with regard to the same things, as blind men are led by the blind, they shall deservedly fall into the ditch of ignorance lying in their path, ever seeking and never finding out the truth.**

**It behooves us, therefore, to avoid their doctrines, and to take careful heed lest we suffer any injury from them** ... therefore says the Spirit of God, You may freely eat from every tree of the garden, that is, 'Eat from every Scripture of the Lord;' but you shall not eat with an uplifted mind, nor touch any heretical discord. For these men do profess that they have themselves the knowledge of good and evil; and **they set their own impious minds above the God** who made them. **They therefore form opinions on what is beyond the limits of the understanding.** For this cause also the apostle says, 'Be not wise beyond what it is fitting to be wise, but be wise prudently,' **that we be not cast forth by eating of the knowledge of these men** (that knowledge which knows more than it should do) **from the paradise of life."**       Against Heresies, Book V, Chapter XX, 2, Irenaeus.

Yes, I believe that if Hal Lindsey had actually been given a choice between John Darby's "school of thought," which was what he was indoctrinated with in his seminary years, and the truth found in the Apostolic Oral Teaching of John, Hal is smart enough that he, too, would have decided to stick with the early church Fathers.

And had he been taught the truth about the reason Darby wanted to come up with an entirely new teaching in the first place; which was that he was upset with his bishop for what he thought was bad treatment that he got, so he struck out at the church's teaching; Hal would have seen that his jumping at the conclusion that Catholicism was the religion God would be so upset about and want to destroy, was in reality just an extension of John Darby's frustration. Hal probably would have at least paused when he saw that poster and thought to himself, "Why would God be so upset with the Catholics when there are other religions on earth that teach folks to worship rats (Hindu), or that Jesus is really not God (Islam), or that teach forms of

Satan Worship (New Age), or that teach that there isn't even a God at all (Atheism)."

And if Hal had read Irenaeus' masterpiece, <u>Against Heresies</u>, and learned that to depart from the Apostolic Oral Teaching, which taught what Jesus taught to His disciples, was the basis of heresy, I truly believe <u>The Late Great Planet Earth</u>, would never have even been written, and what now passes as end times teaching may never have seen the light of day. But as they say, "it is what it is." Fortunately, you and I are now receiving the truth.

**Mystery Babylon**

We talked briefly about the fact that Mystery Babylon, the Harlot, and Babylon were interchangeable in the Apostolic Oral Teaching, and that they all three depict the world system in its entirety. But it is more than that. They depict all of mankind's activities, not just our governance, economics, and false religions. Much as I hate to utter these words, they depict us. Even if we begin something with the noblest of intentions, eventually that something is taken over by corruption, greed, violence, hatred; all of the sins engrained in individuals.

This chapter is the most difficult I have ever written, because in order to do the subject justice I would almost have to include all of the writings from Irenaeus and Hippolytus in order to clarify the message I am trying to impart. Having spent hour upon hour until my eyes were blurry studying their works, I understood that for them it was all so central to the teaching they had received. They knew, and Hippolytus knew that his student (Theophilus, to whom he was writing) already understood completely, that the reason for the tribulation was the destruction of all of the world they, and you and I, consider our normal realm. They understood, as I came to understand as well, that they all three referred to the world as a whole that was not in accord with God's final plan. They understood that it had to be destroyed in order to replace it with the Kingdom of God and all of the righteousness and right judgment that God's Kingdom entails, in every aspect of life. By the time we finish this and the next few chapters, you will see it, too. And I can assure you that once you do see it, everything about the end times will become crystal clear. Maybe even more important, you will have a far greater understanding of the Bible as a whole and the working of God in the world today. And you will be stunned.

# The Cup of the Harlot

As we have discussed, other than the writings we have from the earliest church Fathers, primarily Irenaeus and Hippolytus, the valuable truths in the Apostolic Oral Teaching have been lost. Irenaeus, along with his contemporaries, Tertullian and Justin Martyr, warned adamantly that losing truth could happen if anyone changed anything in the teaching. Irenaeus even subscribed the word "heresy" to teaching anything different than what John had taught Polycarp.

Unfortunately men like Clement of Alexandria and Origin paid no attention to the warning. They were enamored by the Greek Stoic philosophers and how they were interpreting mythology. And not understanding the difference between mythological allegory and historical allegory they opened the flood gates for anyone and everyone to give his own interpretation to the divine scriptures. By the time Augustine came along, the truth, the secrets of interpreting the Old Testament parables and allegory as taught to John and the other apostles by Jesus, was lost, seemingly forever. But God wanted those near the end times to have true understanding, so in His grace He has opened up an important part of that teaching to us.

Much of what was in that Apostolic Oral Teaching that was such a gigantic key to understanding not only the end times but also much of the Old Testament, had to do with the idioms Moses used in his writing of the first five books of the Bible.

Imagine if you will, someone fifteen hundred years from now trying to accurately decipher books that he might come across that were written today. He might have the spelling and the meanings of our words down pat, but how do you think today's idioms might distort his interpretation. Let's consider a few things he might come across in his reading. He might read break a leg, head in the sand, kick the bucket, walking on egg shells, icing on the cake, having a lot of dough, living high on the hog, being a brick shy of a full load, bucket list, got a lemon, sour grapes, fly in the ointment, bought the farm, lived on easy street, feet to the fire, up tight, goose was cooked, or pack rat. Do you think it might be possible if these things were located in strategic places in the text he was reading that he could indeed come up with a totally different interpretation from the original meaning the author had? Obviously. He may, in fact, interpret the text exactly the opposite from what it was suppose to be. And he'd be up a creek without a paddle.

That is exactly what has been happening for the past few thousand years with some crucial scriptures. Then out of the blue a peasant woman plowed up a flagstone that exposed a burial chamber in a field in Syria in 1928. Although the modern Christian community has really paid very little attention to it, what was then discovered was probably of far greater importance than the Dead Sea Scrolls. And the discovery will alter your Biblical view for the rest of your life.

The governor of the region, H. Schoeffler, notified the Bureau of Antiquities in Beirut, whose head, Charles Virolleaud, cleared the tomb the peasant woman had uncovered. In Paris he showed the potsherds he had found to Rene Dussaud. On the basis of these sherds and a drawing of the tomb, Dussaud found significant parallels with Mycenean ware and Cretan tombs. The Academy of Paris then decided to send an archeological expedition to the site. To head the expedition, it chose the thirty year old curator of the Prehistoric and Gallo-Roman Museum of Strasbourg, Claude Schaeffer. What he found when he got to the site was actually a gigantic cemetery, but having common sense, he decided that a city must be nearby.

A few hundred yards east of the cemetery was a hill, so Schaeffer started digging. I'll let him tell the rest:

"I decided to start my excavations on the highest point of the hill, where I had noticed a few traces of walls among the shrubs. Pay dirt was not long in appearing.

In a room divided by three pillars we came upon a large number of clay tablets covered with cuneiform text. We had found the palace library! These writings promise to reveal most valuable information concerning the history of the ancient Near East. Some are written in Babylonian, the diplomatic language of that time, and deal with important government treaties.

To our amazement, we found that the majority of the tablets had been inscribed in a language the existence of which no one had ever surmised! And -- an extraordinary thing -- it is an alphabetical script of 27 cuneiform signs, a real alphabetical document of the second millennium before Christ!"

By Claude Schaeffer.

Excavated ruins at Ras Shamra

What Schaeffer found is now known as the Ras Shamra tablets in the Ugaritic alphabet, and the text of the tablets from the ancient Canaanite city of Ugarit, with their mythological and historical texts, have now opened a new door to the Hebrew Scriptures. In all, there were thousands of tablets with over fourteen hundred of them explaining the Canaanite religion, the most famous being the Baal Cycle, describing the religion of their main God, Baal, which was Satan.

A statuette of Baal from Ugarit

The city turned out to have been inhabited from 6,000 BC to 1,190 BC. You read that correctly. It dates back to 6,000 BC.

We may need to do a refresher course now to put things in perspective. The son of Noah responsible for the Nephilim remaining on earth after the flood was Ham. His son that received the curse from God was Canaan. And Canaan is the uncle of Nimrod. This is important, so let's reread what we read in the earlier chapter:

"The lineage of the post-flood giants can be traced specifically to three of Ham's sons, Cush, Mizraim and Canaan. The first grandson of Ham who receives special designation in Genesis 10 is King Nimrod who led the tower of Babel rebellion. Was he a Nephilim?

*"The sons of Ham: Cush, Mizraim, Put and Canaan. The sons of Cush: Seba, Havilah, Sabtah, Raamah and Sabteca. The sons of Raamah: Sheba and Dedan. Cush was the father of Nimrod, who grew to be a mighty warrior on the earth. He was a mighty hunter before the Lord; that is why it is said, 'Like Nimrod, a mighty hunter before the Lord.' The first centers of his kingdom were Babylon, Erech, Akkad and Calneh, in Shinar. From that land he went to Assyria, where he built Nineveh, Rehoboth Ir, Calah and Resen, which is between Nineveh and Calah; that is the great city. "*

Genesis 10:6-12.

Just as Canaan received a special distinction in his genealogy, Nimrod gets several extra verses, too. Clearly this is someone of special significance. Nimrod was the first murderer and conqueror in the post flood world. He was the founder of the city of Babylon, which became a center of pagan, satanic idolatry, much of it with various versions of Nimrod himself being worshiped as a god. His name, which means "to rebel" or "let us rebel" indicates his disposition. He was an enemy of God and at the time was Satan's main servant on Earth. He is credited for leading the effort to build the Tower of Babel, a religious temple used to access the angelic realm through pagan ritual. The Tower of Babel was also the first attempt at a global government, led by Nimrod, and an attempt for man to reach the spiritual realm and "godhood" without the Lord, to which God swiftly responded by destroying the tower, confusing the languages of all the people of the world and scattering them all over the Earth. Was this grandson of Ham possibly a Nephilim?

It is interesting to note that the above verse states that Nimrod *"began to be a mighty one in the earth."* The term for *"mighty one,"* gibborim, is the same Hebrew phrase used to describe the Nephilim giants in Chapter 6 of Genesis who were *"mighty men."* It is also the same term used to describe the giant Goliath in 1 Samuel 17:51. Was Nimrod a Nephilim?

In mythology, Nimrod is known by many names, among them Gilgamesh and Osiris, who were worshiped as gods. In Sumerian texts he is described as "2/3 god, 1/3 man." The Hebrew word for *"began"* in the verse *"began to be a mighty one in the earth"* is chalal, which means, "to profane, desecrate or pollute oneself, ritually or sexually."

The final piece of evidence we can look at is the Septuagint, the oldest version of the Old Testament. The same verse from Genesis in the Septuagint reads:

*"And [Cush] begot [Nimrod]: he began to be a giant upon the earth. He was a giant hunter before the Lord God; therefore they say, As [Nimrod] the giant hunter before the Lord."*   Genesis 10:8-9 Septuagint (LXX).

So it appears that Nimrod, the grandson of Ham, was very likely a giant containing the Nephilim gene."
From "Nephilim After The Flood" chapter in this book.

Now, we can start putting some things together. We will start with the Bible passage that talks about the Tower of Babel:

*"Now the whole world had one language and a common speech. As people moved eastward, they found a plain in Shinar and settled there. They said to each other, 'Come, let's make bricks and bake them thoroughly.' They used brick instead of stone, and tar for mortar. Then they said, 'Come, let us build ourselves a city, with a tower that reaches to the heavens, so that we may make a name for ourselves; otherwise we will be scattered over the face of the whole earth."*   Genesis 11:1-5.

That seems pretty straightforward, doesn't it? They were going to do four things:
1. Build a city
2. Erect a tower
3. "Make a name" for themselves
4. Avoid being scattered

The only thing that might need interpreting is the "make a name for ourselves" part, which we can assume means that they wanted to become famous. It's an extremely common idiom. But was it always? Yes, it was an idiom, but it did not have a thing to do with becoming famous. Here is where the need for the Apostolic Oral Teaching comes in. Of course, that was lost. What to do, what to do?

Suppose we trust God. By doing that, He just may have a peasant woman uncover something that looks important. And in the treasure trove of tablets we find the meanings of idioms, one of which is "make a name for ourselves."

This is where you need to start reading slower. This is important.

"To make a name" in the Hebrew culture was an idiom for a legitimate custom of a brother of a deceased man who had died without having a son, fathering a son with the deceased brother's widow so that the departed brother would have a son to carry on his name. The practice is called a Levirate marriage. However, with the tablets found in the Ugarit tablets it became clear that the Canaanite practice was far, far different.

The next paragraph is critical. Make sure you completely understand it.

In that cultic practice which had been begun as a ritual prior to the flood, there was a covenant "banquet" that accompanied the "sacred marriage" of a woman, the "Harlot," with her man, her redeemer, lover, or Baal. During the covenant banquet the two were given a cup filled with wine and a very strong sleep inducing narcotic. Its purpose was to get them both highly intoxicated and to put them into a deep sleep meant to symbolize the sleep of death. The couple, after sexual intercourse followed by deep sleep, would then symbolically pass through death and awake in the resurrection. This Canaanite sacred ritual was intended to aid in the conception of a male child which would guarantee the "Harlot" and her "redeemer" a new life in the resurrection. The newborn son, a "name," would carry their "name," which they considered an essential part of their being, after their death.

What Nimrod was planning was the reestablishment of this "sacred marriage" ritual that had been practiced **before the flood** at the site of the tower. This ritual, with a harlot taking a cup with her "redeemer," having sex, entering a deep sleep, with the hope that when they awoke (resurrected) they would have a son who would carry their "name" on forever, was the start of so much. From there, that cup will run throughout the scriptures, ending up in the hands of The Harlot on the beast in Revelation.

Now, we can understand more fully what John was seeing in his vision:

*"There I saw a woman sitting on a scarlet beast that was covered with blasphemous names and had seven heads and ten horns. The woman was dressed in purple and scarlet, and was glittering with gold, precious stones and pearls.* **She held a golden cup in her hand, filled with abominable things and the filth of her adulteries.** *The name written on her forehead was a mystery:*

*Babylon the great*

*the mother of prostitutes*

*and of the abominations of the earth."*  Revelation 17:3-5.

Now we can also better understand what Hippolytus was talking about when we quoted from him, especially when we know that the harlot in the Canaanite "sacred marriage" ritual was called a "virgin," and the ritual was suppose to eliminate the bereavement of a widowed "queen." Here is again what Hippolytus told us earlier:

"But as the task before us was to speak of the harlot, be thou with us, O blessed Isaiah. Let us mark what thou sayest about Babylon.

> *'Go down, sit in the dust, Virgin Daughter Babylon;*
> *sit on the ground without a throne, queen city of the Babylonians.*
> *No more will you be called tender or delicate.*
> *Take millstones and grind flour; take off your veil.*
> *Lift up your skirts, bare your legs, and wade through the streams.*
> *Your nakedness will be exposed and your shame uncovered.*

*I will take vengeance; I will spare no one.*

*Our Redeemer, the Lord Almighty is his name,
is the Holy One of Israel.'*                                Isaiah 47:1-4.

    We can see now why Irenaeus and Hippolytus had such a clear understanding of such things as the meaning of the imagery in Revelation. They had been given it by Jesus himself through John and Polycarp. Those mentored by the other apostles knew the truth, too. There was no need to manufacture new interpretations. And it is easy to understand how Irenaeus would get so incensed at his contemporaries who thought the Greek philosophers knew better, and so tried to emulate them. We can be sure that Irenaeus was livid as he wrote his masterpiece, <u>Against Heresies</u>.

    However, God obviously knew the Apostolic Oral Teaching would be lost in only two hundred years. The fact is, He probably planned it that way. Remember, His ways are higher than our ways. And I feel confident that just like the peasant woman, God can have others in the future uncover the parts of the lost teaching for the benefit of His true children that He wants to truly understand those things.

    I will say, though, that I still think it sad when I see a needless chasm built between the true followers of Jesus within the Protestant Church and the true followers within the Catholic Church because someone sees a poster of Rome in an airport and jumps to the erroneous conclusion that the Catholic Church is the false religion God is so upset with, and a pope will be the false prophet. Knowing the truth, that the Harlot in Revelation is the same thing as Babylon and Mystery Babylon, and that all three are symbolic of the world system that is opposed to God's system, points up how far off base we can get by trying to come up with our own interpretations. Without the knowledge of such things as historic idioms or future changes in the world, the chances are probably a thousand to one that we might ever stumble on a correct interpretation of an image we read about in Revelation. But that is the accepted and expected way of doing things in our modern Church of Laodicea, and that probably will not change.

    Before we get back into being taught the Apostolic Oral Teaching about the end times, I had mentioned that the **Cup of The Harlot** was key to our understanding many things in the Bible, so let's briefly look at a few examples.

The first example is one we could take an entire chapter on; the image of the Israelite captivity in Egypt. But I'll just let you ponder that it all started with Joseph having a **cup** put in Benjamin's sack. It was that event that led to the figurative four hundred year deep sleep of the nation of Israel, followed by its resurrection, the parting of the sea, and the trek to the mountain of God. The phrase I have coined for myself for such an event is an "orchestrated shadow."

Once we understand the meaning of the cup we see it in all the Bible:

> *"You have gone the way of your sister;*
> *so I will put her **cup** into your hand.'*
> *This is what the Sovereign Lord says:*
> *'You will drink your sister's **cup**,*
> *a **cup** large and deep;*
> *it will bring scorn and derision,*
> *for it holds so much.*
> *You will be filled with drunkenness and sorrow,*
> *the **cup** of ruin and desolation,*
> *the **cup** of your sister Samaria."*   Ezekiel 23:31-33.

And:

> *"Rejoice and be glad, Daughter Edom,*
> *you who live in the land of Uz.*
> *But to you also the **cup** will be passed;*
> *you will be drunk and stripped naked."*   Lamentations 4:21.

And:

> *"Awake, awake! Rise up, Jerusalem,*
> *you who have drunk from the hand of the Lord*
> *the **cup** of his wrath, you who have drained to its dregs*
> *the **goblet** that makes people stagger.*
> *Among all the children she bore there was none to guide her;*
> *among all the children she reared*
> *there was none to take her by the hand."*   Isaiah 51:17-18.

And:

> *"Flee from Babylon! Run for your lives!*
> *Do not be destroyed because of her sins.*
> *It is time for the Lord's vengeance;*
> *he will repay her what she deserves.*
> *Babylon was a gold **cup** in the Lord's hand;*
> *she made the whole earth drunk.*
> *The nations drank her wine;*
> *therefore they have now gone mad.*
> *Babylon will suddenly fall and be broken.*
> *Wail over her."*            Jeremiah 51:6-8.

And:

> *"It is God who judges:*
> *He brings one down, he exalts another.*
> *In the hand of the Lord is a **cup***
> *full of foaming wine mixed with spices;*
> *he pours it out, and all the wicked of the earth*
> *drink it down to its very dregs."*         Psalm 75:7-8.

And:

> *"You cannot drink the **cup** of the Lord*
> *and the **cup** of demons too;*
> *you cannot have a part in both the Lord's table*
> *and the table of demons."*            1 Corinthians 10:21.

As you can see, that cup is everywhere. These are just a few examples. Well. I suppose we should include:

> *"If anyone worships the beast and its image and receives its mark on their forehead or on their hand, they, too, will drink the wine of God's fury, which has been poured full strength into the **cup** of his wrath."*
>                                                            Revelation 14:9-10.

As an aside, there were two other nuggets that jumped out at me as I delved into the phenomenal Ugarit Tablets discovery that I found thrilling. The first was the fact that El Shaddai is a derivation of a Semitic stem that appears in the Akkadian shadû that meant "mountain." I kept thinking about God leading the Israelites out of Egypt to the mountain, to Him.

Also, the Baal Cycle Tablets explained in great detail how Satan's domain is the sea. We could list hundreds of places in the Bible where that knowledge makes reading the scriptures more exciting. Think about the red Sea parting so the redeemed could cross over, or Jesus calming the sea and even walking on it, or the first beast we studied earlier coming out of the sea, or most importantly, as we will see at the end of revelation when we discuss heaven, there will be no sea at all there.

Getting back to the idiom we have discussed in this chapter about "making a name" actually dealing with the Nephilim introduced Canaanite "sacred marriage" rite; the picture that sent chills through me was of the events Christ Himself orchestrated. First, He put together His Last Supper and had each disciple, and now us, drink from His **cup**. Then later that night:

> *"Going a little farther, he fell with his face to the ground and prayed, 'My Father, if it is possible, may this **cup** be taken from me. Yet not as I will, but as you will."* Matthew 26:39.

He drank that **cup** from the Father.
The next day:

> *"They brought Jesus to the place called Golgotha (which means 'the place of the skull'). Then they offered him **wine mixed with myrrh**, but he did not take it."* Mark 15:22-23.

He refused this world's cup.
He then died an agonizing death, entering that deep sleep.
But He was resurrected.
So that he could "make His name" through the rebirth of you and me. By this he showed Satan, and us, now that we fully understand, that He did what Satan's Nephilim led crowd could only fantasize about.
He is God.

# The Great Tribulation

Hippolytus spent a lot of time in his treatise making it very clear to his student, Theophilus, that the four beasts in Daniel's vision were exactly the same as the four parts of the statue in Nebuchadnezzar's dream. Both the beasts and the parts of the statue represented the Babylonian, Medo-Persian, Greek, and Roman empires. However, by saying that they would "arise" again, the same action was depicted as Christ arising from the grave. So although they were past empires, they will also arise and be in place as national powers during the end times.

Actually, though, we were told in Revelation of eight empires, not just four, on which the Harlot sits:

*"This calls for a mind with wisdom. The seven heads are seven hills on which the woman sits. They are also seven kings. Five have fallen, one is, the other has not yet come; but when he does come, he must remain for only a little while. The beast who once was, and now is not, is an eighth king. He belongs to the seven and is going to his destruction."* Revelation 17:9-11.

The kingdoms referred to here that had fallen at the point in time John was writing Revelation are Egypt, Assyria, Babylon, Medo-Persia, and Greece. The one that John says "is" would naturally be the Roman Empire that ruled in John's day. The seventh, *"the other has not yet come; but when he does come, he must remain for only a little while"* refers to the one world government we discussed a few chapters back that will be put in place following the destruction of WWIII. The antichrist will at some point head up that government, but it will *"remain for only a little while"* because forty two months before Jesus returns the antichrist will change that government into not only a dictatorship, but a government like the first five mentioned; a government structure in which he will be worshipped as a god. Additionally we are learning that the "world government" the antichrist will initially take over will basically be a culmination of all the governments of the world in the past.

We know from our earlier study that the antichrist will be Jewish, from the tribe of Dan. Whether or not he will actually have come from Israel, we don't know. We do know that when he changes that government into his personal theocracy with himself as god, he will move the headquarters to Jerusalem because Irenaeus told us:

"He shall remove his kingdom into that city (Jerusalem), and shall sit in the temple of God, leading astray those who worship him, as if he were Christ." From Against Heresies, by Irenaeus.

And at that time he will have hoodwinked quite a lot of the Jews who will make him their "king," their "messiah," which was one of his big goals.

With him in his inner circle will be seven underling kings, or as Irenaeus called them, "potentates." These will be the seven who remained after the antichrist did away with three of their cohorts, the heads of Egypt, Libya, and Ethiopia. We learned this from Hippolytus when he said:

"And under this was signified none other than Antichrist, who is also himself to raise the kingdom of the Jews. He says that three horns are plucked up by the root by him, the three kings of Egypt, and Libya, and Ethiopia, whom he cuts off in the array of battle. And he, after gaining terrible power over all, being nevertheless a tyrant, shall stir up tribulation and persecution against men, exalting himself against them." Hippolytus.

There is a quick side trip that I want to take at this point. Normally my favorite version of the Bible is the NIV. Its translation of Daniel, concerning the ten toes of the statue says:

*"And just as you saw the iron mixed with baked clay, so the people will be a mixture and will not remain united, any more than iron mixes with clay."* Daniel 2:43.

Now, however, let's read the King James Version of that very same scripture:

*"And whereas thou sawest iron mixed with miry clay,* **they** *shall mingle themselves with the* **seed of men***: but they shall not cleave one to another, even as iron is not mixed with clay."* Daniel 2:43.

What a difference that makes. The "they" obviously is referring to the ten kings. What imagery that evokes concerning the possibility of Nephilim being involved. Read it again, and let what is being said in that translation really sink in. To me, there is no other possible meaning but that something other than normal humans are mingling their seed **"with the seed of men."**

It conjures up all kinds of scenarios concerning the ten original underlings of the antichrist. And it brings to mind what we studied about demonic UFO abductions and the thought of the possible creation of new Nephilim. Unfortunately, I have searched and searched but have found none of the writings of Irenaeus or Hippolytus, or any of their contemporaries, that specifically address this issue.

My question is, why was the meaning changed so drastically in most of the later Biblical versions that we now use? I have found no suitable answer. It is as if they were scrubbed of the Nephilim inference. A few modern versions, like the American Standard and the New King James Version, do still have the **"seed"** phrase. At any rate, I will not stay on this topic since we have no answers, but I do find it fascinating, and it could actually be quite important. I will leave it for you to ponder.

Getting back to the scenario the Apostolic Oral Teaching lays out, we found out that the government of the antichrist and his seven underling kings will be what will be responsible for bringing about the destruction of the world system; Babylon, the Harlot, and Mystery Babylon:

"With respect, then, to the particular judgment in the torments that are to come upon it (The Harlot and Mystery Babylon) in the last times **by the hand of the tyrants who shall arise then**, the clearest statement has been given in these passages."     Treatise on Christ and Antichrist, by Hippolytus.

We are closing in on being able to see if we can put all of this into some kind of form that makes sense, to see how things will actually play out, using the Apostolic Oral Teaching and not speculation. To help us, though, we can also use one of the most important things other than the scriptures that God has given us. I am talking about God's "orchestrated shadows."

# Orchestrated Shadows

God's Word is utterly phenomenal. Of course, you know that. But what most people don't consider is that even the historical part of the Bible is so much deeper than we have imagined. Yes, all of the stories in the Old Testament actually happened. They are real history, and every detail is true. But from what I can see, almost all of them, if not all of them, were orchestrated by the powerful and intelligent Creator of everything to tell us something. And normally they tell us about things that were prophetic, or to explain not only what God was going to accomplish, but why He was going to do something. That's right; God has controlled the actions of entire nations to present us with shadows of things that had not taken place up until that time.

In <u>Unlocking God's Secrets</u> I wrote about one of my very favorite shadows, the positioning of the Israelite tribes while they were in the desert. I won't take the time here to cover all the details, but in Numbers 2 God told Moses exactly how he wanted each of the twelve tribes to be positioned when they made camp at night. In the center He wanted the Ark of the Covenant and the tribe of Levi, the priests. To the east were the tribes of Judah, Issachar, and Zebulun. To the north were the tribes of Dan, Asher, and Naphtali. To the west were Ephraim, Manasseh, and Benjamin. And to the south were the tribes of Rueben, Simeon, and Gad.

The exciting thing is that when you add up the populations of each of those tribes, and draw it out on paper, it forms a perfect cross. Incredible. God created a human cross that traveled across the desert for forty years, going to Jerusalem, where Jesus was going to suffer and die on one.

And if that were not enough, God positioned the tribes so that the banners of the four outside tribes were the four facets of Jesus, the Lion (King), the Eagle (Divinity), the Ox (Servant), a the face of a man (Humanity). I still get chills thinking about looking down at that lighted cross at night from the heavens, as each of those families burned their camp fires. The word awesome is not adequate. This was an "orchestrated shadow."

We mentioned earlier how the entire Egyptian captivity was an orchestrated shadow of the satanic "sacred marriage" that Nimrod wanted to reestablish at the Tower of Babel. The fact is that within the entire exodus story are literally scores of shadows, each one as wondrous as the next.

And virtually all of the stories in the Old Testament, although actual historical events, were divinely orchestrated to present for us something God wants us to see. What is exciting to me is that God not only continued that pattern of communicating with us into the New Testament, but He has not stopped that method right up until today. And one of His recently orchestrated shadows gives us an interesting glimpse of the end times. I documented this orchestrated shadow in my second book:

## The Martinique Shadow

This may be one of the most incredible events of modern time. I promise that you will be totally amazed, so much so that you will probably never forget this reading. One of the most startling things to me about this story, and there are many, is that although it occurred only about a hundred years ago, and was front page news around the world for months, very few of our generation even know about it. Ponder what could be the reason for this as you read it. That in itself may cause you to shudder.

Please know that I have spent many hours researching what I am about to share with you, to the point of going over such things as old newspaper accounts of the events, and I will tell you that as astonishing as parts of this story may sound, everything I will write did in fact happen. I hope you are seated firmly, because you are about to be blown away.

Our story begins on the beautiful Caribbean island of Martinique in 1902. Although traditional Catholic and Protestant churches had been a part of that French island's culture for many years, what few Christian believers remained had become quite apathetic towards the majority view on the island which held that the Christian religion was out of date. The dwindling population of believers could be described as lukewarm at best. Most of the citizens either did not believe in God at all, or if they did believe He existed, He had just become an object for ridicule and mockery.

There was, however, a small group of new believers who were on fire for God. They had come to their beliefs under the teaching and evangelism of an itinerant missionary from Barbados named John H. Hartman. Several times a year Rev. Hartman would travel from island to island on a small inter-island steamer to visit his various congregations in the Caribbean, including the little church that he had planted on the island of Martinique. The year 1902, though, was different.

In a journal written by Dr. V. Raymond Edman, former missionary to Ecuador, who was for many years the beloved and highly respected president of Wheaton College, we can read Rev. Hartman's own words:

"Only once did my wife, Mrs. Hartman, ever ask me not to go on one of those trips. Many a time she was ill with some tropical fever, to be sure; but only on one occasion did she beg me not to go as I had planned. I explained to her that I had no alternative but to go. The steamer went only once a month. The previous month I had sent letters to each congregation along the way to inform them that on the boat's next trip I would come for some services. The steamer remained in a given harbor for a day or two, sometimes more. Each local congregation knew approximately the day of arrival and would send word about my coming to the members and friends scattered in the towns, villages and plantations. In those days we had no wireless or radio service, and, of course, no air mail. I had to go, or else disappoint every congregation throughout the islands."

But on this one occasion, Mrs. Hartman expressed great apprehension for him. Though she was seldom discouraged, worried, or blue, she had a foreboding about this trip, scheduled for early May, 1902, and she felt that if he started out he would never return. It was such a strong impression, that Rev. Hartman reluctantly agreed to stay in Barbados.

Back on the island of Martinique, things had progressively gotten uglier. Rev. Hartman later related further to Dr. Edman:

"With this mounting wickedness and depravity, there came increasingly violent persecution of the believers. They were subject to physical harm and imprisonment as well as insolence and insults from their fellow citizens, filled with strong drink and heady with sordid pleasures. Finally the persecution grew so intense that the Christians felt they could no longer remain in the city. As a result they gathered together what few belongings they could take with them and went as a group from St. Pierre. They obeyed literally the words of the Savior, 'When ye depart out of that house or city, shake off the dust of your feet When they persecute you in this city, flee ye into another' (Matthew 10:14, 23)."

The anti God feelings on Martinique seemed to be played out even more forcefully during the Christian holiday seasons, and 1902's season of Lent and Easter saw the depravity hit new lows. The things that happened made some of the shameful things we might see today at Mardi Gras seem tame in comparison.

In fact, we read from Days and Nights in the Tropics, by Dean Harris, which was published 1905,

"In parody of the Christ's journey from Pilate's house to Calvary, with a rope around its neck they dragged a living pig outside the city. Here they nailed it to a cross, lifted it on high, and with shouts and curses, apostrophized it. They hailed it as Jesus Christ, crowned its wretched head with thorns, pierced its side and put a board above it with the inscription 'J.C., King of the Christians,' and yelling and dancing like fiends, carried it through the streets.

Then, at about the same hour, another procession of human devils, ascended the mountain behind the city, uprooted a great crucifix that had stood there for many years, and amid obscene rites and blasphemous songs, cast the sacred figure into the crater, their leader yelling as it sank out of sight, 'Go where Thou deservest to go, into Thine own hell.'"

At the same time that these atrocities were occurring, there were two missionaries in Canada who felt a strong pull to go to Martinique as two witnesses of the Gospel. They boarded a ship and headed for the Caribbean. When their ship reached its destination, the immigration officer naturally asked them what their plans were on the island. When told that they planned to preach about Jesus, he refused their entry, making them remain on board the ship until it left the harbor. Martinique had no desire to hear the Gospel.
Early in the morning of May 8, 1902, the Canadian missionaries' ship pulled out of the harbor. As it was leaving, the steamship that should have been carrying Rev. Hartman came into port.

It was the Day of Ascension, the day of celebration held annually forty days after Easter Sunday to commemorate the ascension of Christ into heaven. What new ideas the blasphemous citizenry had for that afternoon to try to top their earlier activities during Easter we can not know. What we do know is reported to us by the people on a cable repair ship that had the city in direct view.

At exactly 7:52 that morning of the Day of Ascension, the mountain behind the city violently split in half and a dense black cloud shot out horizontally. A second black cloud rolled upwards, forming a gigantic mushroom cloud, completely darkening the sky for a fifty mile radius. The initial speed of both clouds was later calculated to be over 420 miles per hour.

According to Wikipedia:

"The horizontal cloud hugged the ground and sped down towards the city of Saint-Pierre, appearing black and heavy, glowing hot from the inside. It consisted of superheated steam and volcanic gases and dust, with temperatures exceeding 1075 C. In under a minute it reached and covered the entire city, instantly igniting everything flammable it came in contact with.

A rush of wind followed, this time towards the mountain. Then came a half-hour downpour of muddy rain mixed with ashes. For the next several hours, all communication with the city was severed. Nobody knew what was happening, nor who had authority over the island, as the governor was unreachable and his status unknown.

One eyewitness said 'the mountain was blown to pieces, there was no warning,' while another said 'it was like a giant oil refinery.' One person even went as far to say that 'the town vanished before our eyes.' A warship approached the shore at about 12:30, but the intense heat prevented it from landing until about 3 PM. The city burned for several more days."

The two missionaries from Canada who were turned away witnessed the unbelievable sight from miles away. The steamship Rev. Hartman was suppose to be on was totally destroyed, as was every other ship in the harbor. Only one resident in the city survived to tell the tale. The rest of the population of over 30,000 people perished, incinerated in the first few seconds, as was virtually all of the animal and bird life. The sea literally boiled for miles out from the island. The lone survivor in the city was a murderer who had been in a dungeon like jail cell under the ground. The air in his underground chamber literally roasted his skin, but he lived to relate his story.

The small Christian church watched the devastation from their new home. The ship carrying the two Canadian Christian witnesses was burning from stem to stern when it reached the next island of St. Lucia; however, the two missionaries were not injured. Fire fell from the eruption down on neighboring islands as far as 125 miles away, from the volcano that was Mt. Pelee, the mountain where the large crucifix had been tossed in six weeks earlier, with the heinous shout, "Go where Thou deservest to go, into Thine own hell."

The editor of The Dominica Guardian, on May 28, 1902, wrote,

"The profanities on last Good Friday at St. Pierre were but the repetitions of similar profanities and sacrilegiousness of which we know too much. But an outraged Divinity having hushed up the actors forever we will say no more about them."

Rev. John H. Hartman and his small congregation of believers were reunited, and Martinique is today the lush paradise it was intended to be.
        From Musings from Me and My Master by Bob Morley.

In my research I was astounded to find that, as far as I know, no other person has ever looked at the events of the Mt. Pelee Ascension Day eruption in this light of searching for Types and Shadows. Interestingly, you and I may be the first people on earth ever to do so.

My belief is that God did not stop communicating to us with the writing of the last word in Revelation. We know that God "is the same yesterday, today, and forever," and since His communication was relatively constant up until two thousand years ago, it seems to make sense that He probably did not stop then. We also know that up until today He does continue to communicate to mankind in prayer, situational direction, dreams, visions, etc. Before you jump up and down, though, please be certain that I realize that the Bible is the final word on any matter. And know also that it would be easy to go way overboard in trying to read things into every historical event. But when something seems to have God's hand so openly on it, even down to the timing being on the Day of Ascension, it might be worthwhile to explore some possibilities.

Our Father orchestrated historical events to tell us things in the shadows or pictures within the events themselves, such as those in the book of Ruth that most Christians are familiar with. Those "shadows" were a form of prophecy. The people involved had no idea that they were living out prophetic dramas, but they certainly were. We can be confident that Abraham had no idea when he was told to take his son, Isaac, up on a mountain and sacrifice him that what he was doing was a picture of God Himself having to take Jesus, His Son, up the very same mountain hundreds of years later to sacrifice Him as a substitution for sinful mankind. After 15,000 hours of research I have come to believe that virtually every event described in the Bible contains these shadows, including even the miracles of Christ, our Savior.

For instance, although I will not go into all the details now, even the two stories of the feedings of the multitudes are full of such shadows, indicating the old and new covenants. For example, the two baskets used to pick up the remaining fish were different Hebrew words, one describing a basket used exclusively by Jews, and the other describing one used by Gentiles. Reread those miracles sometime and notice how even the numbers are different. Twelve of the Jewish baskets were retrieved in one feeding, obviously representing the twelve tribes of Israel, whereas seven of the Gentile baskets were filled at the end of the other feeding, representing the seven churches, as in the seven churches Jesus wrote letters to in Revelation.

With the knowledge that God indeed orchestrated all of the Biblical events in order to tell us things, my feeling is that some events since then could, in fact, be loaded with "types and shadows" and prophecy. The story we saw that happened in Martinique in 1902 may be a prime example. As you read the accounts, you probably saw the wrath of God and Judgment Day played out in that story, but could there have been more? Although no one else in the past hundred years seems to have noticed, I for one believe there well might be much more.

God's overall story to us is a fairly simple one in many regards, and because of that, most Biblical stories contain types and shadows that portray the same themes over and over. Personally, I see many of the exact same ones in the Martinique story. You may feel that what I am going to share is a stretch, but humor me for a moment. Below are the "types and shadows" that jumped out at me:

1 - The wrath of God and Judgment Day. That one is too obvious to discuss.
2 - Could the traditional church on the island represent the end time church that Jesus said He would spit out of His mouth in His letter to the Church of

Laodicea in Revelation? As we know, that church, which is probably our church age, was said to be lukewarm. It will become a completely apostate (unbelieving) church during the tribulation according to the book of Revelation.

3 - Increasingly violent persecution of the true Christians like we know will occur during the tribulation.

4 - I see that small church of on-fire believers that was led to leave as a shadow of the resurrection/rapture. We know that event will occur immediately before God shows His wrath at the end of the tribulation

5 - One of the most obvious "types" in the Martinique story is that of the two Canadian men who came to witness, but whose message was not wanted. They clearly represent the Two Witnesses in Revelation, Enoch and Elijah, who will be sent to preach the Gospel but will be hated to the point that their killing is a time for celebration.

6 - Speaking of that small band of believers that left before the eruption in our story, could Rev. Hartman represent the Holy Spirit? He obviously was the overseer of the small church.

7 - The leader of the blasphemous citizens is obviously a "type" of the antichrist.

8 - And the defiant act that he committed with the pig was definitely a shadow of the "abomination that causes desolation" spoken of in places such as Daniel, Mark, Matthew, and Revelation.

9 - The actual fire itself seems extremely representative, since God tells us over and over that He will cleanse the earth of sin the second time with fire, not a flood. The heat of the fire on Martinique surpassed a thousand degrees centigrade. Everything was completely destroyed.

10 - And in mentioning the fire, notice that after the total "cleansing" on Martinique occurred, the island came back as a completely lush paradise. This to me is a "shadow" of what we are told will happen to the earth after it is cleansed by fire when the Millennial Kingdom is over, so that heaven can then be on this earth.

11 - Another "type" that springs to mind is the murderer in the dungeon who survives the devastation. I can see him as representing Satan. At the end of the tribulation, when unbelievers are destroyed, Satan is put in a dungeon and allowed to live on until the end of the Millennial Kingdom, when he is released for a short time.

12 - The mountain splitting in two is a perfect picture of what we are told will happen to the Mount of Olives on the day that Jesus will return.
13 - What about Jesus? Is there a "type" of Him in this story? I actually see Him twice. First, I think the crucifix that was thrown into the pit represented what happened to him for three days following His crucifixion. Second, I see the forceful eruption on the Day of Ascension as representing His power, which we seem to forget to think about way too much.

Virtually every story, event, parable and miracle in the Bible is rich with the symbolisms of "types and shadows" which foretell future events and people. God orchestrated things that way up until two thousand years ago in order to prophesy events that were to come. Did the Father change His way of doing things after John wrote the last word in Revelation? I don't believe He did. Hebrews 13:8 tells us, *"Jesus is the same today and yesterday and forever."* It is still His earth. It is still "His story." Those in the world today who don't take advantage of God's grace, and rush to the feet of Jesus now, will someday experience the same destruction that the citizens of Saint-Pierre, Martinique, did in 1902. God has given mankind thousands and thousands of prophecies and shadows so that man would understand the future and run to Him before it is too late. Our loving Father has even orchestrated history, His story, to try to reach the children He so dearly loves.

From <u>Musings from Me and My Master</u> by Bob Morley.

# Hard Times

We have looked at the seals and trumpets up to the sixth trumpet, and although using the timing of Rabbi Samuel ben Judah's 1917 as being the starting point for the trumpets, since we do not have the luxury of looking backward from the complete finish of the second coming, the things we described about the trumpets are still speculative and may not be correct. Only time will tell for sure.

It seems, however, that the sixth trumpet will be the next event, and will be WWIII, which will be the most devastating war imaginable, with a third of the world's population dying in that nuclear war. It will begin around the Euphrates River, quite probably starting with an Israeli-Muslim confrontation and then escalating. From what we will learn a little later, we are fairly certain that Israel will have been on the winning side of the sixth trumpet war.

Following the devastation of WWIII, the sentiment of the world that remains will be to create a type of one world government and one world religion to prevent future wars, and it will use an existing organization that had been on the decline or stagnant prior to that war to be the basis of it. Individual nations will still exist, however, so it will not be a total one world government. Ten nations will be the central part of the organization, three of which will be Egypt, Libya, and Ethiopia, indicating that the organization may be primarily a Mediterranean or Mid Eastern confederation of some sort.

We also know that four other nations or confederations of nations will be in existence, represented by the four beasts in Daniel's dream, and although they may have lost much of their power and clout during the sixth trumpet war, they will remain, even into the Millennial Kingdom after Christ's second coming. They will be subjugated, at least to some degree, by the antichrist's ruling government.

The two witnesses spoken of in Revelation will in some manner make their appearance. How that will unfold and play out, we are not told, but the Apostolic Oral Teaching is clear that they will be Enoch and Elijah, and will signal the beginning of the seven year tribulation. They will be on the scene for 42 months before they are killed.

Either before or during that first 42 month period the antichrist, who will be Jewish from the tribe of Dan, will move into a leadership role of the one world government organization. He will immediately have some type of trouble with Egypt, Libya, and Ethiopia and will conquer them in a war. Also during that time period the antichrist will move his headquarters to Jerusalem and will rebuild the Jewish temple. Remember, the Apostolic Oral Teaching taught us that it would be the antichrist who would rebuild the temple, not the Jews. During those 42 months the antichrist will push for his subjects to almost worship his organization.

At the end of the first 42 months the antichrist will go into the temple and declare himself to be the christ, the messiah of the Jews. Many of the Jews will fall for that lie and worship him. He will then demand that the entire world worship him, and will begin an all out campaign of persecution against the Christians, as well as any Jews who do not comply. Many will be killed. During this time we can see that the antichrist will have his hands full trying to get all of the nations of the world into full agreement that he is divine.

Knowing the power the antichrist will have over the world, and since the antichrist will be ruling from Jerusalem, we can be certain that Israel was not subjected to nuclear attack during the sixth trumpet war; otherwise due to the small area that Israel has, the entire nation would have become uninhabitable. This can also lead us to know that Israel was probably on the winning side of WWIII. And it is probably her military might that gives the antichrist his power.

Since the antichrist and his seven "potentates" will come to hate the entire world system, as represented by the Harlot, Babylon, and Mystery Babylon, they will be the instrument used for its destruction. We learned:

"These (the ten kings) shall make war with the Lamb, and the Lamb shall overcome them, because He is the Lord of lords and the King of kings. It is manifest, therefore, that of these [potentates], he who is to come shall slay three, and subject the remainder to his power, and that he shall be himself the eighth among them. And **they shall lay Babylon waste, and burn her with fire**, and shall give their kingdom to the beast, and put the Church to flight."      Against Heresies, book 5 chapter 26, by Irenaeus.

This will be a terrible time in the world. Jesus told us:

> *"For then there will be great distress, unequaled from the beginning of the world until now—and never to be equaled again."*     Matthew 24:21.

    One of John Darby's better traits was that he had a soft spot in his heart for the Jewish people. So when he decided that the lady's dream in which she supposedly saw Christians going to heaven before the tribulation was a revelation from God that the rapture would occur before the tribulation started and the church would not be on earth when it happened, it allowed him to "invent" a scenario in which the Jews would be the ones persecuted by the antichrist instead of the Christians, as had been taught for eighteen hundred years, thus providing a happy end for the tribulation story in which Jesus would return in the nick of time to save the Jewish people. Yes, it made for a happy ending for the Jews, but the problem was that there was no truth to it. It was not what Jesus taught His disciples would happen, as we now know from studying the Apostolic Oral Teaching.

    The highly respected Justin Martyr, a church Father and contemporary of Irenaeus, said in <u>The Second Apology of Justin for the Christians, Addressed to the Roman Senate</u>, chapter CX:

"He (Jesus) shall come from heaven with glory, when the man of apostasy, who speaks strange things against the Most High, shall venture to do unlawful deeds on the earth **against us the Christians**, who, having learned the true worship of God from **the law**, and **the word which went forth from Jerusalem by means of the apostles of Jesus**."     Justin Martyr.

    In that short quote we see that Justin Martyr was convinced that the **truth** was found in two sources; first the **Bible**, which he referred to as **"the law,"** and secondly the **teaching Jesus gave His disciples** that was not written down in the Bible, which he called **"the word which went forth from Jerusalem by means of the apostles of Jesus,"** which we now call the Apostolic Oral Teaching.

    We also saw in that quote that Justin Martyr was saying that Jesus taught His disciples that the persecution would be against the Christians, not the Jews, as Darby's newly invented scenario depicts, and as is taught by virtually every single prophecy teacher today. Additionally, Justin Martyr was telling us that the true Christians during the tribulation will have learned the truth from both the Bible and the Apostolic Oral Teaching. That is exactly what you are receiving in this book when you read the quotes of Irenaeus and Hippolytus.

And may I state as emphatically as I can that, after reading the **truth** presented in this book, if you decide to continue to believe John Darby's interpretations of the end times, as presented by the so called modern "scholars" that you see on TV, or even the ministers and teachers in your local churches who recite what they have heard from those "scholars," you are going to be making a terrible mistake.

You now are being given the truth from Jesus Himself, through the quotes from the early Fathers who still had the teaching He had given John and His other disciples, so my heartfelt advice is to not only reject the modern teaching, but to not even subject your ears to it any longer. It is the "heresy" that Satan wants you to pay attention to and believe. Don't give him that satisfaction, even though you may be ridiculed by your circle of Christian friends who have not had the opportunity to learn what you are now learning. Justin Martyr is telling us that should the tribulation occur in our lifetime, we will not be alone. The true end time Christians will be on the same page in their beliefs, and according to Justin Martyr, those beliefs will have come from the Bible and the Apostolic Oral Teaching, not man's latest interpretations that are in vogue at this moment.

Please, therefore, share the truth with your friends; otherwise they may be being set up for the Great Delusion that we will delve into a little later. This is not a game. If you are a minister or a teacher in any capacity of the end times, I strongly urge you to immediately scrap what we have been taught in the past. I am convinced that you, like me, would never want to have a student be led down the wrong path, the path to the Church of Laodicea that Jesus will spit out of His mouth. Spend the time to learn from the giants of the faith from the Church of Philadelphia (1730 to 1900) and especially the Church of Smyrna (100 to 313 AD), which still had the oral lessons Jesus taught His disciples. We need to reverently heed the words of Hippolytus:

**"We, too, who are rightly instructed in what was declared aforetime by them, speak not of our own capacity. For we do not**

**attempt to made any change one way or another among ourselves in the words that were spoken of old by them**, …; for that is a common benefit for both parties: **for him who speaks, in holding in memory and setting forth correctly things <u>uttered</u> of old; and for him who hears, in giving attention to the things spoken.**

Since, then, in this **there is a work assigned to both parties together, to him who speaks, that he speak forth faithfully without regard to risk, and to him who hears, that he hear and receive in faith that which is spoken**, I beseech you to strive together with me in prayer to God."

Treatise on Christ and Antichrist, number 2, by Hippolytus.

We can only hope that when Darby said of the early church Fathers that "their views and statements weigh with me not one feather," that he did not realize that those church Fathers knew better than to try to interpret the allegory in Revelation, because they knew that the truth had indeed been passed down to them from the Lord through the Apostle John. It is bad enough that Darby irreverently discarded the beliefs and teaching of eighteen hundred years, in order to try to discredit the church's teaching as a kind of back door slap at the bishop who he thought had wronged him, but it would be unthinkable to believe that Darby had created such a foolish invention, with the conscious knowledge that he was saying that Jesus Himself was wrong and he, Darby, knew better.

So, we will give Darby the benefit of the doubt and assume that he concocted his theory because he deep down wanted the best for the Jewish people that he cared about. Let us assume that he felt "the apple of God's eye" deserved better than they received in Covenant Theology, which basically stated that God no longer cared about the Jews and had completely replaced them in His mind with the church.

Of course, any type of replacement Theology is erroneous, too, because if we look at the closing chapters of Ezekiel we find that God will still keep the promise He made to the patriarchs and He will divide up Israel, the land He had set aside for their descendants, into twelve separate tracts for the twelve Jewish tribes. Obviously, when Jesus returns, Israel will recognize their true Messiah.

Prior to that return, however, John's teaching reveals to us that the Jews will fall for the antichrist's lies and miracles. They will indeed make him their king and worship him as god. A problem looms large that many, many people who say they are Christians will ignorantly follow the lead of most of the Jews, and fall in lock step behind the antichrist. Let's face the facts; the vast majority of the supposed two billion folks on planet earth who might say they are Christian do not have the foggiest idea about what Christianity is all about. If asked, unfortunately, most will say they are Christian because they think Jesus was a good man with good teaching, even though they really don't even know what He taught. And since most have never read a single chapter in the Bible, they obviously have no knowledge at all of the prophecies found in places like Daniel and Revelation. Thus, the Great Delusion. For, continuing on with the above quote from Jesus:

*"For then there will be great distress, unequaled from the beginning of the world until now—and never to be equaled again.*
*If those days had not been cut short, no one would survive, but for the sake of the **elect** those days will be shortened. At that time if anyone says to you, 'Look, here is the Messiah!' or, 'There he is!' do not believe it. For false messiahs and false prophets will appear and perform great signs and wonders to deceive, if possible, even the **elect**. See, I have told you ahead of time.*
*So if anyone tells you, 'There he is, out in the wilderness,' do not go out; or, 'Here he is, in the inner rooms,' do not believe it. For as lightning that comes from the east is visible even in the west, so will be the coming of the Son of Man."*                                             Matthew 24:21-27.

As a quick aside, I highlighted the word "elect" in that quote for a reason. Some believers in Darby's dipensationalism and the pre-trib rapture will deny that the "elect" Jesus was talking about in those verses were Christians. They will say with a straight face that the "elect" in that quote refers to Israel. The truth, however, is that the Greek word translated as "elect" is "eklektos," which is found seven times in the New Testament and always refers to the church or to individual Christians, except once in 1st Timothy 5:21 where it mentions *"the elect angels."* But this is nothing new. I have found more times than I would have wished, that people will twist all sorts of passages to try to make them fit their preconceived beliefs, rather than actually using the scriptures to formulate their beliefs. I have been saddened to see it.

Irenaeus, on the other hand was not only saddened to see that happen, but became downright angry about it. In fact, we can almost see the anger boil over when he wrote about how men in his day tried to conform the scriptures to their way of thinking:

"And it is not only from the writings of the evangelists and the apostles that they endeavor to derive proofs for their opinions by means of **perverse interpretations and deceitful expositions**: they deal in the same way with the law and the prophets, which contain many parables and allegories that can frequently be drawn into various senses, according to the kind of exegesis to which they are subjected. And others of them, with great craftiness, **adapted such parts of Scripture to their own figments**, lead away captives from the truth.

Such, then, is their system, which neither the prophets announced, nor the Lord taught, nor the apostles delivered, **but of which they boast that beyond all others they have a perfect knowledge**. They gather their views from other sources than the Scriptures; and, to use a common proverb, they strive to weave ropes of sand, while they endeavor to adapt with an air of probability to their own peculiar assertions the parables of the Lord, the sayings of the prophets, and the words of the apostles, in order that their scheme may not seem altogether without support. In doing so, however, they disregard the order and the connection of the Scriptures, and so far as in them lies, **dismember and destroy the truth**. By **transferring passages, and dressing them up anew, and making one thing out of another, they succeed in deluding many through their wickedly adapting the oracles of the Lord to their opinions**. These persons patch together old wives' fables, and then endeavor, by violently drawing away from their proper connection, words, expressions, and parables whenever found, to adapt the oracles of God to their **baseless fictions**."

Against Heresies, Book 1, chapter 8, #1, and 3, #6, Irenaeus.

But leaving the fact that people try to change the meaning of words like "elect" in order to make them fit their "baseless fictions," what we can see happening next during the tribulation, according to what the Apostolic Oral Teaching tells us, is that the Jews will see the antichrist as the person who protects them from their enemies, possibly due to a role he played in the sixth trumpet war, although that, of course, is pure speculation. At any rate, the Jews messed up the first time Jesus came because they were only looking for a king who would defeat their enemies, not realizing that their own sacred texts had told them that their Messiah would come first as a humble servant. And since most of Israel's Jews today are even less informed of their own scriptures than their forefathers were two thousand years ago, they will make the wrong choice yet again. They will believe the antichrist's lies, possibly because of the miracles the Bible tells us he will perform.

There is something we need also to understand. We Christians, knowing that Israel is the "apple of God's eye," and knowing that they worship the same God we do, and knowing that Jesus came through their heritage, normally feel very "simpatico" towards them. We know that one day, when God opens their eyes, they will be our brothers and sisters in Christ. What we need to get through our heads is that for the most part that love relationship is a one way street. Most Jews believe that deep down all Christians hate them, and that Christians have been the cause of all their problems for the last two thousand years.

Mike Evans, a Messianic Jew, tells of his Jewish mother teaching him those exact things as truths to never be forgotten. Now, knowing that most of the Jews in Israel still believe that, Mike, through his wonderful "Jewish Prayer Team" organization, has recently bought a large building a few blocks from Old Jerusalem which will house an interactive museum that will teach the Jews who visit it about the love shown to them during the Holocaust by such Christians as Corrie ten Boom's family, Dietrich Bonhoeffer, Harry Truman, Raoul Wallenberg, and many others.

You may be wondering how the Jews could truly not see that Christians are their friends. Well, let's list a few names. Adolf Hitler, Heinrich Himmler, Reinhard Heydrich, Joseph Goebbels, Adolf Eichmann. Now, pretend you are a Jew and you read over that list. What words would come to your mind in association with those names? How about evil, murder, torture, persecution, death camps, slaughter, hatred, cruel, suffering, heinous, killers, misery, pain, monsters, atrocious, Christian, beastly, torment, depraved, wicked, or obscene? You read that right. Christian would definitely be in your list. And why not? Adolf Hitler, Heinrich Himmler, Reinhard Heydrich, Joseph Goebbels, and Adolf Eichmann all said they were Christians. Of course, you and I know that no one who had truly surrendered his life to the Lordship of Jesus would ever do what those people did. But as a Jew, how would you tell the difference? Or would you even try?

Even today, we have world leaders from here in America like Bill Clinton, Jimmy Carter, George Bush, Barack Obama, Condoleezza Rice, John Kerry, and Hillary Clinton who all are defined as Christians, and all claim to be the friend and ally of Israel, but whose actions all side with the people whose chief goal in life, as stated clearly by their revered leader Yasser Arafat, is the total destruction of all the Jewish people. These American leaders have all pushed hard for Israel to give up part of the land God promised the descendants of Jacob to the Palestinians, a people who dream of wiping Israel off the map. As a Jew, would you feel that Christians were your brothers and sisters? We are so naïve not to understand this.

I mention this because when the antichrist and his potentates begin their mass persecution and murder of the Christians, most of the Jewish people will not see that as being out of the ordinary for their messiah. Of course, there will be some who will openly rebel at the persecution of the Christians, and for that they will be persecuted as well. And, as it was in Germany during the Holocaust, when Christians literally sang their hymns in churches louder and louder in order to drown out the screams of the Jews as the trains went by on the way to Hitler's death camps, there will be Jews who will silently cringe at the persecution of the Christians.

If we doubt that can happen again, let's imagine from what we have learned from the Apostolic Oral Teaching what those days will be like with the antichrist. He will come on the scene talking about true peace for the entire planet, and as a speaker, he will be the best ever heard. Visualize the very best speaker you have ever heard in your life. That person will be a rank amateur compared to the antichrist. He will quickly have most of the world eating out of his hands.

I can imagine that since his first big goal will be to win the Jews over and become their king, once he moves his headquarters to Jerusalem he will really target them with his lies. Let's remember, Satan will have had thirty five hundred years to study their scriptures, and he will know them as well as if he had written them himself. We saw him try to tempt Jesus in the wilderness by quoting scriptures, but since Jesus was the true author of those verses the antichrist was in over his head. But the Jewish people and their rabbi's will be putty in his hands. It is not difficult at all to see how they could be clamoring for the antichrist to admit that he was their messiah long before he actually makes that lying declaration. And not only will he easily convince the religious Jews of that day, but with his miracle working power, he will bring the secular Jews into his camp as well. So, when he does build a temple and then stands in it and states that he is divine, a spontaneous eruption of joy and celebration will occur, the likes of which we have never seen.

After that, since he has also had a few thousand years to learn the New Testament backwards and forwards, he will do the same thing with most of the "in name only" Christian population. And at the same time he will be gaining believers among the followers of all the other religions of the world as well. This should be fairly easy for him since he was the inventor of all of those religions, including New Age, Atheism, Islam, etc.

This guy will be a real smooth talker. And since he will have the world media at his disposal, I can see where he will make FDR's fireside chats that caused a nation to follow his line of thinking, be comparable to a test pattern versus an IMAX movie. As we saw Hitler being able to bring thousands to tears or to rage, the antichrist will be able to illicit any emotion from the largest of audiences.

His problem will be the true Christians, the ones who truly have a relationship with the Lord; the ones with the precious Holy Spirit within them, telling them to beware, letting them know that this is the one Jesus and His disciples warned about. These are the "elect" who will know better, the "elect" who will not be deceived. These are the ones who would die for their Savior. And many, if not most, actually will. These will be Christians of the same mind set as the saints of the Church of Smyrna who Jesus only commended in His letter to them in Revelation. These will believe as Justin Martyr did when he faced the Prefect Rusticus in Rome, in A.D. 165, with six companions, Chariton, Charito, Evelpostos, Pæon, Hierax, and Liberianos. We still have the authentic account of their martyrdom:

"The Prefect Rusticus says: Approach and sacrifice, all of you, to the gods. Justin says: No one in his right mind gives up piety for impiety. The Prefect Rusticus says: If you do not obey, you will be tortured without mercy. Justin replies: That is our desire, to be tortured for Our Lord, Jesus Christ, and so to be saved, for that will give us salvation and firm confidence at the more terrible universal tribunal of Our Lord and Savior. And all the martyrs said: Do as you wish; for we are Christians, and we do not sacrifice to idols. The Prefect Rusticus read the sentence: Those who do not wish to sacrifice to the gods and to obey the emperor will be scourged and beheaded

according to the laws. The holy martyrs glorifying God betook themselves to the customary place, where they were beheaded and consummated their martyrdom confessing their Savior."
From "Corpus Apologetarum", III, Jena, 1879, 266-78; P.G., VI, 1565-72.

In those days the Christians knew that there was an excellent chance that they would be killed for their faith. They were living in a time like that of the coming tribulation. In fact, Justin Martyr wrote about his thoughts on the subject prior to his own martyrdom about 165 AD:

"For you are aware that the prophetic word says, 'And his wife shall be like a fruitful vine.' Now it is evident that no one can terrify or subdue us who have believed in Jesus over all the world. For it is plain that, though beheaded, and crucified, and thrown to wild beasts, and chains, and fire, and all other kinds of torture, we do not give up our confession; but the more such things happen, the more do others and in larger numbers become faithful, and worshippers of God through the name of Jesus."
The Second Apology of Justin for the Christians, Chapter CX, Justin Martyr.

Justin Martyr was the same type of Christian Hippolytus described when he told us what the Apostle John taught concerning the verse he had written in Revelation that says:

*"And the dragon saw and persecuted the woman (the church) which brought forth the man-child. And to the woman were given **two wings of the great eagle**, that she might fly into the wilderness, where she is nourished for a time, and times, and half a time, from the face of the serpent."*
Revelation 12:13-14.

Yes, the bane for the antichrist, the ones Hippolytus told us who, like those who died in his and Justin Martyr's day in the Roman arena, will be:

"possessed of no other defense than the **two wings of the great eagle**, that is to say, **the faith of Jesus Christ**, who, in stretching forth His holy hands on the holy tree, **unfolded two wings**, the right and the left, and called to Him all who believed upon Him, and covered them as a hen her chickens."
Treatise on Christ and Antichrist, by Hippolytus.

# The Just Ending

It is quite possible that both WWI and WWII were orchestrated shadows of the end times. Consider that both world wars were so close together, as probably will be true of the sixth trumpet war and the final war we know as Armageddon. Hitler could obviously be a type of the antichrist, pure evil with oratorical skills that could incite a people to follow him. We saw thousands of both Jews and Christians killed in Hitler's death camps. We witnessed evil. We saw kings of the east in the form of Japan come to Hitler's aide, but to no avail. We saw nations rise up to defeat him. And just as Hitler fell, the same is in store for the antichrist. But it will be a bad time for forty two months until that happens. The Bible tells us:

*"The great day of the Lord is near—near and coming quickly.*
  *The cry on the day of the Lord is bitter;*
  *the Mighty Warrior shouts his battle cry.*

*That day will be a day of wrath—a day of distress and anguish,*
  *a day of trouble and ruin, a day of darkness and gloom,*
  *a day of clouds and blackness—a day of trumpet and battle cry*
  *against the fortified cities and against the corner towers.*

 *'I will bring such distress on all people*
  *that they will grope about like those who are blind,*
  *because they have sinned against the Lord.*
  *Their blood will be poured out*
  *like dust and their entrails like dung.*
  *Neither their silver nor their gold will be able to save them*
  *on the day of the Lord's wrath.'*

*In the fire of his jealousy the whole earth will be consumed,*
  *for he will make a sudden end of all who live on the earth."*
Zephaniah 1:14-18.

Those forty two months will obviously be terrible.

Concerning that scripture, however, we should investigate something about the very last sentence. It says that, *"the **whole** earth will be consumed,"* and there will be *"a sudden end of **all** who live on the earth."* Since we know that at the end of the tribulation Jesus will return and reign in His kingdom on earth, obviously the **whole** earth will not be consumed and there will not be an end to **all** who live on the earth. So, what gives?

One of the things that God does in the Bible is use synecdoches in order to make a powerful impact on what He is telling us. I can hear you now. A what? That definitely is not a word we use every day around the house. Dictionary.com defines a synecdoche as "a figure of speech in which a part is used for the whole or the whole for a part, the special for the general or the general for the special. When used in literature, a synecdoche will add to the visual imagery of the passage and enhance the reader's experience."

For instance, if I were to write that "the world was giving Joe a hard time," you would understand what I meant. Obviously the entire world was not bothering poor Joe. The synecdoche, however, painted a more vivid picture than if I had written that "a leaky fountain pen and a ringing telephone were giving Joe a hard time." By saying, "the world was giving Joe a hard time," I was using a whole for a part, the entire world for his pen and phone.

We can find synecdoches throughout scripture. For instance we read:

*"Your Majesty, you are the king of kings. The God of heaven has given you dominion and power and might and glory; in your hands he has placed **all mankind and the beasts of the field and the birds in the sky. Wherever they live, he has made you ruler over them all**. You are that head of gold."*
Daniel 2:37-38.

Obviously Nebuchadnezzar did not rule over every man, beast and bird on earth. And the same is true of the Medo-Persian Empire described in the next verse:

*"After you, another kingdom will arise, inferior to yours. Next, a third kingdom, one of bronze, will rule over **the whole earth**."*     Daniel 2:39.

We know without being told that there were nations that empire did not rule over. We actually can find synecdoches throughout the entire Bible, for example, in talking about John the Baptist we read:

*"The **whole Judean countryside** and **all the people of Jerusalem** went out to him. Confessing their sins, they were baptized by him in the Jordan River."* Mark 1:5.

We have no problem at all understanding that not every single person who lived in Jerusalem went to the Jordan River to be baptized by John the Baptist. However, since John Darby came up with the ridiculous idea that unless somehow told otherwise through the scripture, we should take the verses in Revelation completely literally, such as:

*"It was given authority over **every tribe, people, language and nation**."* Revelation 13:7.

What I am getting to is the fact that although the antichrist will be evil and powerful, he will not be nearly as powerful as we have been taught, and his rule will not cover the entire world. We will see that the Apostolic Oral Teaching will bear that out. There will still be nations that the antichrist will not control. Maybe those nations started out thinking it would be good to become a part of a one world government, but as those nations got to see the antichrist in action, they backed away from him. Or maybe they never were a part of his confederation to begin with. The scripture only mentioned ten nations, and three of them he put down rather quickly. We just can not guess what the exact situation will be, and the Apostolic Oral Teaching does not even give us any clues. But we can be positive that there will be nations which will oppose him.

Let's first read John's allegorical account in Revelation of the end of the antichrist:

*"I saw heaven standing open and there before me was a white horse, whose rider is called Faithful and True. With justice he judges and wages war. His eyes are like blazing fire, and on his head are many crowns. He has a name written on him that no one knows but he himself. He is dressed in a robe dipped in blood, and his name is the Word of God. The armies of*

*heaven were following him, riding on white horses and dressed in fine linen, white and clean. Coming out of his mouth is a sharp sword with which to strike down the nations. "He will rule them with an iron scepter." He treads the winepress of the fury of the wrath of God Almighty. On his robe and on his thigh he has this name written: king of kings and lord of lords.*

*And I saw an angel standing in the sun, who cried in a loud voice to all the birds flying in midair, 'Come, gather together for the great supper of God, so that you may eat the flesh of kings, generals, and the mighty, of horses and their riders, and the flesh of all people, free and slave, great and small.'*

*Then I saw the beast and the kings of the earth and their armies gathered together to wage war against the rider on the horse and his army. But the beast was captured, and with it the false prophet who had performed the signs on its behalf. With these signs he had deluded those who had received the mark of the beast and worshiped its image. The two of them were thrown alive into the fiery lake of burning sulfur. The rest were killed with the sword coming out of the mouth of the rider on the horse, and all the birds gorged themselves on their flesh."* Revelation 19:11-21.

For most of my Christian life I never even tried to figure out from those verses how the antichrist would meet his end. I suppose I had a mental image of Jesus riding on a white horse in the sky with His army of saints riding behind Him and the antichrist on the ground exhorting his army to fire upon Jesus and His troops. In fact, I can imagine wondering why people would obey the antichrist while seeing with their own eyes that Jesus was coming and obviously was God. You may have had the same type of imagery. Quite honestly, I never tried to consider how those last few minutes would really play out. It was all so surreal to me, but having been indoctrinated in Darby's school of thought, I never questioned that it would happen exactly as it was written. Darby had said to take it literally, so those who taught me taught the same, and I naturally just mentally said, OK.

Now that we have seen the truth, the interpretations of John's visions by John himself in the exact words he taught Polycarp, who passed those words on to Irenaeus, we might suspect that there may be a more earthly explanation of how those scriptural images will really play out.

In fact, Hippolytus, in explaining how the antichrist will meet his end, quotes Ezekiel:

*"Therefore this is what the Sovereign Lord says:*

> *Because you think you are wise, as wise as a god,*
> ***I am going to bring foreigners against you,***
> ***the most ruthless of nations;***
> *they will draw their swords against your beauty and wisdom*
> *and pierce your shining splendor.*
> *They will bring you down to the pit,*
> *and you will die a violent death in the heart of the seas.*
> *Will you then say, 'I am a god,'*
> *in the presence of those who kill you?*
> *You will be but a mortal, not a god,*
> *in the hands of those who slay you.*
> *You will die the death of the uncircumcised*
> ***at the hands of foreigners.***

*I have spoken, declares the Sovereign Lord."*     Ezekiel 28:6-10.
Treatise on Christ and Antichrist, by Hippolytus.

By quoting Ezekiel, Hippolytus is telling us that there will be nations who will go against the antichrist, the same as nations went against Hitler. And he will be killed. We also read that he *"will die a violent death in the heart of the seas."* Do we think that the antichrist will be killed in a navel battle? Let's recall the short discussion we had about the often used Biblical reference to the sea. As we recall, the sea was the domain of Satan in the original Canaanite (Nephilim) religion.

What I am seeing in all of this is "comfortable shoes." For me, the end times are making more sense. It is not all so surreal. As with almost every other Biblical event, God is using His creation, not something we would think of as supernatural. Of course, when we ponder it only for a brief second, it is still quite supernatural how God orchestrates events. And wonderful.

As to what nations are going to be involved in this last war that we know of as Armageddon, we could only guess, and in so doing, as we have seen we will probably be wrong. But it does seem from what the scripture tells us that the antichrist will elicit help from "the kings of the east," kind of like what we saw in the orchestrated shadow of WWII when Japan came in to help Hitler. What nations are these we can only surmise. China, North Korea, maybe. Of course, we don't know for sure when all of this will take place, or the relative strengths of different nations following the sixth trumpet war, or the political landscape. And what about the nations opposing the antichrist? Are they Christian nations? They were in WWII. But again, only time will tell. The Apostolic Oral Teaching does not tell us, but I'm sure we will all have our ideas on the possibilities, which is natural. But let's not throw them out as gospel truth, because our personal thoughts are certainly not that.

We do know that things will get pretty much out of control because Jesus tells us:

*"If those days had not been cut short, no one would survive."*
Matthew 24:22.

Something must happen to stop what could indeed be the destruction of mankind at his own hands through uncontrolled nuclear activity. We all know that there exists today enough nuclear bombs to destroy the world many times over, so something must be done to put a stop to the carnage.

# Off We Go

It is at this time that I find myself standing without my "comfortable shoes," because the events to come next can only be described as supernatural. Although throughout most of history God has used what we consider the "natural" to play out "His story," there have been some occasions when that has not been the case. We can think of both Elijah and Enoch being taken without dying, the virgin birth of Jesus, the raising of the dead by Jesus, and His own resurrection. These were not "ho hum" events. These were eye poppers. And at the stopping of Armageddon there will be several of them occurring almost at once. Jesus had said that the events of the end times would be like birth pains, coming together faster and faster, and with greater magnitude, until the resulting birth takes place. And it is at this time when the culmination of everything occurs. The "birth," the second coming of the Lord to finally establish His Kingdom, is truly at hand at this moment in time that we have come to in our study. Jesus said:

> "**Immediately after** the distress of those days
> 'the sun will be darkened, and the moon will not give its light;
> the stars will fall from the sky, and the heavenly bodies will be shaken.'
> Then will appear the sign of the Son of Man in heaven. And then all the peoples of the earth will mourn when they see the Son of Man coming on the clouds of heaven, with power and great glory."
> 
> Revelation 24:29-30.

WOW!!! WOW!!!
We were told that it would happen like this the day Jesus left the earth. He was with His disciples and God's Word says:

> "He was taken up before their very eyes, and a cloud hid him from their sight. They were looking intently up into the sky as he was going, when suddenly two men dressed in white stood beside them. 'Men of Galilee,' they said, 'why do you stand here looking into the sky? This same Jesus, who has been taken from you into heaven, will come back in the same way you have seen him go into heaven.'
> 
> Acts 1:9-11.

And we have come to the point in our study where that prophecy will be fulfilled. Wow!!! But *"all the peoples of the earth will mourn when they see the Son of Man coming on the clouds of heaven, with power and great glory."* And this "all" is not a synecdoche. This all means **all** will mourn, because at this same moment, in the next verse, Jesus says of those who will be rejoicing at His return:

*"And he will send his angels with a loud trumpet call, and they will gather his **elect** from the four winds, from one end of the heavens to the other."* Matthew 24:31.

This is the rapture. This is when:

*"We who are still alive and are left will be caught up together with them in the clouds to meet the Lord in the air."* 1 Thessalonians 4:17.

Halleluiah!!!

The moment Christians constantly talk about, and oftentimes wish for. Although not as important as Christ's return as King of kings and Lord of lords, it is the thought of this moment that makes my mind get a little giddy. And I start thinking about the Air Force Song, "Off we go into the wild blue yonder, climbing high into the sun (Son)."

John's allegorical description of this moment to come paints this picture:

*"I looked, and there before me was a white cloud, and seated on the cloud was one like a son of man with a crown of gold on his head and a sharp sickle in his hand. Then another angel came out of the temple and called in a loud voice to him who was sitting on the cloud, 'Take your sickle and reap, because the time to reap has come, for the harvest of the earth is ripe.' So he who was seated on the cloud swung his sickle over the earth, and the earth was harvested."* Revelation 14:14-16.

The Apostle Paul had told us about this moment with a little more detail:

*"... the dead in Christ will rise first. After that, we who are still alive and are left will be caught up together with them in the clouds to meet the Lord in the air. And so we will be with the Lord forever. Therefore encourage yourselves with these words."*        1 Thessalonians 4:16-17.

When we looked at this verse earlier we learned that the Greek word, "eis apantesin" (to meet, as in *'to meet the Lord in the air'*) actually means, "to meet an incoming official such as a newly appointed governor, with honor and praise, in order to escort him into the city." And this is what we will now do. We, together with the resurrected saints, will meet Jesus with what must naturally be unbelievably heart felt praise and worship, such as was never approached by the people of Jerusalem on the day Jesus rode in on a donkey on that first Palm Sunday. This throng of believers will be so much in love with their Savior on this day, and exalt Him so highly, that the universe itself might quake from the emotion of it all. And as we bow down and worship the King, we will be escorting Him to His new Kingdom.

Close your eyes and just imagine the power of that incredible moment. The moment all creation has longed for. Shed tears if you like. You will then.

And it is at that moment when those alive will see again their departed loved ones, for the dead in Christ will have risen first. What a scene. What emotion. No one in either camp will be able to restrain the emotions. The tears of joy will flood the sky. Those left on earth may be in for a torrential down pouring of not rain, but unbridled tears.

There has never been, and probably never will be again, such an emotionally charged, joyful time in all of the expanse of the universe. It is in this moment that the "hope" of Christianity will become reality, not only for us saints, but for Jesus Himself, for we read in His Word:

*"For the joy set before him he endured the cross, scorning its shame."*
Hebrews 12:2.

It was the joy of this moment that caused Jesus to voluntarily leave His throne in heaven and become a mere mortal man. It was for the joy of this moment that Jesus was strengthened enough to "drink the cup" and submit his very human body to the most excruciatingly painful hours of torture imaginable. It was for this moment of seeing you in the crowd, locking eyes with you in love.

# Non Stop Action

So many things will be happening at the end at the same time or in such rapid succession that they all may occur within a few minutes, or a few hours. It may take a few days, but it will be fast, because the birth pains we read so much about in the Bible will have come to their conclusion. And much of it, quite frankly, we will not fully understand until we witness it unfold, because of its supernatural nature that we as yet can not relate to.

Irenaeus talks of this very end time:

"Those nations however, who did not of themselves raise up their eyes unto heaven, nor returned thanks to their Maker, nor wished to behold the light of truth, but who were like blind mice concealed in the depths of ignorance, the Word justly reckons *'as waste water from a sink, and as the turning-weight of a balance— in fact, as nothing'* (Isaiah 40:15); so far useful and serviceable to the just, as stubble conduces towards the growth of the wheat, and its straw, by means of combustion, serves for working gold. And therefore, **when in the <u>end</u> the Church shall be suddenly caught up from this**, it is said, *'there shall be tribulation such as has not been since the beginning, neither shall be.'* (Matthew 24:21). For this is the last contest of the righteous, in which, when they overcome they are crowned with incorruption."     <u>Against Heresies</u>, Book V, Chapter 29 (1), Irenaeus.

And naturally, we hear from Hippolytus about this moment:

"Concerning the resurrection and the kingdom of the saints, Daniel says, *'And many of them that sleep in the dust of the earth shall arise.'* Isaiah says, *'The dead men shall arise, and they that are in their tombs shall awake; for the dew from thee is healing to them.'* The Lord says, *'Many in that day shall hear the voice of the Son of God, and they that hear shall live.'* And the prophet says, *'Awake, thou that sleep, and arise from the dead, and Christ shall give thee light.'* And John says, *'Blessed and holy is he that hath part in the first resurrection: on such the second death hath no power.'* ... And again the Lord says, *'Then shall the righteous shine forth as the sun shineth in his glory.'* And to the saints He will say, *'Come, ye blessed of my*

*Father, inherit the kingdom prepared for you from the foundation of the world.'*

Concerning the resurrection of the righteous, Paul also speaks thus in writing to the Thessalonians: *'We would not have you to be ignorant concerning them which are asleep, that ye sorrow not even as others which have no hope. For if we believe that Jesus died and rose again, even so them also which sleep in Jesus will God bring with Him. For this we say unto you by the word of the Lord, that we which are alive (and) remain unto the coming of the Lord, shall not prevent them which are asleep. For the Lord Himself shall descend from heaven with a shout, with the voice and trump of God, and the dead in Christ shall rise first. Then we which are alive (and) remain shall be caught up together with them in the clouds to meet the Lord in the air; and so shall we ever be with the Lord.'*

These things, then, I have set shortly before thee, O Theophilus, drawing them from Scripture itself, in order that, maintaining in faith what is written, and anticipating the things that are to be, thou may keep thyself void of offence both toward God and toward men, *'looking for that blessed hope and appearing of our God and Savior,'* when, having raised the saints among us, He will rejoice with them, glorifying the Father. To Him be the glory unto the endless ages of the ages. Amen."

Treatise on Christ and Antichrist, 65-67, by Hippolytus.

At the same time this resurrection/rapture is occurring, something else will be going on that we need to seriously look into. It will change how we foresee the Millennial Kingdom that is to come.

Immediately after John tells us what he sees in his vision about the rapture of the *"elect,"* he describes another group:

*"Another angel came out of the temple in heaven, and he too had a sharp sickle. Still another angel,* **who had charge of the fire***, came from the altar and called in a loud voice to him who had the sharp sickle, 'Take your sharp sickle and gather the clusters of grapes from the earth's vine, because its grapes are ripe.' The angel swung his sickle on the earth, gathered its grapes and threw them into the great winepress of God's wrath."*

Revelation 14:17-19.

In this section John is talking about the same group that Jesus talked about when He said:

> *"He put before them another parable: 'The kingdom of heaven may be compared to someone who sowed good seed in his field; but while everybody was asleep, an enemy came and sowed weeds among the wheat, and then went away. So when the plants came up and bore grain, then the weeds appeared as well. And the slaves of the householder came and said to him, "Master, did you not sow good seed in your field? Where, then, did these weeds come from?" He answered, "An enemy has done this." The slaves said to him, "Then do you want us to go and gather them?" But he replied, "No; for in gathering the weeds you would uproot the wheat along with them. Let both of them grow together until the harvest; and at harvest time I will tell the reapers, 'Collect the weeds first and bind them in bundles **to be burned**, but gather the wheat into my barn."*
> *Then he left the crowds and went into the house. And his disciples approached him, saying, 'Explain to us the parable of the weeds of the field.' He answered, 'The one who sows the good seed is the Son of Man; the field is the world, and the good seed are the children of the kingdom; the weeds are **the children of the evil one**, and the enemy who sowed them is the devil; the harvest is the end of the age, and the reapers are angels."*
> Matthew 13:24-31, 36-39 (NRSV).

We have been taught by today's end time scholars that this group of people are all of the people in the world who are not believers. But is that really the case? I firmly believe those "scholars" are once again way off base, and there are two reasons for that.

First, on looking at how Jesus describes them, He says that they are *"the children of the evil one."* We know that the only children *"the evil one"* has are Nephilim and their offspring who bear that seed. All other babies born are children of God. This then is my first reason for believing the harvesting of this group is the final harvesting of the results of *"the apostasy of the angels"* that was the reason for the flood.

In the second place, and even more convincing for me, is that in both the Revelation section and the parable of Jesus, their end is the fire. Let's look again at what happens at the end of Armageddon to the antichrist and the false prophet and their army:

> *"The two of them were thrown alive into the **fiery lake** of burning sulfur. The rest were killed with the sword coming out of the mouth of the rider on the horse."*  Revelation 19:21.

Now let's look at Jesus' words in another place:

> *"Then he will say to those on his left, 'Depart from me, you who are cursed, into **the eternal fire prepared for the devil and his angels**."*  Matthew 25:41.

And another scripture:

> *"And the devil, who deceived them, was thrown into the **lake of burning sulfur**, where the beast and the false prophet had been thrown."*  Revelation 20:10.

We know that at the end of the Millennial Kingdom all of the dead will be judged at what is called the White Throne Judgment, for we read:

> *"Then I saw a great white throne and him who was seated on it. ... And I saw the dead, great and small, standing before the throne, and books were opened. Another book was opened, which is the book of life. The dead were judged according to what they had done as recorded in the books. The **lake of fire is the second death**. Anyone whose name was not found written in the book of life was thrown into **the lake of fire."***  Revelation 20:11-12, 14-15.

The point is that normal folks are first judged before a sentence of the second death (lake of fire) is given. Normal humans get their day in court. The devil and his angels have already been judged. They can be thrown in the fire whenever Jesus desires. In other words, had the second group that John saw been normal humans, they would have later been given their day in court at the White Throne Judgment, and not summarily tossed into the fire as the devil, his angels, and their offspring could be. It is like we Americans are granted the right of "due process." Normal people have been granted that right by God in the heavenly realm as well.

I started out this book explaining in detail the Nephilim, not because I know what part they will play during the tribulation, because I do not. It does, however, seem clear that they will play some part, even if only being the antichrist and his ten kings who we saw in Daniel 2:43 who, *"shall mingle themselves with the seed of men."*

Interestingly, although the Apostolic Oral Teaching tells us to not even bother guessing at the name of the antichrist in reference to the number 666 because we will guess wrong; Irenaeus does tell us some truly fascinating things about that number 666 which directly relate to what we are talking about. Read his words slowly and really think about what he is saying:

"And there is therefore in this beast (antichrist), when he comes, a recapitulation made of all sorts of iniquity and of every deceit, in order that all apostate power, flowing into and being shut up in him, **may be sent into the furnace of fire**. Fittingly, therefore, shall his name possess the number six hundred and sixty-six, **since he sums up in his own person all the commixture of wickedness which took place previous to the deluge, due to the apostasy of the angels.** For Noah was six hundred years old when the deluge came upon the earth, sweeping away the rebellious world, for the sake of that most infamous generation which lived in the times of Noah. And [Antichrist] also sums up every error of devised idols since the flood, together with the slaying of the prophets and the cutting off of the just. For that image which was set up by Nebuchadnezzar had indeed a height of sixty cubits, while the breadth was six cubits; on account of which Ananias, Azarias, and Misaël (Shadrach, Meshach, and Abednego), when they did not worship it, were cast into a furnace of fire, pointing out prophetically, by what happened to them, the wrath against the righteous which shall arise towards the [time of the] end. For that image, taken as a whole, was a prefiguring of this man's coming, decreeing that he should undoubtedly himself alone be worshipped by all men. Thus, then, the six hundred years of Noah, in whose time the deluge occurred because of the apostasy, and the number of the cubits of the image for which these just men were sent into the fiery furnace, do indicate the number of the name of that man in whom is concentrated the whole apostasy of six thousand years, and unrighteousness, and wickedness, and false prophecy, and deception; for which things' sake a cataclysm of fire shall also come [upon the earth]."

Against Heresies, Book V, Chapter 29 (2), Irenaeus.

I could write an entire book about what Irenaeus talks about in that one paragraph. You may want to read it again. In it he tells us that the antichrist will be a Nephilim like the ones who were the cause of the flood, which allows him to be immediately sent to the fire without a judgment day. He tells us that Shadrach, Meshach, and Abednego being thrown into the furnace was a shadow of the Christians being persecuted by the antichrist for not worshipping him. He gives us the reason behind the number 666 being applied to the antichrist's name. He shows us that the entire world system, Mystery Babylon, is concentrated in the antichrist. And he tells us the reason for the cleansing of the earth by fire which will occur at the end of the Millennial Kingdom. And there are many other lesser nuggets in that one paragraph which came down to him from the Apostle John through Polycarp. And knowing that, remember, we also know that the information in that paragraph actually originated with Jesus teaching His disciples. What an interesting paragraph. And one that by itself completely discredits all modern end times teaching.

But back to what I was saying about the reason I felt we needed to spend so much time discussing the reality of the Nephilim. It was not because I had insight into their overall role during the tribulation years, but because I could see the overarching importance of this section of the Revelation scripture which discusses the Nephilim being thrown in the fire, and not normal human unbelievers as we have been taught for years in relation to the upcoming thousand year reign of Christ.

You see, with the knowledge that it is not the normal, unbelieving folks who are thrown into the fire, but the Nephilim, we can now understand that those normal unbelieving people who survive the tribulation years will be a part of the Millennial reign of Christ. This will become even more apparent when we discuss that thousand year period in detail a little later. But the point we need to be aware of now is that this fact is in direct opposition to the modern teaching which asserts that only the Jews, along with the righteous dead and raptured, will populate the earth during that thousand year period.

This new understanding of who really will be alive in the Millennial Kingdom, as we will see, will explain a lot about the Millennial Kingdom that the modern teaching must gloss over because it has no explanation. And as we will see, the modern teaching has no explanation of those things we will discuss simply because it is dead wrong on its basic assumptions, assumptions which are in conflict with the Apostolic Oral Teaching. Irenaeus, Polycarp, Justin Martyr, Tertullian, Hippolytus, and others from that Church of Smyrna "Era of Persecution," which Jesus had nothing but praise for in His second Revelation letter, were so correct when they declared that any teaching which contradicted the Apostolic Oral Teaching was heretical teaching. And although our church leaders today do not understand it because they have not learned what you and I have learned already in this book, it is that heretical teaching which is taught today by virtually ever person who teaches anything about the end times. Sound the alarm, my friend.

There is another event that will be occurring simultaneously to the resurrection/rapture, the second coming of Christ, and the tares (Nephilim) being thrown into the fire. Let's read about it:

*"And I saw an angel coming down out of heaven, having the key to the Abyss and holding in his hand a great chain. He seized the dragon, that ancient serpent, who is the devil, or Satan, and bound him for a thousand years. He threw him into the Abyss, and locked and sealed it over him, to keep him from deceiving the nations anymore until the thousand years were ended. After that, he must be set free for a short time."* Revelation 20:1-3.

We can be fairly certain that this angel is the archangel, Michael, who earlier had defeated Satan and tossed him out of heaven at the beginning of the Great Tribulation. That earlier battle was explained:

*"Then war broke out in heaven. Michael and his angels fought against the dragon, and the dragon and his angels fought back. But he was not strong enough, and they lost their place in heaven. The great dragon was hurled down—that ancient serpent called the devil, or Satan, who leads the whole world astray. He was hurled to the earth, and his angels with him.*

*Then I heard a loud voice in heaven say:*

*'Now have come the salvation and the power*

*and the kingdom of our God, and the authority of his Messiah.*
*For the accuser of our brothers and sisters, who accuses them*
    *before our God day and night, has been hurled down.*
*They triumphed over him*
    *by the blood of the Lamb and by the word of their testimony;*
    *they did not love their lives so much as to shrink from death.*
*Therefore rejoice, you heavens and you who dwell in them!*
*But woe to the earth and the sea, because*
    *the devil has gone down to you!*
*He is filled with fury, because he knows that his time is short.'*

*When the dragon saw that he had been hurled to the earth, he pursued the woman* (the church) *who had given birth to the male child. The woman was given the two wings of a great eagle* (faith) ..."     Revelation 12: 7-14.

Whether or not we will actually see Michael defeat Satan and lock him away, we can't say. That obviously will be happening in the spiritual realm. Personally, I doubt it, but your guess is as good as mine. Unfortunately, the Apostolic Oral Teaching on that matter was either never written down or has been lost during the ages, but isn't it fantastic to know that Satan will be gone during the Millennial Kingdom?

# The Jews

Although much of Israel will have been blinded by the lies of the antichrist, and they will have made him their king, we can be sure that there will remain a remnant of the Jewish people who will be sickened by this man and continue to worship the One true God, as has been the case throughout history. And we can imagine that these Godly men and women, much as the remnant of true followers of Jesus, will have been put under the antichrist's sword of persecution. And as with the true followers of Christ, many of them will not have submitted when persecuted, and will have faced martyrdom.

It is at this point that we may have a question. The Jews have not realized that Jesus is their Messiah, they do not obviously worship Jesus, so will they be resurrected at the resurrection/rapture or will they not be seen again until they appear before the White Throne for judgment? Many point to the words of Jesus which say:

*"I am the way and the truth and the life. No one comes to the Father except through me."* John 14:6.

The thinking by most is that the Jews, because of those words, do not have a chance of making it. The thinking is that only the Messianic Jews will make it. This is true of both of the main theological groups today, those who follow what we know of as Covenant Theology, and those who follow John Darby's Dispensational Theology. Both theologies really give no hope for Jews, especially for those who have lived since Jesus came. Some will give a little leeway to those who lived prior to Jesus, stating that they didn't know any better. Of course it is hard to dismiss such things as Moses and Elijah visiting Jesus on the Mount of Transfiguration, or Jesus telling us plainly:

*"I say to you that many will come from the east and the west, and will take their places at the feast with Abraham, Isaac and Jacob in the kingdom of heaven."* Matthew 8:11.

Of course, many will reluctantly concede that some of the Jews prior to the time of Jesus will be saved, but they can pull out a bunch of verses to prove that after Jesus came everything for the Jews changed drastically, and unless they convert to Christianity they too, are condemned to hell:

*"he who has the Son has life; he who does not have the Son of God does not have life,"* and *"no one who denies the Son has the Father; whoever acknowledges the Son has the Father also."*     1 John 5:12; 2:23.

The question, then, is a truly tough one; although our modern church has decided on its belief, and it is to follow the latter position.

Fortunately, you and I do not have to guess, for on this matter the Apostolic Oral Teaching, which originated with Jesus teaching His disciples, has been preserved for us to study and be taught by. Normally in this book, for brevity sake, I have tried to pull out of that teaching a few sentences or paragraphs that are easy to follow and that answer specific questions relating to the end times. This question is so extremely weighty, however, that it is probably best if we look at what was written in a more scholarly fashion by including much more of the Apostolic Oral Teaching than we have looked at on other subjects in this book. I will, however, highlight some of the phrases that jump out at me. Please do not, though, think that by doing so I am giving less importance to any of the other material. Read the below, then, understanding as you are reading how extremely privileged you are to be able to drink in wisdom that has been lost or hidden from our fellow believing brothers and sisters:

"1. All things therefore are of one and the same substance, that is, **from one and the same God**; as also the Lord says to the disciples Therefore every scribe, which is instructed unto the kingdom of heaven, is like a man that is a householder, which brings forth out of his treasure things new and old. Matthew 13:52. He did not teach that he who brought forth the old was one, and he that brought forth the new, another; but that **they were one and the same.** For the Lord is the good man of the house, who rules the entire house of His Father; and who delivers a law suited both for slaves and those who are as yet undisciplined; and gives fitting precepts to those that are free, and have been justified by faith, as well as throws His own inheritance open to those that are sons. And He called His disciples scribes and teachers of the kingdom of heaven; of whom also He elsewhere says to the Jews: Behold, I send unto you wise men, and scribes, and teachers; and some of them you shall kill, and persecute from city to city. Matthew 23:34. Now, without contradiction, He means by those things which are brought forth from the treasure new and old, the two covenants; the old, that giving of the law which took place formerly; and He points out as the new, that manner of life required by the Gospel, of which David says, Sing unto the Lord a new song; and Esaias, Sing unto the Lord a new hymn. His beginning (initium), His name is glorified from the height of the earth: they declare His powers in the isles. And Jeremiah says: Behold, I will make a new covenant, not as I made with your fathers Jeremiah 31:31 in Mount Horeb. **But one and the same householder produced both covenants**, the Word of God, our Lord Jesus Christ, who spoke with both Abraham and Moses, and who has restored us anew to liberty, and has multiplied that grace which is from Himself.

2. He declares: For in this place is One greater than the temple. Matthew 12:6. But [the words] greater and less are not applied to those things which have nothing in common between themselves, and are of an opposite nature, and mutually repugnant; **but are used in the case of those of the same substance, and which possess properties in common**, but merely differ in number and size; such as water from water, and light from light, and grace from grace. Greater, therefore, is that legislation which has been given in order to liberty than that given in order to bondage; and therefore it has also been diffused, not throughout one nation [only], but over the whole world. **For one and the same Lord**, who is greater than the temple, greater than Solomon, and greater than Jonah, **confers gifts upon men, that is, His own presence, and the <u>resurrection from the dead</u>; but He does not change God, nor proclaim another Father, but that very same one**, who always has more to measure out to those of His household. And as their love towards God increases, He bestows more and greater [gifts]; as also the Lord said to His disciples: You shall see greater things than these. John 1:50. And Paul declares: Not that I have already attained, or that I am justified, or already have been made perfect. For we know in part, and we prophesy in part; but when that which is perfect has come, the things which are in part shall be done away. As, therefore, when that which is perfect has come, **we shall not see another Father, but Him whom we now desire to see'** ('for blessed are

the pure in heart: for they shall see God Matthew 5:8); **neither shall we look for another Christ and Son of God, but Him who [was born] of the Virgin Mary, who also suffered, in whom too we trust, and whom we love**; as Esaias says: **And they shall say in that day, Behold our Lord God, in whom we have trusted, and we have rejoiced in our salvation;** Isaiah 25:9 and Peter says in his Epistle: **Whom, not seeing, you love; in whom, though now you see Him not, you have believed,** you shall rejoice with joy unspeakable;' 1 Peter 1:8 'neither do we receive another Holy Spirit, besides Him who is with us, and who cries, Abba, Father; Romans 8:15 and we shall make increase in the very same things [as now], and shall make progress, so that no longer through a glass, or by means of enigmas, but face to face, we shall enjoy the gifts of God—so also now, receiving more than the temple, and more than Solomon, that is, the advent of the Son of God, **we have not been taught another God besides the Framer and the Maker of all, who has been pointed out to us from the beginning; <u>nor another Christ, the Son of God, besides Him who was foretold by the prophets.</u>**

3. <u>**For the new covenant having been known and preached by the prophets, He who was to carry it out according to the good pleasure of the Father was also preached, having been revealed to men as God pleased**</u>; **that they might always make progress through believing in Him,** and by means of the [successive] covenants, should gradually attain to perfect salvation. For there is one salvation and one God; but the precepts which form the man are numerous, and the steps which lead man to God are not a few. It is allowable for an earthly and temporal king, though he is [but] a man, to grant to his subjects greater advantages at times: shall not this then be lawful for God, since He is [ever] the same, and is always willing to confer a greater [degree of] grace upon the human race, and to honor continually with many gifts those who please Him? But if this be to make progress, [namely,] to find out another Father besides Him who was preached from the beginning; and again, besides him who is imagined to have been discovered in the second place, to find out a third other, — then the progress of this man will consist in his also proceeding from a third to a fourth; and from this, again, to another and another: and thus he who thinks that he is always making progress of such a kind, will never rest in one God. For, being driven away from Him who truly is [God], and being turned

backwards, he shall be for ever seeking, yet shall never find out God; 2 Timothy 3:7. but shall continually swim in an abyss without limits, unless, being converted by repentance, he return to the place from which he had been cast out, confessing one God, the Father, the Creator, and **believing [in Him] who was declared by the law and the prophets, who was borne witness to by Christ**, as He did Himself declare to those who were accusing His disciples of not observing the tradition of the elders: Why do you make void the law of God by reason of your tradition? For God said, Honor your father and mother; and, Whosoever curses father or mother, let him die the death. Matthew 15:3-4. And again, He says to them a second time: And you have made void the word of God by reason of your tradition; Christ confessing in the plainest manner Him to be Father and God, who said in the law, Honor your father and mother; that it may be well with you. For the true God did confess the commandment of the law as the word of God, and called no one else God besides His own Father."

Against Heresies, Book IV, Chapter 9.

"1. Now in the last days, when the fullness of the time of liberty had arrived, **the Word Himself did by Himself wash away the filth of the daughters of Zion,** Isaiah 4:4 **when He washed the disciples' feet with His own hands.** John 13:5 For this is the end of the human race inheriting God; that as in the beginning, by means of our first [parents], we were all brought into bondage, by being made subject to death; so at last, by means of the New Man, **all who from the beginning [were His] disciples, having been cleansed and washed from things pertaining to death, should come to the life of God.** For He who washed the feet of the disciples sanctified the entire body, and rendered it clean. For this reason, too, <u>He administered food to them in a recumbent posture, indicating that those who were lying in the earth were they to whom He came to impart life</u>. As Jeremiah declares, <u>The holy Lord remembered His dead Israel, who slept in the land of sepulture;</u> and He descended to them to make known to them His salvation, that they might be saved. For this reason also were the eyes of the disciples weighed down when Christ's passion was approaching; and when, in the first instance, the Lord found them sleeping, He let it pass—thus indicating the patience of God in regard to the state of slumber in which men lay; but coming the second time, He aroused them, and made them stand up, in token that His passion is the arousing of His sleeping disciples, on whose account He also descended into the lower parts of the earth, Ephesians 4:9 to behold with His eyes the state of those who were resting from their labors, in reference to whom He did also declare to the disciples: Many prophets and righteous men have desired to see and hear what you see and hear.

2. **For it was not merely for those who believed on Him in the time of Tiberius Cæsar that Christ came, nor did the Father exercise His providence for the men only who are now alive, <u>but for all men altogether, who from the beginning, according to their capacity, in their generation have both feared and loved God, and practiced justice and piety towards their neighbors, and have earnestly desired to see Christ, and to hear His voice.</u> Wherefore <u>He shall, at His second coming, first rouse from their sleep all persons of this description, and shall raise them up, as well as the rest who shall be judged, and give them a place in His kingdom.</u> For it is truly one God who directed the patriarchs towards His dispensations, and has justified the circumcision by faith, and the uncircumcision through faith.** Romans 3:30 For as in the first we were prefigured, so, on the other hand, are they represented in us, that is, in the Church, and receive the recompense for those things which they accomplished." <u>Against Heresies</u>, Book IV, Chapter 22.

"1. For thus it had behooved the sons of Abraham [to be], whom God has raised up to him from the stones, Matthew 3:9 and caused to take a place beside him who was made the chief and the forerunner of our faith (who did also receive the covenant of circumcision, after that justification by faith which had pertained to him, when he was yet in uncircumcision, so that in him both covenants might be prefigured, that he might be the father of all who follow the Word of God, and who sustain a life of pilgrimage in this world, that is, of those who from among the circumcision and of those from among the uncircumcision are faithful, even as also Christ Ephesians 2:20 is the chief corner-stone sustaining all things); and **He gathered into the one faith of Abraham those who, from either covenant, are eligible for God's building.** But this faith which is in uncircumcision, as connecting the end with the beginning, has been made [both] the first and the last. For, as I have shown, it existed in Abraham antecedently to circumcision, as it also did in the rest of the righteous who pleased God: and in these last times, it again sprang up among mankind through the coming of the Lord. But circumcision and the law of works occupied the intervening period.

2. This fact is indeed set forth by many other [occurrences], but typically by [the history of] Thamar, Judah's daughter-in-law. Genesis 38:28, etc. For when she had conceived twins, one of them put forth his hand first; and as the midwife supposed that he was the first-born, she bound a scarlet token on his hand. But after this had been done, and he had drawn back his hand, his brother Phares came forth the first; then, after him, Zara, upon whom was the scarlet line, [was born] the second: the Scripture clearly pointing out that people which possessed the scarlet sign, that is, faith in a state of circumcision, which was shown beforehand, indeed, in the patriarchs first; but after that withdrawn, that his brother might be born; and also, in like manner, him who was the elder, as being born in the second place, [him] who was distinguished by the scarlet token which was on him, that is, the passion of the Just One, which was prefigured from the beginning in Abel, and described by the prophets, but perfected in the last times in the Son of God.

3. For it was requisite that certain facts should be announced beforehand by the fathers in a paternal manner, and others prefigured by the prophets in a legal one, but others, described after the form of Christ, by those who have received the adoption; while in one God are all things shown forth. **For although Abraham was one, he did in himself prefigure the two covenants, in which some indeed have sown, while others have reaped; for it is said, In this is the saying true, that it is one 'people' who sows, but another who shall reap; John 4:37 but it is one God who bestows things suitable upon both**— seed to the sower, but bread for the reaper to eat. Just as it is one that plants, and another who waters, but one God who gives the increase. 1 Corinthians 3:7 **For the patriarchs and prophets sowed the word [concerning] Christ, but the Church reaped, that is, received the fruit. For this reason, too, do these very men (the prophets) also pray to have a dwelling-place in it, as Jeremiah says, Who will give me in the desert the last dwelling-place? in order that both the sower and the reaper may rejoice together in the kingdom of Christ, who is present with all those who were from the beginning approved by God, who granted them His Word to be present with them."**

<u>Against Heresies</u>, Book IV, Chapter 25.

"**1. After this fashion also did a presbyter, a disciple of the apostles, reason with respect to the two testaments, proving that both were truly from one and the same God.** For [he maintained] that there was no other God besides Him who made and fashioned us, and that the discourse of those men has no foundation who affirm that this world of ours was made either by angels, or by any other power whatsoever, or by another God. For if a man be once moved away from the Creator of all things, and if he grant that this creation to which we belong was formed by any other or through any other [than the one God], he must of necessity fall into much inconsistency, and many contradictions of this sort; to which he will [be able to] furnish no explanations which can be regarded as either probable or true. And, for this reason, those who introduce other doctrines conceal from us the opinion which they themselves hold respecting God, because they are aware of the untenable and absurd nature of their doctrine, and are afraid lest, should they be vanquished, they should have some difficulty in making good their escape. But if any one believes in [only] one God, who also made all things by the Word, as Moses likewise says, God said, Let there be light: and there was light; Genesis 1:3 and as we read in the Gospel, All things were made by Him; and without Him was nothing made; John 1:3 and the Apostle Paul [says] in like manner, There is one Lord, one faith, one baptism, one God and Father, who is above all, and through all, and in us all Ephesians 4:5-6 — this man will first of all hold the head, from which the whole body is compacted and bound together, and, through means of every joint according to the measure of the ministration of each several part, makes increase of the body to the edification of itself in love. Ephesians 4:16; Colossians 2:19 **And then shall every word also seem consistent to him, if he for his part diligently read the Scriptures in company with those who are presbyters in the Church, among whom is the <u>apostolic doctrine</u>, as I have pointed out.**

**2. For all the apostles taught that there were indeed two testaments among the two peoples; but that it was one and the same God who appointed both for the advantage of those men (for whose sakes the testaments were given) who were to believe in God**, I have proved in the third book **from the very teaching of the apostles; and that <u>the first testament was not given without reason, or to no purpose, or in an</u>**

**accidental sort of manner; but that it subdued those to whom it was given to the service of God, for their benefit** (for God needs no service from men), and exhibited a type of heavenly things, inasmuch as **man was not yet able to see the things of God through means of immediate vision**; and foreshadowed the images of those things which [now actually] exist in the Church, in order that our faith might be firmly established; and contained a prophecy of things to come, in order that man might learn that God has foreknowledge of all things."    <u>Against Heresies</u>, Book IV, Chapter 32.

So, what we have learned by reading the words of the above sections of the Apostolic Oral Teaching is that the Christ the Jews await, the Christ that has always been taught, worshipped, and loved by the Jewish Religion, but was not recognized because the eyes of the Jews have been blinded for our sake, is the exact same Christ Jesus we Christians have been fortunate enough to have seen because our eyes were opened by God.

Yes, Jesus is the Way, the only Way to the Father, and in a different manner, both the Jews and the Christians possess that Way.

I understand that there will be some who, even after reading the words of the Apostolic Oral Teaching, will not accept this truth. Their complete indoctrination of the false teaching that the Jews are doomed will not allow them to step back and see the big picture and admit that what they have believed for so long is wrong. I understand that completely. But if you are one of those, please don't take the time to write me with all of the scriptures you think you have found that back up your thinking. I have already read and studied each and every one of them many times. In fact, in the past I used them myself to try to prove that very same erroneous position.

Please instead, really and truly let the Word of God sink in which says:

*"I do not want you to be ignorant of this mystery, brothers and sisters, so that you may not be conceited: Israel has experienced a hardening in part until the full number of the Gentiles has come in, and in this way **all Israel will be saved**. As it is written:*

*'The deliverer will come from Zion;*
  *he will turn godlessness away from Jacob.*
*And this is my covenant with them*
  *when I take away their sins.'*

*As far as the gospel is concerned,* **they are enemies for your sake**; *but* **as far as election is concerned, they are loved on account of the patriarchs, for God's gifts and his call are irrevocable**. *Just as you who were at one time disobedient to God have now received mercy as a result of their disobedience, so they too have now become disobedient in order that they too may now receive mercy as a result of God's mercy to you. For God has bound everyone over to disobedience so that he may have mercy on them all."* Romans 11:25-32.

We need to fully understand what has been done for us: **"they (the Jews) are enemies for <u>your</u> sake."** That is it. Had the Jews not been blinded by God beforehand, they would have recognized Jesus when He rode into Jerusalem, made Him their King, and the story would have ended right there and then. You and I, the gentile nations who had never believed in the One true God, would have been cut off without a chance. It was to give you and me a chance to use our free will and accept Jesus as our Lord and Savior that **the Jews were blinded <u>by</u> God**. We see it first right after the Israelites came out of the slavery of Egypt:

*"Moses summoned all the Israelites and said to them: 'Your eyes have seen all that the Lord did in Egypt to Pharaoh, to all his officials and to all his land. With your own eyes you saw those great trials, those signs and great wonders. But to this day* **the <u>Lord</u> has not given you a mind that understands or eyes that see or ears that hear***."* Deuteronomy 29:2-4.

Then we also read in Isaiah:

*"Then I heard the voice of the Lord saying,*
*'Whom shall I send? And who will go for us?'*
*And I said, 'Here am I. Send me!'*
*He said, 'Go and tell this people* (the Jews)*:*
*"Be ever hearing, but never understanding;*
  *be ever seeing, but never perceiving.'*
*Make the heart of this people calloused;*
  *make their ears dull and* **close their eyes***.*
*Otherwise they might see with their eyes,*

*hear with their ears, understand with their hearts, and turn and be healed."* Isaiah 6:8-10.

And we find in Romans that it was all done for us: **"they (the Jews) are enemies for your sake."** So we must remember these words:

*"Again I ask: Did they stumble so as to fall beyond recovery? Not at all! Rather, because of their transgression, salvation has come to the Gentiles to make Israel envious. But if their transgression means riches for the world, and their loss means riches for the Gentiles, how much greater riches will their full inclusion bring?"* Romans 11:11-12.

And even to this day:

*"But their minds were made dull, for to this day the same veil remains when the old covenant is read. It has not been removed, because only in Christ is it taken away.* **Even to this day when Moses is read, a veil covers their hearts.***"* 2 Corinthians 3:14-15.

God caused the blindness of the Jews, although they were and are His chosen people, the apple of His eye, because He loved us and made a way for you and me to have eternal life. And still today that veil over their eyes exists, allowing more and more Gentiles the time to come to their Savior.

So the next time you drive by a Synagog and see a Jewish mother or father walking out after spending time worshipping the Christ they are not yet allowed to see, give thanks to God for His plan which allowed us eternal life. No more should we shake our head, believing that God has stopped loving them, or worse yet, shake our fist at them as most of the world does. It is through their continued obedience, in the face of blindness, that some non Jew will next week close his or her eyes, repent, and come to Jesus.

Had the Apostolic Oral Teaching that fortunately still survives not been ignored so blatantly by the church for the past two thousand years, maybe fewer innocent Jews would have been persecuted so harshly all over the world, to the point of atrocious murdering. But in the end:

*"The days are coming,' declares the Lord,*
*'when I will make a new covenant with the people of Israel*

*and with the people of Judah.
It will not be like the covenant I made with their ancestors…
This is the covenant I will make with the people of Israel
after that time,' declares the Lord. 'I will put my law in their minds
and write it on their hearts.
I will be their God, and they will be my people.
No longer will they teach their neighbor, or say to one another,
"Know the Lord," because they will all know me,
from the least of them to the greatest,' declares the Lord.
'For I will forgive their wickedness
and will remember their sins no more.'
This is what the Lord says,
'he who appoints the sun to shine by day,
who decrees the moon and stars to shine by night,
who stirs up the sea so that its waves roar –
the Lord Almighty is his name:
Only if these decrees vanish from my sight,' declares the Lord,
'will Israel ever cease being a nation before me.'
This is what the Lord says:
'Only if the heavens above can be measured
and the foundations of the earth below be searched out will I reject
all the descendants of Israel because of all they have done,'
 declares the Lord."*                 Jeremiah 31:31-32, 33-37.

You and I will witness this on the day of the resurrection/rapture.
Oh, what a glorious day.

# It Ends At Jerusalem

Hardly a day goes by without the fairly small city of Jerusalem making its way into virtually all the newspapers of the world. Interesting, isn't it? Jerusalem is not anywhere to be found on any list of the world's largest cities. It is definitely not a center of world power like Washington or Moscow. And we could not call it a hub of world finance. But there it is in front of us day after day. It is on TV. It is in the magazines. It is spattered all over the internet blog sites. There is something about Jerusalem that is almost mystical in the way the people of the world are drawn to it in their thinking. And lest we think that is something relatively new since the recreation of the nation of Israel in 1948, it is not. It has been fought over sixteen times in its history, destroyed twice, besieged 23 times, attacked 52 times, and captured and recaptured 44 times. The reason; it is actually the center of all creation. It is the "City of God." Jones' Dictionary of <u>Old Testament Proper Names</u> states that Jerusalem means "Foundation of Peace," although it has not seen that "peace" yet.

The Bible has nearly 800 references to Jerusalem. Since there are 31,102 verses in the Bible, that means that we read about Jerusalem on average every fourth verse we read in God's Word. Wow! Looking at Jerusalem like that is incredible.

*"Great is the Lord, and most worthy of praise,*
   *in **the city of our God, his holy mountain**.*
*Beautiful in its loftiness,*
   *the joy of the whole earth,*
*like the heights of Zaphon is Mount Zion,*
   ***the city of the Great King***.
*God is in her citadels;*
   *he has shown himself to be her fortress.*
*As we have heard, so we have seen*
   *in **the city of the Lord Almighty**,*
   *in **the city of our God**:*
*God makes her secure forever."*                Psalm 48:1-3, 8.

> *"For the Lord has chosen Zion,*
>> *he has desired it for his dwelling."*      Psalm 132:13.

> *"His tent is in Salem,*
>> *his dwelling place in Zion."*      Psalm 76:2.

> *"Praise be to the Lord from Zion,*
>> *to him who dwells in Jerusalem."*      Psalm 135:21.

> *"From Zion, perfect in beauty,*
>> *God shines forth."*      Psalm 50:2.

> *"Jerusalem, for it is **the city of the Great King**."*      Matthew 5:35.

> *"in Jerusalem, which I have chosen ...,*
>> *I will put my Name forever."*      2 Chronicles 33:7.

> *"My Name will remain in Jerusalem forever."*      2 Chronicles 33:4.

> *"and they will call you the City of the Lord,*
>> *Zion of the Holy One of Israel."*      Isaiah 60:14.

We could go on and on with scriptural examples showing how God views Jerusalem as His special place in all the earth. Yes, it is a mystical place. It is the City of God.

There is a fascinating story in the Bible of a time when Jerusalem was under siege by the Assyrians. And it is so relevant to our discussion and where we are in our journey into the study of the end times we were never taught that I am going to sit back and let this story unfold for you the way God intended it to. In other words, without further verbiage from me, let's just read the story in its entirety. We will pick it up at the point where the Assyrians have already conquered the Northern tribes and have now mounted a campaign against those living in Jerusalem, which is ruled by one of the few good kings, King Hezekiah. They have sent word to Hezekiah, basically saying, "Surrender and we'll treat you good, or oppose us and be destroyed;"

"When King Hezekiah heard this, he tore his clothes and put on sackcloth and went into the temple of the Lord. He sent Eliakim the palace administrator, Shebna the secretary and the leading priests, all wearing sackcloth, to the prophet Isaiah son of Amoz. They told him, 'This is what Hezekiah says: This day is a day of distress and rebuke and disgrace, as when children come to the moment of birth and there is no strength to deliver them. It may be that the Lord your God will hear all the words of the field commander, whom **his master, the king of Assyria, has sent to ridicule the living God**, and that he will rebuke him for the words the Lord your God has heard. Therefore pray for the remnant that still survives.'

When King Hezekiah's officials came to Isaiah, Isaiah said to them, 'Tell your master, "This is what the Lord says: Do not be afraid of what you have heard—those words with which the underlings of the king of Assyria have blasphemed me. Listen! When he hears a certain report, I will make him want to return to his own country, and there I will have him cut down with the sword."

When the field commander heard that the king of Assyria had left Lachish, he withdrew and found the king fighting against Libnah.

Now **Sennacherib** received a report that Tirhakah, the king of Cush **(Egypt)**, was marching out to fight against him. So he again sent messengers to Hezekiah with this word: 'Say to Hezekiah king of Judah: Do not let the god you depend on deceive you when he says, "Jerusalem will not be given into the hands of the king of Assyria." Surely you have heard what the kings of Assyria have done to all the countries, destroying them completely. And will you be delivered? Did the gods of the nations that were destroyed by my predecessors deliver them—the gods of Gozan, Harran, Rezeph and the people of Eden who were in Tel Assar? Where is the king of Hamath or the king of Arpad? Where are the kings of Lair, Sepharvaim, Hena and Ivvah?'

Hezekiah received the letter from the messengers and read it. Then he went up to the temple of the Lord and spread it out before the Lord. And Hezekiah prayed to the Lord: 'Lord, the God of Israel, enthroned between the cherubim, you alone are God over all the kingdoms of the earth. You have made heaven and earth. Give ear, Lord, and hear; open your eyes, Lord, and see; listen to the words Sennacherib has sent to ridicule the living God.

It is true, Lord, that the Assyrian kings have laid waste these nations and their lands. They have thrown their gods into the fire and destroyed them, for they were not gods but only wood and stone, fashioned by human hands. Now, Lord our God, deliver us from his hand, so that all the kingdoms of the earth may know that you alone, Lord, are God.'

Then Isaiah son of Amoz sent a message to Hezekiah: 'This is what the Lord, the God of Israel, says: I have heard your prayer concerning Sennacherib king of Assyria. This is the word that the Lord has spoken against him:

"Virgin Daughter Zion despises you and mocks you.
    Daughter Jerusalem tosses her head as you flee.
    Who is it you have ridiculed and blasphemed?
    Against whom have you raised your voice and lifted your eyes in pride?
    Against the Holy One of Israel!

By your messengers **you have ridiculed the Lord.**
    **And you have said**, "With my many chariots
    I have ascended the heights of the mountains,
    the utmost heights of Lebanon.
    **I have cut down its tallest cedar**s, the choicest of its junipers.
    I have reached its remotest parts, the finest of its forests.
    I have dug wells in foreign lands and drunk the water there.
    With the soles of my feet I have dried up all the streams of Egypt.

Have you not heard? Long ago I ordained it. In days of old I planned it;
    now I have brought it to pass, that you have turned fortified cities
    into piles of stone.
    Their people, drained of power, are dismayed and put to shame.
    They are like plants in the field, like tender green shoots,
    like grass sprouting on the roof, scorched before it grows up.

But I know where you are and when you come and go
    and how you rage against me.
    Because you rage against me

and because your insolence has reached my ears,
I will put my hook in your nose and my bit in your mouth,
and I will make you return by the way you came.

This will be the sign for you, Hezekiah:

This year you will eat what grows by itself,
and the second year what springs from that.
But in the third year sow and reap,
plant vineyards and eat their fruit.
Once more a remnant of the kingdom of Judah
will take root below and bear fruit above.
For out of Jerusalem will come a remnant,
and out of Mount Zion a band of survivors.

The zeal of the Lord Almighty will accomplish this.

Therefore this is what the Lord says concerning the king of Assyria:

**He will not enter this city** or shoot an arrow here.
He will not come before it with shield or build a siege ramp against it.
By the way that he came he will return;
**he will not enter this city**, declares the Lord.
**I will defend this city and save it,
for my sake** and **for the sake of David my servant.**'

That night **the angel of the Lord went out and put to death a hundred and eighty-five thousand in the Assyrian camp**. When the people got up the next morning—there were all the dead bodies! So Sennacherib king of Assyria broke camp and withdrew. He returned to Nineveh and stayed there.
One day, while he was worshiping in the temple of his god Nisrok, his sons Adrammelek and Sharezer killed him with the sword, and they escaped to the land of Ararat. And Esarhaddon his son succeeded him as king."

2 Kings 19.

Most Biblical scholars and teachers break the thirty nine books of the Old Testament into groups of books:

1) Law – Genesis to Deuteronomy (5)
2) History – Joshua to Esther (12)
3) Poetry – Job to Song of Solomon (5)
4) Major Prophets – Isaiah to Daniel (5)
5) Minor Prophets – Hosea to Malachi (12)

In a small way, I understand why they do that, and maybe there is a little value in doing it, but to me they are all basically the same; they were all written by God Himself, and they are all chocked full of prophecy, types, and shadows. By categorizing the books as they do, they tend to leave some folks with the impression that if you want to find prophetic writing you need to concentrate on the last seventeen books of the Old Testament, with special emphasis on Isaiah through Daniel. What a shame. Some of the most profound yet overlooked prophecies are in the first twenty two books. The above nineteenth chapter that we just read from the "history Book," 2 Kings, is a prime example. There are so many prophetic nuggets in that chapter that we could spend a hundred pages delving into them. For time's sake, however, we will just touch on a few gigantic truths we need to pull from that chapter.

I highlighted the part where God says to the Assyrian king, *"you have ridiculed the Lord. And you have said, I have cut down its tallest cedars"* because that brings us full circle, back to The Cup of The Harlot. Back to the Tower of Babel and the Satanic ritual of the harlot and her "redeemer" getting drunk from the cup, having sex, and then going to sleep in order to "make a name for themselves" by producing a son who will live on after them.

Most Christians are familiar with the Messianic scriptures in Isaiah that say:

> *"The people walking in darkness have seen a great light;*
>     *on those living in the land of deep darkness a light has dawned.*
> *You have enlarged the nation and increased their joy;*
>     *they rejoice before you as people rejoice at the harvest,*
>     *as warriors rejoice when dividing the plunder.*

> *For as in the day of Midian's defeat, you have shattered*
> > *the yoke that burdens them, the bar across their shoulders,*
> > > *the rod of their oppressor.*
> *Every warrior's boot used in battle and every garment rolled in blood*
> > *will be destined for burning, will be fuel for the fire.*
> **For to us a child is born, to us a son is given,**
> > **and the government will be on his shoulders.**
> **And he will be called Wonderful Counselor, Mighty God,**
> > **Everlasting Father, Prince of Peace.**
> **Of the greatness of his government and peace there will be no end.**
> > **He will reign on David's throne and over his kingdom, establishing and upholding it with justice and righteousness from that time on and forever.**
> *The zeal of the Lord Almighty will accomplish this."*     Isaiah 9:2-7.

However, there is something important in the next few verses when we truly examine them. Our Bibles say:

> *"The Lord has sent a message against Jacob; it will fall on Israel.*
> *All the people will know it—Ephraim and the inhabitants of Samaria—*
> > *who say with pride and arrogance of heart,*
> *"The bricks have fallen down, but we will rebuild with dressed stone;*
> > *the fig trees have been felled,*
> > > *but **we will replace them with cedars**."*     Isaiah 9:8-10.

Unfortunately we don't see the full meaning of those verses in our current translations; however, if we search out the matter deeper we find that the translation in the Septuagint version of this text, which was the Greek translation into Greek between 300 BC and 200 BC and used by the early church, has a phrase at the end which is quite profound. It reads:

> *"The Lord has sent death upon Jacob, and it has come upon Israel. And all the people of Ephraim, and they that dwelt in Samaria shall know, who say in their pride and lofty heart, The bricks are fallen down, but come, let us hew stones, **and cut down sycamores and cedars, and let us build for ourselves a tower**."*     Isaiah 9:8-10, LXX, Brenton's translation.

You see, when we look at that 2 Kings story we can see that the thing God still finds detestable is The Cup of The Harlot. And for reinstituting that ceremonial act, Satan will receive God's full wrath. Satan overstepped his boundaries when he brought it about the very first time. It was that ceremonial act that the Nephilim had performed prior to the flood. But more than that, it was the ceremony that depicted the real life "apostasy of the angels" talked about in Jude in God's Word, in <u>The Book of Enoch</u>, in <u>The Book of Jubilees</u>, and in the Apostolic Oral Teaching, that resulted in the initial creation of the Nephilim.

And we see in that Septuagint translation that in the end times God will be seeing in the mostly secular nation of Israel the mental building of that tower and drinking of that cup. So, God will enact His terrible punishment, and the drinking The Cup of The Harlot will finally come to an end.

Another thing I will mention about that 2 Kings story is that when we look into the meaning of the Assyrian king's name in that chapter we find that Sennacherib astonishingly means **"the moon god."** Could this give credence to the notion that the man who will be the antichrist will be the person the Muslims believe to be their Mahdi? Let's look at some facts.

As we all know, Islam worships a god named "Allah." The Muslims claim that Allah in pre-Islamic times was the Biblical God of the Patriarchs, prophets, and apostles. But, was "Allah" the Biblical God, or a pagan god in Arabia during pre-Islamic times? False religious claims often fall apart in the light of hard sciences such as archeology, and as we will see, the hard evidence is obvious that the god Allah was a pagan deity. In fact, he was the moon god who was married to the sun goddess and the stars were his daughters.

Archaeologists have uncovered temples to the moon god throughout the Middle East. From the mountains of Turkey to the banks of the Nile, the most wide-spread religion of the ancient world was the worship of the moon god. In the first literate civilization, the Sumerians have left us thousands of clay tablets in which they described their religious beliefs. The ancient Sumerians worshipped a moon god, whose symbol was the crescent moon. Given the amount of artifacts concerning the worship of this moon god, it is clear that this was the dominant religion in Samaria. The cult of the moon god was the most popular religion throughout ancient Mesopotamia.

In ancient Syria and Canna, the moon god was usually represented by the moon in its crescent phase. At times the full moon was placed inside the crescent moon to emphasize all the phases of the moon. The sun goddess was his wife and the stars were their daughters. For example, Istar was a daughter. In the Ugaritic texts that we looked at earlier and learned about the cup of the harlot, the moon god was sometimes called Kusuh. In Persia, as well as in Egypt, the moon god is depicted on wall murals and on the heads of statues. He was the Judge of men and gods.

The Old Testament constantly rebuked the worship of the moon god and when Israel fell into idolatry, it was usually the cult of the moon god. As a matter of fact, everywhere in the ancient world, including the habitats of the Jews, the symbol of the crescent moon can be found on seal impressions, pottery, amulets, clay tablets, cylinders, weights, earrings, necklaces, wall murals, etc. Even bread was baked in the form of a crescent as an act of devotion to the moon god.

A temple of the moon god has been excavated in Ur by Sir Leonard Woolley. He dug up many examples of moon worship in Ur and these are now displayed in the British Museum. Also, in the 1950's a major temple to the moon god was excavated at Hazer in Palestine. Two idols of the moon god were found. Each was a statue of a man sitting upon a throne with a crescent moon carved on his chest. The accompanying inscriptions make it clear that these were idols of the moon god. Several smaller statues were also found which were identified by their inscriptions as the "daughters" of the moon god.

Thousands of inscriptions from walls and rocks in Northern Arabia have also been collected. Reliefs and bowls used in worship of the "daughters of Allah" have also been discovered. The three daughters, al-Lat, al-Uzza and Manat are sometimes depicted together with Allah the moon god represented by a crescent moon above them. The archeological evidence demonstrates that the dominant religion of Arabia was the cult of the moon god.

When the popularity of the moon god waned elsewhere, the Arabs remained true to their conviction that the moon god was the greatest of all gods. While they worshipped 360 gods at the Kabah in Mecca, the moon god was the chief deity. Mecca was, in fact, built as a shrine for the moon god. This is what made it the most sacred site of Arabian paganism.

The evidence reveals that the temple of the moon god was active even in the Christian era. Evidence gathered from Arabia demonstrates that moon god worship was clearly active even in Muhammad's day and was still the dominant cult. According to numerous inscriptions, while the name of the moon god was normally Sin, his title was al-ilah, "the deity," meaning that he was the chief or high god among the gods. The god Il or Ilah was originally a phase of the moon god. The moon god was called al-ilah, meaning "the god," which was shortened to Allah in pre-Islamic times. The pagan Arabs even used Allah in the names they gave to their children. For example, both Muhammad's father and uncle had Allah as part of their names.

The fact that they were given such names by their pagan parents proves that Allah was the title for the moon god even in Muhammad's day. Under Mohammed's teaching, the relatively anonymous Ilah, became Al-Ilah, The God, or Allah, the Supreme Being. Muhammad was raised in the religion of the moon god Allah. But he went one step further than his fellow pagan Arabs. While they believed that Allah, the moon god, was the greatest of all gods and the supreme deity in a pantheon of deities, Muhammad decided that Allah was not only the greatest god but the only god. This is seen from the fact that the first point of the Muslim creed is not, "Allah is great" but "Allah is the greatest," that is, he is the greatest among the gods. Why would Muhammad say that Allah is the "greatest" except in a polytheistic context? Interestingly, the pagan Arabs never accused Muhammad of preaching a different Allah than the one they already worshipped. This "Allah" was the moon god according to all the archeological evidence. Muhammad, therefore, attempted to have it both ways. To the pagans, he said that he still believed in the moon god Allah. To the Jews and the Christians, he said that Allah was their God too. But both the Jews and the Christians of his day knew better and that is why they rejected his god Allah as a false god.

Al-Kindi, one of the early Christian apologists against Islam, pointed out that Islam and its god Allah did not come from the Bible but from the paganism. They did not worship the God of the Bible but the moon god. The Arabs worshipped the moon god as a supreme deity, not the God of Abraham, Isaac, and Jacob. While the moon god was greater than all other gods and goddesses, this was still a polytheistic pantheon of deities. Now that we have the actual idols of the moon god, it is no longer possible to avoid the fact that Allah was a pagan god in pre-Islamic times.

Is it any wonder then that the symbol of Islam is the crescent moon? That a crescent moon sits on top of their mosques and minarets? That a crescent moon is found on the flags of Islamic nations? That the Muslims fast during the month which begins and ends with the appearance of the crescent moon in the sky?

The pagan Arabs worshipped the moon god Allah by praying toward Mecca several times a day; making a pilgrimage to Mecca; running around the temple of the moon god called the Kabah; kissing the black stone; killing an animal in sacrifice to the moon god; throwing stones at the devil; fasting for the month which begins and ends with the crescent moon.

The Muslim's claim that Allah is the God of the Bible and that Islam arose from the religion of the prophets and apostles is refuted by solid, overwhelming archeological evidence. Islam is nothing more than a revival of the ancient moon god cult. It has taken the symbols, the rites, the ceremonies, and even the name of its god from the ancient pagan religion of the moon god. As such, it is sheer idolatry, but as I said earlier, I feel like "one calling out in the wilderness," for even Pope Francis and Chrislamists like Rick Warren can not see this fact. Catholics and protestants should be outraged that these men, along with all the media, elevate Islam to equal footing with the two religions of the one true God, Judaism and Christianity. But political correctness, fear, and ignorance will win out. Those voices crying in the wilderness are seldom heard. Thank God some heard and paid attention to John the Baptist.

But now, a few pages earlier, in the scripture we read from 2 Kings, we find that the name of the king of Assyria meant "the moon god," which quite frankly makes all the sense in the world when we understand that God called both the antichrist and Satan, Assyrians. The moon god, the Assyrian, Gog, Satan, and the antichrist who is possessed by Satan in the final forty two months; they are all one and the same. They are all Lucifer, the angel spoken of in scripture:

> *"How you have fallen from heaven,*
>   *morning star, son of the dawn!*
> *You have been cast down to the earth,*
>   *you who once laid low the nations!*
> *You said in your heart,*
>   *'I will ascend to the heavens;*

*I will raise my throne*
  *above the stars of God;*
*I will sit enthroned on the mount of assembly,*
  *on the utmost heights of Mount Zaphon.*
*I will ascend above the tops of the clouds;*
  *I will make myself like the Most High.'*
*But you are brought down to the realm of the dead,*
  *to the depths of the pit.*

*Those who see you stare at you,*
  *they ponder your fate:*
*'Is this the man who shook the earth*
  *and made kingdoms tremble,*
*the man who made the world a wilderness,*
  *who overthrew its cities*
  *and would not let his captives go home?'*

*All the kings of the nations lie in state,*
  *each in his own tomb.*
*But you are cast out of your tomb*
  *like a rejected branch;*
*you are covered with the slain,*
  *with those pierced by the sword,*
  *those who descend to the stones of the pit.*
*Like a corpse trampled underfoot,*
  *you will not join them in burial,*
*for you have destroyed your land*
  *and killed your people.*

*Let the offspring of the wicked*
  *never be mentioned again.*
*Prepare a place to slaughter his children*
  *for the sins of their ancestors;*
*they are not to rise to inherit the land*
  *and cover the earth with their cities.*

> *'I will rise up against them,'*
>   *declares the Lord Almighty.*
> *'I will wipe out Babylon's name and survivors,*
>   *her offspring and descendants,' declares the Lord.*
> *'I will turn her into a place for owls*
>   *and into swampland;*
> *I will sweep her with the broom of destruction,'*
>   *declares the Lord Almighty.*
>
> *The Lord Almighty has sworn,*
>
> *'Surely, as I have planned, so it will be,*
>   *and as I have purposed, so it will happen.*
> *I will crush **the Assyrian** in my land;*
>   *on my mountains I will trample him down.*
> *His yoke will be taken from my people,*
>   *and his burden removed from their shoulders.'*
>
> **This is the plan determined for the whole world;**
>   **this is the hand stretched out over all nations.**
> **For the Lord Almighty has purposed, and who can thwart him?**
>   **His hand is stretched out, and who can turn it back?"**
>
> Isaiah 14:12-27.

    I find it interesting in the story from 2 Kings that although the armies of the Kingdom of Egypt, which is normally a depiction of the flesh in the Bible, are headed toward the king of Assyria, King Sennacherib, the moon god, Satan, God did not use that nation to conquer him. We know that God will use the nations to kill the antichrist, but this is different. This is spiritual, and must be handled with the spiritual. So *"the angel of the Lord went out and put to death a hundred and eighty-five thousand in the Assyrian camp."*

    It is pure speculation on my part, but it seems that when Satan sees the antichrist killed he will lose any semblance of sanity he might have had and be out to destroy the whole world, especially Jerusalem. But in that story we read. ***"he will not enter this city, declares the Lord. I will defend this city and save it, for my sake and for the sake of David my servant."***

So, my thinking is that it all ends at the city gate. We read:

*"They were trampled in the winepress **outside the city**, and blood flowed out of the press, rising as high as the horses' bridles for a distance of **1,600 stadia**."* Revelation 14:20.

1,600 stadia is 180 miles, the distance by the Jericho Road from Mount Megiddo, the location of Armageddon, to the gates of Jerusalem. It ends there.

*"And I saw an angel coming down out of heaven, having the key to the Abyss and holding in his hand a great chain. He seized the dragon, that ancient serpent, who is the devil, or Satan, and bound him for a thousand years. He threw him into the Abyss, and locked and sealed it over him, to keep him from deceiving the nations anymore until the thousand years were ended."* Revelation 20:1-3.

The words of Jesus resound;
*"Immediately after the distress of those days*

> *'the sun will be darkened,*
> *and the moon will not give its light;*
> *the stars will fall from the sky,*
> *and the heavenly bodies will be shaken.'*

*Then will appear the sign of the Son of Man in heaven. And then all the peoples of the earth will mourn when they see the Son of Man coming on the clouds of heaven, with power and great glory. And he will send his angels with a loud trumpet call, and they will gather his elect from the four winds, from one end of the heavens to the other."* Matthew 24:29-31.

And you and I, whether resurrected or raptured, will meet and escort Jesus, our savior, the King of kings, into Jerusalem, the City of God, the capital city of our Lord's new kingdom on earth.

# King of Kings

I must admit that this is the chapter I have been looking forward to from the beginning. To most of us the thousand year reign of Jesus has been just as mystifying as our concept of heaven, but after learning the truth from the Apostolic Oral Teaching, our life in the Millennial Kingdom has become to me like those old comfortable shoes. I think I can now see what life will actually be like. It is as if the fog of allegory has been lifted and I truly am pleased with what I see. I believe you will be as well.

Quite frankly, John does not give us a lot to go on in Revelation concerning this time in the history of mankind, for all he says about it is:

*"I saw thrones on which were seated those who had been given authority to judge. And I saw the souls of those who had been beheaded because of their testimony about Jesus and because of the word of God. They had not worshiped the beast or its image and had not received its mark on their foreheads or their hands. They came to life and reigned with Christ a thousand years. (The rest of the dead did not come to life until the thousand years were ended.) This is the first resurrection. Blessed and holy are those who share in the first resurrection. The second death has no power over them, but they will be priests of God and of Christ and will reign with him for a thousand years."* Revelation 20:4-6.

That is all John wrote concerning the thousand year period after the tribulation is over and Jesus has returned to reign as King over the entire earth. But we now know so much more.

One of the most interesting things for me was finding out that the tares in the parable by Jesus were Nephilim. That is huge; because that means that **everyone** who lives through the seven tribulation years will enter the Millennium Kingdom, not just those who had been believers in Jesus or Jews who were saved at the end of the tribulation. No, the fact is that people from all beliefs and nationalities will join us in the next section of the history of mankind. There will be Muslims, Hindus, Buddhists, New Agers, and Atheists; Spanish, Vietnamese, Argentinians, Canadians, Chinese, South Africans, Russians, Australian, Mexicans, and Swiss. And all the nations will still be nations.

We shouldn't be surprised to find that the nations will still exist. Earlier we read what Daniel saw in his vision of the four beasts or empires:

*"Then I continued to watch because of the boastful words the horn was speaking. I kept looking until the beast was slain and its body destroyed and thrown into the blazing fire. (The other beasts had been stripped of their authority, but were allowed to live for a period of time.)"* Daniel 7:11-12.

As we know, that final beast, the empire of the antichrist, was slain when Jesus returned, so if the other beasts (empires) were *"allowed to live for a period of time,"* that time period has to be during the Millennial Reign of Christ.

We will look at the other nations during the Millennium a little later, but first we need to focus on Israel, from where Jesus will be ruling the world. Let's read God's Word;

*"I myself will gather the remnant of my flock out of all the countries where I have driven them and will bring them back to their pasture, where they will be fruitful and increase in number. I will place shepherds over them who will tend them, and they will no longer be afraid or terrified, nor will any be missing,' declares the Lord.*

*'The days are coming,' declares the Lord, 'when I will raise up for David a righteous Branch, a King who will reign wisely and do what is just and right in the land. In his days Judah will be saved and Israel will live in safety. This is the name by which he will be called: The Lord Our Righteous Savior.*

*'So then, the days are coming,' declares the Lord, 'when people will no longer say, "As surely as the Lord lives, who brought the Israelites up out of Egypt," but they will say, "As surely as the Lord lives, who brought the descendants of Israel up out of the land of the north and out of all the countries where he had banished them." Then they will live in their own land."* Jeremiah 23:3-8.

This return to the land of Israel by all of the remnants of all the tribes has not taken place yet. Yes, we have seen Jews coming back to their land, but the above passage is talking about God bringing back **all** the Jews at the beginning of the Millennium. Most of them had fallen for the lies of the antichrist during the tribulation years, but it is at the beginning of the Millennium when God will finally take the veil from their eyes so that they will be able to see the truth; that Jesus Christ is their true Messiah, their true King. Blessed are we gentiles that they had been blinded for a period of time in order that we might have the chance of salvation, but it is at the beginning of the Millennium when it will be Israel's turn to be blessed. The days of continual persecution and the holocaust will be over and they will now live in their own land in safety and prosperity, forever. What a glorious day for Israel.

There is a story of a miracle in the Gospel of John that I believe is a shadow of the blindness Israel experienced. Jesus and His disciples were walking along when we take up the story. Let's read the highlights:

*"As he went along, he saw a man blind from birth. His disciples asked him, 'Rabbi, who sinned, this man or his parents, that he was born blind?'*

*'Neither this man nor his parents sinned,' said Jesus, 'but this happened so that the works of God might be displayed in him.'*

*After saying this, he spit on the ground, made some mud with the saliva, and put it on the man's eyes. 'Go,' he told him, 'wash in the Pool of Siloam' (this word means 'Sent'). So the man went and washed, and came home seeing.*

*His neighbors and those who had formerly seen him begging asked, 'Isn't this the same man who used to sit and beg?' Some claimed that he was.*

*Others said, 'No, he only looks like him.'*

*But he himself insisted, 'I am the man.'*

*'How then were your eyes opened?' they asked.*

*He replied, 'The man they call Jesus made some mud and put it on my eyes. He told me to go to Siloam and wash. So I went and washed, and then I could see.'*

*They brought to the Pharisees the man who had been blind. Now the day on which Jesus had made the mud and opened the man's eyes was a Sabbath. Therefore the Pharisees also asked him how he had received his sight. 'He put mud on my eyes,' the man replied, 'and I washed, and now I see.'*

*'One thing I do know. I was blind but now I see!'*

*To this they replied, 'You were steeped in sin at birth; how dare you lecture us!' And they threw him out.*

*Jesus heard that they had thrown him out, and when he found him, he said, 'Do you believe in the Son of Man?'*
*'Who is he, sir?' the man asked. 'Tell me so that I may believe in him.'*
*Jesus said, 'You have now seen him; in fact, he is the one speaking with you.'*
*Then the man said, 'Lord, I believe,' and he worshiped him."*
John 9:1-3, 6-11, 13-15, 25, 34-38.

One thing that is important to note is that this miracle occurred on the Sabbath, the day of rest. That is symbolic of the Millennium, the seventh thousand year period in Biblical time. Also, among other things, we can see from the beginning of the story that the blind man had not been blinded because of his or his parents' sin, as is also the case with the Jews, *"but this happened so that the works of God might be displayed in him."* And in the end, when the veil of blindness is lifted and the man sees who gave him his sight, he believes and worships. So will Israel.

As we saw, Israel will in all probability be the big winner in the sixth trumpet war, World War III. And in so doing, they will probably increase their territory, possibly to the boundaries that God originally promised them. The original covenant given to Abraham was passed on to his grandson Jacob, the man whose name God changed to Israel. In that covenant, God promised:

*"On that day the Lord made a covenant with Abram and said, 'To your descendants I give this land, from the Wadi of Egypt to the great river, the Euphrates— the land of the Kenites, Kenizzites, Kadmonites, Hittites, Perizzites, Rephaites, Amorites, Canaanites, Girgashites and Jebusites."*
Genesis 15:18-21.

This territory covers part of Egypt, all the way to the Euphrates River, including Lebanon, and most of Syria, Jordan, and Iraq. And we know that the promised boundaries given in the Abrahamic Covenant are the same ones

Israel later received through Abraham's grandson, Jacob, for we read God tell Jacob at the same time He changed his name to Israel;

> *"The land I gave to Abraham and Isaac I also give to you, and I will give this land to your descendants after you."*           Genesis 35:12.

Although the entire land described in the covenant will certainly comprise the nation of Israel during the Millennium, when we look at a futuristic depiction of the land that each of the tribes will be allotted according to Ezekiel's vision, we see that the area only encompasses the eastern portion of the full land mass that according to the covenant will eventually be Israel.

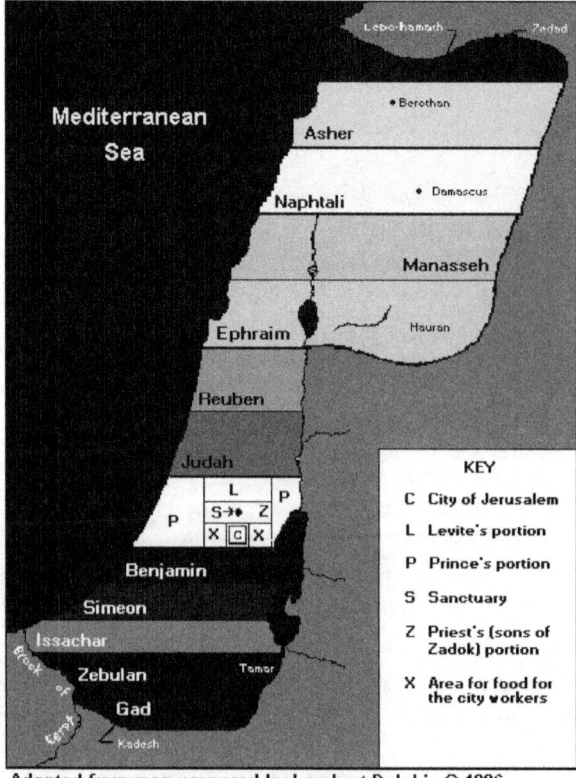

Adapted from map prepared by Lambert Dolphin ☉ 1996

We might note in that map that the tribe of Dan from which the antichrist will come, although seemingly out of God's good graces prior to the second coming of Christ, will again be included in the Millennial Kingdom allotment of land for each of the Jewish tribes within the nation of Israel. Note also that the tribal allocation map does indeed include the land that we now know as Lebanon and Syria.

An interesting side topic is that it seems to me that the entire land area that might belong to Israel during the Millennium, stretching all the way to the Euphrates River, is almost the exact same territory that originally was the Garden of Eden, of which we read:

*"A river watering the garden flowed from Eden; from there it was separated into four headwaters. The name of the first is the Pishon; it winds through the entire land of Havilah, where there is gold. (The gold of that land is good; aromatic resin and onyx are also there.) The name of the second river is the Gihon; it winds through the entire land of Cush. The name of the third river is the Tigris; it runs along the east side of Ashur. And the fourth river is the Euphrates."* Genesis 2:10-14.

Whether or not the boundaries of the Garden of Eden and the boundaries of the land given the Israelites by God are in fact identical, we can not be completely sure; however, the similarities to me are striking.

One of the things that I find interesting is the notion that Revelation is almost the reverse of Genesis, in that in Genesis we start out with God being with man in the Garden of Eden, Satan being introduced, and the downfall of man; whereas in Revelation we see man being redeemed, Satan done away with, and God and man again being together in a paradise situation. If indeed the entire land area that Israel will end up with is actually the same land area as the original Garden of Eden, it just strengthens that thought of Revelation being the mirror image of Genesis.

Another point to ponder is that when John is told to measure the New Jerusalem at the end of the Millennium, when that glorious city comes down from heaven to exist on earth throughout eternity, John finds that it is about fourteen hundred miles long and wide, which is about the length of the Euphrates River, which is listed as the eastern boundary for both the Garden of Eden and the land given to Jacob (Israel) by God in covenant. There is no doubt that that land is Holy Land.

With that in mind, we may be looking at why there is a discrepancy between the total land area given the Jews and the land divided and allocated to each of the Jewish tribes during the Millennium. It is possible that Israel will not receive its full territory until the Millennial Kingdom has ended and what we know as heaven has begun. But, of course, that is just speculation. Neither the Bible nor the Apostolic Oral Teaching fills us in on those details.

At any rate, the center of everything will be Jerusalem:

> *"For Zion's sake I will not keep silent,*
> > *for Jerusalem's sake I will not remain quiet,*
> > *till her vindication shines out like the dawn,*
> > *her salvation like a blazing torch.*
> 
> *The nations will see your vindication,*
> > *and all kings your glory;*
> > *you will be called by a new name*
> > *that the mouth of the Lord will bestow.*
> 
> *You will be a crown of splendor in the Lord's hand,*
> > *a royal diadem in the hand of your God.*
> 
> *No longer will they call you Deserted,*
> > *or name your land Desolate.*
> 
> *But you will be called Hephzibah [my delight is in her],*
> > *and your land Beulah [married];*
> > *for the Lord will take delight in you,*
> > *and your land will be married.*
> 
> *As a young man marries a young woman,*
> > *so will your Builder marry you;*
> > *as a bridegroom rejoices over his bride,*
> > *so will your God rejoice over you.*
> 
> *I have posted watchmen on your walls, Jerusalem;*
> > *they will never be silent day or night.*
> 
> *You who call on the Lord,*
> > *give yourselves no rest,*
> > *and give him no rest till he establishes Jerusalem*
> > *and makes her the praise of the earth."*   Isaiah 62:1-7.

Yes, Israel will be a big part of the Millennial Kingdom. We can see their fulfillment as "one nation under God:"

> *"In that day the deaf will hear the words of the scroll,*
> *and out of gloom and darkness the eyes of the blind will see.*
> *Once more the humble will rejoice in the Lord;*
> *the needy will rejoice in the Holy One of Israel.*
> *The ruthless will vanish, the mockers will disappear,*
> *and all who have an eye for evil will be cut down—*
> *those who with a word make someone out to be guilty,*
> *who ensnare the defender in court*
> *and with false testimony deprive the innocent of justice.*
>
> *Therefore this is what the Lord, who redeemed Abraham,*
> *says to the descendants of Jacob:*
>
> *'No longer will Jacob be ashamed;*
> *no longer will their faces grow pale.*
> *When they see among them their children, the work of my hands,*
> *they will keep my name holy; they will acknowledge the holiness of the Holy One of Jacob, and will stand in awe of the God of Israel."*   Isaiah 29:18-23.

But what about the rest of the nations of the world? Since we saw that the tares that were destroyed by fire were the Nephilim and the souls of the Nephilim (the demons), we know that those who survived the tribulation, in addition to the Jewish people, were non-believers of different religions from Muslims to Hindus to Atheists. And they populate all the existing nations of that day. What about them?

The days of gaining salvation by faith in Jesus will be over then. Jesus will be reigning in Jerusalem as King of kings and Lord of lords. It is obvious that those who had denied Him before He returned would not now just be able to see the truth of His divinity as He sits on His throne, and still be saved by just acknowledging what they obviously are seeing. Things don't work that way.

And if Jesus is King of kings, will those kings ruling under Him be the same non-believers who were ruling over those nations before His return?

No, the Bible is clear that it will be the resurrected and raptured Christians who will rule and reign with Christ. And the Apostolic Oral Teaching does not deviate from that truth:

"For the first appearance of our Lord in the flesh took place in Bethlehem, under Augustus, and He suffered in the thirty-third year. And 6,000 years must needs be accomplished, in order that the Sabbath may come, the rest, the holy day 'on which God rested from all His works.' For the Sabbath is the type and emblem of the **future kingdom of the saints, when they 'shall reign with Christ,'** when He comes from heaven, as John says in his Apocalypse: for 'a day with the Lord is as a thousand years.' Since, then, in six days God made all things, it follows that 6,000 years must be fulfilled. And they are not yet fulfilled, as John says: 'five are fallen; one is,' that is, the sixth; 'the other is not yet come.'"

Commentary on Daniel, 2.4, Hippolytus.

So, what about those previous non-believers populating those nations being ruled by the saints; those folks in the town, cities, counties, states, and nations who then will be directly under the rule of King Jesus through His appointed resurrected and raptured ambassadors who will be "ruling and reigning" with Him and for Him? If those prior non-believers can't now just have "faith," do they have any hope? Even they would understand that it is too late to rely on the promise of Romans 10:9, which says, *"If you declare with your mouth, "Jesus is Lord," and believe in your heart that God raised him from the dead, you will be saved."* Any fool would know that Jesus is Lord and that God raised Him from the dead at that point, because He will be in plain view of the entire world. So, did God provide them another option?

Actually, God takes a full nine chapters at the end of Ezekiel to not only describe the division of the land of Israel during the Millennium, but also the particulars of the Millennial Temple down to the minutest of detail. Also in detail in those chapters are the animal sacrifices that will be performed at that temple on a daily basis. Those sacrifices have been a source of puzzlement and mystery for the past two thousand years.

But with what you and I now know from the unveiling of the truth about who the tares in Revelation 14 really are, that mystery is now over. It is only because we now understand the importance of the Nephilim in the entire Bible story, culminating with those important words in Revelation in which the tares are put to the fire, a fire of destruction mere humans could not be subjected to because they had not at that point had their day in court at the White Throne Judgment, that you and I can see the truth about who the inhabitants of the world will be at the start of the millennium. And quite frankly, it is mainly because of that truth that I spent so much time in this book on the subject of the Nephilim. It is such a shame that our churches completely ignore the topic of the Nephilim. Had they explored the Nephilim head on, it may even have been a clue for our church leaders as to why Darby's "school of thought," that is now memorized and spewed out in virtually every pulpit, was faulty from the get go.

But now you and I can unlock the mystery of the animal sacrifices in the Millennium. First, let's refresh our thinking as to what animal sacrifices were all about to begin with. God's very first prophecy was,

*"You are free to eat from any tree in the garden; but you must not eat from the tree of the knowledge of good and evil, for when you eat of it you will surely die."* Genesis 2:16-17.

This prophecy stated clearly that if His creation, mankind, experienced sin, he would surely die. That death referred to eternal death. And God does not change. That statement by God is just as true today as it was in the Garden of Eden. God later said:

*"For the life of a creature is in the blood, and I have given it to you to make atonement for yourselves on the altar; it is the blood that makes atonement for one's life."* Leviticus 17:11.

Of course, you and I know that the shedding of blood on the cross by Jesus was our ultimate atonement for sin, but until that time came, God gave the Israelites a method by which they could daily atone for their sins, and that atonement was through the redemptive sacrifice of a clean animal, which not only was a picture of the sacrifice of the pure Lamb of God, Jesus, which was to come and which you and I can choose to accept or reject, but was for the Jews an atonement for sins for a truly repentive soul. That was all the Jews had as their hope for receiving eternal life. And God honored His word.

The only hope for eternal life for people like David, who had Bathsheba's husband, Uriah the Hittite, murdered, just so he could be with her, or the eleven brothers of Joseph who sold him into slavery and lied to their father, Jacob, about it, or virtually any other characters in the Old Testament who sinned, was in God's promise of the atonement brought about by the sacrifices on the altar of clean animals as replacements for themselves. They did not have the everlasting sacrifice of Jesus on the cross like you and I do today. And the same will be true of those unbelievers who live through the tribulation. Their time for redemption by the blood of Jesus will have past. But God is a loving God, and since He has never officially done away with the redemptive value of the Old Covenant, that covenant will be their option for gaining entrance into eternal life.

In that Old Covenant, once the tabernacle had been constructed exactly as He told them, God laid out instructions as to how the Israelites were to substitute an animal's blood for their own blood on the Day of Atonement. There were actually to be three animals involved, a bull and two goats.

*"Aaron is to offer the bull for his own sin offering to make atonement for himself and his household. Then he is to take the two goats and present them before the Lord at the entrance to the Tent of Meeting. He is to cast lots for the two goats - one lot for the Lord and the other for the scapegoat. Aaron is to bring the goat whose lot falls to the Lord and sacrifice it for a sin offering. But the goat chosen by lot as the scapegoat shall be presented alive before the Lord to be used for making atonement by sending it into the desert as a scapegoat."* Leviticus 16:6-10.

The word "scapegoat", by the way, was first coined by William Tyndale when he combined "escape goat" into "scapegoat" in 1530 AD, when he translated the first English Bible from the Latin Vulgate. At any rate, as you and I know, all three animals mentioned above were types of Jesus. There has been some erroneous teaching that the scapegoat represents Satan; however, Satan can obviously never take away the sin nature from man. The confusion occurred because the original Hebrew describing the scapegoat says "the other goat for Azazel." "Azazel" literally means, "the one to be sent away." We can find Satan referred to as Azazel in <u>The Book of Enoch</u> we studied earlier. The Book of Enoch was actually referring to Satan also as "one to be sent away." However, that goat is a type of Jesus.

God goes on with his instructions by saying that after the bull is killed for the sins of the High Priest,

*"He is to take some of the bull's blood and with his finger sprinkle it on the front of the atonement cover; then he shall sprinkle some of it with his finger seven times before the atonement cover. He shall then slaughter the goat for the sin offering for the people and take its blood behind the curtain and do with it as he did with the bull's blood: He shall sprinkle it on the atonement cover and in front of it."* Leviticus 16:14-15.

Lest we start wondering why all this killing and bloodshed was necessary, let's remember that God's first prophecy was that once man's sin nature was manifested, *"You shall surely die."*

And since God told us man's life and the soul *"is in the blood,"* man's own blood, or adequate substitutionary blood, must be shed. This entire shadow showed that God had already devised the plan *"from the foundation of the world"* to fulfill the prophecy and still allow us to live. We need also to realize that the death referred to in the prophecy was our spiritual death. The death we experience on earth is itself a shadow of the more important and devastating spiritual death. Earthly death is only a transition from our fleshly selves to our spiritual selves, our real selves.

God's instruction continued, after the sacrifice of the bull and the goat, and after the blood of both had been presented to God at the Mercy Seat and found acceptable to substitute for the needed death of both the priest and the people,

*"He shall take some of the bull's blood and some of the goats blood and put it on all the horns of the altar. He shall sprinkle some of the blood on it with his finger seven times to cleanse it and to consecrate it from the uncleanness of the Israelites."* Leviticus 16:18-19.

The above act finalized the acceptance of the substitutions for dying, which allowed for the forgiveness of any prior sins and the sending of them away. Therefore, God then said,

*"He shall bring forward the live goat. He is to lay both hands on the head of the live goat and confess over it all the wickedness and rebellion of*

*the Israelites - all their sins - and put them on the goat's head. He shall send the goat away into the desert. ... The goat will carry on itself all their sins to a solitary place."* Leviticus 16:20-22.

As we said, all three of these animals represented Jesus and what was accomplished on the cross. His death was first of all for Himself, because, since He was fully human He had to have the sin nature inside Him. Some "scholars" argue that point, referring to His divinity, but Hebrews 4:15 says very clearly about Jesus, *"we have one who has been tempted in every way, just as we are, yet was without sin."* Had there been no sin nature in Him, He could not have been tempted. In fact, to put an end to that debate God tells us in James 1:13, *"God cannot be tempted by evil."* Therefore, since Jesus was tempted, the humanity of Jesus, with its necessary sin nature, had to die. The shadow of the bull's death represented that necessary death.

The second animal, the sacrificed goat which was God's lot, was a shadow of the death of Jesus that was a completely acceptable substitution for us. The sin in mankind could in no way be brought into the presence of God, just as darkness could not come into the presence of light. God, being Holy could not allow sin to be brought to the Mercy Seat. Jesus, however, took all of mankind's sin, for we read in 2 Corinthians 5:21, *"God made Him who had no sin to be sin for us."* His crucifixion, therefore, like the scapegoat, took our sins,

*"As far as the east is from the west, so far has He removed our transgressions from us."* Psalm 103:12.

So, during the Millennium, when Christ's sacrifice will not be available to them as their substitutional atonement, the peoples of the world will be required to revert to the original hope that was never cancelled in the Old Covenant.

I think we can be certain that this requirement will be much easier for the Jewish people who will then see that their religion had all the time been pointing to Jesus being their Messiah, than for some of the other groups who will be living at that time. Let's face the facts and reverse the tables for a second. Suppose a life long follower of Jesus survived the tribulation only to find that the Islamic Mahdi was the one in charge of the world. What do you think his reaction would be? I can assure you that mine would be rebellion.

And I think we can be pretty sure that a life long Muslim who finds Jesus in charge following the tribulation, instead of the Mahdi that he expected, will be just as rebellious to the idea. Some will never get over it, as we will see at the end of the Millennium when Satan is set loose one final time. And during the Millennium we can see that this will be a continual concern for Jesus throughout those thousand years. We get a glimpse of this in scripture:

*"If any of the peoples of the earth do not go up to Jerusalem to worship the King, the Lord Almighty, they will have no rain. If the Egyptian people do not go up and take part, they will have no rain. The Lord[a] will bring on them the plague he inflicts on the nations that do not go up to celebrate the Festival of Tabernacles. This will be the punishment of Egypt and the punishment of all the nations that do not go up to celebrate the Festival of Tabernacles."* Zechariah 14:17-19.

Unlike the picture painted by most who talk about the Millennial Reign of Christ, everything will not always be a bed of roses during that time. I find that when God really wants to make a point in the Bible He will repeat something three times. And in Revelation we find God explain to us three times that Jesus will be ruling with an "iron scepter," the idiom used in those days much like "ruling with an iron fist" is today.

*"She gave birth to a son, a male child, who 'will rule all the nations with an **iron scepter**."* Revelation 12:5.

*"Coming out of his mouth is a sharp sword with which to strike down the nations. 'He will rule them with an **iron scepter**."* Revelation 19:15.

Plus, those saints put in authority over towns, cities, counties, states, and nations, will be given the same authority and expected to use it:

*"To the one who is victorious and does my will to the end, I will give authority over the nations - that one 'will rule them with an **iron scepter** and will dash them to pieces like pottery' - just as I have received authority from my Father."* Revelation 2:26-27.

Yes, Jesus will be ruling from Jerusalem as King of kings, and He will expect the kings under Him to make sure that the people they rule over will follow His edicts, and that includes worship.

> *"In the last days the mountain of the Lord's temple will be established as the highest of the mountains; it will be exalted above the hills, and all nations will stream to it."*     Isaiah 2:2.

Fortunately, most of the people will understand for the first time the truth about God and Jesus:

> *"Many peoples will come and say,*
>    *'Come, let us go up to the mountain of the Lord,*
>      *to the temple of the God of Jacob.*
> *He will teach us his ways,*
>    *so that we may walk in his paths.'*
> *The law will go out from Zion,*
>    *the word of the Lord from Jerusalem.*
> *He will judge between the nations*
>    *and will settle disputes for many peoples.*
> *They will beat their swords into plowshares*
>    *and their spears into pruning hooks.*
> *Nation will not take up sword against nation,*
>    *nor will they train for war anymore."*     Isaiah 2:3-4.

Those people will gladly make the journey to the center of everything:

> *"This is what the Sovereign Lord says: This is Jerusalem, which I have set in the center of the nations, with countries all around her."*     Ezekiel 5:5.

But there will also be altars or places of worship in the other nations as well. One is mention pertaining to Egypt"

> *"In that day there will be an altar to the Lord in the heart of Egypt, and a monument to the Lord at its border. It will be a sign and witness to the Lord Almighty in the land of Egypt."*     Isaiah 19:19-20.

I have wondered if *"an altar to the Lord in the heart of Egypt, and a monument to the Lord at its border"* might not have already been erected. Saying that reminded me of a time when I was a small boy. My dear mother who has been in heaven with the Lord for several years now was the Sunday School Superintendent for the younger ages up to age twelve at the First Baptist Church that was so integral to our lives in the small mountain town I grew up in, Brevard, North Carolina. She use to tell Bible stories with her "flannel board" and then had little songs we children would sing. One of her favorites, and mine, was:

> "Zacchaeus was a wee little man
> And a wee little man was he
> He climbed up in a sycamore tree
> For the Lord he wanted to see
> And as the Savior passed that way
> He looked up in that tree
> And He said, "Zacchaeus, you come down!
> For I'm going to your house today
> For I'm going to your house to stay"

You may be old enough to remember that song and those innocent days in the fifties. If so, you are fortunate. At any rate, once I was old enough to realize how God orchestrated events throughout history, I could imagine God having that sycamore tree planted years before the event was to occur, and putting angels in charge of that seedling to make sure no one ever bothered it. I can see now how God is so instrumental in even the minutest of details of the events that are important to "His Story."

At any rate, I can see the same attention to detail, and even more so in the structure that I have a feeling could be the altar He told us would exist in Egypt during the Millennial Reign of Jesus, one that I believe to be undoubtedly the most phenomenal structure ever created on earth. We could search our dictionaries for a word or phrase that would be a remotely adequate superlative to describe the awesomeness of this building, but there is none. I am talking about the Great Pyramid of Giza.

Estimated to have been built about 2200 BC, the Great Pyramid is different from all the other pyramids in Egypt. For one thing it's made of stone, not bricks, and is the only one that's not solid. There is a series of passageways and several chambers inside. All of the 80 or so other pyramids which were built later are vastly inferior copies. And unlike the Great Pyramid, they were all used as gigantic headstones covering the tombs of the Pharaohs. The Great Pyramid, however, never served as a tomb. Its purpose, as I have inferred, may still be for a future time.

Each face of this phenomenal structure is an exact equilateral triangle. If we use 25.025 inches, which is the Hebrew Cubit, we find that every side of the four triangles is exactly 365.2422 cubits long, an exact solar year. When we consider that this building was constructed 4,600 years ago without modern equipment and computers, such accuracy is almost mind boggling. But as we will see, that is nothing compared to what else we are going to discover.

By the way, everything the Egyptians built was based on the Egyptian Cubit, with the exception of the Great Pyramid of Giza, which was based on the Hebrew Sacred Cubit. There's only one possible reason for this; the Egyptians did not design the Great Pyramid of Giza.

The ancient Egyptians called the pyramid the "Pillar of Enoch," and Enoch's fingerprints are all over it. Did you ever wonder why Enoch lived 365 years? The same number of days in our solar year. More precisely if we go back to the <u>Book of Enoch</u> that we studied earlier in regards to the Nephilim, we find that Enoch lived 365 years 88 days and 9 hours. Or 365.242 years. Did you see that? The exact same number of years Enoch lived is exactly the length of each of the four triangles that make up the Great Pyramid. This is out of this world phenomenal. You see, God had it planned that way. He made Enoch live the exact length of our solar year and then He took him. But Where? Normally you could express someone's life from birth to death with a straight line. But with Enoch you can't. His line would be a circle and if you take 365.242 years and reduced them to sacred inches you get the Enoch circle. This same circle can be measured in the Anti-chamber within the King's chamber complex that we will mention momentarily. It is a "Map" room that gives us the key to interpreting the whole message in the Pyramid. One inch equals one year, as in Enoch's life.

While being the oldest structure on the face of the earth, the Great Pyramid is the most accurately oriented, being laid out almost exactly due north, south, east, and west. Modern man's best effort, the Paris Observatory, is six minutes of a degree off true north. The Great Pyramid is only three minutes deviant. Many architects and engineers who have studied the

Pyramid's structure contend that, with all our vaunted technological prowess, we could not build the structure today.

The Great Pyramid is huge, built on a thirteen acre base, and was incredibly made level to within less than one inch. Think about what you just read, this thing has a thirteen acre base, and it is level to within an inch. I doubt that most modern structures are that level, and none of them are anywhere near that size. It is so big that it took nine hundred million cubic feet of granite blocks to construct. Modern engineers can't explain how the workers managed to fit those huge blocks together so carefully in building a monument nearly 500 feet high. Some of the larger ones, in fact, weighed nearly 80 tons, or the weight of three jumbo jets. There is not a machine on earth today that could lift such a mammoth weight.

Like 20th century bridge designs, the entire structure rests on four foundation stones that fit into sockets cut into the bedrock. These stones are designed to compensate for changes in temperature. They keep the pyramid perfectly square and level at all times, and in fact it is exactly square on every course. The Great Pyramid of Giza is several football fields long, and naturally subject to expansion and contraction movements from heat and cold, as well as earthquakes, settling, and other such phenomena. So without the cornerstones having balls and sockets built into them there would have been major damage in the last 4,200 years since it was completed. What a remarkable feat of engineering.

The pyramid originally had a face of polished white limestone consisting of 115,000 stones finished on all six sides to within .01 inch of perfectly straight. You read that right, one hundredth of an inch. Measurements like that are hard to duplicate in a modern scientific laboratory, and we are discussing several ton rocks cut with vastly inferior tools to what our normal local stone mason might have in his truck. Then these gigantic stones were cut on a bevel with such accuracy that they fit together with seams of less than 1/50th of an inch. In other words, you could not get a razor blade into any of the seams. And again, we are talking about the seams of 115,000 gigantic rocks cut and then put together.

They were then cemented together and polished to a high sheen. It's said that the pyramid shone as if made of light itself and could be seen from over a hundred miles away.

Interesting also is the fact that air shafts keep the temperature inside at exactly 68 degrees, the same as the mean temperature of Earth.

The structure is huge. It is thirty times larger than the Empire State Building and the Pyramid's features can actually be seen from the moon. A highway lane eight feet wide and four inches thick could be built from San Francisco to New York and put inside the Great Pyramid. What makes the size even more remarkable to me is that it is the oldest structure in existence, having been built over 4,200 years ago.

And speaking of the pyramid's size, only a solid stone mountain could endure the Pyramid's immense weight. And indeed, a flat solid granite mountain happens to be located just beneath the surface of the ground directly under the Pyramid. Coincidence? I doubt it.

The Great Pyramid of Giza faces due North more accurately than we can position buildings today so that each side faces the four cardinal points of the compass. Its shadow has predicted equinoxes and solstices. In fact, on one day in history the angle of the passageway looking up from the bottom pointed directly at the North Star. If you could have drawn a line straight up from the pyramid into the sky on that day you would have intersected the exact center of our galaxy. That day was the vernal equinox in 2141 BC. Such an alignment happens only once every 26,000 years. Since the Great Pyramid was built in 2200 BC, the builders obviously knew when this event would occur and planned their construction accordingly.

But the builders incredibly knew a lot of things that don't make sense that they could know. For instance, they knew the exact center of Earth's land mass, for that is incredibly where they built their monument. Equal amounts of land are contained in each of the quadrants drawn off its four corners. I'll say it again for you to take in slowly and ponder; the Pyramid is located at the exact center of the Earth's land mass. That is, its East-West axis corresponds to the longest land parallel across the Earth, passing through Africa, Asia, and America. Similarly, the longest land meridian on Earth, through Asia, Africa, Europa, and Antarctica, also passes right through the Pyramid. Since the Earth has enough land area to provide 3 billion possible building sites for the Pyramid, the odds of it having been built where it is at random, in the very center of the earth, are 1 in 3 billion. And since the entire world had not been mapped in 2200 BC, it seems fairly obvious to me that the builders knew a lot more than the smartest normal man of that time.

They also understood mathematical systems and equations long before the rest of mankind. Muse on this a while: the height of the Pyramid's apex is 5,812.98 inches, and each side is 9,131 inches from corner to corner (in a straight line). If the circumference of the Pyramid is divided by twice its height (the diameter of a circle is twice the radius), the result is 3.14159, which just happens to be pi. Incredibly, this calculation is accurate to six digits. So the Pyramid is a square circle, and thus pi was designed into it 4,200 years ago. Without going into many more illustrations such as this, I can tell you that pi is demonstrated many times throughout the Pyramid.

It seems that these geniuses also knew the average height of land above sea level, with Miami being low and the Himalayas being high, which only recently can be measured by modern day satellites and computers. That average height of land above sea level is 5,449 inches, which is the exact height of the Pyramid.

One strange feature worth noting is that all four sides of the Pyramid are very slightly and evenly bowed in, or concave. This effect, which cannot be detected by looking at the Pyramid from the ground, was discovered around 1940 by a pilot taking aerial photos to check certain measurements. As measured by today's laser instruments, all of these perfectly cut and intentionally bowed stone blocks duplicate exactly the curvature of the earth. The radius of this bow is equal to the radius of the Earth. In thinking about such awesome ingredients of the Great Pyramid, the only words that come to my mind are "mind boggling."

I'm sure you are getting the picture by now. Questions must be asked. Who was alive at that time that could have accomplished this feat of architecture and construction? And who was alive then that could have known things that no other living being in 2200 BC could have known?

The only possible answer seems to be the Nephilim, those that God told us in Genesis 6:4, "They were the heroes of old, men of renown." The King James Version of that verse used the words "mighty men." It is said that they had supernatural knowledge and abilities, as well as phenomenal strength. Speaking of their abilities, Jewish tradition teaches us that Nephilim could not only levitate themselves but also other objects. In my opinion the Nephilim were the perfect candidates to answer the questions about who truly built the Great Pyramid. But let's continue our investigation.

A single entrance on the North side opens into a passageway that slopes down 150 feet to the base where it descends another 200 feet into the bedrock on a line that's straight to within 1/4 of an inch over its 350 ft. length. The passageway, several chambers, and all the air vents were pre-cut into the stones before they were placed and appeared in their finished form as the stones were fit together.

As I mentioned earlier, the "sacred cubit" was the unit of measure used in building the Great Pyramid; the only time it was used in Egyptian architecture. Its length is 25 pyramid inches, which is about the same as the inch used today in the US. These units of measure were carved into the wall, and can serve to decode the pyramid's dimensions. For instance, multiplying the sacred cubit times 10 million equals the polar radius of earth. Multiplying the total weight of the Pyramid by 1000 trillion equals the weight of planet Earth.

These markers that were carved into the wall, however, tell us even more than that. As I said, I believe that even if the Nephilim built the Great Pyramid, and since they were quite obviously very much against God, it was that same God who was directing them in their effort. Just as in most historical events, it was God's purposes that were ultimately being served. The first clue to that is that the main passageway descends at an angle of 26 degrees 18 minutes and 9 seconds. This is called the Christ angle because a line drawn from the Pyramid to Bethlehem is 26 degrees 18 minutes and 9 seconds from true north.

I used the term main passageway in the above paragraph because there are actually three passageways. Picture if you will the main passageway descending straight downward at the Christ angle of a little over 26 degrees from an opening in the north side of the pyramid. At a point down that passageway there is another passageway that starts and ascends upward toward the middle of the pyramid. This passageway rises until it becomes a wider hallway known as the grand gallery that leads into a chamber called the king's chamber. And at the beginning of that hallway another passageway leads off in a horizontal direction, ending in a smaller chamber called the queen's chamber.

Robert Menzies, in 1865 thought that the various passageways were constructed according to a chronological scale of a geometric inch to a year. For example if you start at a certain point in the descending passage and this is represented by a certain year, than every inch you move represents one year forward.

In order to have a chronology, though, there must be a starting point. Let us see how this was determined in the great pyramid. If we start from the outside of the north entrance and move down the descending passage about

40 feet, we come to the markers, which are a series of so called "scored lines". These are straight knife-edge lines cut into the blocks from roof to floor. They are on each side of the passage and directly opposite each other.

Earlier I mentioned that the descending passage is in exact alignment of true north. We also saw that in the last 5,000 years, only at one time did the North Star line up exactly with the descending passage and shine directly down. This occurred in 2141 BC and the North Star at that time was Draconis, also called the dragon star. The North Star changes gradually over long periods of time because of the precession of the earth on its axis, like a spinning top. Also only at that time, the star cluster known as the Pleiades in the constellation Taurus was in alignment with the scored lines. Thus this is the date that Robert Menzies and most other scholars accept as the starting date at the first scored lines. Measurements in inches from the scored lines represent chronology in years. Thus we count one year for every inch we move from the scored lines, starting at 2141 BC.

If we move down the descending passageway to the beginning of the ascending passageway, we have moved a distance of 688 inches. If each inch represents one year and we add 688 years to the start date of 2141 BC we see that we have arrived at the year 1453 BC, which is accepted as the date of the exodus of the Israelites from Egypt.

Now, hang on to your hats for this one. When we move up the ascending passageway toward the king's chamber we find that when we reach the 1485 inch mark we are at the opening to the grand gallery. That makes a lot of sense because 1453 BC minus 1485 years equals 33 AD. Obviously things changed drastically in both our dimension and the unseen world, the spiritual dimension, after the completed work of salvation that occurred with the crucifixion and the defeat of death by Jesus when He left the tomb and arose to glory.

The hand of God in the creation of the Great Pyramid is unmistakable.

If you have read either <u>Unlocking God's Secrets</u> or <u>Musings from Me and My Master</u> you know of my passion for studying "Types and Shadows," both within the Word of God itself and in history, which truly is "His story." And it is at this point in the ascending passageway to the king's chamber that I see a shadow. For it is at this point, equivalent to the year 33 AD, that the passageway to the queen's chamber juts off in a horizontal direction. Could it be that the passageway to the queen's chamber is a shadow of the church, since the true church is the bride of Christ? I think so.

At any rate, if we move up the grand gallery to its end, to the entrance of the king's chamber we travel another 1881 inches. This brings us to the year 1914, the date of the beginning of the First World War which was the first time in over 2,500 years that Israel was not ruled by a foreign power. For it was during this war that England's General Lord Allenby, commander of the Allied Expeditionary Army, decided to walk into Jerusalem as a servant after taking it rather than riding into the city as a conqueror.

It would take volumes to cover all of the phenomenal things that are in the Great Pyramid, including much more on the chronology within the passageways, but the investigation for the purposes of this book does not need to be that detailed. I would, however, like to briefly cover three other facts concerning this great structure, the most outstanding and mysterious building ever erected on earth.

First, it contains one piece of furniture, a box the same size as the Ark of the Covenant. It is located in the King's Chamber. The box is too big to fit through the passageway, so it had to have been placed there as the pyramid was built, over 1000 years before God gave Moses the Ark's dimensions.

Second, as we have written extensively about in the past, we know that each Hebrew letter has a numerical value. The Pyramid's height in inches equals is 5449, which just happens to be the sum of all the letters in the Hebrew text of Isaiah 19:19-20. I find that to be extremely fascinating because that is the passage we read earlier,

*"In that day there will be an altar to the LORD in the heart of Egypt, and a monument to the LORD at its border. It will be a sign and witness to the LORD Almighty in the land of Egypt. When they cry out to the LORD because of their oppressors, he will send them a savior and defender, and he will rescue them."* Isaiah 19:19-20.

Interestingly, The Hebrew word translated as *"sign"* in this Scripture is "oth," which can refer to a sign, or a monument.

Finally, we should really think about the fact that originally the Great Pyramid was to have a solid gold capstone that was a scale model of the pyramid itself. It was never put in place because the builders rejected it. Only on a pyramid can a capstone also be the head of the corner.

Jesus Himself, the rock of our salvation, quoting from the very center chapter in the Bible, Psalm 118:22, said,

*"The stone the builders rejected has become the capstone; the Lord has done this, and it is marvelous in our eyes."*          Matthew 21:42.

The Nephilim, Satan's children, and the vast majority of the world's population in 2200 BC, rejected the One True God. Talking to them and those who follow in their footsteps today, Jesus continued on after He quoted the above words, to say,

*"Therefore I tell you that the kingdom of God will be taken away from you and given to a people who will produce its fruit. He who falls on this stone will be broken to pieces, but he on whom it falls will be crushed."*
         Matthew 21:43-44.

Hopefully, you and I both do fall on this stone, Jesus, with praise worship, and complete love, and are broken in such a way that our reliance for everything in our lives is totally on Him. If that is not already the case in your life, I strongly urge you to close your eyes this very moment, and surrender every single thing in your life to your Savior. Realize, after reading about the wonders of just this one building, and thinking about the scope of all the wonders in all of creation, that all of your knowledge and ability is absolutely nothing compared to His. So give that "nothing" over to Him entirely. Allow Him to make of you what He has planned for you to be from the creation of the world.

I must warn you, however, that just closing your eyes and saying it, even though with the utmost of emotion, will not make it so. You must then live it, every day and every hour, to the utmost of your ability. If you do that, and I assure you that the precious Holy Spirit will help you, your life will gain meaning far beyond yourself, and far beyond just this mortal life. Into the Millennium and reaching into all of eternity to come, your life will be awesomely molded into one that will have purpose that no one can today even imagine. You will live God's purpose.

The beginning is the closing your eyes. But then continue with daily study of His Word, capped off with a pressing into Him through prayer. Practice obedience and truly cast off sin with a passion, which is abundantly more important than our church of Laodicea teaches. Do these things and the living structure God will make of your life will far exceed the Great Pyramid.

# Into Heaven

There is so much to talk about regarding the time we know as the Millennial Reign of Christ that it would take an entire book just to crack the surface, but the point that I want to get across is that in both that thousand years and beyond into heaven, God will continue to use His creation. He did not create the world and all the magnificent universes just to toss them away after a mere six or seven thousand Biblical years. And this realization has birthed in me that feeling I have lightly characterized as standing in comfortable shoes. Yes, I understand fully that there is an unseen world, and eventually it will be meshed with the one we now know, but I do not now believe that the surreal and unearthly will hit us like a ton of bricks. I now believe that much of the allegory in the Bible pertaining to future events will turn out to be something that we will be comfortable with. For instance, we are told of the Millennium,

> *"Never again will there be in it an infant who lives but a few days, or an old man who does not live out his years; the one who dies at a hundred will be thought a mere child; the one who fails to reach a hundred will be considered accursed."* Isaiah 65:20.

Often I have heard it preached that God will be doing away with death at the start of the Millennium, but in reading that verse from Isaiah we can see that is not the case. People will only be living longer. Death will not have mysteriously, miraculously, and supernaturally been done away with during the Millennium. And I believe the gigantic increase in life expectancies will occur because of the drastic reduction in murders and suicides caused by the demons, those hateful souls of the Nephilim, having been destroyed, plus enormous strides in medicine will be made.

An example of the latter jumped out at me this past week. A fourteen year old high school student, Jack Andraka from Maryland, was astounded that a good family friend who he looked at as his uncle seemed to go almost overnight from the picture of health to death from pancreatic cancer. It made no sense whatsoever to young Jack; so he got on the internet and started Googling information on the deadly pancreatic cancer.

What he found was that the detection system for pancreatic cancer was sixty years old and cost $800 to administer. And at that, by the time it gave any results, it was too late. Pancreatic cancer was never detected in time to do anything about it.

Jack kept digging on Google and looking up what he did not know on Wikipedia on-line. He started out as an inquisitive fourteen year old and ended up, using only those two internet sources, developing a paper strip sensor that detects mesothelin, a protein found in most pancreatic cancers that is not found in healthy people. For this gigantic medical advancement a then Jack Andraka was the 2012 Intel Science Fair grand prize winner. And hold on to your hat; the cancer detector Jack came up with costs only three cents and takes less than five minutes to determine. Officials at Intel have said that Andraka's method is more than 90 percent accurate in detecting the presence of mesothelin. He has patented his method of sensing pancreatic cancer and is communicating with companies about developing an over-the-counter test. This is huge.

I watched a talk Jack gave, and what struck me was a point he made near the end. Jack said, "There are millions of us;" talking about inquisitive teenagers who know how to research anything on-line. I believe he is right, and I believe this brainpower will be unleashed as never before in the next few years, and we will see life expectancies rise dramatically almost overnight. Yes, God is doing it, but He is doing it through His creation. It won't come about as a supernatural miracle. It will come about through God's plan, utilizing what He created at the beginning. As for me, it is like I am standing in Cliff Claven's "comfortable shoes."

There is one change that we are told of that we may wonder about, though. Could the following things mentioned in Isaiah happen without supernatural intervention?

> *"The wolf will live with the lamb,*
>   *the leopard will lie down with the goat,*
> *the calf and the lion and the yearling together;*
>   *and a little child will lead them.*
> *The cow will feed with the bear,*
>   *their young will lie down together,*
>   *and the lion will eat straw like the ox."*       Isaiah 11:6-7.

We learned earlier that Papias was a contemporary of Polycarp, and one of the Apostle John's students as well. Therefore, Papias taught the Apostolic Oral Teaching, and referring to this mysterious scripture in Isaiah, Papias said:

"In like manner, [He said] that a grain of wheat would produce ten thousand ears, and that every ear would have ten thousand grains, and every grain would yield ten pounds of clear, pure, fine flour; and that apples, and seeds, and grass would produce in similar proportions; and that **all animals, feeding then only on the productions of the earth, would become peaceable and harmonious, and be in perfect subjection to man."**
Fragments of Papias, IV.

So Papias is telling us that Jesus taught the apostles that it will be because of the overabundance of natural food that animals which are now meat eaters will basically become vegetarians. I guess we will just have to see how that comes about ourselves. Quite frankly, I kind of hope that there will be a little bit of supernatural intervention as well, before I try to interact up close and in personal with a tiger or lion.

As I mentioned earlier, there is so much I would love to discuss about the Millennium and heaven that are talked about in the Apostolic Oral Teaching, but it would take a book to do it. Maybe, if God lets me live long enough and I feel the nudge to do it, I will write such a book and share the exciting things I have learned. However, this book's purpose, of course, was primarily to cover the end time teaching up to the return of Jesus, so we will save all of those nuggets until a later date and hopefully give them the time and attention they deserve. I did, though, want you to see that the Millennium may very well not be as other worldly as we may have been led to believe.

The Millennium has been referred to as the first step into heaven, and I think we can understand why. It will be a transitionary period from our current age to the eternal age we know as heaven. One of the things that will need to be accomplished during that time will be the decision concerning who the participants in heaven will be. And the end of the Millennium, we know already that Satan will be released once more, to determine that.

A human's reason for living is to answer the question about who that person chooses, God or Satan. And by releasing Satan one final time the people in the Millennium will definitively determine that. Jesus, of course will have ruled the earth for a thousand years, and His reign will have been righteous. We can read.

*"A shoot will come up from the stump of Jesse;*
*from his roots a Branch will bear fruit.*
*The Spirit of the Lord will rest on him—*
*the Spirit of wisdom and of understanding,*
*the Spirit of counsel and of might,*
*the Spirit of the knowledge and fear of the Lord—*
*and he will delight in the fear of the Lord.*

*He will not judge by what he sees with his eyes,*
*or decide by what he hears with his ears;*
*but with righteousness he will judge the needy,*
*with justice he will give decisions for the poor of the earth.*
*He will strike the earth with the rod of his mouth;*
*with the breath of his lips he will slay the wicked.*
*Righteousness will be his belt*
*and faithfulness the sash around his waist."* Isaiah 11:1-5.

We would think that a ruler like that would win over everyone to His side. But as was the case when Jesus walked the earth the first time, many will be put off by His righteousness. The sin nature in people will still be in play, even though Satan will have been bound and the demons destroyed. Man will still have the capacity to sin. James, the half brother of Jesus and the head of the first church in Jerusalem, stated it clearly:

*"When tempted, no one should say, 'God is tempting me.' For God cannot be tempted by evil, nor does he tempt anyone; but each person is tempted when they are dragged away* **by their own evil desire** *and enticed. Then, after desire has conceived, it gives birth to sin; and sin, when it is full-grown, gives birth to death."* James 1:13-15.

So, even without the demons help, man will choose the wrong path.

around since God only knows, were not created with the gift of eternal life. For proof, let's read the definitive verses from God's Word about the most famous angel, Lucifer (Satan himself):

"*This is what the Sovereign Lord says:*

> *'You were the seal of perfection,*
> > *full of wisdom and perfect in beauty.*
> 
> *You were in Eden, the garden of God;*
> > *every precious stone adorned you:*
> > *carnelian, chrysolite and emerald,*
> > *topaz, onyx and jasper,*
> > *lapis lazuli, turquoise and beryl.*
> 
> *Your settings and mountings were made of gold;*
> > *on the day you were created they were prepared.*
> 
> *You were anointed as a guardian cherub,*
> > *for so I ordained you.*
> 
> *You were on the holy mount of God;*
> > *you walked among the fiery stones.*
> 
> *You were blameless in your ways*
> > *from the day you were created*
> > *till wickedness was found in you.*
> 
> *Through your widespread trade*
> > *you were filled with violence, and you sinned.*
> 
> *So I drove you in disgrace from the mount of God,*
> > *and I expelled you, guardian cherub,*
> > *from among the fiery stones.*
> 
> *Your heart became proud*
> > *on account of your beauty,*
> > *and you corrupted your wisdom because of your splendor.*
> 
> *So I threw you to the earth;*
> > *I made a spectacle of you before kings.*
> 
> *By your many sins and dishonest trade*
> > *you have desecrated your sanctuaries.*
> 
> *So I made a fire come out from you, and it consumed you,*
> > *and I reduced you to ashes on the ground*
> > *in the sight of all who were watching.*

> *All the nations who knew you are appalled at you;*
>   *you have come to a horrible end*
>     *and **will be no more.**"*                         Ezekiel 28:11-19.

No one, neither man nor angel, will receive the precious gift of eternal life until the beginning of the period called heaven. Eternity. The last line of that scripture tells us at that time even Satan and his gang **"will be no more."**

It is not at all pleasant to realize that many will make the wrong choice and never experience eternal life. But for those who do choose God, the ending is both happy and glorious:

*"Then I saw 'a new heaven and a new earth,' for the first heaven and the first earth had passed away, and there was no longer any sea. I saw the Holy City, the new Jerusalem, coming down out of heaven from God, prepared as a bride beautifully dressed for her husband. And I heard a loud voice from the throne saying,* **'Look! God's dwelling place is now among the people, and he will dwell with them. They will be his people, and God himself will be with them and be their God. He will wipe every tear from their eyes. There will be no more death or mourning or crying or pain, for the old order of things has passed away.'**

*He who was seated on the throne said, 'I am making everything new!' Then he said, 'Write this down, for these words are trustworthy and true.'*

*He said to me: 'It is done. I am the Alpha and the Omega, the Beginning and the End. To the thirsty I will give water without cost from the spring of the water of life.* **Those who are victorious will inherit all this, and I will be their God and they will be my children. But the cowardly, the unbelieving, the vile, the murderers, the sexually immoral, those who practice magic arts, the idolaters and all liars—they will be consigned to the fiery lake of burning sulfur. This is the second death.'**

*One of the seven angels who had the seven bowls full of the seven last plagues came and said to me, 'Come, I will show you the bride, the wife of the Lamb.' And he carried me away in the Spirit to a mountain great and high, and showed me the Holy City, Jerusalem, coming down out of heaven from God. It shone with the glory of God, and its brilliance was like that of a very precious jewel, like a jasper, clear as crystal. It had a great, high wall with twelve gates, and with twelve angels at the gates. On the gates were written the names of the twelve tribes of Israel. There were three gates on the* east, three on the north, three on the south and three on the west. *The wall of the city had twelve foundations, and on them were the names of the twelve apostles of the Lamb.*

*The angel who talked with me had a measuring rod of gold to measure the city, its gates and its walls. The city was laid out like a square, as long as it was wide. He measured the city with the rod and found it to be 12,000 stadia in length, and as wide and high as it is long* (This is the 1,400 miles we discussed; the length of the Euphrates River, the boundary of the Garden of Eden and the land promised to Israel.). *The angel measured the wall using human measurement, and it was 144 cubits thick. The wall was made of jasper, and the city of pure gold, as pure as glass. The foundations of the city walls were decorated with every kind of precious stone. The first foundation was jasper, the second sapphire, the third agate, the fourth emerald, the fifth onyx, the sixth ruby, the seventh chrysolite, the eighth beryl, the ninth topaz, the tenth turquoise, the eleventh jacinth, and the twelfth amethyst. The twelve gates were twelve pearls, each gate made of a single pearl. The great street of the city was of gold, as pure as transparent glass.*

*I did not see a temple in the city, because the Lord God Almighty and the Lamb are its temple. The city does not need the sun or the moon to shine on it, for the glory of God gives it light, and the Lamb is its lamp. The nations will walk by its light, and the kings of the earth will bring their splendor into it. On no day will its gates ever be shut, for there will be no night there. The glory and honor of the nations will be brought into it. Nothing impure will ever enter it, nor will anyone who does what is shameful or deceitful, but only those whose names are written in the Lamb's book of life.*

*Then the angel showed me the river of the water of life, as clear as crystal, flowing from the throne of God and of the Lamb down the middle of the great street of the city. On each side of the river stood the tree of life, bearing twelve crops of fruit, yielding its fruit every month. And the leaves of the tree are for the healing of the nations. No longer will there be any curse. The throne of God and of the Lamb will be in the city, and his servants will serve him. They will see his face, and his name will be on their foreheads. There will be no more night. They will not need the light of a lamp or the light of the sun, for the Lord God will give them light. And they will reign for ever and ever.*

*The angel said to me, 'These words are trustworthy and true. The Lord, the God who inspires the prophets, sent his angel to show his servants the things that must soon take place.'*

*'Look, I am coming soon! Blessed is the one who keeps the words of the prophecy written in this scroll.'*

*I, John, am the one who heard and saw these things. And when I had heard and seen them, I fell down to worship at the feet of the angel who had been showing them to me. But he said to me, 'Don't do that! I am a fellow servant with you and with your fellow prophets and with all who keep the words of this scroll. Worship God!'*

*Then he told me, 'Do not seal up the words of the prophecy of this scroll, because the time is near. Let the one who does wrong continue to do wrong; let the vile person continue to be vile; let the one who does right continue to do right; and let the holy person continue to be holy.*

*Look, I am coming soon! My reward is with me, and I will give to each person according to what they have done. I am the Alpha and the Omega, the First and the Last, the Beginning and the End.*

*Blessed are those who wash their robes, that they may have the right to the tree of life and may go through the gates into the city. Outside are the dogs, those who practice magic arts, the sexually immoral, the murderers, the idolaters and everyone who loves and practices falsehood.*

*I, Jesus, have sent my angel to give you this testimony for the churches. I am the Root and the Offspring of David, and the bright Morning Star.'*

*The Spirit and the bride say, "Come!" And let the one who hears say, "Come!" Let the one who is thirsty come; and let the one who wishes take the free gift of the water of life.*

*I warn everyone who hears the words of the prophecy of this scroll: If anyone adds anything to them, God will add to that person the plagues described in this scroll. And if anyone takes words away from this scroll of prophecy, God will take away from that person any share in the tree of life and in the Holy City, which are described in this scroll.*

*He who testifies to these things says, "Yes, I am coming soon."*
*Amen. Come, Lord Jesus.*
*The grace of the Lord Jesus be with God's people. Amen."*

Revelation 21 & 22.

# Final Thoughts from Me and God

A good friend in Mississippi, and a true brother in Christ, Tom Moore, recently reminded me of a major event in Polycarp's life that we would do well to examine. As we have discussed, as a young man Polycarp sat at the feet of the Apostle John and soaked up everything he taught. John was so pleased with his student that before he died he made Polycarp the Bishop of the Church of Smyrna, the church Jesus had nothing but praise for in His letters to the seven churches in Revelation. As he got older Polycarp was revered and considered the leader of all of the churches in Asia Minor.

We have a letter from Ignatius to Polycarp that was written in 108 AD:

"...to Polycarp, bishop of the Smyrnaeans...So approving am I of your godly mind, which is as it were, grounded upon an unmovable rock, that my praise exceeds all bounds...Do not let those who appear to be trustworthy yet who teach strange doctrines baffle you. Stand firm, like an anvil...Grace will be...always...with Polycarp." Letter to Polycarp. Ignatius.

And we, of course, have words from his student, Irenaeus;

"But Polycarp also was not only instructed by apostles, and conversed with many who had seen Christ, but was also, by apostles in Asia, appointed bishop of the Church in Smyrna...always taught the things which he had learned from the apostles, and which the Church has handed down, and which alone are true. To these things all the Asiatic Churches testify, as do also those men who have succeeded Polycarp down to the present time."
Against Heresies, III, 3 and 4, Irenaeus.

The event Tom Moore reminded me of occurred about a year before Polycarp was martyred. Earlier, there had been a bishop in Rome named Sixtus who had tried to distance the Christians from the Jews in the eyes of the Roman government because the Jews had rebelled against the Roman Empire and were being hunted down and killed. In so doing Sixtus had done away with the remembrance of the Passover and instead started celebrating Christ's resurrection on a pagan holiday, Easter.

In what are known as "Fragments of the Lost Writings of Irenaeus," he mentions that this change from Passover to Easter was continued by Roman bishops after Sixtus:

"And the presbyters preceding Sorer in the government of the Church which thou dost now rule--I mean, Anicetus and Pius, Hyginus and Telesphorus, and Sixtus--did neither themselves observe it [after that fashion], nor permit those with them to do so."  Irenaeus.

About a year before he was martyred, Polycarp of Smyrna went to Rome to deal with various heretics there, and he tried to persuade Bishop Anicetus not to switch from Passover to Easter Sunday. Irenaeus, in those "Fragments of the Lost Writings" records this:

"And when the blessed Polycarp was sojourning in Rome in the time of Anicetus, although a slight controversy had arisen among them as to certain other points…For neither could Anicetus persuade Polycarp to forego the observance [in his own way], inasmuch as these things had been always observed by John the disciple of our Lord, and by other apostles with whom he had been conversant; nor, on the other hand, could Polycarp succeed in persuading Anicetus to keep [the observance in his way], for he maintained that he was bound to adhere to the usage of the presbyters who preceded him. And in this state of affairs they held fellowship with each other; and Anicetus conceded to Polycarp in the Church the celebration of the Eucharist, by way of showing him respect"  Irenaeus.

In the end, the Roman churches celebrated Easter and the churches in Asia Minor continued to celebrate Passover, as Jesus, the Apostles, and all those who learned directly from them had always done. This difference existed between the two factions long after Polycarp was killed, until 325 AD when Easter was set as the orthodox practice of the Catholic Church.

Prior to that date we have a letter from a later Bishop of Smyrna, Polycrates, to Roman Bishop Victor, still arguing about changing the Passover to what became Easter Sunday. In it he quoted Polycarp:

"I, therefore, brethren, who have lived sixty-five years in the Lord, and have met with the brethren throughout the world, and have gone through every Holy Scripture, am not affrighted by terrifying words. For those greater than I have said 'We ought to obey God rather than man."
Letter to Victor, Polycrates.

Yes, of course, **"We ought to obey God rather than man."**
We would think that admonishment would be self evident throughout the entire Christian church. Unfortunately that is not the case. I have a friend who is currently a pastor who initially attended another denomination's seminary. Before he could get his degree he was supposed to write a paper answering the question, "Which is more important: revelation, the Bible, or church tradition?" He was not allowed to graduate because he stated firmly in his writing that the Bible was clearly above the other two in importance. The answer demanded by the seminary was that all three were of equal importance.

I submit that it is because of that thinking which, whether admitted or not, predominates our church, that we have become the Church of Laodicea. Let's reread what Jesus said in His letter to us:

*"These are the words of the Amen, the faithful and true witness, the ruler of God's creation. I know your deeds, that you are neither cold nor hot. I wish you were either one or the other! So, because you are lukewarm— neither hot nor cold—**I am about to spit you out of my mouth**. You say, 'I am rich; I have acquired wealth and do not need a thing.' But you do not realize that you are wretched, pitiful, poor, blind and naked. I counsel you to buy from me gold refined in the fire, so you can become rich; and white clothes to wear, so you can cover your shameful nakedness; and salve to put on your eyes, so you can see."* Revelation 3:14-18.

Lukewarm. That is our problem. Lukewarm in our passion for God and His way of doing things.

We do not see the need for *"white clothes to wear,"* which represents righteousness. And we do not think we need gold, which Biblically represents "the divine nature." It is kingly. It represents the character, quality, and works of King Jesus. Yes, we are *"wretched, pitiful, poor, blind and naked "*

I mentioned at the beginning of this book that the purpose of my initial search into the writings of the Christian giants from the church eras of the Church of Philadelphia (1730 -1900) and the Church of Smyrna (100-313) was to determine what they thought and taught and how they acted from the way our church age teaches and acts. I found the answer, and it was startlingly apparent. I will give it to you in one concise sentence, but first I will briefly mention three of the several things that have brought us to this "lukewarm" state.

The first can be found in Polycarp's fight to keep the Passover and refuse the more politically correct celebration of Easter. His overriding reason for his passion was not what we might think. He could not foresee the over commercialization to come of the holiday, and the focus on Easter bunnies and eggs, although we can be sure he would have wept if he had. Polycarp knew that Easter was a festival observance of springtime resurrection and fertility that long predated Christianity. The thought behind it went all the way back to Nimrod, The Cup of The Harlot ceremony, and the method of worship by the Nephilim before the flood. It went back to the idea of "creating a name for themselves" without God being involved.

But even more important than those things to Polycarp was his knowledge that Paul had taught in his Apostolic Oral Teaching and instructed the first century church to keep a memorial to Christ's death, not to His resurrection. Paul knew that we Christians needed to keep our focus on Jesus, not on our own salvation. The Passover was a memorial to the crucifixion of Jesus. Easter was a celebration of our salvation. And Paul knew and taught that our salvation was not the high point of God's plan.

The second thing I found in researching our lukewarm state was the mentality found in the teaching of the pre tribulation rapture. We could afford to be lukewarm because we were going to be beamed out of here before the tough times came. We did not need to develop a dependency on "the wings of an eagle" (Jesus) in preparation for what might well be our martyrdom, and worse, the witnessing of the torture and killing of our loved ones, including even our own children. No, somehow we were going to get better treatment than that, probably because we deserved better. "Jesus is not going to slap around His bride, the church, right before the marriage supper." Never mind that Polycarp and Irenaeus saw their brothers and sisters fed live to the lions. And never mind that more good devout Christians are being martyred this year than in any time in history. No, as for me, I'm out of here.

And the third thing I'll mention on this partial list of contributing factors to our lukewarmness has to do with the increased teaching of our lack of personal responsibility in God's plan. With the full embracing of such new doctrinal man made traditions as "once saved, always saved," we have now even evolved to the point that the most liberal among us are now incredibly teaching that we should not even try to stop sinning because that is the job of the Holy Spirit within us, and we should not show such lack of faith in His work that we would interfere. Yes, unbelievably it has come to that. We started out not talking about sin in church so as to not drive people away. We were "people friendly" churches. Now we celebrate that we are such special people that we are entitled to the Holy Spirit driving sin out of our life with no effort at all on our part, and in the timing He sees fit. We have finally arrived at the point in which we have absolutely no responsibility whatsoever in God's plan but to say we are a Christian. The era of "cheap grace" has arrived in all its glory. So go ahead and sin. It's the Holy Spirits job to get rid of it, not ours.

I know I will sound like a completely old fashion, out of date and out of touch preacher from the nineteenth century, like Charles Finney, but I will state emphatically that sin is a gigantic deal to God, and it is our responsibility to get it out of our lives immediately. When Jesus started His sermons with the word, "repent," He meant it. An extremely big part of the Greek word, "pistevo," which is translated in our Bible as "believe," is the part that says we will "obey totally and completely the One followed."

OK, I'll stop preaching, although I could go on and on. The concise sentence that is the defining difference between our church age and the ages of the churches of Philadelphia and Smyrna is this: "their focus was on God, our focus is on me."

The great news, though, is also found in the letter to the church of Laodicea in which Jesus showed nothing but condemnation.

*"Those whom I love I rebuke and discipline. So **be earnest and repent**. Here I am! I stand at the door and knock. If anyone hears my voice and opens the door, I will come in and eat with that person, and they with me.*

*To the one who is **victorious**, I will give the right to sit with me on my throne, just as I was victorious and sat down with my Father on his throne. Whoever has ears, let them hear what the Spirit says to the churches."*

Revelation 3:19-22.

The great news is that we are individuals, and Jesus will treat us as such. We do not have to be swept away with the church as a whole. If we are *earnest* for God by loving *"the LORD your God with all your heart, all your soul, all your strength, and all your mind."*(Luke 10:27), which is every part of our being; if we repent, meaning not only to say we are sorry, ask forgiveness for, and turn away from our sins; and if we are victorious over sin and all things dealing with the enemy; Jesus promises that we will sit *"down with my Father on his throne."* What a glorious promise. But just as with every promise in the Bible, there are "if's" involved, even though the Church of Laodicea does not ever tell us about them.

You and I can do it. By developing a passion and a love for Him, and abiding with Him in daily prayer, and learning from Him in Bible study, you and I can one day give each other a knowing wink as we see each other sitting near Jesus with the Father on the throne.

Yes, there is grace; a wonderful, glorious grace. We could not possibly get there had Jesus not paid the ultimate price for us. But since He did indeed pay that horrible price, we do have grace. He did His part. For Jesus, *"it is finished."* And He is rooting for us to be *"victorious."* He is our biggest cheer leader. How could we not love Him with every fiber of our being? How could we not desire to "**obey God rather than man**?"

## Final Thoughts from God

*"Woe to the shepherds who are destroying and scattering the sheep of my pasture!" declares the Lord. Therefore this is what the Lord, the God of Israel, says to the shepherds who tend my people: "Because you have scattered my flock and driven them away and have not bestowed care on them, I will bestow punishment on you for the evil you have done," declares the Lord. "I myself will gather the remnant of my flock out of all the countries where I have driven them and will bring them back to their pasture, where they will be fruitful and increase in number. I will place shepherds over them who will tend them, and they will no longer be afraid or terrified, nor will any be missing," declares the Lord.*

"The days are coming," declares the Lord,
    "when I will raise up for David a righteous Branch,
a King who will reign wisely
    and do what is just and right in the land.
In his days Judah will be saved
    and Israel will live in safety.
This is the name by which he will be called:
    The Lord Our Righteous Savior.

"So then, the days are coming," declares the Lord, "when people will no longer say, 'As surely as the Lord lives, who brought the Israelites up out of Egypt,' but they will say, 'As surely as the Lord lives, who brought the descendants of Israel up out of the land of the north and out of all the countries where he had banished them.' Then they will live in their own land."

Concerning the prophets:

My heart is broken within me;
    all my bones tremble.
I am like a drunken man,
    like a strong man overcome by wine,
    because of the Lord and his holy words.
The land is full of adulterers;
    because of the curse[b] the land lies parched
    and the pastures in the wilderness are withered.
The prophets follow an evil course
    and use their power unjustly.

"Both prophet and priest are godless;
    even in my temple I find their wickedness,"
    declares the Lord.
"Therefore their path will become slippery;
    they will be banished to darkness
    and there they will fall.
I will bring disaster on them
    in the year they are punished," declares the Lord.

*"Among the prophets of Samaria
        I saw this repulsive thing:
They prophesied by Baal
        and led my people Israel astray.
And among the prophets of Jerusalem
        I have seen something horrible:
                They commit adultery and live a lie.
They strengthen the hands of evildoers,
        so that not one of them turns from their wickedness.
They are all like Sodom to me;
        the people of Jerusalem are like Gomorrah."*

Therefore this is what the Lord Almighty says concerning the prophets:

*"I will make them eat bitter food
        and drink poisoned water,
because from the prophets of Jerusalem
        ungodliness has spread throughout the land."*

This is what the Lord Almighty says:

*"Do not listen to what the prophets are prophesying to you;
        they fill you with false hopes.
They speak visions from their own minds,
        not from the mouth of the Lord.
They keep saying to those who despise me,
        'The Lord says: You will have peace.'
And to all who follow the stubbornness of their hearts
        they say, 'No harm will come to you.'
But which of them has stood in the council of the Lord
        to see or to hear his word?
                Who has listened and heard his word?
See, the storm of the Lord
        will burst out in wrath,
a whirlwind swirling down
        on the heads of the wicked.*

> *The anger of the Lord will not turn back*
> >  *until he fully accomplishes*
> >  *the purposes of his heart.*
> *In days to come*
> >  *you will understand it clearly.*
> *I did not send these prophets,*
> >  *yet they have run with their message;*
> *I did not speak to them,*
> >  *yet they have prophesied.*
> *But if they had stood in my council,*
> >  *they would have proclaimed my words to my people*
> >  *and would have turned them from their evil ways*
> >  *and from their evil deeds.*
>
> *"Am I only a God nearby,"*
> >  *declares the Lord,*
> >  *"and not a God far away?*
> *Who can hide in secret places*
> >  *so that I cannot see them?"*
> >  *declares the Lord.*
> *"Do not I fill heaven and earth?"*
> >  *declares the Lord.*

"I have heard what the prophets say who prophesy lies in my name. They say, 'I had a dream! I had a dream!' 26 How long will this continue in the hearts of these lying prophets, who prophesy the delusions of their own minds? They think the dreams they tell one another will make my people forget my name, just as their ancestors forgot my name through Baal worship. Let the prophet who has a dream recount the dream, but let the one who has my word speak it faithfully. For what has straw to do with grain?" declares the Lord. "Is not my word like fire," declares the Lord, "and like a hammer that breaks a rock in pieces?

"Therefore," declares the Lord, "I am against the prophets who steal from one another words supposedly from me. Yes," declares the Lord, "I am against the prophets who wag their own tongues and yet declare, 'The Lord declares.' Indeed, I am against those who prophesy false dreams," *declares the Lord. "They tell them and lead my people astray with their reckless lies, yet I did not send or appoint them. They do not benefit these people in the least," declares the Lord.*

*"When these people, or a prophet or a priest, ask you, 'What is the message from the Lord?' say to them, 'What message? I will forsake you, declares the Lord.' If a prophet or a priest or anyone else claims, 'This is a message from the Lord,' I will punish them and their household. This is what each of you keeps saying to your friends and other Israelites: 'What is the Lord's answer?' or 'What has the Lord spoken?' But you must not mention 'a message from the Lord' again, because each one's word becomes their own message. So you distort the words of the living God, the Lord Almighty, our God. This is what you keep saying to a prophet: 'What is the Lord's answer to you?' or 'What has the Lord spoken?' Although you claim, 'This is a message from the Lord,' this is what the Lord says: You used the words, 'This is a message from the Lord,' even though I told you that you must not claim, 'This is a message from the Lord.' Therefore, I will surely forget you and cast you out of my presence along with the city I gave to you and your ancestors. I will bring on you everlasting disgrace— everlasting shame that will not be forgotten."*                    Jeremiah 23.

# About the Author and His Books

Although Bob Morley's educational background at the University of North Carolina was in psychology, his overriding passion is the study of all things pertaining to God, as is obvious in all of his books.

**Unlocking God's Secrets** was the culmination of over thirteen thousand hours of intensive research and study into that passion. It has been described as the most comprehensive single book about God and Christianity ever written, and is a must read for any truth seeker. Virtually every single page contains something that will cause both the novice and the scholar to say, "Wow!"

**Musings from Me and My Master** is an exciting collection of seventy articles that stir every emotion within the reader, and causes deep thinking as only this author can. In it can be found Biblical prophecies and shadows that may never have been seen before, along with a pleasant mixture of miracles and personal insights.

**Wonder No More** is a fabulous tool for bringing people to the truth through a uniquely provable method that leaves no possibility for doubts. It proves God's existence the way God told us to do it. And it was deliberately created to be extremely short, concise, and inexpensive for that very purpose.

**The Cup of The Harlot** may well be the most definitive study of the true interpretation of end times prophecy as explained by the Apostle John himself to his student, Polycarp, after he had written Revelation. The book reveals how far afield we have gone by giving credibility to man's ideas about what the Revelation images could mean, rather than following the true divine interpretations that John laid out in the Apostolic Oral Teaching.

All four books will continue to be available from Amazon.com and other fine retailers for years to come.

Bob and his wife, Barbara, happily reside in Ormond Beach, Florida. They have four daughters and nine grandchildren.
Bob can be reached at **morley120@juno.com**.

The following pages give totally **unsolicited** comments about Bob's books.

## Unsolicited Comments about Bob Morley's Books

The difference between you and the seminary professors that I sat under is that they know God academically, but are not empowered by Him. You are like those in Acts 4 who were recognized as being "with Jesus". God uses you in his writing. There is a giftedness and an empowering that was always lacking by my professors. **Senior Pastor Dan P.**

This is the most well researched and written book I ever read. **Jim E.**

I was blown away with the detail, the wit, the easiness of reading your book. It is definitely what I call a "twicer," has to be read more than once…so much to grasp. **Randy T.**

The book will be close to my heart for the rest of my life. It changed my life. **Tom M.**

The kind of book I enjoy really digging into, gleaning nuggets of wisdom from. I'm particularly intrigued by the Three Hundred Thirty Two Prophecies. **Zig Z.**

I am in awe. I am humbled. I am speechless. **Tondra B.**

I ordered several to send to friends. **AnnMarie L.**

There is so much research, etc. I can't find the words to express myself. I ordered more copies. All I can say is WOW. I am truly amazed. **Eleonor B.**

I really enjoyed the book… Could not put it down… I plan to buy several and give to family and friends as well as my church. **Pat F.**

I think it is a "WOW" and a tremendous learning tool. **Charlie C.**

This I know was truly inspired by our Lord, and I can't imagine all of the time that went in all of the research of it. **Corky G.**

What can I say but Wow. Very interesting and provocative. **Fred S.**

## Unsolicited Comments about Bob Morley's Books

This book is truly amazing! I have a friend that I grew up with that is in prison now that I'm going to send a copy of this book to. **John W**.

I am ordering 25 copies to give out to friends and pastors. **Allie M**.

Your book is wonderful. **Melodye D**.

I am giving this book to my son and praying that the Holy Spirit will use it in his life as He did in mine. **Gloria C**.

Awesome!!!!!! **Jay D**.

Your references to historic alliances elsewhere in the world and here in the United States have made me much more attentive. Perhaps it is the best time in history to be hyper-focused on God's prophecy. **Ben O**.

I love your book. It flows so nice it is hard to put down. **Kathy V**.

Rarely has a book been brought to my attention more than yours. The last book this heavily recommended was The Shack. **Jason W**.

Enthralling. **Charles H**.

Your book is awesome – and I certainly believe that the Holy Spirit dictated that to you. There are really no words to describe the way the book affected me. **Sandra J**.

It is a wonderful book. **Ed C**.

Thank you for providing me with a book to answer many of my questions regarding the Word of God. **Fannie E**.

I can hardly put it down. It is incredible!!!!!! **Wanda J**.

# Unsolicited Comments about Bob Morley's Books

THANK YOU for your obedience in writing the book Unlocking God's Secrets. I have been able to do little else other than read this book since I bought it. My life with my Lord has been forever changed. My walk is permanently marked. I am stirred in a way that only the Holy Spirit can stir in my spirit. I see my purpose so clearly now and hope to be used to lead others to this truth. Thank you so very much!! **Sharron M.**

Thank you for you efforts and your faithfulness. Reading the Bible without studying it is difficult, at least for me. Your book has given me the desire to further study the Word. I now look at it as total truth with purpose in each word. I have already purchased 10 more copies for two of my employees and some of my friends. I thank God for you. **Tony C.**

I have read Unlocking God's Secrets from front to back and will read it again and again and utilize it for study and confirmation. I wish I could describe how important it has been for me. I treasure this book. **Chuck H.**

I loved your book. Thank you for all of your research, study, and time. It is an amazing book. My eyes have been opened so much. **Gerri Ann M.**

I am almost finished with the book and want everyone I know to have a chance to read it. You really have made a difference in my life. **Shirley H.**

I was in tears last night when I read about the twelve tribes of Israel and the cross formation they made. What a God we have the privilege of serving. Thanks so much for the labor of love you've poured into this book. Thanks for letting the Lord use you so mightily. **Peter K.**

I'm really enjoying the content and wanted you to know that your message is true and fascinating. Thank you for your efforts. Your message is very timely in our world today. **Joyce R.**

I want to thank you so very much, from the bottom of my heart for your book. Bob, your book has taught me more than all the preachers and teachers I have ever studied with. **Ray T.**

# Unsolicited Comments about Bob Morley's Books

You did a fantastic job on your research. **Ann K**.

Thank you for the incredible time it must have taken you to put this book together. **Jan H**.

It is important that every believer read this important work. **Pete K**.

"Unlocking Gods Secrets" Wow, you certainly unlocked something in me. I am not much of a reader. I don't think I have ever read a whole book in my life, but I read yours cover to cover in 2 days. All the prophecies were great but the part that really touched me was chapter 27, where you talked about the "engagement period" with Jesus. **Jay P**.

Wish I had time never to lay it down!! **Jean H**.

The book is fascinating! I would recommend it to all. A great gift. I'll be giving several this year! **Jamie**.

I am enjoying your book; it is driving a deeper study for me. **Paul D**.

Your book is awesome! My friend, Betty, just called me 15 minutes ago!!! WOW is she on fire! She just finished the book, ran out and got 3 more copies, (that is all she could find). I also got my Jewish friend hooked on it last weekend! He sat here and read about half of it! **Joanne J**.

I don't know which of my neighbors has it now but the cover is getting pretty tattered and worn from handing it around. **Jim L**.

I love your book and have been sharing it with others. **Dale C**.

Your book has made a great impression on my fiancé's daughter. And this is really something special. **Mac**.

I am making a list of my friends and family to have this book for Christmas gifts from my family. **Becky S**.

# Unsolicited Comments about Bob Morley's Books

I can't imagine the amount of time you must have spent in research and study. It is a book that will bless readers for years to come. **Vaona H.**

I loved it. I was just amazed. Your book was very easy to read and the information astounding. **Debby C.**

The best book I have ever read. Wow!!! **Betty C.**

One of the greatest books that I have ever read. I couldn't put it down. I am telling everybody about this book. It is really a "Wow" book. I am giving them for Christmas presents. **Lynda J.**

I continue to be enthralled with your writings. I feel that you are blessed with such an ability and such knowledge. It humbles me. **C H.**

I just finished reading the last page of your book. I was wanting to read more. You are soooo blessed to have the ability to search out the matter and pass knowledge on to us. God bless you. **Thomas M.**

The structure and prose are excellent. The logic is pure - inspired and inspiring. The book is awesome! Thank you. **Neil N.**

Your book is a must read but it is an intense read. Wow is all I can say. God has a special place for you. **Sharon T. B.**

So much information to take in! I can't imagine the amount of research you do, but I, for one, loved it all. So many things that I had wondered about, you touched on. The info about the Nephilim was new to me, but I see it clearly, especially the part about how Satan can't be everywhere at once. It makes sense. You laid that out so clearly. You are an intelligent man who is using his brain to bring great glory to God. **Ann D.**

I am amazed at the depth of your research and writing. The Lord must be using you to uncover understanding and insight that 99.9% of the church is unaware. May the Lord bless the church through your work. **J.C. B.**

Printed in Great Britain
by Amazon